AQA English Literature B

Great Clarendon Street, Oxford, OX2 6DP, United Kingdom

Oxford University Press is a department of the University of Oxford. It furthers the University's objective of excellence in research, scholarship, and education by publishing worldwide. Oxford is a registered trade mark of Oxford University Press in the UK and in certain other countries

First published in 2015

British Library Cataloguing in Publication Data

Data available

ISBN 978-019-833748-5

10 9 8 7 6 5 4 3 2 1

Printed in Great Britain by Ashford Print and Publishing Services, Gosport.

Acknowledgements

The authors and publisher are grateful for permission to reprint extracts from the following copyright material:

The Authorized Version of the Bible (*The King James Bible*), the rights in which are vested in the Crown, are reproduced by permission of the Crown's Patentee, Cambridge University Press.

Kate Atkinson: *When Will There Be Good News?* (Transworld, 2008), reprinted by permission of The Random House Publishing Group.

Margaret Atwood: *The Handmaid's Tale* (Vintage 1996), copyright © O W Toad 1985, reprinted by permission of The Random House Group and Curtis Brown Ltd, London, on behalf of the author.

John Betjeman: 'Ireland with Emily' from *New Bats in Old Belfries* (John Murray, 1945) and 'The Arrest of Oscar Wilde at the Cadogan Hotel' from *Continual Dew: a little book of bourgeois verse* (John Murray, 1937), reprinted by permission of the publishers.

Michael Billington: review of a production of *The Taming of the Shrew* at the Globe Theatre, *The Guardian*, 5 July 2012, copyright © Guardian News and Media Ltd 2012, reprinted by permission of GNM Ltd.

NoViolet Bulawayo: *We Need New Names* (Chatto & Windus, 2013), copyright © NoViolet Bulawayo 2013, reprinted by permission of The Random House Publishing Group.

Raymond Chandler: *Farewell My Lovely* (Penguin, 2005), copyright © Raymond Chandler 1953, *The Simple Art of Murder: Short Stories* (Hamish Hamilton, 1950), copyright © Raymond Chandler 1950, and *The Long Goodbye* (Penguin, 1959) copyright © Raymond Chandler 1953, all reprinted by permission of Penguin Books Ltd.

Agatha Christie: *Five Little Pigs* (HarperCollins, 2013), copyright © Agatha Christie 1942, and *The Murder of Roger Ackroyd* (HarperCollins, 2013), copyright © Agatha Christie 1926, reprinted by permission of HarperCollins Publishers Ltd.

Jim Crace: *Harvest* (Picador, 2013), copyright © Jim Crace 2013, reprinted by permission of Pan Macmillan UK, and the author c/o David Godwin Associates.

Helen Dunmore: *The Betrayal* (Penguin, 2010), copyright © Helen Dunmore 2010, reprinted by permission of Penguin Books Ltd.

Richard Ford: 'Abyss' from *A Multitude of Sins* (Vintage, 2002), copyright © Richard Ford 1996, reprinted by permission of the author c/o Rogers, Coleridge & White Ltd, 20 Powis Mews, London W11 1JN.

Robert Frost: 'The Road Not Taken', copyright © 1916, 1969 by Henry Holt & Company, copyright © 1944 by Robert Frost, from *The Poetry of Robert Frost* edited by Edward Connery Lathem (Cape, 1971), reprinted by permission of The Random House Publishing Group and Henry Holt & Company, LLC. All rights reserved.

Helen Gardner: on *Othello* from 'The Noble Moor' in *Proceedings of the British Academy* vol. 41 (1955), p.189-205, reprinted by permission of the British Academy.

Graham Greene: *Brighton Rock* (Penguin, 1971), copyright © Graham Greene 1938, reprinted by permission of David Higham Associates.

Tony Harrison: 'Them and [uz]' and 'National Trust' from *Selected Poems* (Penguin, 2006), copyright © Tony Harrison 2006, reprinted by permission of the author.

Weblinks are included throughout this book. Please note that Oxford University Press is not responsible for third-party content and although all links were correct at the time of publication, the content and location of the material may change over time.

Khaled Hosseini: *The Kite Runner* (Bloomsbury, 2004), copyright © Khaled Hosseini 2004, reprinted by permission of the publishers, Bloomsbury Publishing Plc.

Simon Kelner: 'Banksy perfectly embodies our transitory age, but who cares? ...' *The Independent*, 16 April 2014, copyright © The Independent 2014, reprinted by permission of the Independent.

Philip Larkin: 'Going, Going' from *High Windows* (Faber, 1974) and Philip Larkin: 'Sunny Prestatyn' from *The Whitsun Weddings* (Faber, 1994), reprinted by permission of Faber & Faber Ltd.

Andrea Levy: *Small Island* (Headline Review, 2004), copyright © Andrea Levy 2004, reprinted by permission of the Headline Publishing Group.

F L Lucas: *Greek Drama for the Common Reader* (Chatto & Windus, 1967), reprinted by permission of The Random House Publishing Group and Oliver Lucas.

Ian McEwan: *Atonement* (Cape, 2001), copyright © Ian McEwan 2001, reprinted by permission of The Random House Publishing Group.

George Orwell: 'Tribune, 1946' from *Decline of the English Murder and Other Essays* (Penguin, 1965, 2009), reprinted by permission of A M Heath for Bill Hamilton as the Literary Executor of the Estate of the Late Sonia Brownell Orwell and Penguin Books Ltd.

Ross Parker and Hughie Charles: 'There'll Always Be an England', words and music by Ross Parker and Hughie Charles, copyright © 1939 Chester Music Ltd trading as Dash Music Co, reprinted by permission of Chester Music Ltd trading as Dash Music Co. All rights reserved. International copyright secured.

Image acknowledgements:

Cover: © Lee Avison/Trevillion Images; **p28:** Cordelia's Portion, 1866 (w/c, gouache & pastel on paper), Brown, Ford Madox (1821-93)/© Lady Lever Art Gallery, National Museums Liverpool/ Bridgeman Images; **p29:** King Lear and the Fool in the Storm, c.1851, Dyce, William (1806-64)/© Scottish National Gallery, Edinburgh/Bridgeman Images; **p30:** © Robbie Jack/Corbis; **p34:** © Geraint Lewis/Alamy; **p38:** W. Eugene Smith/The LIFE Picture Collection/Getty Images; **p39:** © cineclassico/Alamy; **p52:** Isabella and the Pot of Basil, 1867 (oil on canvas), Hunt, William Holman (1827-1910)/Private Collection/Photo © Christie's Images/Bridgeman Images; **p57:** The Friar, detail from The Canterbury Tales, by Geoffrey Chaucer (c.1342-1400) Ellesmere Manuscript, facsimile edition, 1911 (for original detail see 128933), English School, (15th century) (after)/Private Collection/Bridgeman Images; **p79:** © Geraint Lewis/Alamy; **p85:** © Roger Cracknell 01/classic/Alamy; **p93:** REX/Ray Tang; **p94:** © Robbie Jack/Robbie Jack/Corbis; **p116:** St. George and the Dragon, c.1470 (oil on canvas) (for detail see 85548), Uccello, Paolo (1397-1475)/National Gallery, London, UK/Bridgeman Images; **p122:** © GL Archive/Alamy; **p129:** © Lordprice Collection/Alamy; **p140:** © Heritage Image Partnership Ltd/Alamy; **p161:** Mary Evans Picture Library; **p169:** Slave Trade, engraved by John Raphael Smith, pub. by S. Morgan, London, 1814 (mezzotint with later colouring) (pair of 120643), Morland, George (1763-1804) (after)/Private Collection/© Michael Graham-Stewart/Bridgeman Images; **p215:** © Bruce McGowan/Alamy

Although we have made every effort to trace and contact all copyright holders before publication this has not been possible in all cases. If notified, the publisher will rectify any errors or omissions at the earliest opportunity.

Page layout by Phoenix Photosetting.

Contents

How to use this book

A strong principle behind this book, and indeed the specification which it supports, is that A Level English Literature, at both AS and A level, involves more than simply the study of a named collection of set texts. For this reason, it is important that you use this book carefully – even though parts of it will cover options that you (and/or your teachers) have chosen not to study specifically.

The best way to demonstrate this is to look at the book's structure and how it relates to AQA English Literature Specification B.

Chapter 1 provides an introduction to the specification (at both AS and A level). This introductory chapter should be read by all students early on in the course.

Near the end of the book, Chapters 27–33 deal with topics that relate directly to the NEA (or coursework) component of A level. *However*, they have a much wider importance than this. These chapters deal with critical ideas and theories which are of relevance to both AS and A-level students – in all the exams that they take. This is because the Literature B specification requires you at all times to debate critical ideas. It is recommended that you start looking at these chapters early on in your course, and to have completed them all by the time you take your first examination. Obviously you will want to look again closely at the most relevant chapters if you are preparing coursework for A level.

The central chapters of this book deal with the examined components and involve options. Chapters 2–8 deal with 'Option 1A: Aspects of tragedy', and Chapters 9–15 deal with 'Option 1B: Aspects of comedy'. As an AS and/or A-level student, you will work through one of these options. Remember to read through all of the content in all of the chapters in your chosen option, even if your specific set text is not being covered. Although these chapters often deal with set texts, they are always looking more widely at aspects of the whole genre.

Chapters 16–20, and 21–26 are for A-Level students only (although AS students might like to look at what the full A Level has to offer). Again, there is a choice between two genres in the options being provided. Chapters 16-20 deal with 'Option 2A: Elements of crime writing' and Chapters 21–26 deal with 'Option 2B: Elements of political and social protest writing'. As with the Tragedy/Comedy options, you are strongly advised to read all of the chapters that apply to your choice of genre. Thinking about all of the set-text choices, rather than just your own, will broaden your understanding of the genre as a whole.

The label 'Key term', used within this book, indicates that each term listed is important. The first time that each key term is used in the book, it has been emboldened in the main text and defined briefly in the margin. Many subsequent appearances of each key term throughout the rest of the book have also been emboldened, to emphasize that they are key terms. However, because four of the sections in this book are optional, sometimes the key term margin definitions have been repeated to ensure that, whichever option(s) you choose, you receive the same background information. In addition, all of the separate key term definitions have been gathered together and repeated alphabetically on pages 264–267, as a glossary, for easy reference.

When it comes to revision for your exams, you should re-use this book sensibly – focusing on specific aspects that you are revising at the time. At this point, the glossary will also be of importance, by helping you to develop a critical vocabulary specific to this course.

A note on spelling

Certain words, for example 'specialized' and 'organized' have been spelt with 'ize' throughout this book. It is equally acceptable to spell these words and others with 'ise'.

An introduction to AQA English Literature Specification B

1

The specification's philosophy

It is tempting – when looking for the first time at an English Literature course – to launch straight into a review of the components and set books, and to ignore the fact that the whole specification may have an organizing set of ideas and approaches which you need to know first.

That is certainly the case with this specification, which is not just built around three components (two components at AS), but has some over-arching concepts that are well worth understanding before you start your study – and should be borne in mind throughout.

This chapter will:

- outline some underlying principles behind this specification
- introduce the choices within the specification
- introduce you to the key idea of 'significance' in this specification
- show you how the Assessment Objectives in this specification are organized
- introduce you to some of the most important skills needed for studying A/AS Level English Literature.

Ways of reading

This specification is designed to show you as an A-level literature student that there is no single way to read texts, but several ways. The pleasure and interest that come from reading closely, involve understanding that meanings in texts are not closed and fixed, but are open to several interpretations at the same time. Knowing that meanings are negotiated in many different ways, liberates you as a reader to explore alternative views and to be confident in your own judgements.

A focus on genre

If you are willing to accept that there are different ways of reading texts, which lead to different meanings and interpretations, then the idea of looking at texts through a certain 'lens' is a useful one. Our language is full of metaphors connected with *seeing*, in the sense of *understanding and interpreting*; a phrase such as 'I see what you mean' shows this.

This specification offers you various lenses, or filters, through which you can look at texts. In the examined components, the lenses are generic ones: in other words, you will be exploring your chosen texts through having first chosen a **genre** in which the text somehow fits. Note, though, that both of the examined components contain qualifiers in their titles. You are not being told that the text you study belongs to a certain genre; you are being asked to explore to what extent you can find elements or aspects of a genre within your text.

In other words, your chosen set texts do not definitively belong to a genre – but they may relate to one to a certain extent, depending on what you are specifically focusing on at the time.

Key term

Genre. A way of categorizing texts. Genres can be arranged around ways of writing (such as poetry/drama/prose), around content (such as crime, politics) around purpose (such as satire) and so on. In a most general sense, genre involves grouping texts by type – and so connecting texts. There are many ways of grouping literary texts. They can be grouped in many ways through their connections with other texts, with which they have things in common. In most cases, generic groupings are not fixed, so thinking about genre involves connecting with other texts.

A focus on theory

It should be clear by now that studying literature is not a factual process designed to find the 'truth'. If thinking about genre is one set of lenses through which you can look, another set involves understanding that there are different schools of critical thought which use different starting points, or theories, to look at texts.

Your NEA (non-exam assessment, once known as coursework) deals directly with some theoretical approaches to reading literature, and provides you with an anthology of critical reading to work with. A section of this book is devoted to exploring some of the main issues in this critical reading.

Sometimes when you are studying a linear course, with numbered components, it is easy to think that this is the required sequence of study – that you complete Component 1 first before going on to Component 2, and so on. That is certainly not the case with this course. You are strongly recommended to read through your Critical Anthology, and its associated material, at the start of this course, and to go back to it frequently throughout the course. At some points you will be required to work specifically with your Anthology while you carry out your two NEA pieces of work, but the value of the Anthology as an aid to supporting your ways of reading means that it should be constantly at your side.

Finding significance

The underlying principles introduced briefly above all lead to you being assessed on how well you can find meanings in texts, using all of the methods of analysis that the subject, and this specification's own emphasis, require.

A word that you will find frequently on your exam papers, in your teachers' questions and in this book, is **significance**. It is used not in a general sense of 'importance', but in a more specific sense to do with the study of possible meanings, or signification. Significance involves weighing up all of the potential contributions to the ways in which a text can be analysed (such as the way the text is constructed and written, contexts that can be applied, aspects of genre, and possible theoretical approaches) and then finding potential meanings and interpretations.

> **Key term**
>
> **Significance.** Your course of study, and this book designed to aid you in your course of study, are aimed at helping you to become an independent and active reader who can find relevant significances in your literary reading. Significance involves weighing up all the potential contributions to how a text can be analysed.

The Assessment Objectives

This specification offers you various routes to follow in your English Literature course. However, these routes have to be delivered within the framework of a national system. In the detail of your course you will soon understand that there are rules about things such as how many texts you study, when they were written, whether they are poetry, prose or drama, and so on. The permutations for these rules are quite complex and will be worked out for you by your teachers. The other part of the framework is the Assessment Objectives, which are the nationwide rules about the skills that must be covered in your course.

As you read about the Assessment Objectives below, the key thing to remember at this stage is that they are all assessed in all questions, so although you need to understand what they are and what you are required to do about them, you do not need to worry about whether they operate in some questions and not in others.

Assessment Objective 1 (AO1)

Within AO1 you are required to *articulate informed, personal and creative responses to literary texts, using associated concepts and terminology, and coherent, accurate written expression*. This Assessment Objective describes, then, the need for good writing and a use of terminology appropriate to the task you are doing.

Assessment Objective 2 (AO2)

AO2 requires you to *analyse ways in which meanings are shaped in literary texts*. This Assessment Objective describes the need to analyse authorial methods of writing, with the shaping of meanings a key idea here, indicating that you should link an author's ways of writing with the meanings that arise from them. Just listing a set of effects is not what is required.

Assessment Objective 3 (AO3)

AO3 requires you to *demonstrate understanding of the significance and influence of the contexts in which literary texts are written and received*. This specification is so closely linked to contexts in its references to genre and theory (see above) that if you answer the questions, you will be dealing with contexts.

Assessment Objective 4 (AO4)

AO4 requires you to *explore connections across literary texts*. Again, if you are working within a genre, then you are clearly connecting your text with others. There is a requirement here to show an understanding of the typical features of a genre, and then you can show the extent to which your text has typical aspects or elements of that genre.

Assessment Objective 5 (AO5)

AO5 requires you to *explore literary texts informed by different interpretations*. Again it should be clear that if you are working within ideas of genres and theories, there cannot be a single fixed interpretation, and if the question you are answering is framed as a debate, then you will need to consider different possible ways of interpreting your texts.

Specification design: various choices

This specification has, in all of its components, quite a large degree of choice. If you are working as part of a group in a school or college, these choices – especially those concerning the dates of texts – will be made for you. In the outline below, for the sake of simplicity, these are not given in detail.

Component 1 Literary genres

Option 1A: Aspects of tragedy **or** Option 1B: Aspects of comedy

These are two separate exams, of which you will study for one. They are closed-book exams, which means that you cannot take copies of the texts into the exam room. Whichever option you study, you will work on a compulsory Shakespeare play, another play and one further text. This means that two of your three texts in this component are plays, and that the study of drama is central to both tragedy and comedy.

Your final exam will include:

- writing about a Shakespeare extract and its relation to the play
- an essay on the same Shakespeare play
- an essay on two other texts.

In this book, there is detailed coverage of both tragedy and comedy.

Component 2 Texts and genres

Option 2A: Elements of crime writing **or** Option 2B: Elements of political and social protest writing

Again, there are two separate exams (of which you will study for one), but this time they are open-book exams, which means that you can take clean copies of your texts into the exam room. Whichever option you study, you will study three texts: one prose text written after 2000, one poetry text and one other text. In this exam you will also write about an 'unseen' text, which will relate to the genre you are studying.

Your final exam will include:

- writing about an unseen text or extract
- an essay on a single set text
- an essay on two other texts.

This book contains a section on each of these genres.

Component 3 NEA: Theory and independence

This component is a non-exam assessment (NEA), which was previously known as coursework. In this component you will write about two texts: one poetry and one prose. You will be working independently on your two tasks, and each task will have a link to the AQA Critical Anthology.

Your final NEA will include writing about:

- one poetry text in connection with at least one critical theory
- one prose text in connection with at least one critical theory.

All of the topics in the Critical Anthology are covered in this book. Remember that the theories can be applied to exam work as well as the NEA.

AS level

An AS-level specification runs alongside the A level one. The rules for AS level and its relationship to A level are common to all subjects.

The AS level in this specification relates to Component 1 of the A level. This means that you will study either 'Aspects of tragedy' or 'Aspects of comedy'. There will be two exam papers. The first involves the study of a Shakespeare play, plus another play. The second involves the study of a prose text and a poetry text.

This means that there will be parts of this book (those devoted to Component 2) that are not relevant to AS. What must be stressed, however, is the value of working with the material on critical theory, even though there is no NEA at AS level. This theoretical material will help you in your study of the set books at AS.

Laying the foundations for your Literature course

An opening exercise

Poems offer a good starting point for thinking about the skills that you need for studying English literature, because they are in many ways complete texts. Short poems can be especially useful, because they can be quickly processed on a first reading and then re-read several times. As you will see below, the constant re-reading of texts can open up meanings.

The following text is a poem by Alexander Pope. Read it aloud several times.

Epigram Engraved on the Collar of a Dog which I Gave to His Royal Highness

I am his Highness' dog at Kew:
Pray tell me, sir, whose dog are you?

Alexander Pope

Study tip

Poetry needs to be heard as well as seen. Practise reading poetry aloud, at least in your head, so that the significance of rhythm and rhyme becomes clear.

Asking questions

You face problems when first reading challenging texts – and A-level texts *are* challenging – because their meanings (note the plural here) will not always be immediately apparent. You should not feel, though, that you must come up with a full and complete understanding of the text and its possibilities right away. Instead, you would do better to have the confidence, and the skills, to know what questions to ask about the text, and how to go about answering them.

Sometimes you will find answers to your questions through your own thinking; sometimes you will consult an 'expert' such as your teacher or a critic; and probably most frequently as an A-level student, you will talk about it collectively in class.

Activity

Write out the Alexander Pope poem above on a blank piece of paper, then list a set of questions that will help you to understand the poem. When you have done this, collaborate with at least one other person to make a fuller list of questions. Finally, return to the book and look at the commentary below.

As with many activities in this book, it is best to carry out the activity yourself first, rather than simply jumping to the commentary.

Commentary

Here are some of the more obvious questions that may appear on your collective list:

1. What is an epigram?
2. What was actually given to the king?
3. Who is 'I' in the poem? Who is 'Sir'?
4. Who was Alexander Pope?
5. Who was 'His Royal Highness'?
6. What is Kew?
7. Why are dogs central to this poem?
8. Who is 'you' at the end of the poem?
9. What does the poem actually mean?

You may well have other questions, but in answering those above you can begin to understand some of the concepts and skills you need for this course.

Within some of the following explanations, you will find references to the Assessment Objectives. Note these for now, but do not do any more than that at this stage.

Key terms

Metaphor / Metaphorical. A literary technique that involves the transfer of meaning, with one thing described as being another (e.g. education is a journey, as in the metaphor 'I'm stuck' or ' I am making good progress'). There are many types of metaphor, but in a broad sense metaphor involves the linking of something with something else that is otherwise not related to it.

Reflexivity. The act of referring to yourself. In a literary sense, it involves texts showing and knowing that they are texts.

Representation / Representational. The process of showing versions of the world, rather than the real world itself. Literature can only ever be representational.

Satire / Satirical. A **genre** that criticizes people or systems, usually in a comic or witty way.

1. **What is an epigram?** An epigram is a short poem that uses **satire** to make a point (AO1). This text therefore connects with other texts through **genre** (AO4). The word 'genre' can be used here in two distinct ways. One refers to the structure of the poem, so is a technical connection (AO2), and one refers to the content of the poem, which is a contextual connection (AO3). Note also that the title of the poem refers to its own nature by labelling itself an epigram (AO2). This **reflexivity**, along with the fact that the title of the poem is almost as long as the poem itself, suggests that the author is in some ways playing with the reader's expectations.
2. **What was actually given to the king?** In reality nothing, as this is a fictional text, but if we go along with the world of **representation**, then several answers appear possible. It could be that the king was given a new dog, or a collar for a dog he already owns, or even the text of the poem which is engraved on the collar. This ambiguity, which arises out of the deliberate use of narrative voice (AO2) opens up several possible interpretations (AO5). This openness to interpretation is a feature you will come across repeatedly during your course.
3. **Who is 'I' in the poem? Who is 'Sir'?** There are two 'I's in the poem, one in the title and one in the body of the poem. Because of this structure (AO2), it would be wrong to assume that the first 'I' has to be the same as the second. There is considerable ambiguity around both voices, with one voice written and one represented as spoken – except of course, on another level, they are both written (AO5). Equally ambiguous is the reference to 'Sir'. It is marked off from the rest of the sentence by the commas either side of it (AO2). When you read the poem aloud these make you pause, but although this 'Sir' is addressed directly by the voice in the poem, no special clue is given about who it might be. See later for a further discussion of this.
4. **Who was Alexander Pope?** This question refers directly to the author's biography for help with the puzzle of the poem (AO3). This can sometimes be relevant – and here, it probably is – but beware, in working with this specification, of giving too much importance to details in the life of the author. Pope was a politically active poet; his favoured party, the Tories, had lost out to the Whigs in terms of power and influence. He had an axe to grind.
5. **Who was 'His Royal Highness'?** This is another historically based question, which seeks answers in factual contexts (AO3). George II was king at the time the poem was written in the 1730s, and he supported political groups and ideas that Pope disliked.
6. **What is Kew?** Kew was a royal palace on the edge of London, one of many royal palaces in use at the time. In that sense it was a seat of government (AO3). Why refer to this palace? The clue here lies in what the name sets up in the second line. Whenever a rhyme is completed (AO2), a special emphasis is placed on the sound completing the rhyme. Repeat the poem aloud, and you will hear that the word 'you', at the end of the poem, has a special importance.
7. **Why are dogs central to this poem?** They are mentioned both in the title of the poem and in the poem itself. Indeed, on one level, the poem is spoken by a dog – not such a strange thing when you consider the prominence of talking animals in children's literature, for example. But as an already experienced reader, you will almost certainly be wondering if there is more to these dogs than the literal. In other words, are they **metaphors**

(AO1/2)? One of the most challenging tasks for students of literature is to work out whether a text means literally what it says, or whether it is possible to find a wider **significance** (AO1/2/3/4/5) in what is written. Here we need to draw on some cultural knowledge about how dogs are perceived. Generally they are seen as blindly obedient, following orders and doing what their masters command. And if we want to keep going with some of the historical references we saw earlier (AO3), a particularly popular sort of dog in posh society in the 1700s was the lap-dog, which had no real purpose beyond fawning on its master.

8. **Who is 'you' at the end of the poem?** We have already noticed that the poem has a lot of **pronouns** (AO1/2), but we do not know who, specifically, they refer to. Also we have noticed that the word 'you' completes both the poem and the rhyme. Placed where it is, it would seem to contain a lot of potential significance. This significance can arise out of its possible reference points (AO5). The most obvious and literal 'you', in the world of talking dogs, is another dog. But if we leave it there, the poem is hardly satirical. If, though, we regard these dogs as representing certain humans, meanings begin to open up. The speaker proudly says that he (presumably) belongs to the king and asks 'sir' whom he belongs to? This sense of being owned by others is clearly significant. There is also another possible 'you', however, and that is the king himself. Who else, after all, is going to read the dog's collar?

9. **What does the poem actually mean?** It should be clear by now that this question has not really been framed properly, because the question carries the implication of looking for one 'right' answer. It would be much better instead to ask the question: What significance can you find in this poem? We have many clues in the contexts (AO3) to the poem, and in its genre (AO1/4), that this funny little poem carries lots of potentially serious meanings (AO5). The construction of the poem (AO2) also leads us to this conclusion. Overall, it suggests that the world of politics is based on fawning flattery and that nobody is immune from this. Public servants (courtiers then, a wider group now) look for preferment rather than policy. Politicians are almost proud of being uncritical as they jockey for the role of favourite. And if we see the ambiguity of 'you' at the end of the poem, even the person at the very top, 'His Highness', is not really the master, but is subservient to others. If this poem were stuck in time, and merely a historical document, we would probably not bother to read it any more. But because what Pope says still resonates now, and we can see in his simple little poem an acute observation on the ways in which organizations work today (nationally, locally, institutionally), we continue to read the poem with contemporary significances in mind.

Key term

Pronoun. A word that stands for and replaces a noun.

Why the term 'significance' is at the heart of this specification

When looking at the question 'Why are dogs central to this poem?' above, you will notice that when the word '**significance**' is used, all of the Assessment Objectives are seen to apply. This holistic view of English literature, with all aspects of the subject being applied at the same time, places the idea of significance right at the heart of this specification. It is worth, therefore, understanding how the term is used – not only in this book but in the questions you will be asked as part of your final assessments.

Link

This specification encourages interpretation. The Critical Anthology which you need to use for your NEA is discussed later in this book (see Chapter 27 pages 217–218). Make sure that you are familiar with at least some of these critical ideas early on in your course.

Key term

Semiotics. The study of signs and how they work. Signs can be visual (a red light on a traffic light worldwide means stop) and can also be verbal (a Rolls Royce car, at least in British culture, could signify social class and wealth for example). Semiotics, then, looks at the significance of connotations.

In general usage, the word 'significance' can mean 'importance' or 'noteworthiness', but here it is being used in a very specific and academic way, deriving from **semiotics**. Signs (such as road signs, for example) are ways of representing the world. A sign, say a number 30 in a circle, has the signification or meaning of 'you may travel at a maximum speed of 30 mph in this area'. The motorist must interpret the sign and know what it means. So significance, in the way it is used in this specification, involves finding interpretations and making meanings. Road signs are intended to be unambiguous – otherwise chaos would reign – but in literature, as we have seen in the poem above, ambiguity can be seen as a positive. That is why questions which ask you to discuss the significance of something, are asking you to debate possible ideas – not to give a predetermined answer.

Activity

To make sure that you understand the key term 'significance', map out in note form a response to the following question: 'What is the significance of dogs in Pope's poem as a whole?'

When you have done this, look at the commentary below.

Link

For more about the role of narrative when we read, look at the NEA section of this book (Chapters 29 and 30).

Commentary

The whole poem is configured around dogs. The narrative that the poem tells is about the gift of a collar, or even a dog, to the king. Genre and implications of power suggest that this is a satirical poem with dogs at the heart of the possible meanings. Dogs can represent servility, and the seeking of approval. They can suggest political corruption. There is the sense that we are all dogs in that we all follow masters; that even the king is not really as powerful as he thinks; that all power is corrupt and empty; and so on.

Significance: a short walk or a whole life

To conclude this introductory work, and to focus particularly on significance, let's look at a much-anthologized poem by Robert Frost, sometimes entitled 'The Road Not Taken'. The metaphor of the journey is used in many literary texts, as well as films. So-called 'road' novels and films are a distinct genre in themselves. Frequently, the road and the journey serve as literal settings for action to take place, but as the journey progresses we become aware that characters are learning from their experiences and being changed as people, usually becoming wiser and more knowledgeable. As the journey develops, so does the individual.

Did you know?

Lines and phrases from 'The Road Not Taken' are often quoted in self-help books and management training, in order to suggest that unconventional people are the ones who succeed in life.

In this poem, Frost gives us a variant on the road theme: a person is standing at a crossroads, deciding which path to take. The idea of the crossroads is, of course, a common one in everyday life – we frequently refer to ourselves and others as being at a crossroads, when we are referring to potentially life-changing decisions.

Activity

Read the poem opposite. What different possible **significances** can you find in the way Frost uses the 'Two roads' in this poem? Make a note of where you are applying the Assessment Objectives when you answer this question.

The Road Not Taken

Two roads diverged in a yellow wood,
And sorry I could not travel both
And be one traveler, long I stood
And looked down one as far as I could
To where it bent in the undergrowth.

Then took the other, as just as fair,
And having perhaps the better claim,
Because it was grassy and wanted wear;
Though as for that the passing there
Had worn them really about the same.

And both that morning equally lay
In leaves no step had trodden black.
Oh, I kept the first for another day!
Yet knowing how way leads on to way,
I doubted if I should ever come back.

I shall be telling this with a sigh
Somewhere ages and ages hence:
Two roads diverged in a wood, and I –
I took the one less traveled by,
And that has made all the difference.

Robert Frost, 1920

Commentary

If you read this poem a number of times, its apparent simplicity becomes ever more complex. Clearly one way to read it is to stay with the idea promoted in self-help books (AO3) that it is a road poem (AO4) about having the courage to make unconventional life choices, to do what most people will not do. But the more you read the poem, the more problematic that simple reading becomes (AO5).

Where poems are so clearly structured (AO2) in their stanza patterns, it can often help to take one stanza at a time and look at the way the argument moves forward. This poem has four stanzas of five lines each.

Stanza 1: The dilemma is set up: there are two paths, and although the speaker (who we will assume is male) would like to travel down both, he knows that he can choose only one. Nonetheless, he takes his time and tries to peer ahead down one route to see if it is worth taking. The possible significance here involves understanding that the poem can be interpreted as being about a whole life rather than just a short walk.

Stanza 2: The narrator chooses the path that is less worn, but it's a close-run thing between the two. The two paths are not that different. The significance here could be that it is not the dramatically different choices that are difficult to make, but the ones which are nearly the same.

Stanza 3: Again the narrator tells us that there is not much to choose between the two paths: on 'that morning' they were in fact identical. He decides to keep one for another day (so it is not a major decision), while at the same time knowing that he probably won't ever come back to take the other path. The little word 'Oh' makes it all sound rather unimportant. The significance here could be to do with the way in which we can tell ourselves that our life choices are reversible, when in truth they are not. And deep down, we know they are not.

Stanza 4: In poetry, final stanzas often carry the most significance, because they create some sort of conclusion to an argument. In this stanza, we find the famous lines, often quoted out of context:

> I took the one less traveled by,
> And that has made all the difference.

Taken in isolation, it is possible to see why these lines can be used to encourage individuality and risk-taking. They are put in a different context, though, by the two lines that precede them. The chronology of the poem – its time sequence – makes reference to the present, the future and, in the last lines, a sort of future/past. Out of context, of course the final two lines look confident and definitive, but in context there is much more ambiguity. The fact that the speaker knows he will be 'telling this with a sigh' makes the choice seem far less obviously 'right'. A sigh certainly seems to suggest regret, for example.

So one way of reading this conclusion to the poem is to say that 'The Road Not Taken' is not so much about making life choices, but about how in retrospect we give more importance to what we see as key moments in our life than they really deserve. In this reading, the **significance** of these final lines differs from the way they are commonly interpreted; the journey of life is not about vital choices, it is about accepting that you have to live with the consequences of what you do.

Not surprisingly, this poem has received a huge amount of critical response. Whatever their reading of the poem, most critics see the crossroads as highly significant. Just to add to the ambiguity, though, Frost himself warned readers to be wary of reading the poem too simply as a moral tale, saying it was 'more tricky' than that. He said it was in part about his friend and fellow poet Edward Thomas, who was horribly indecisive and could not even choose which path to take on a walk without making a fuss about it.

Link

The NEA/coursework section of this book (Chapters 27–33) looks at different ways of reading texts. It is well worth referring to throughout your study.

Extension activity

1. Look up the following article about Frost's poem, from the *Guardian* in 2011. What is your response to it? http://www.theguardian.com/books/2011/jul/29/robert-frost-edward-thomas-poetry
2. To understand more about **significance**, **genre**, **metaphor** and other ideas introduced in this chapter, research more widely the ways in which animals, and in particular journeys, are used in representational texts. A starting point could be to research and watch some road movies. In literature, from the *Odyssey* and *Aeneid* onwards, there are countless examples of texts organized around journeys. Cormac McCarthy's *The Road* is a recent example of a novel. Philip Larkin's poem 'No Road' is worth reading. Your research in these areas could lead to some possible texts to study for your non-exam assessment (coursework).
3. Consider the ideas about eco-criticism that are in your Critical Anthology and in the NEA/coursework section of this book. How could 'The Road Not Taken' be interpreted through the lens of eco-criticism?

Summary

This introductory chapter has established some of the underlying principles behind the way in which AQA English Literature Specification B works. In particular, it has focused on the holistic way in which the subject is approached, and the importance of finding **significance** in what you read.

Component 1 Literary genres

Option 1A: Aspects of tragedy

2 Tragedy: an introduction

This chapter introduces you to the study of tragedy within this specification. The course as a whole aims to encourage you to develop your interest in, and enjoyment of, literature and literary studies, and for the 'Aspects of tragedy' option you will:

- read widely and independently set texts and others that you have selected for yourself
- engage critically and creatively with a substantial body of texts and ways of responding to them
- develop and effectively apply your knowledge of literary analysis and evaluation
- explore the contexts of the tragedies you are reading and others' interpretations of them.

Aspects of tragedy: some initial concepts

Tragedy has a long tradition in literature, with its origins in the ancient world and with a special emphasis on drama. Although there are variations, at the core of all the set texts is often a tragic hero who is flawed in some way, who suffers and causes suffering. In all the texts there is an interplay between what might be seen as tragic villains and tragic victims.

Some tragic features will be more in evidence in some texts than in others, and you will need to understand how particular aspects of the tragic **genre** are used and how they work in your chosen texts. The absence of any one of these aspects can be as significant as its presence.

As the AS and A-level specifications show, there can be no exhaustive list of the possible aspects of tragedy, but areas that might be considered include:

- the type of tragic text itself, whether it is classical and about public figures, like *King Lear*, or domestic and about representations of ordinary people, as in *Tess of the d'Urbervilles*
- the settings for the tragedy, both places and times
- the protagonists' journey towards death, their flaws (such as pride and folly), their blindness and their insight, their discovery and learning, their mixture of good and evil
- the role of the tragic villain or opponent, who directly affects the fortune of the hero, who engages in a contest of power and is partly responsible for the hero's demise
- the presence of fate and how the hero's end can be seen as inevitable
- how the hero's behaviour affects the world around him or her, creating chaos and affecting the lives of others
- the **significance** of violence and revenge, humour and moments of happiness
- the structural pattern of the text as it moves through complication to catastrophe, from order to disorder, through climax to resolution, from the hero's prosperity and happiness to his or her tragic end
- the use of plots and sub-plots
- the way language is used to heighten the tragedy
- ultimately, how the tragedy affects the audience, acts as a commentary on the real world, and moves the audience through pity and fear to an understanding of the human condition.

Connecting across the A level

The concepts described above make a good checklist for any student exploring 'Aspects of tragedy', but you will also make your own decisions and reach your own views about the texts. Later in the course, your views might be shaped by other aspects of your studies. For example, you may find that studying 'Elements of political and social protest writing' or 'Elements of crime writing' informs your views about tragedy.

The most important thing to remember is that you should always be ready to make connections and to examine tragedy from a variety of angles and perspectives.

Discussing tragedy

Tragedy is a genre of literature that ends with the death of the main character. In principle, there are two main kinds of tragedy:

- The form written by classical Greek dramatists (such as Sophocles, Aeschylus and Euripides) and later refined by Shakespeare and his contemporaries, in which the audience witnesses terrible chaos and breakdown in society. We may usefully label this **classical** or **epic tragedy**
- The type usually known as **modern** or **domestic tragedy**. This may initially seem less ambitious than classical or epic tragedy, but it confronts many of the same issues. It usually involves the breakdown of a family, showing the corruption and chaos that lurk beneath apparent domestic order. This type of tragedy was established in the nineteenth century by writers such as Henrik Ibsen and August Strindberg, and was later developed by twentieth-century playwrights such as Tennessee Williams and Arthur Miller. More recent plays are often labelled **contemporary tragedy**.

Tragedies are ambitious texts because they carry huge subject matter and themes. In most dramas of this type, three aspects are emphasized: suffering, chaos and death.

- Suffering is what the characters must endure in a tragedy. The audience watches how the suffering is created and how the central characters deal with it.
- Chaos (which we might also term **disorder**) can be personal, social and political. In some tragedies the central character breaks down; in others the whole of society disintegrates, while several tragedies show both the characters and their society falling apart and collapsing. Chaos usually leads to death.
- At the end of the story, both cast and audience are left staring at the reality of death and the disintegration which follows it. Tragedies offer a bleak vision of life, since they concentrate on failure, conflict and disaster.

Activity

With a partner, make a list of all of the events, dramas, stories, films, songs, television programmes and computer games that you can think of which involve aspects of tragedy. Share some of these with your class. What common features can you identify? What makes the storyline particularly tragic?

Commentary

You will probably have thought of the titles of a number of well-known plays, novels, films, and so on. You may also have thought of many powerful real-life stories which have ended in death. For example, the destruction of New York's World Trade Centre on 11 September 2001, the killing of hostages, and the early deaths of famous people such as Peaches Geldof and Amy Winehouse.

Link

Your reading of the tragedies that you study will also be informed by the critical methods and ideas which you will learn about from the NEA Critical Anthology (see Chapters 27–33).

Key terms

Classical tragedy. Plays written in ancient Greece or Rome, or in a similar style.

Contemporary tragedy. Plays written in the late twentieth or twenty-first centuries.

Disorder. The inversion or destruction of the normal order in a society.

Domestic tragedy. A drama set in a household, apparently without grand or ambitious themes.

Epic tragedy. Plays with a grand or ambitious theme.

Modern tragedy. Plays written in the late nineteenth or twentieth century.

Key term

Conventions. The accepted rules, structures and customs that we expect to see in a specific genre of writing.

Sometimes whole events are labelled 'tragedies', such as the disappearance of Malaysian Airlines flight MH570 in March 2014. However, in these cases we are often using the term 'tragedy' quite loosely. In everyday use it can refer to accidents, disastrous events that move us, examples of outrageously bad luck, and even sporting failure.. When we consider the literary genre of tragedy, though, we need to see it working within certain **conventions**.

Tragedy in literature

Tragedy is a specific genre of literature which operates within a set of conventions. In terms of dramatic tragedy, which you will look at first, these conventions have helped to define what happens on stage, and why writers construct tragedies in certain ways.

One of the things the audience should feel when watching a tragedy is that somehow the world is a worse place without the tragic hero being part of it. As we continue through this unit, keep in mind the popular and everyday ideas of tragedy, but try to compare them with the literary genre of tragedy. You will need to examine these literary conventions within your exam answers, and comment on their occurrence in the texts you study.

Conclusion

In this first chapter, you have been introduced to tragedy as an important literary genre, and have seen some of the various forms it can take. You will have noted issues such as the importance of the tragic hero, and have understood initial aspects of the structure of tragedy.

Tragedy: concepts and theories

3

Introduction

In this chapter you will:

- study further the concepts and theories behind tragedy, so that you can make informed responses to texts
- begin to analyse the ways in which established authorial methods shape meanings in tragedies, and apply these concepts and theories to your chosen exam texts
- consider concepts and theories from the medieval and Renaissance periods.

Tragedies may have been performed in other parts of the world in ancient times, but the western tradition began in ancient Greece.

One of the most important discussions of the theory or concept behind tragedy is to be found in Aristotle's *Poetics*. In this work, the philosopher Aristotle attempts to define and understand how the **genre** of tragedy works. He begins to define it by commenting that a tragic drama is the '**imitation** of an action that is admirable, complete and possesses **magnitude**'. He also notes that tragedy is a form of drama that excites the emotions of 'pity and fear'. Its action should be 'single' and 'complete', presenting a 'reversal of fortune', involving persons who are 'held in great esteem', and it should be written in 'language made pleasurable'.

From these ideas, Aristotle identifies six core components of tragedy:

- plot
- character/characterization
- diction
- reasoning
- spectacle
- lyric poetry.

The features of tragedy established by Aristotle influenced later Athenian writers, and to a certain extent the work of Shakespeare and his contemporaries – and even new tragedies which you can see today.

As you have already learned, most tragedies are based on a serious exploration of an event that causes the downfall of a central character. In narrative prose, or even poetry, writers have to explain everything for the reader, but drama is more flexible in its interpretation. Obviously, the way actors look, their interaction with an audience, their facial expressions and their movement and gestures will all give other indications of how the drama can be interpreted, beyond the words of the script alone.

Tragedy also deals with the issue of fortune or chance. According to Aristotle, events in tragedies do not happen just by chance. They happen because of the circumstances which the characters find themselves in.

Aristotle's theories about tragedy: a summary

Aristotle's theories about tragedy are summarized below. Although they cannot be applied to every tragedy you encounter, the model he suggests is a useful one to keep in mind when you study tragedy:

- The **protagonist**, or central character, is a man or woman of high rank, power or fortune. The protagonist can be noble (of noble birth) or show wisdom (by virtue of their birth).
- He or she undergoes a catastrophe (Greek *peripeteia*) – which is usually a reversal of fortune.
- He or she must suffer beyond what most people ever endure in their lives. His or her suffering causes pity (for the protagonist) and fear (in the audience themselves).

Key terms

Characterization. The way in which an author creates and uses characters, and why.

Diction. In the sense in which Aristotle uses it, this means the composition of the verse.

Imitation. In Aristotle's theory, this means acting like or being like the real world.

Lyric poetry. The medium in which classical drama is written.

Magnitude. The presence of the ambition in tragedy to deal with an event that is sufficiently serious.

Plot. The chain of causes and circumstances that connect the various events and place them in some sort of relationship with each other.

Protagonist. In dramatic terms, the first major character who offers a particular view. The protagonist is often seen in opposition to the **antagonist**. ▶

Key term

Reasoning. The case being staged and the opinions being put forward by the characters.

Did you know?

The word 'tragedy' has its origins in the Greek phrase *trago idia* from *tragos* (goat) and *aeidein* (to sing). So 'tragedy' literally means 'goat song'. This may be because songs were sung before goats were led to an altar for sacrifice, or because actors who played satyrs (who featured in early tragedies) wore goat costumes.

Did you know?

In ancient Greece, watching tragedies was regarded in part as an educational process, because citizens would learn from them about codes of behaviour, and what constituted heroism or human failure.

- His or her downfall is caused by a series of bad choices, made as a result of a tragic flaw (*hamartia*) in his or her character. The most common flaw is excessive pride, or *hubris*. Often, a bad choice inverts the natural order of things.
- There is usually a scene in which the protagonist comes to understand his or her own flaw and why events have gone the way they have. There is then a recognition of the *hamartia*.
- This moment provides the *catharsis* or emotional release for the audience.

These theories are not rules or criteria for measuring the degree to which a play is a tragedy. They are there to help you think about the concepts and effects of tragedy.

The concept of *catharsis*

Aristotle further suggested that when writing tragedy, dramatists should be aiming to arouse pity and fear in the audience so as to purge or purify these emotions. *Catharsis* (or purification) is the term Aristotle applies to the way Greek tragedies worked – they should purge or sweep away the pity and fear brought about by the tragic action being performed. This emotional release purifies the mind and body. In this way, Aristotle argued, the audience would learn how to behave and to conduct their lives.

Not all readers and observers of drama agree with the concept of *catharsis*. The German dramatist and poet Bertolt Brecht (1898–1956) suggested that rather than having the effect of purging emotions in this way, tragedies should make people think about how to change the world for the better. Brecht considered the idea of purification to be an outmoded one.

Activity

Consider the overall story in Shakespeare's *Othello* or *King Lear*. Bearing in mind what you have read about the theory of tragedy as described in Aristotle's *Poetics*, try answering the following questions:

1. Is the story an imitation of an action that is serious?
2. Does the story have magnitude?
3. Is the story complete in itself?
4. Does the story arouse the emotions of pity and fear in you?
5. Does the story contain persons who are renowned and of superior attainments?
6. Is an experience of *catharsis* (a purging of the pity and fear) offered in the story?
7. Do you think Brecht's theory about tragedy has some relevance here as well?

Commentary

In *Othello*, the play *is* an imitation of an action that is serious. It involves the accusation that Othello's wife is unfaithful to him, and culminates in the death of Othello, his wife Desdemona, and a number of other characters. The play has a certain magnitude: it is set in glamorous and exotic Venice and Cyprus and contains characters of high status. Othello is a Moor (one of the play's central issues is that of race) but he is also a successful military general in the service of the state. Desdemona is the daughter of Brabantio, a Venetian senator, so is also of high status. Therefore, they are persons renowned and of superior attainments. The play reaches a full resolution: the surviving characters must negotiate their way in the new order of a Venice without Othello.

The murder of Desdemona does arouse fear and pity within us as an audience, because we know that she is innocent and that Othello is mistaken. Othello's downfall and death are more ambivalent; is he too easily fooled?

In the case of *King Lear*, Lear's division of Britain is a serious act that has magnitude. Lear and many of the other characters are obviously of high status. Like *Othello*, the play also reaches some sort of resolution: the surviving characters must move forward in a new order after Lear and Cordelia's deaths.

Lear's destruction also arouses fear and pity within us as an audience, because we see him making wrong decisions. Kent and Albany's final words, however, leave us wondering what lessons can be learned and whether humanity can ever flourish again.

The concepts of *hubris* and *hamartia*

Aristotle saw the 'tragic pleasure of pity and fear' as being the most distinctive thing about a tragedy. He notes that in order for the tragic hero to arouse such feelings in an audience, he or she cannot be either all good or bad, but importantly must be someone with whom the audience can identify. If the tragic hero is superior in some specific way (perhaps a king or a general), then the tragedy and pleasure of pity and fear will be intensified for the audience watching. Put another way, the tragedy is more intense because the hero has further to fall. Kings like Lear make great subject matter in tragedy, because they begin at the top of the hierarchy of human society.

As we have seen, according to Aristotle the disastrous results are often brought about by the tragic hero making a mistake based on a tragic flaw in his or her character. For Othello, his mistake is to put absolute trust in his lieutenant Iago, who is spinning a web of deceit. For Lear, it is his decision to divide Britain and seek the wrong kind of love from his daughters. Aristotle named this *hubris*, a kind of excessive pride that causes the hero to ignore divine or other important warnings, or to break moral codes. For example, many characters warn Othello of his self-deception, but he chooses to ignore them. In *King Lear*, Cordelia warns Lear of the mistake he is making. This error breaks the established and 'natural' order. The mistake that is made is termed *hamartia,* which can refer both to a tragic error and a tragic flaw.

The critic Karen Newman uses the term 'contrary to nature' about the marriage of Othello and Desdemona. What she means here is that sometimes tragic events occur because the characters and situations 'invert' or 'break' the natural order. This idea of what is a 'natural order' is related to the **ideology** of the time in which the play was written. In many tragedies, the natural order is broken irreversibly. In *King Lear*, Lear abdicates, dividing up the island of Britain. This inverts 'natural' kingship and causes chaos.

One final point here is that, because the tragic hero's suffering is greater than is warranted by the actual offence, the audience feels pity. They realize that they could have behaved in exactly the same way, and therefore feel sorry for the character enduring the suffering.

Activity

Consider the concepts of *catharsis*, *hubris* and *hamartia*. Where are they to be seen in the play you are studying? Discuss how relevant you feel these ideas are in the twenty-first century. Are there any high-status leaders in history, or media stars in the contemporary world, to whom we might apply these terms?

Key term

Ideology. A view of the world held by a particular group of people at a particular time.

Aristotle's deductions

By now you should begin to see how Aristotle's arguments relate to *Othello* or *King Lear*. Read the following conclusions which he reaches about the structure of tragedies:

- Any decent people should not be seen undergoing a change from good fortune to bad fortune – this does not evoke fear or pity, but disgust.
- Nor should depraved people be seen undergoing a change from bad fortune to good fortune – this is the least tragic of all: it has none of the right effects, since it is neither agreeable, nor does it evoke pity or fear.
- Nor again should a wicked person fall from good fortune to bad fortune – that kind of structure would be agreeable, but would not excite pity and fear.
- It follows that a well-formed plot will involve a change not to good fortune from bad fortune, but from good fortune to bad fortune – and this must be due not to depravity but to a serious error.
- The best tragedies are constructed around a few households, and any others whose lot it has been to experience something terrible – or to perform some terrible action.

Activity

Considering the above statements and all that you have learned so far about tragedy and tragic heroes, take a piece of A3 paper and sketch the tragic hero from the tragedy you are studying. Now add all of the components that feed into the construction of the tragedy. You should find that some of the components are internal and connected with the hero's character: place these *inside* your figure. Some components will be external, connected with events in society: place these *around* your figure.

Present your sketch to the rest of your class. Discuss whether one of these components has an overriding influence, or whether they all input equally into the character's downfall.

Did you know?

A sub-genre of drama from Shakespeare's time, derived from the work of the Roman playwright Seneca, is called revenge tragedy. Components of this are used by Shakespeare in his own plays, notably in *Hamlet*.

Aspects of revenge can be found in *Othello* (in the character of Iago), and many strands in *King Lear* relate to revenge. You may also discover ideas about revenge in *Richard II*, and revenge-related acts in *Death of a Salesman* and *A Streetcar Named Desire*. Keep the concept of revenge in mind as you study these texts.

The concept of revenge

Revenge is an important concept in many tragedies – both in Classical Greek drama and in the work of Shakespeare and his contemporaries. Watching characters gaining revenge on those who have done them some harm was popular viewing – and the process of revenge can sometimes form an integral part of a tragedy.

The difficulty with revenge in a Christian worldview is that it is regarded as being inconsistent with Christian beliefs. Christianity promotes the idea of forgiveness rather than revenge, which is sometimes seen as more of a pagan or Old Testament concept. This, however, did not stop the theme of revenge from becoming central to the popularity of plays. There is a notion that we like to see wrongdoers get their come-uppance; it is a human trait to want to see the downfall or punishment of someone who has done you wrong.

Medieval tragedy and the wheel of fortune

In medieval times, when Greek tragedy was still unknown in Western Europe, people also considered in detail what tragedy was about. Tragedy was perceived as a reversal of fortune for particular characters, who experienced a fall from a high position.

Medieval societies had a concept of Fortune, **personified** as Dame Fortune, a blindfolded woman who turned a wheel at her own whim. Human beings were positioned around the wheel. The top of the wheel represented the best fortune to be had, while those at the bottom of the wheel had the worst fortune. However, the wheel could turn at any point, so that those at the top could suddenly find themselves at the bottom, and vice versa.

Much drama in the medieval period had a religious origin, with the main tragic stories being the Fall of Lucifer and the temptation of Adam and Eve, with their expulsion from Paradise. Sometimes the characters in the plays make the wrong decisions out of pride. From these types of plays, the more complex tragedies of the Renaissance evolved.

Key term

Personification. The attribution of human feelings or ideas to a non-human concept.

Did you know?

Tragic episodes formed major components of medieval mystery and morality plays, which were performed in places as diverse as Cornwall, York, Chester and Wakefield.

Tragedy: not comedy

You have probably seen the image of two masks representing the two main strands of drama: comedy and tragedy. One other productive way of thinking about tragedy is to see it as a comedy that goes wrong. Shakespearean comedies, in particular, may be considered in this connection. Usually, a comedy of this type will begin in an 'old world', with the characters who inhabit it encountering a particular problem (for example, the lovers in *A Midsummer Night's Dream*, who wish to escape Athenian law, or the twins Sebastian and Viola being shipwrecked off the coast of Illyria in *Twelfth Night*).

Such characters usually escape to the 'Green World' (so-called because it is usually in a forest or wood – as in *A Midsummer Night's Dream* or *As You Like It* – or in a strange new country, as in *Twelfth Night*). The Green World is beyond the reaches of law, order and civilization, and therefore anarchy, chaos and an inverted social order exist. Confusion, disguise and mistaken identity are rife, which means that lovers are given the wrong partners and events become disordered. In most comedies this **disorder** is eventually resolved and the characters progress to a 'new world', in which the confusion of the past is negated. Very often this resolution is given new impetus by a marriage, or multiple marriages, between the main characters.

You should be able to see that tragedies sometimes follow the same structure as comedies, except that in tragedy the confusion of the Green World continues, spiralling downwards and taking all the characters with it. Confusion and mistaken identity are not resolved in time, and death follows. A new world is eventually created, but some characters have had to die before it can be constructed.

Conclusion

In this section you have explored some critical theories and concepts that should allow you to write more confidently about aspects of tragedy. The core concepts of *catharsis*, *hubris* and *hamartia* can become a regular part of your vocabulary when you discuss tragedies.

4 Shakespearean tragedy: *Othello* and *King Lear*

In this chapter you will:

- further understand the **significance** of the context in which tragedies are written and received
- start to apply the ideas of tragic heroes and villains to the texts you are studying
- focus on either *Othello* or *King Lear* as the Shakespearean tragedy you will study.

Othello

The way that 'tragedy can strike' and seem like 'a bad dream' can be seen in one of Shakespeare's most famous tragedies, *The Tragedy of Othello: The Moor of Venice*, which was written between 1602 and 1604. *Othello* has many of the characteristics of a typical Shakespearean tragedy. Notice the full title: the Elizabethan audience first watching the drama would have no difficulty in recognizing that the play was a tragedy, since the term indicated that it would be about the death of a great or noble person.

Another important point to note about the title of this play is that Othello is described as a Moor. The Moors were Muslim inhabitants of northern Africa, mainly in Algeria and Morocco. Othello would therefore not have been born a Christian, which is a contrast to most other Shakespearean heroes. Moors were black-skinned, and by making Othello a tragic hero, Shakespeare was doing something original for his time.

In the play, the life of Othello (the tragic hero) descends into chaos or disorder when he is misled by his friend and lieutenant, Iago (the villain) into believing that his wife Desdemona (the victim) is unfaithful. Iago's motives for manipulating Othello are varied and often inconsistent, but they include his own jealousy and his belief that he has been passed over for promotion in favour of Cassio. At one point in the play, Othello uses the word 'chaos', although the tone is a loving one. Desdemona has just left the stage and he tenderly says:

> I do love thee, and when I love thee not
> Chaos is come again.

The language here is predictive of their fate, and these words have a grim irony later on in the drama. After being misled by Iago, Othello is filled with rage, doubt and fear. His nobility then gives way to the chaos of desire for revenge on those who have hurt him. Tragedy strikes Othello from nowhere, and when he finds out about the supposed affair between Desdemona and Cassio, he acts instantly.

Chaos and disorder in *Othello*

Othello is presented as a very noble and thoughtful man, who has the ability to cope with the racist slurs made against him by Brabantio. Structurally, however, Shakespeare is setting up Othello for a fall. This is the way that many playwrights construct tragedy, and you will see it over and over again. In some ways, Shakespeare wishes to present Othello as someone who is naïve about the way the world operates – hence Helen Gardner's observation about Othello's 'inadequacy' as a noble hero.

What you may also have noticed in the text is that there has been some notable change in the social order, and it is this change that leads to the destruction of human life. In *Othello*, the change in the social order is the marriage between Othello and Desdemona – a black man and a white woman.

Iago, recognizing that he has some considerable power and influence over Othello, manipulates information and events, so that Othello will believe anything that he says. We see that Iago is a recognizable type of tragic villain, who causes catastrophe for his own ends. Early on, he lies, telling Brabantio that Othello has bewitched his daughter. Later, he spreads the lie that Cassio is a drunk, and tells Othello that Desdemona gave Cassio her handkerchief as a symbol of her love for him.

Iago is frequently labelled as 'honest' by other characters, and often speaks to the audience in **soliloquies** or **asides** in which we learn of his possible objectives – possible, because Iago's motives often seem confused. Iago is the character who helps along the disorder for his own ends.

Did you know?

Traditionally, characters are regarded as necessarily telling the truth as they see it in their soliloquies and asides, although Iago's inconsistencies make it more complicated in his case.

Different readings of *Othello*

It is important to remember that the opinions of successive generations of readers about *Othello* are always influenced by the time period in which they are writing and by the trends of literary scholarship. For example, someone writing in the eighteenth century about interracial marriage would probably have a very different view from someone writing in the twenty-first century. Therefore, you should read all criticism with a degree of scepticism – keeping an open mind and constantly looking back at the text itself.

One of the most influential commentators on Shakespeare's tragedies was A. C. Bradley (1851–1935). Bradley took a very character-driven approach towards tragedy, which has since been heavily criticized. Nevertheless, in his famous book *Shakespearean Tragedy*, originally published in 1904, Bradley makes many helpful points about the play, which have implications for other tragedies as well. Here are some examples:

> Of all Shakespeare's tragedies, I would answer, not even excepting *King Lear*, *Othello* is the most painfully exciting and the most terrible. From the moment when the temptation of the hero begins, the reader's heart and mind are held in a vice, experiencing the extremes of pity and fear, sympathy and repulsion, sickening hope and dreadful expectation.
>
> … There is no subject more exciting than sexual jealousy rising to the pitch of passion; and there can hardly be any spectacle at once so engrossing and so painful as that of a great nature suffering the torment of this passion, and driven by it to a crime which is also a hideous blunder.
>
> A. C. Bradley (1904), *Shakespearean Tragedy*, pp.143–144

Bradley was writing at the beginning of the twentieth century. A critic writing in the middle of that century, Helen Gardner, has this to say about Othello:

> Othello is like a hero of the ancient world in that he is not a man like us, but a man recognized as extraordinary. He seems born to do great deeds and live in legend. He has the obvious heroic qualities of courage and strength, and no actor can attempt the role who is not physically impressive. He has the heroic capacity for passion. But the thing that most sets him apart is his solitariness. He is a stranger, a man of alien race, without ties of nature or natural duties. His value is not in what the world thinks of him, although the world rates him highly, and does not derive in any way from his station. It is inherent. He is, in a sense, a 'self-made man', the product of a certain kind of life which he has chosen to lead.
>
> Anne Ridler (ed.) (1970) *Shakespearean Criticism 1935–1970*, pp.352–353.

Key terms

Aside. A brief soliloquy, where – within a longer sequence of dialogue – a character speaks a short line aside, as if privately, to the audience – revealing their true thoughts about events on stage.

Soliloquy. A speech where a character tells or confesses thoughts to the audience, unheard by other characters. Soliloquies are often used in tragedies because they tell us why particular characters are doing something. In films, this is often presented as a voice-over to imitate the thoughts inside a character's mind.

Link

For ideas on aspects of power in literary texts, see the chapter on Marxism and Feminism, Chapter 28.

A more recent interpretation of the play is offered by Karen Newman, who explores the connection between race and sexuality in the play. Many prejudices and stereotypes are turned upside-down by the marriage of Othello and Desdemona:

> In *Othello*, the black Moor and the fair Desdemona are united in a marriage which all the other characters view as unthinkable. Shakespeare uses their assumption to generate the plot itself – Iago's ploy to string Roderigo along is his assurance that Desdemona could not, contrary to nature, long love a black man. Even his manipulation of Othello depends on the Moor's own prejudices against his blackness and belief that the fair Desdemona would prefer the white Cassio.
>
> Karen Newman in J. E. Howard and M. F. O'Conner (eds.) (1987) *Shakespeare Reproduced: The Text in History*, p.144

Sean McEvoy, in his book *Shakespeare: The Basics* notes that:

> Othello is an outsider in Venice and unsure of its ways. Desdemona is a young woman who has been kept apart from male society and politics. Their love is not grounded in the reality of how their society operates, and so it founders when it comes into contact with that world in its purest form: Iago.
>
> Sean McEvoy (2000), *Shakespeare: The Basics*, p.216

Link

For more ideas on feminist criticism see Chapter 28, pages 220–223.

From this you can see that differences of interpretation are part of literary studies. The critics here give an indication of ways in which you can write about tragedy. You should also begin to note that tragedies can be viewed from lots of different perspectives: through character, structure, culture, power, identity and gender.

Activity

Briefly discuss the critical views of *Othello* quoted above. What does each have to offer you as a student now?

Performances and images of Othello, Iago and Desdemona

Just as there are differences between critics, so there are different ways for performers to present the play. These change with each generation, because there are always new contexts and new ways of interpreting the text to coincide with what is happening in the world. All theatre performances or film versions of *Othello* in some way reflect the cultural, social, political and economic period in which they are produced.

However, in some ways the tragedies of Shakespeare and his contemporaries are paradoxically easier to set in different time periods, compared with the **domestic tragedies** you will read about later. This is because the domestic tragedies are very specific in time and place.

The dramatic structure of tragedy

We already know that tragedies usually contain a hero, a villain and a victim, but there are other structural elements we can consider. One further complication to the structure of most tragedies is the moment where the tragic heroes undergo a process of review and self-evaluation – realizing what their fault has been, and how they might have prevented the worst events from happening.

This process of understanding often occurs after the climax and before the eventual resolution. The resolution signals the dawn of a new period of time in the imagined world of the play, and it is hoped that the same mistakes will not be made.

The Tragedy of Othello: The Moor of Venice has a recognizable five-part dramatic structure which is used over and over again in tragedies that you will read, research and perform. Put simply, this consists of:

- introduction
- complication
- climax
- understanding
- resolution.

As you continue in this unit, you will find other ways of explaining the structure and development of a tragedy, but these are some of the initial concepts.

In *Othello*, these structural components are easily recognizable. The play contains perhaps two climaxes to the action. The first is the point where Othello smothers and kills Desdemona, mistakenly thinking that she has been unfaithful to him; the second is where Othello takes his own life. Both of these sequences are very dramatic, and most of the audience would agree that they are where the actual moments of tragedy occur.

King Lear

King Lear was written in 1605. Lear was a mythological pre-Roman Celtic king. The play's earliest version was titled *The True Chronicle of the History of King Lear and His Three Daughters*, but it was later known as *The Tragedy of King Lear*. Shakespeare's *King Lear* (as it has come to be known) is an **epic tragedy** with a large cast of characters, who are listed below.

LEAR, King of Britain
KING OF FRANCE
DUKE OF BURGUNDY
DUKE OF CORNWALL, husband to Regan
DUKE OF ALBANY, husband to Goneril
EARL OF KENT
EARL OF GLOUCESTER
EDGAR, son to Gloucester
EDMUND, bastard son to Gloucester
CURAN, a courtier
OSWALD, steward to Goneril
OLD MAN, tenant to Gloucester
DOCTOR
FOOL
AN OFFICER, employed by Edmund
GENTLEMAN, attendant on Cordelia
HERALD
SERVANTS TO CORNWALL
GONERIL, daughter to Lear
REGAN, daughter to Lear
CORDELIA, daughter to Lear
KNIGHTS OF LEAR'S TRAIN
OFFICERS
MESSENGERS
SOLDIERS
ATTENDANTS
SCENE: Britain

Activity

Study the above list of characters with a partner, then answer the following questions.

1. What does the list tell you about the epic qualities of this tragedy?
2. What do we learn about the setting?
3. What relationships do you think Lear has with the other characters in the play?
4. Can you predict what goes wrong?
5. What do you think the role of Edmund and the Fool in the drama might be?

Commentary

The list of *dramatis personæ* can tell us a lot about the nature of this tragedy. You probably noticed that *King Lear* has a lot more characters than other tragedies you may have encountered. You will have also noticed that the country, 'Britain', is the location for *King Lear* – the exact place is not specified, but it somehow seems 'epic' and 'grand'. The Laurence Olivier version of *King Lear* sets the play against a backdrop of Stonehenge.

King Lear is the tragic hero who has three daughters. Two of them have husbands, and it seems these might somehow be significant to the tragedy. Cordelia has no husband. Lear's relationship with his daughters is thus likely to be important in the tragedy. Gloucester and his relationships also seem important. You would be correct in identifying him as significant, since he forms the **sub-plot** of the tragedy.

Key term

Sub-plot. An additional or second plot that often parallels events of the main plot of the tragedy.

Predicting what might go wrong is difficult, but you may have picked up on the illegitimacy of Edmund ('bastard son') and also the presence of a Fool. Illegitimacy is a problem in tragedies from Shakespeare's time, because it was considered as being against the normal order of things. In much literature, fools often have an insight into events, even though they may seem stupid or naïve.

King Lear, then, is likely to be a tragedy that depicts some aspect of misplaced ambition testing the nobility of the tragic hero, causing him to ask fundamental questions about life and resulting in the breakdown of conventional social bonds.

The main plot

King Lear abdicates as ruler of Britain, a clear alteration in the social order. His loving daughter Cordelia is banished and Lear hands over all his responsibilities to his selfish daughters Goneril and Regan. A vicious power struggle develops, and Lear is driven out of doors into a storm. He confronts a chaotic universe in which the state, family, nature and reason have all been thrown into confusion. There is a match between his personal madness and the madness of the state of Britain around him. He asks whether there is any justice or order in the world, whether there is anything that distinguishes human beings from animals. Lear goes mad, but is in many ways more clear-sighted at the end of the play than he was at the beginning.

The painting 'Cordelia's Portion' (1866) by Ford Madox Brown. It shows King Lear deciding the future of his kingdom on abdicating as ruler. Cordelia is portrayed on the right and Goneril and Regan on the left.

The sub-plot

The sub-plot of the play focuses on another old man, Gloucester, who is the father of the illegitimate Edmund. His eyes are ripped out as a punishment for helping King Lear in defiance of Goneril and Regan.

What the sub-plot does in a tragedy is to expand the audience's awareness of a world falling apart: we witness another character going through the same anxiety and pain. In *King Lear*, the sub-plot works as a parallel to the main plot because both Lear and Gloucester have to struggle physically to reach Dover. Lear is mad and Gloucester has been blinded, so the audience sees both old men progressing through a terrifying world that will ultimately end in death. The complexity of the sub-plot allows the drama to explore more themes.

Lear and a devolved Britain

When King Lear decides to divide up the kingdom of Britain into three parts, he enacts a type of devolution of power. Shakespeare seems to suggest that this is an 'unnatural' state of affairs. Our first impression of Lear might be that, although he seems outwardly confident about what he is doing, this procedure may not be the best plan. Shakespeare makes good use of **asides** in the first scene to show how Cordelia feels about events.

The error that Lear makes is two-fold: the division of the island of Britain is seen as a mistake, but so is his craving for false flattery from his daughters.

Study tip

Compare Cordelia to other determined young women you may encounter in the literature you study for this specification.

The storm and Lear's madness

In Act 3 of the play, Lear has to confront a storm. The storm is literal, but it is also metaphorical – representing the storm inside him, and the storm in the island of Britain. It represents Lear's state of confusion, but is also a natural process to which everyone is subject. The storm therefore hints at our mortality and the brevity of our lives. Some critics have observed that the storm is part of the process of justice in the play – Nature and even God himself seem angry about events and demonstrate their power to Lear.

One view is that Lear has been mad from the start of the play. However, his madness is functional, allowing him to progress towards **enlightenment** and understanding. The first stage of obvious madness is when he is ranting at the weather. The second stage is the so-called 'trial scene' (which is a **parody** of his former powers). The third stage is when his personality disintegrates. Finally he becomes weak, serene and gentle, paradoxically demonstrating a new kind of strength, though it has taken much suffering to reach this stage.

The painting 'King Lear and the Fool in the Storm' (1851) by William Dyce. Lear is ranting against the storm.

The concepts of Nature and the natural appear throughout the play, and to an extent, Lear is obsessed with them: he breaks the natural order and suffers the consequences. When he becomes mad, he wishes for a return to the natural order, but this can't be found because his world has been so badly broken by his actions.

Tragic villains and tragic victims

Two tragic villains in *King Lear* are two of Lear's daughters. Goneril is the eldest daughter and the wife of Albany. The fact that she is a woman with amoral qualities suggests that she too is working against the natural order, since women were expected more than men to uphold moral standards. Goneril has masculine qualities, taking military power away from her husband and challenging Lear's authority. She thus confronts the **patriarchal** order. She also begins an affair with Edmund.

Regan is Lear's middle daughter and is the wife of the Duke of Cornwall. Like Goneril, her main traits are ingratitude, cruelty and aggression. Like her sister, she is therefore 'unnatural'. The third villainous force within the tragedy is Edmund, who is discussed later.

Key terms

Enlightenment. A state of wisdom or knowledge, usually based on fact and experience rather than belief or superstition.

Parody. This is the copying of a specific text (or **genre**) for a comic and sometimes satirical effect.

Patriarchy. A social system run by men for the benefit of men.

Greg Hicks as King Lear and Geoffrey Freshwater as the blinded Earl of Gloucester in the RSC production of *King Lear*, directed by David Farr

Cordelia's route to becoming a tragic victim begins early on in the play, when she is disowned by Lear after refusing to flatter him. In this sense, her fate is sealed. However, she is considered virtuous by all the good characters in the play. Her loyalty to Lear remains steadfast, even though he is cruel towards her.

Although much of the focus is on the main plot, the sub-plot of Gloucester is also highly tragic. Gloucester is part a tragic hero, part tragic victim. He works as a double of Lear in the play. His story echoes that of Lear's, with his arrogance, his belief in the goodness of Edmund rather than Edgar, his literal blinding, and his ultimate display of courage.

The function of the fool: comedy in tragedy

One important figure who actively observes the tragic processes in the play is Lear's Fool. Fools were traditionally employed to entertain royal courts, and often they alone were allowed to speak the truth when others could not for fear of reprisals. This is certainly the case with the Fool in *King Lear*, who offers moments of comedy and wit that are, for a modern audience, quite complex. The jokes he tells offer moments of insight into what is happening. The Fool only appears in the first half of the play – we later learn of his hanging.

Some observers have commented that the Fool is a kind of **alter-ego** of Lear, and that he acts as a 'walking conscience' in the play – commenting on events. Lear's intimacy with the Fool might suggest how foolish the king is, but the Fool's humour sometimes suggests that joking about things is no help either in stemming the inevitable tide of misfortune.

Key term

Alter-ego. A second self, similar to but in crucial respects different from the first person.

Activity

Read some of the Fool's speeches and analyse the ways in which he creates humour and satirizes Lear's behaviour. You may wish to consider what insight the Fool has into Lear's decisions, and why Shakespeare chose to remove him from the rest of the play.

Commentary

You will see that Lear has a friendship with his Fool and that he is dependent upon him to some extent. The Fool works as a commentator. Crucially, the Fool sees Goneril and Regan for what they really are. His wit seems to resonate with the audience at the bleakest moments in the play. Perhaps Shakespeare removes him from the text simply because events become too tragic. The Fool's absence and hanging complete the suffering: this world is one where even Fools are cruelly dispatched.

Illegitimacy in *King Lear*

Gloucester's acknowledgement of an illegitimate son (Edmund) seems something of an embarrassment in the play. When Gloucester brings Edmund to the court, this is viewed as being disastrous to the order of things. Edmund, however, is a new kind of character in Shakespearean tragedy: he seems very modern, and is not connected to the traditional bonds of hierarchy, family or allegiance. We might go so far as to say he is almost a tragic **anti-hero**.

In the way that Edmund refers to Nature as his 'Goddess', we can see that Edmund is unaffected by the old order. He questions why he is treated unfairly, and considers in detail the word 'bastard' and what it means. When he says 'I grow, I prosper', it is as if Shakespeare gives him a sense of himself that we do not normally encounter in tragedies. However, he is a villainous character who enacts revenge against Edgar, Gloucester, Albany and Regan. He very often shares his intentions with the audience in **soliloquies**, so in this sense he has some similarities to Iago in *Othello*.

Edmund is often regarded as one of the most original characters in any Shakespearean tragedy. He has qualities of Renaissance individualism, meaning he is not interested in following the old medieval order. It will be productive for you to consider the differences between Edmund and Edgar in the play.

Key term

Anti-hero. A character with heroic or attractive qualities who does not fit the usual criteria for heroism.

Did you know?

In Shakespeare's time – and to an extent, in the dark-age world described in *King Lear* – the bonds of family, hierarchy and heritage were highly prized, so a legitimate line of inheritance was considered highly important.

Different readings of *King Lear*

Different readers of *King Lear* will have varying views on the play. Some will focus on the question of how much Lear has learned – and whether there is added **significance** to the fact that his dying words are not about himself. Others will explore the many and varied possibilities created by applying aspects of gender theory to the play.

This play in particular considers political issues of power and control. Some readers have looked at the tragedy of *King Lear* through a psychoanalytical lens. They note that there are no mother figures in the play – and that the kind of love Lear craves might have been given to him by a partner. The way in which he asks for love and care from his daughters is a reversal of the normal role of a parent – and is thus unnatural.

Link

See the earlier discussion of Iago's soliloquies on pages 24–25.

Conclusion

Othello and *King Lear* both show the fall of respected, high-status characters who have made crucial errors of judgement. These decisions have ramifications for them and for the whole of the society around them. The disorder of their own lives prompts disorder in the wider world.

This is one type of tragedy. You will now consider a selection of other types of tragedy.

5 Dramatic tragedy: *Richard II*, *Death of a Salesman* and *A Streetcar Named Desire*

In this chapter you will be introduced to:

- further drama choices – *Richard II* or *Death of a Salesman*
- the additional choice of *A Streetcar Named Desire* if you are taking AS
- alternative ways in which dramatists have explored tragedy in both political and domestic settings
- ways of connecting these plays to other tragedies.

Richard II: the end of kings?

Although this is often categorized as a history play, its original title was *The Tragedie of King Richard the Second*. It can be seen, therefore, as both a tragedy and a history.

The play takes as its theme the problem of whether the **divine right** of kings can ever be questioned. The play shows that kings are not divine or superhuman, but that they are – in the end – merely human like the rest of us. Shakespeare appears to be depicting a process where a country calls into question the right of a particular monarch to rule.

Richard II can be read as a political power struggle, although it is one that begins with Richard making some poor decisions. These decisions have an effect on his own life, his function as a king and on the unity of England. The tragedy is therefore a personal one, but it also affects the nation state. Along the way, other figures are embroiled in the wider tragedy of the age. As we know, suffering – both personal and societal – is part of the tragic process.

Key terms

Banishment. A form of punishment where an individual is forced to stay away from a particular area, or even to stay out of the country, on pain of death.

Divine right. The idea that kings are anointed by God; this was reinforced by the religious order in the coronation ceremony.

Did you know?

William Shakespeare wrote *Richard II* in 1595. It is based on the real life of Richard II, who ruled England between 1377 and 1390.

Setting up the tragedy

Activity

Read Act 1 of *Richard II* again and then answer the following questions:

1. What is the dispute between Henry Bolingbroke and Thomas Mowbray?
2. How does King Richard suggest that it should be resolved?
3. What tragic decision does the king make?
4. How does this set the tragic processes in motion?

Commentary

The dispute at the start of the play is something that the king needs to sort out right away. Instead, he seems to relish its intricacies: this is Richard's first mistake. The dispute itself is over an accusation by Bolingbroke that Mowbray has squandered money given to him by King Richard for the king's soldiers. Furthermore, Bolingbroke accuses Mowbray of the murder of the Duke of Gloucester. Perhaps a little half-heartedly, Richard encourages them to resolve their differences, but they will not. Therefore they challenge each other to a duel.

At the duel, Richard interrupts them and sentences both combatants to **banishment** from England. Mowbray is banished forever, but Richard seems to show some favour towards Bolingbroke (first sentencing him to ten years, then reducing it eventually to six years).

Mowbray predicts that the king will fall because of Bolingbroke. The king clearly makes a number of strategic errors at the start of the play, which set tragic processes in motion.

Activity

In performances of the play, Richard is generally depicted as somewhat effeminate or weak, and at the same time arrogant and prone to vanity. Choose two of his speeches in the early part of the play and see whether you can present them in this way. How do you think this might affect an audience's reaction to his character?

A key character at the start of the play is John of Gaunt. He is one of the king's advisors and is the father of Henry Bolingbroke. John of Gaunt suggests that Richard himself was responsible for the murder of the Duke of Gloucester. An old man, he is devastated that his son should be sent away to exile, and begins to see what England will become. As he is dying, he reflects on events.

Activity

Read John of Gaunt's speech beginning 'Methinks I am a prophet new-inspired' to 'How happy were my ensuing death!' (Act 2 Scene 1). Consider the following questions about this speech:

1. How is England presented here?
2. What is English success dependent on?
3. What have kings been like in the past?
4. What does John of Gaunt fear?
5. What about the rest of Britain and Ireland?

When you have answered these questions, consider Gaunt's wider significance to the play.

Commentary

You may recognize parts of Gaunt's speech because it is very famous. England is celebrated as a paradise. We know that this is ominous because paradise is linked to the Fall of Man – and that is what both John of Gaunt and we suspect will happen. England's success has been due to its isolation as an island – although it appears now that danger might come from within, rather than externally. The country's independence and strength have been derived from its kings and its Christian faith but, as we know, this may be subject to question. John of Gaunt now fears 'shameful conquest of itself'. We might note that England is perhaps used interchangeably here with Britain – remembering that Wales and Ireland were subject to England's **colonization** project – something we witness in the play.

After this, John of Gaunt argues with Richard about his decisions and predicts what will come. As Gaunt is dying, Richard seizes all of his resources and wealth, and uses them to fund a war in Ireland. In essence, this is another marker of Richard's downfall. He should have listened to Gaunt's wise words and statesmanship. There is also an implication that the conquest of Ireland should not be begun when there is disaffection at home. However, Richard believes that war against Ireland will help to unify the country. It is while Richard is away waging war that Henry Bolingbroke returns from his banishment.

Key term

Colonization. The process whereby one country or group of countries seeks to take over another.

Richard back in England

Act 3 Scene 2 is a crucial sequence in the play, when Richard returns from Ireland. He is jubilant to be back home on English soil, but events soon begin to unravel for him. There is news about Bolingbroke's return, and then the realization that the Welsh will no longer support him. At this point, Richard begins to acknowledge that serious events are in motion and that he is likely to be deposed. Richard's monologues here offer insights into what he is thinking.

Activity

Look at Richard's speech below. What issues are raised here about the nature of kingship, and is it possible to see Richard as a tragic figure?

> No matter where; of comfort no man speak:
> Let's talk of graves, of worms, and epitaphs;
> Make dust our paper and with rainy eyes
> Write sorrow on the bosom of the earth,
> Let's choose executors and talk of wills:
> And yet not so, for what can we bequeath
> Save our deposed bodies to the ground?
> Our lands, our lives and all are Bolingbroke's,
> And nothing can we call our own but death
> And that small model of the barren earth
> Which serves as paste and cover to our bones.
> For God's sake, let us sit upon the ground
> And tell sad stories of the death of kings;
> How some have been deposed; some slain in war,
> Some haunted by the ghosts they have deposed;
> Some poison'd by their wives: some sleeping kill'd;
> All murder'd: for within the hollow crown
> That rounds the mortal temples of a king
> Keeps Death his court

The RSC production of *Richard II* from 2013, directed by Gregory Doran. Nigel Lindsay (on the left) is Bolingbroke and David Tennant, playing Richard II, is being forced to hand over his crown.

Commentary

This speech seems to suggest that Richard is already aware of his fate, and that he is part of a wider process of political change. He realizes by the end of it that the crown is 'hollow', because it can easily be taken from him – and he is aware that this is what Bolingbroke is now intent on doing. At this point, Richard shows an awareness of the direction his life is taking, but whether you would say this is tragic depends on the critical stance you take.

To some critics, his poetry and his regal bearing make us feel pity for him. To others he is self-indulgent, temperamental and for the sake of the country needs to be removed so that it can be governed differently (if not necessarily for the good of all). How the part is performed will reveal the director's and actor's interpretation of the role. In this play, unlike some other tragedies, the roles of hero and villain are ambiguous, and therefore are much more reliant on stage interpretations.

Activity

Look again at Act 3 Scene 4. Here you will see Queen Isabel and her First Lady walking in a garden. They overhear the gossip of two gardeners who are talking about events in the play. Try to answer the following questions about this sequence:

1. How does Shakespeare present the gardeners?
2. Why is this sequence different to the rest of the tragedy here?
3. What are they chatting about?
4. What comparison is made between the garden and England?
5. What is Queen Isabel's reaction to their observations?
6. How do the gardeners respond?

Commentary

Shakespeare shifts the focus at this point to comments on events from two low-status characters, as well as the queen and her lady. The gardeners are presented as getting on with the task in hand – maintaining the garden, despite the wider tragedy playing out in England. They chat about the garden but compare it to the 'garden' of England, which is 'choked up'. They know that Bolingbroke has seized the 'wasteful King' and that he is 'deposed'. Isabel is shocked at their reaction but the Gardener says he is speaking 'no more than everyone doth know'. This sequence is dramatically significant because it allows for a pause in the tragedy, and at the same time allows the audience to see a symbolic representation of events.

The cycle of tragedy and treachery

At the end of the play York's son, the Duke of Aumerle, plans a rebellion against the new king, Henry Bolingbroke. Sir Piers Exton enters the prison where Richard is held and murders Richard, thereby ridding Henry Bolingbroke of his 'living fear'. However, despite this, Bolingbroke has throughout the play maintained a level of respect for Richard. Feeling guilty, Henry vows to journey to Jerusalem to atone for his part in the tragedy. There is an implication that further tragedy will follow – and it does, in the next play in Shakespeare's sequence, *Henry IV, Part One*.

Different readings

In his reading of the play, *The King's Two Bodies* (1998), the critic Ernst Kantorowicz observed that the play constantly considers Richard as having two bodies: one natural body and one **body politic** – his body as a king. Bolingbroke, meanwhile, is a new kind of leader with a fresh philosophy about what kings should be.

Richard (like Lear) closely conforms to the characteristics of the classical tragic hero. He has unshakeable faith in his own divinity, and an arrogance that is self-destructive. Although some critics have observed that he suffers from a lack of humour, there are points when he does laugh at himself, but his stubbornness prevents this humour from redeeming him.

Some readers have also commented that Richard's actions against John of Gaunt are motiveless, which makes his tragic fate seem set. Richard believes too much in his own powers and rights, and it is this that marks him out as a tragic figure.

Key term

Body politic. The nation, symbolized by the monarch as head of state.

Modern domestic tragedy

Although less epic in scale than *King Lear*, *Othello*, or *Richard II*, so-called **domestic tragedies** can still be very powerful, and can appeal to contemporary audiences because they deal with modern issues, such as materialism, consumerism and alienation.

Modern domestic tragedy becomes issue-led drama. This means that the tragedy looks at a particular issue and examines its effect on the central characters. Most modern domestic tragedies focus on **anti-heroes**, who do not quite fit the society in which they live. Whereas **epic tragedy** tends to look at how the world somehow brings tragic events upon the lead character, and the ways in which their 'fatal flaw' causes their downfall, many modern domestic tragedies complicate these principles.

Modern domestic tragedies can still have the effects on the audience noted by Aristotle, but they also cause the audience to question the establishment and assumptions about life. Most characters in these tragedies face some kind of predicament. Some playwrights in modern drama try to subvert normal values – breaking established conventions of drama as well as subject matter.

Structurally, the plays are usually much tighter – most only have three acts or are divided into scenes alone. You should also expect to see much more emphasis in the stage directions on exactly what the set should look like, as well as a greater focus on costumes, sound, lighting, movement and how particular sections of the text are to be spoken. This is because modern playwrights tend to be more concerned with this, and because technology in the theatre has progressed.

You might expect to see the following elements in modern domestic tragedy:

- Anti-heroes are depicted.
- Characters are ordinary people – not the 'great' men or women of earlier tragedies.
- Although family life is central, it is presented as somehow inadequate and diseased. This inadequacy undermines faith and belief in the whole order of society.
- The world can be full of deceit, and prizes or dreams turn out to be illusory.
- Often characters are vying and manoeuvring for control.
- There is often an emphasis on psychological aspects. The disorder of the world sometimes matches a disorder of the mind.
- Whereas deaths are usually shown onstage in earlier tragedies, in modern domestic drama they usually happen offstage (or are concealed).
- If earlier tragedies looked 'outwards', modern domestic tragedies look more 'inwards'.
- Usually, there is some element of the past impinging tragically on the present.

Activity

When you begin studying your modern domestic tragedy (either *Death of a Salesman* or, at AS level, *A Streetcar Named Desire*), look at a small section of the play – perhaps two or three pages early in the script. Can you find the above elements in the section you are considering?

Death of a Salesman

The play, first performed in 1949, centres on the life of Willy Loman, a man in his sixties who has spent much of his life on the road as a travelling salesman. He seems once to have been sociable and well liked, but increasing bouts of anxiety and flashbacks have meant that he has become unstable. In the play, he stands in the shadow of his more successful brother Ben, and is then sacked from his job when he requests a post off the road back in New York.

Willy has high hopes for his two sons, Happy and Biff, who were popular at school. Happy is the younger son, and lies to his father to make himself look successful. Biff, the older brother, is 34 and is still unsettled, without a career. Willy's wife, Linda, has to struggle to make ends meet. We learn that in the past Willy had an affair while out on the road, which was discovered by Biff.

A 'get-rich-quick' deal or better prospects are always on the horizon, but never quite reached. Biff decides to confront his father and tell him the truth. Willy wants to be liked, believing that this will bring success and the **American Dream** to him and his family. He postures and bluffs his way into believing in the mythology of success, while drowning in his own failure. But in an emotional scene with Biff, he acknowledges his own failure and the ways in which society has failed him. Willy takes his own life.

Key term

American Dream. The idea that everyone has opportunities, in the comparatively new country of America, to achieve material success and financial rewards.

Miller's authorial method

By the time Miller came to write *Death of a Salesman*, cinema had become an important genre, and this tragedy is much influenced by a technique commonly used in film: flashback. Flashback allows the playwright to take the audience back in time and observe events that took place before the beginning of the play on stage, with the added suggestion that some of these events take place, in part, inside Willy's head rather than in reality. Miller uses this technique throughout *Death of a Salesman*, and his skill as a playwright is to deftly write the transitions between the present and past in the play. This method of writing helps the audience to understand the reasons behind Willy's psychological problems.

Unlike most modern dramas, Miller's play only has two acts – Miller calls these 'Certain Private Conversations in Two Acts', although there is a third section to the play, labelled 'Requiem'. This takes place at Willy's funeral and represents the new world in which the characters must exist and work, after the death of the main character. Nobody but Willy's immediate friends and family turn up, which shows that regardless of how well Willy thought he was liked, very few people either cared about him or remembered him. Happy thinks that Willy did not die in vain, but Biff comments that, 'He had the wrong dreams. All, all, wrong.' This is a comment on Willy, but it might also seem to be a comment on the widely held American wish to be liked, to have material goods and to chase a false dream of prosperity. In this way, domestic dramas can lead to comments and observations on wider issues and themes.

In **modern tragedy**, irony is an important device. *Death of a Salesman* is filled with ironic lines and observations. In the 'Requiem', Willy's dream of owning his own house is realized, but only after his death (this is a reference to his earlier observations that he will be 'worth more dead than alive'). Linda has paid the last mortgage payment that morning, but Willy is not there to enjoy the achievement. As well as being tragic, this is hugely ironic. His death may well set up his sons for a better life. It is a very noble and heroic act – terms which should make you think of earlier tragedies.

Did you know?

Music was used in classical drama, and most probably also during tragedies performed in the time of Shakespeare and his contemporaries. Miller's *Death of a Salesman* also makes use of music to advance and enhance the tragedy – suggesting symbolic ideas as well as creating atmosphere.

The actors Arthur Kennedy (on the left) and Lee J. Cobb in a scene from Arthur Miller's play *Death of a Salesman*.

Activity

Answer the following questions about *Death of a Salesman*:

1. What organizing or structural devices does Miller use? Find examples of them.
2. How do the surviving characters cope after Willy's death? How much truth do they acknowledge?
3. How does Miller use music to signal and enhance the tragedy?
4. Are there moments when the usual dramatic realism is suspended by Miller? What is the significance of the dream-like scenes?
5. What is the significance of the scenes enacted inside Willy's head?

Different readings

Death of a Salesman is considered to be one of the most important American plays of the twentieth century. The critic Ronald Harman, in *All the World's a Stage*, says that 'the play is universal because it is particular'. This is an interesting comment to make about a tragedy, because it suggests that the very specific setting of characters and place appeals to us as an audience since we see something of ourselves in it. Therefore, it may be that modern domestic tragedies are set in particular contexts, but that they can still be universal.

A Streetcar Named Desire

If you are working towards the AS qualification, then you can study *A Streetcar Named Desire*, a 1947 play by the American playwright Tennessee Williams. As in many of Williams's plays there is a dangerous (for the time) sense of repressed desire, and of sexuality that is outside the norm.

Setting

The play is set in New Orleans. Blanche DuBois has fantasies of refinement and grandeur, but these ideas are smashed by her brother-in-law Stanley Kowalski, whose animalistic nature both attracts and repels her. This forms the basis of the tragedy, and tragic events occur driven by sexual frustration and violence. Blanche keeps up a façade of respectability and decorum, which makes her attractive to men, but underneath this she is an alcoholic and is deluded about her position in life.

The title of the play is derived from the moment when she arrives in New Orleans to visit her sister, and takes a streetcar (an urban railway or tram) to 'Desire', a suburb and terminus for the tram. However, 'desire' becomes a crucial aspect of the play. Compared to elsewhere in the South (which is predominantly rural), the urban intensity of the city seems to unnerve Blanche and, as the drama unfolds, Williams reveals much about Blanche's tragic past.

There are other symbolic names in the play, of both people and places. Stanley and Stella Kowalski live, for example, in Elysian Fields – this was the name of a place in Greek mythology reserved for the heroic dead.

The advertising poster for the 1951 film version of *A Streetcar Named Desire*, directed by Elia Kazan and starring Marlon Brando as Stanley and Vivien Leigh as Blanche

Blanche

Blanche's life is filled with fantasy and illusion. Her tragic flaw is that she believes in the false veneer she creates for own her life, but there is little reality to it.

Activity

With a partner, explore the things we learn about Blanche's tragic past, but do not actually see on stage. As well as noting what is revealed, comment on how it might affect her character and present identity. You should also comment on Williams's methods of revealing this information. Most of it is found in Scenes One and Two of the play.

Consider the following areas:

- The loss of Belle Reve plantation at Laurel.
- The time she took off from her work as an English teacher.
- The brief marriage with Alan Grey.
- Grey's homosexuality and suicide.

Stanley and Stella

While the tragedy's initial focus is on Blanche DuBois, in the middle of the play we also see the lifestyle of Stanley and Stella Kowalski. They have a difficult and troubling relationship, which may have tragic repercussions.

Activity

Look at some of the sequences when Stanley and Stella are together on stage, and then come to some decisions in response to the following questions:

1. What are the main characteristics of Stanley?
2. What are the main characteristics of Stella?
3. Are the two of them in love?
4. Is sexual passion implied between them?
5. What does Stanley reveal to Blanche about Stella?

Commentary

Williams presents Stanley as animalistic, brutal and rough, yet at the same time, shows a sensual side to him. He is a blue-collar worker (a working-class person who performs manual labour) and is frustrated with his job. Stella is self-effacing and lets others take control. Despite their differences, a passionate sexuality is implied. Stella seems to put up with Stanley's brutality, knowing that his male prowess is what attracted her to him in the first place. Stanley explains to Blanche that Stella is pregnant, something that Blanche already seems to sense about her sister. Although they seem to be in love, Williams is able to indicate cracks in their relationship.

Williams's authorial method

Williams's text is obviously a modern play, and the way the drama is structured on the page indicates this. He makes prolific use of stage directions, and it is very important to consider these when writing about his drama. What is written in the script can be read by the actor (and student) but is not necessarily performed on the stage.

The main style of Williams's work is dramatic naturalism. However, he is not averse to melodramatic flashes that invoke an older style of drama. You will see some of this in Blanche's sighs, hand gestures and screams.

Key term

Motifs. Repeated elements that usually have a symbolic function.

Williams uses a number of recurring **motifs** in his play. Blanche is often seen avoiding the light, as if this will reveal her true identity. She also spends much time bathing, perhaps hoping she can cleanse herself of her past. You may like to investigate other symbols that Williams uses, including shadows, polka music and meat.

The ending of the play

The ending of *A Streetcar Named Desire* is one of the most famous endings in modern drama. Although Blanche's death is not indicated, she must endure another kind of tragedy – being locked away in an institution after she suffers a breakdown.

Activity

Re-read the section from where the Doctor says 'Miss DuBois' until the 'Curtain'. What do you notice about the play's tragic ending?

Commentary

This is a powerful and alternative kind of ending for a modern, domestic tragedy. The decline in Blanche, the result of her tragic past and of her recent encounter with Stanley, reaches its climax here. Williams elects not to have her die, which would have been the conventional thing to do within the genre. Instead, she is to be cut off from her family and incarcerated in an institution. In this way, Williams pushes the form of tragedy, by saying that it does not always have to culminate in death. In fact, here, death might have been a release for Blanche. She is instead doomed to undergo further suffering.

The Matron and the Doctor differ in their response to Blanche. The Matron seems to have seen her type before, whereas the Doctor (perhaps more naively) helps her. These 'strangers' are helping her once again – and that is what she has become used to, even from her earliest arrival in New Orleans when she was recommended to take the streetcar named Desire. There is an implication here too that we cannot always rely on family – we sometimes have to rely on strangers to help us.

When Eunice brings Stella's child, there is hope for the future with a new generation. However, despite the tragedy of Blanche's hospitalization, the men quickly carry on with their game. Williams seems to be commenting here that, despite tragedy for some, things soon go back to normal for others. There is an echo of Stanley and Stella's earlier passion, but this has been destroyed by the rape and perhaps by their new responsibilities as parents. Stella's sobs seem to be as much for this, as for her sister.

Williams is careful with the detail of his authorial method. We note that the trumpets (normally a celebratory instrument) are 'muted' here. Steve's confirmation of the type of poker being played has a double meaning. It denotes the direction the game will take but also what life throws at you. Stanley as 'stud' may well be playing a game here – as the audience knows.

Different readings

A Streetcar Named Desire is usually read as a tragedy about the central characters coping with their personal demons and the pressures of the modern world. The tragedy is often therefore seen as being about the shattering of romantic illusions, both by the past and the present.

Another perspective is offered by considering the tragedy along class lines, with class barriers being crossed in sexual encounters. Blanche and Stella are obviously of a higher social class than Stanley, although both of them have been 'levelled' by their experiences. Stanley's family is made up of more-recent migrants to the United States, and he is a new kind of man, not having the old allegiances of his wife and her sister.

Some productions in the past have tried to steer the audience's sympathy away from Blanche (who, it is argued, does not deserve any sympathy) and direct it towards Stanley. However, more recent productions have placed this sympathy back with Blanche. The play has also been read as a study in cruelty – this strand is generated in both Blanche and Stanley.

Another critical theme in the play is desire itself: Blanche is driven by desire. It is what forced her to leave her job and drove her out of town. She also has a physical desire for Stanley, which is not driven by intellectual interest in him, but purely by sexual feelings. Blanche appears to be unable to find balance, and a place for desire in her life. She either abandons it or pursues it to destruction. This is at the heart of the tragedy.

Conclusion

This chapter has introduced you to the different kinds of tragedy you may study. It has also outlined some further concepts and ideas surrounding tragedy – focusing primarily on political and domestic dramas.

6 Prose tragedy: *Tess of the d'Urbervilles, The Great Gatsby* and *The Remains of the Day*

In this chapter you will:

- examine the aspect of tragedy in prose fiction
- explore the ways in which Thomas Hardy, F. Scott Fitzgerald and Kazuo Ishiguro present tragic figures within their work.

Introduction

Some writers have taken tragic **motifs** and elements and used them within prose fiction; such fiction allows for a longer and more sustained development of the tragedy. Novels are most often written about characters who are at odds with the society in which they find themselves. Usually, the society constructed in novels is a complex one where many changes occur. These changes affect not only the central character of the novel – contributing to a tragic downfall – but can also affect other characters. Sometimes the tragedy of an individual is representative of a wider tragedy occurring in that society at a particular point in time. You will see this in *Tess of the d'Urbervilles*, *The Great Gatsby* and *The Remains of the Day*.

When you read a prose tragedy, you may like to consider how the tragic structure is both similar to and different from that found in drama.

Tess of the d'Urbervilles: a novel about change

Tess of the d'Urbervilles: A Pure Woman Faithfully Presented was written by the English novelist Thomas Hardy (1840–1928) and published in 1891. Hardy imagined the Dorset-centred world of his novel to be part of the old Anglo-Saxon kingdom of 'Wessex', a term that has come to be applied to his construction of this space.

Hardy was always interested in the status and position of women in society, and to an extent, he champions their cause in his novels, where he looks at issues of gender and sexuality. He was writing at a time when there were substantial changes in the status and rights of women, and sometimes, as Hardy realized, attitudes towards women led to tragic consequences. Hardy was arguing that gender and sexuality are part of life and should not be ignored. His subtitle, claiming that Tess is 'faithfully presented', seems to indicate that he wanted to present these issues in a realistic way. In this sense, the narrative was to be a mirror of the 'Wessex' society he was writing about. In Hardy's fiction, we see tragedy combined with **narrative realism**.

Some critics have said that Hardy's works are about the 'implanted crookedness of things' and that his novels show the indifferent forces that operate in the world and can inflict suffering on human beings. This suggests that although human beings can contribute to their own **destiny**, there is a wider process whereby an unavoidable '**fate**' is in operation and it is hard for characters to fight against it. This may suggest to you a new reading of tragedy, which acknowledges that sometimes misfortunes are not due to an individual character's flaws or lack of insight, but are instead caused by malevolent forces operating on us all – almost as if the gods are playing with us. However, an alternative view would be that the way we deal with these forces does have an impact, and that we can alter our predetermined fate for the better. This is a central debate about the tragedy in *Tess of the d'Urbervilles*.

Key terms

Destiny. The path one takes in life, and its eventual destination, which often seem mysteriously assigned to us.

Fate. A pattern of predetermined and unstoppable events that affect one's life.

Narrative realism. Narrative style that aims to faithfully represent real life.

Did you know?

Hardy grew up in Dorset, and trained to become an architect. He knew the landscape and folklore of the agricultural world of Dorset intimately, and realized it was changing rapidly. Agriculture was becoming more mechanized and people were more socially mobile.

Tess: ideas above her station?

To an extent, Tess Durbeyfield has many similarities to the kind of tragic figures found in dramatic domestic tragedies, in that she is not a high-status figure. She is comparatively ordinary, but, of course, it is her high-status heritage – and in particular her name – which starts the process leading to her downfall. The phrase in the subtitle of Hardy's novel, 'a Pure Woman', is important because it suggests that Tess is genuine and respectable – and is perhaps manipulated by a threatening **patriarchal** society.

The pattern established here is different from some of the other tragedies that you will read on this course, but it is just as powerful. There is a feeling of wasted opportunities, wasted lives, the imposition of social codes, and a depiction of the way in which women's lives (like Tess's) can be destroyed by the behaviour of men.

When Tess is found at the altar stone of Stonehenge, powerful symbolic connections are made. Stonehenge is a symbol of a mythical past, a pagan Britain, and a place where (according to some folkloric belief) the ancient druids made sacrifices. Tess's arrest at the altar stone suggests that in this tragedy she is being sacrificed, in an echo of ancient practices.

Study tip

You may like to think about the similarities between Tess and other female figures in tragedy, such as Desdemona in *Othello* and Cordelia in *King Lear*.

Double standards

One of the ways in which Hardy depicts the causes of Tess's tragedy is through the double moral and sexual standards which her society applied to men and women. Men were held to a very different set of standards (or moral codes) than women.

Activity

With a partner, find the key moments where these double standards are presented in the novel. You may find it useful to draw up a table like the one below, where the structure of Hardy's novel is listed on the left-hand side. When you have completed this table, consider the questions that follow.

Phase	Men	Women
Phase the First: The Maiden (1–11)		
Phase the Second: Maiden No More (12–15)		
Phase the Third: The Rally (16–24)		
Phase the Fourth: The Consequence (25–34)		
Phase the Fifth: The Woman Pays (35–44)		
Phase the Sixth: The Convert (45–52)		
Phase the Seventh: Fulfilment (53–59)		

1. What are the core turning points, in your view?
2. Do these double standards persist to the end of the novel?
3. Are they the direct cause of the tragedy?
4. Do men pay a price as well?

The tragic novel as social critique

One helpful way of understanding *Tess of the d'Urbervilles* is to think of the novel as a piece of social criticism. Tess is perhaps a tragic figure because she rejects conventional behaviour and breaks society's rules, although Hardy obscures the key event of her seduction. Her rule-breaking means that she is highly likely to come to grief. However, Hardy is able to show how farcical and outmoded those rules are, and the novel therefore criticizes the society under scrutiny. To a degree, Hardy seems to be suggesting that society is permanently in disarray and that order is hard to find.

Something else is noticeable here: Hardy seems to read a kind of tragic **significance** into the lives of his characters. Although these may simply be ordinary lives, there is something grand and even high-status about the way his characters operate in response to their circumstances. Therefore we may note a blending or **hybridization** of old and new models of tragedy. Ordinary characters can sometimes have the heroic qualities of classical and Shakespearean characters.

Key terms

Hybridization. The fusion of two or more concepts.

Transition. A process of change or development.

Hardy uses the genre of tragedy to create social criticism related to several areas that he believes need reform and rethinking. Among these are the status and place of women in the legal system, marriage, attitudes towards virginity and sex, **patriarchal** views, and absurd and outmoded laws. Hardy is suggesting that these issues are the cause of Tess's personal tragedy. Numerous other social issues are explored in the text, including changes in the lifestyles of the rural poor, exploitation by urban centres of power, and shifts in population and the economy. These give an indication of the wider tragedy that Hardy sees taking place. As a writer, he seems to have a keen eye on England's **transition** from its pre-industrial period into modernity, and considers that modernity brings about a certain kind of tragedy.

Different readings: Tess, modernism and industrialism

Some observers believe that the reason why Tess suffers and dies is because she goes against traditional Christian ideas.

Tess can be seen as a symbolic **personification** of the natural world. In this sense her rebellion is feral (wild, no longer domesticated) and uncontrolled, and it is this that brings about her tragedy. There are many sequences in the novel where Tess is compared to animals and associated with nature.

An alternative view here is that Tess may be a kind of 'Wessex Eve', who rebels against the order of things. Wessex is therefore constructed as a kind of Paradise (or Garden of Eden), and it Tess's fatal temptation that leads to her downfall.

Activity

Find some textual examples of Tess being compared to or linked with the natural world.

Some critics have argued that the reason why the tragedy happens to Tess is because of the twin factors of modernism and industrialism. It is often perceived that novels such as *Tess of the d'Urbervilles* are about 'the ache of modernism'. This seems to suggest that by the late nineteenth century, traditional ways of working and living were being replaced by more modern aesthetics and beliefs, which brought about a dissatisfaction and dislocation. Modernism was also coupled with growing secularization and a realization that the traditional order was rapidly changing and going into decline. The age-old traditions of the countryside were disappearing rapidly, and it is felt that this brings about a wider tragedy, not only a personal one.

Obviously, part of this shift towards modernism came in the form of industrialization. You may like to re-read the section in *Tess of the d'Urbervilles* about the mechanization of the dairy, and how, in this complex new world, the milk sent to the cities from the countryside has to be watered down because whole milk is too strong for urban tastes. The wider implication here is that Tess is symbolic of an agricultural peasantry being actively destroyed by industrialism.

There is an alternative view, however. The Marxist critic Raymond Williams (1921–1988) in his book *The English Novel: From Dickens to Lawrence* (1970) argues that this is too simplistic a view of the novel, and that Tess is not just a member of the peasantry. She is an educated member of the rural working class and is prevented by mechanisms of repression from realizing her ambition and rising above her origins. Williams argues that the repressive factors are the landed **bourgeoisie** (represented by Alec), **liberal idealism** (represented by Angel), and the general outmoded Christian **moralism** that dominates the community she is part of.

Did you know?

Williams commented on Hardy as a prose tragedian. In *The English Novel*, he wrote that Hardy's work is located in a 'border country that so many of us have been living in: between custom and education, between work and ideas, between love or place and an experience of change' (page 98).

Key terms

Bourgeoisie. The wealthy, middle-class individuals in a society.

Decadence. A process of decay in moral standards, revealed in undignified and wasteful behaviour.

Idealism. A philosophical idea that the ideal state of humanity is possible.

Liberal idealism. A set of philosophical and political ideas concerned with creating a progressive society based on humanity moving from the dark into the light.

Moralism. The promotion of conventional (and usually outmoded) morals or values upheld by a society.

Conclusions

Tess of the d'Urbervilles is a complex prose tragedy that bears much re-reading and thinking about. Although it has many elements that you will have noted in Shakespearean tragedies, the tragedy is not always so personal or caused by the flaws of an individual. It is much more social and related to the accepted morals of the day, which are often found to be redundant and destabilizing. It also contains elements of fate, such as the misplaced letter.

The Great Gatsby: an American tragedy

The Great Gatsby, first published in 1925, was written by F. Scott Fitzgerald (1896–1940). The story is set in the summer of 1922, and follows a wide range of characters who live in the imagined town of West Egg on wealthy Long Island.

It is narrated by Nick Carraway, a friend and neighbour of the young millionaire Jay Gatsby (the 'Great Gatsby' of the title). Gatsby, who is obsessed with Daisy Buchanan, is presented as a mysterious individual, who has working-class roots but pretends he is of a higher class. He appears to have obtained his money through illegal activities, including bootlegging (the illegal production and distribution of alcohol).

There is a cast of supporting characters from West Egg, and poor East Egg, who become embroiled in Gatsby's life and who introduce the themes of upheaval and change during the so-called 'Roaring Twenties' or 'Jazz Age'.

The novel culminates in tragedy with the deaths of Myrtle Wilson, George B. Wilson and Gatsby himself. The novel deals with the **decadence** and **idealism** of the age – partly derived from the aftermath of World War I. The tragedy of the text cautions us to question the nature of the **American Dream**.

One of the underlying themes of the novel is division in society, which Fitzgerald appears to argue is a cause of tragedy. As in Hardy's novels, the social mobility of certain characters (in particular Gatsby himself, and Myrtle Wilson) is also part of the tragic structure. Such characters are, in effect, in places they should not be and cannot sustain, and therefore they pay the price for their actions. One of the major ideas of the novel is the way it critiques the fact that the American Dream is only achievable at great cost.

Before the time of the novel, many people had left Europe with the hope of finding a better, less repressive and more successful life in the United States. Fitzgerald disrupts and questions that hopeful view of America. The novel may also be regarded as being about the question of who wields cultural and political power in America during this era. Obviously the power was thought to reside with the 'old money' of the people of West Egg, but the society depicted is undergoing change, with 'new money' being created by immigrants from elsewhere, and by individuals such as Gatsby re-inventing themselves.

Did you know?

For some members of society, the Jazz Age was a time of parties, dancing and illegal alcohol, but for the vast majority of working-class American citizens, it was full of struggle and poverty.

Titles and names

Fitzgerald had a number of titles in mind for the tragedy that eventually became known as *The Great Gatsby*.

Activity

1. Listed below are some of the titles which Fitzgerald considered for his novel. Look at each title and consider why it might have been suitable. Try to relate the proposed title to the novel's tragic outcome, and say why it might eventually have been rejected.

Potential title	Suitability
Among Ash-Heaps and Millionaires	
On the Road to West Egg	
Under the Red, White, and Blue	
Gold-Hatted Gatsby	
*Trimalchio**	
The High-Bouncing Lover	

* This is a reference to a character in a first-century AD Roman text: Trimalchio is a freed slave who gains money and power.

2. Novelists always choose their characters' names carefully. They often add meaning to characters' names by using symbols, colours and concepts to highlight personality traits or to perform a function within the tragedy. Make a table like the one below and note down any ideas that come into your mind in response to the characters' names. One set of suggestions has been added for you. Note that you may need to do some research here. Do these names inform readers about the way the tragedy will unfold? Is this a sophisticated or clumsy literary technique, in your view?

Name	Interpretation
Daisy Fay Buchanan	e.g. flower, fairy, innocence
Tom Buchanan	
Nick Carraway	
Jay Gatsby	
George B. Wilson	
Myrtle Wilson	
Meyer Wolfsheim	
Jordan Baker	

Destructive passion

One of the core tragic concepts in *The Great Gatsby* is that love and passion for another person can sometimes be catastrophic, and cause disorder and death. This is seen in two cases in the novel. First, the passion between Daisy and Gatsby is presented as destructive. Not only did it previously fail, but it leads to Gatsby's murder by George B. Wilson. The second case of destructive passion in the novel is between Myrtle Wilson and Tom Buchanan. Myrtle is accidentally killed after being hit by Gatsby's car. At this point it is being driven by Daisy, but Gatsby insists he will take the blame for the accident, thereby igniting anger in George B. Wilson.

Activity

Re-read the descriptions of the two destructive moments mentioned above, and look at how Fitzgerald structures the sequences. Ask yourself the following questions about them, and about how destructive passion contributes to their success as pieces of writing.

1. In what ways is this form of tragedy about ordinary people?
2. What impact does the setting have on the tragedy?
3. What was the journey towards death for the **protagonists**?
4. What role do violence and revenge play here?
5. What is the structural pattern of the sequence?
6. How is language used to heighten the power of the tragedy?
7. Are pity and fear still instilled in the audience as they read about the events unfolding?

Share your responses as a group.

A mysterious tragic hero

Some readers find the character of Gatsby hard to pin down. Even Fitzgerald's editor requested that he be made less of a mystery. However, you might want to consider whether the mystery surrounding Gatsby enhances or detracts from his tragic hero status within the book.

Consider:

- the fact that Gatsby is described as a '**Platonic** conception of himself'
- Gatsby's true name and identity
- his role in criminal activities
- his imagined past and connections
- his relationship with his father.

Key term

Platonic. Connected with the thinking of the Greek philosopher Plato. A 'Platonic conception' is an unreal, impossibly ideal version of something.

Activity

What conclusions do you reach about Gatsby's past? Does this past influence the tragic consequences? Is his desire to achieve equal footing with the rich his tragic flaw? Compare and connect Gatsby with other tragic heroes you have encountered in your studies.

Key terms

Midwest. A geographical area of the USA, centred broadly between the Great Lakes in the east and the state lines of North Dakota, South Dakota, Nebraska and Kansas in the west.

Moralistic novel. A novel with a moral message for the reader, usually about how to lead a better life.

Symbol / Symbolized / Symbolism. This involves suggestion or connection between things, rather than direct comparison. A symbol is often repeated, or part of a bigger scheme of suggestion. The meanings of symbols are not fixed.

Link

For a discussion of ecocriticism, see Chapter 32.

Did you know?

The Valley of the Ashes seems to be an incarnation of the landscape imagined in T. S. Eliot's famous poem, *The Waste Land* (1922).

Tragic symbolism

Fitzgerald makes use of **symbols** and **motifs** within his writing to enhance the tragedy, helping us as readers to make connections across the narrative. These symbols and motifs also act as reminders of the tragic conditions operating in the text.

Activity

With a partner, write an explanation of the **significance** of the following recurring elements in the narrative:

- the colour yellow
- the eyes of Dr T. J. Eckleberg
- the green light at the end of the dock
- West and East Egg
- the Valley of the Ashes
- the Plaza Hotel
- the **Midwest**
- Gatsby's mansion.

Share your findings and ideas with other members of your class.

Glamour and squalor in *The Great Gatsby*

The way in which Fitzgerald builds the tragedy in *The Great Gatsby* partially relies on location and place. There are obvious contrasts in the novel between West Egg and the Valley of the Ashes. The mechanization and industrialization that promised so much offer a very different reality. The fact that this is, of course, already a 'tragic' landscape may reinforce the idea that the characters associated with it are also heading towards tragedy. It might be helpful to consider this view of the text from an ecocritical perspective.

Although the Valley of the Ashes is the most potent **representation** of humanity's fall from Eden, it may also be worth looking in detail at the difference between Long Island glamour and New York squalor as presented in the novel. Look in particular at Gatsby's mansion and its ostentatious nature, but also Tom and Myrtle's apartment in New York. Compare Gatsby's mansion and its development with other properties on Long Island.

Different readings: turning to ashes?

One way to think about *The Great Gatsby* is to regard it as a **moralistic novel** that aims to teach its readers something. Thus when Nick returns from the East he wants the world to be 'at a sort of moral attention forever'. While the lives of the characters in the East have literally turned to ashes – matching the Valley of the Ashes – there is an understanding that readers will be morally attentive too. As with the Shakespearean tragedies, we have undergone a form of *catharsis* to understand the virtues and importance of living a moral and decent life – which many of the characters do not. Again, this seems to be a tragedy that warns us about over-ambition.

The Remains of the Day (AS level)

The Remains of the Day by Kazuo Ishiguro was published in 1989. It is an unusual tragedy set in the large country house of an English lord in the period around World War II. In the story a butler, James Stevens, is the flawed character. He falls in love with the housekeeper, Miss Kenton, but because of his inertia and loyalty to his post, he is unable to do anything about it.

The novel is written in a first-person narrative voice, and therefore Ishiguro is able to clearly show Stevens' human flaws and offer a sense of **pathos**. He also makes the reader work hard to supply the ideas that Stevens himself does not express.

> **Key term**
>
> **Pathos.** The depiction of suffering, an appeal to the reader's emotions.

> **Did you know?**
>
> Kazuo Ishiguro was born in Nagasaki, Japan in 1954, but later moved to England.

Stevens' drive

During World War II Stevens has been loyal to Lord Darlington, but when the estate is sold on to his new employer (an American named Mr Farraday), he takes a car and drives to visit Miss Kenton. He discovers that she has been married for 20 years and is expecting her first grandchild. The two characters contemplate the choices they made and wonder how their life would have been if they had admitted their love and married each other. Stevens is forced to accept this loss and now has to fulfill the 'remains of the day' of his life.

Other tragedies in the novel

The relationship between Stevens and Miss Kenton can be seen as the central tragedy of the novel. Although neither of them dies, there is a sense that death beckons. The two of them realize they should have acted sooner. However, a number of other events in the novel are worth investigating as being potentially tragic, at least in some respects:

- Lord Darlington tries to negotiate a settlement between Britain and Germany but this fails, and so causes his social and political decline.
- William Stevens, Stevens' 72-year-old father, is still in service. He suffers a stroke and Stevens is unsure how to respond to this.
- Mr Cardinal, the young journalist, is killed in Belgium during the war.

These events are all set against the wider tragedy of World War II.

Tragic patterns

Several elements contribute to the tragedy in *The Remains of the Day*. In comparison to the large issues that affect characters in, say, *Othello* or *King Lear*, these might seem comparatively small, but they still have a tragic impact. Consider:

- the constraints of the English class system – compare this with Mr Farraday's views
- dignity and service – men like Stevens feel these elements are integral to who they are, and the tragic events suggest that he should have ignored these feelings
- loyalty – despite the damage created by Lord Darlington, Stevens remains loyal, but his loyalty is his undoing
- perspective – while Stevens see events in one way, Miss Kenton views them rather differently.

As Stevens continues his drive, he meets other characters who knew him years ago. These characters work as mirrors, reflecting his life and showing him what it consists of.

Different readings

Even though there are no conventionally tragic deaths in *The Remains of the Day*, many readers find the novel intense and powerful. Characters go through typical tragic emotions as they contemplate their flaws. What really hits home in the novel is that we as readers probably know people like Stevens and Miss Kenton, and we recognize the tragic pattern.

Conclusion

Hardy, Fitzgerald and Ishiguro offer the reader a new understanding of tragedy in these three texts. They show that the novel is a very productive form in which to explore tragedy, and they build upon the conventions established in drama over a number of centuries. In the next chapters we will see how, over time, poets have also used tragedy in their work.

Poetic tragedy: John Keats and Thomas Hardy

7

'Lamia'

'Lamia' was first published in 1820. Like other poets of this period, John Keats was fascinated with the range of tragedies that were to be found in Greek mythology. What he attempts to do in the poem is to breathe life into an old story and make it relevant again for his readers. Such tragedies often have quite intricate plots, and events in them are sometimes quite strange and disturbing.

In the Lamia story, the god Hermes (a son of Zeus) hears about a nymph and decides to search for her. Instead of finding the nymph, he comes across what is termed a Lamia (a beautiful queen from Libya who can change into a child-eating demon or vampire). This Lamia reveals the nymph to Hermes, and in return he restores her human form. Hermes and his nymph depart.

Lamia seeks a young man from Corinth (in eastern Greece) called Lycius. Lycius and Lamia fall in love. However, tragedy occurs when the sage (or philosopher) Apollonius reveals Lamia's true identity at their wedding feast. Lamia disappears and Lycius dies of grief.

In this chapter you will:

- examine poems with tragic themes written by John Keats or Thomas Hardy
- explore Keats's and Hardy's authorial methods in shaping these tragedies
- make connections to other tragedies you have read in this option of the specification.

Did you know?

John Keats (1795–1821) was an English Romantic poet. Many of his poems look at legendary figures, re-invented classical legends, and medieval or 'fairie' romance, and are concerned with the importance of direct experience.

Activity

Read the section of the poem that first describes Hermes' meeting with Lamia, beginning 'She was a gordian shape of dazzling hue'; and ending 'Like a stoop'd falcon ere he takes his prey'. Then answer the following questions.

1. How do the author's methods here contribute to a picture of Lamia?
2. Which image is most striking?
3. What verse form is being used here?
4. Does any of this indicate a tragic dimension to the poem?

Commentary

Lamia is presented as being both snake-like and also as having 'fairie' and elfin (or elf-like) qualities. Thus she is both repulsive and attractive. There are indications of what she can do when Keats writes of her being 'touch'd with miseries'. Many of the images are striking, but one of the most effective is the description of her 'rainbow-side'. Much of the description leads us to believe that she will be a tragic force in the poem. You will note that the poem is written in **heroic couplets** which, with their predictable stress pattern, reinforce the message of the poem and help to make the tragedy seem inevitable.

Key term

Heroic couplets. A verse form found in epic poetry, where the lines are in rhyming pairs.

The tragedy of promiscuity

In the nineteenth century, many readers thought that figures like Lamia hunted for men. This would have been shocking because of the idea of female promiscuity: women were not expected to behave in such a predatory way, or to have sexual feelings.

As you read the poem, make notes on how this promiscuity is explored by Keats and whether he intends it to be shocking or merely truthful. One of the key strands in Keats's poem is that as well as presenting Lamia in this way, he also shows that she is a woman who has needs. In some of his correspondence,

Did you know?

Lamia is a very old story and was used by generations of mothers to 'scare' children into good behaviour – as a kind of female bogeyman. Many Christian writers warned against the seductive nature of Lamia-type creatures, and there was some belief that they could act as 'reproductive spirits', magically becoming pregnant.

Keats wrote that he hoped the poem 'would start a fire in people and give them either an unpleasant or pleasant sensation'.

Activity

Look at the final section of the poem, from 'By her glad Lycius sitting, in chief place' to the end. How do you respond to this sequence?

Commentary

Apollonius is Lycius' teacher, so the closeness of the tragedy is enhanced. Much of the tragic power of this section is brought about by the dialogue and Lycius' reaction to what he has discovered.

You may notice that a lot of the imagery is based on eyes and sight. This may be ironic – to point out Lycius' blindness to the truth. To echo the discovery of Lamia's serpent-like past, look at how many words Keats uses beginning with the letter 's'. These seem to reinforce the evil in Lamia at the end, prefiguring Lycius' death. The serpent imagery also connects with the biblical imagery of the Garden of Eden, when Satan comes to tempt Eve in the form of a snake.

Lycius' death is dealt with abruptly and quickly, which emphasizes its impact and potentially shocks the reader. This may be one of the 'unpleasant sensations' Keats was seeking.

Conclusion

The poem uses a different model of tragedy than much of what you have encountered before. Although the characters are high-status figures in that they operate in the ancient, mythical past, Keats seems keen to present them as ordinary people who happen to be operating in this mythical world. Lamia's flaw is her secret identity, while Lycius' flaw is his naivety in becoming involved with a woman he does not really know. You may like to consider whether the poem's tragedy resists or supports the **patriarchal** order of the day.

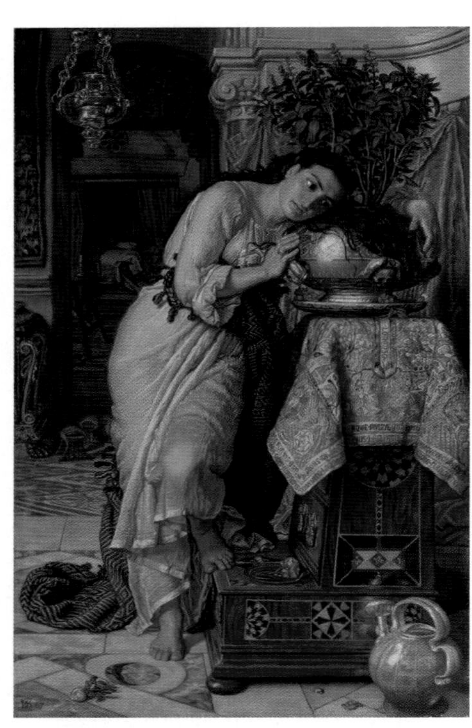

A painting by William Holman Hunt, depicting a scene from Keats' poem 'Isabella, or The Pot of Basil'.

Isabella is caressing the basil pot in which she has buried the severed head of her lover, Lorenzo, who has been murdered by her brothers.

'Isabella, or The Pot of Basil'

With 'Lamia', you have seen how Keats has taken one older tragedy and re-invented it for his nineteenth-century readers. To some degree, it is true that there are only so many tragic stories that can be told. What makes them different and new is how a particular writer re-shapes the story.

The tragic story of 'Isabella, or The Pot of Basil' is based on a time-tested narrative idea: the heroine is a woman whose family want her to marry someone of high social status, but she would prefer to marry someone else. Determined women like her are usually a starting point for tragedy, because, in earlier times, they countered the perceived natural order of things – women were not expected to take control of their lives, but to be passive.

In this case, Isabella's lover Lorenzo is an employee of one of her two brothers, and as they see it, he is not fit for her. The brothers murder and bury him. However, Lorenzo's ghost comes to tell Isabella of this, and she recovers the body and reburies the head in a pot of basil. In the past, the herb basil was thought to have been found growing on the cross of Christ, and there were several legends that it guaranteed safe passage for the dead.

In the story, however, the brothers take away the pot of basil from Isabella, and she dies of grief. Not only does Isabella have to suffer the tragedy of knowing her lover is dead, but she also has to endure the fact that the relic containing his head (which might be able to sustain her in carrying on with life) is also taken from her. It is this final act that causes her death.

Activity

To begin to understand the poem, go through it and write a few words in response to each stanza. For example, see the following in response to the first five stanzas:

Isabella and Lorenzo could not sleep in the same place

↓

But their love grew more tender

↓

He longed to hear her morning step upon the stair

↓

They fantasize about each other

↓

Isabella falls sick with love.

When you encounter difficult sections of the poem, this is often a productive thing to do as it can help you sort through the core ideas in each of the stanzas. Once you have established the core argument, the rest of the poem becomes easier to understand.

Did you know?

The notion of the headless lover was a popular idea in the Romantic movement, in that it influenced other poets and painters. The Pre-Raphaelites were a group of painters heavily influenced by Keats's tragic poems. You will find images of Isabella by searching on the Internet and looking at the paintings of William Holman Hunt, John White Alexander and John Everett Millais. The Pre-Raphaelite painters wanted a return to intense colour and complex compositions. You might like to think of them as a useful match for the poetry of Keats.

Conclusion

With 'Isabella, or The Pot of Basil', we see that Keats has constructed another kind of tragedy, one that should give you new insights into the genre. Long narrative poems of this type offer plenty of opportunities for different interpretations and show that, despite the apparently distant medieval setting, such a tragedy can have a contemporary relevance.

'La Belle Dame sans Merci'

By now, you will have started to understand how Keats has adapted and used the genre of tragedy for poetic purposes. We have so far looked at two longer narrative poems. The final poem you are required to study is shorter and its tragedy is therefore, in some ways, more intense.

An indication of the content of the poem comes from its title, which is in French and translates as 'The Beautiful Lady without Mercy (or Pity)'.

Activity

Read the poem a couple of times and try to work out the central plot. Then see if you can find any elfin or faerie imagery. Answer the following questions.

1. Who is asking the questions at the beginning of the poem?
2. What effect does the elfin and faerie imagery have?
3. What is the warning offered in the dream?
4. What do you find tragic about this poem?

Commentary

The first voice in the poem is an anonymous one, which asks questions of the Knight in the opening two stanzas. The Knight then responds to these questions and explains his predicament. There is much elfin and faerie imagery in the poem, which seems to reinforce both the magical nature of the beautiful woman and the danger. It seems that there ought to be no fusion between the faerie world and the human world – and therefore the implication is that this is what brings about the tragedy.

You may wish to compare the elfin and faerie imagery used here with that found in 'Lamia'. The poem is potentially about two kinds of tragic love. It could be about unrequited (or unreturned) love. At the same time, it could also be about impossible love: when two people meet and fall in love but cannot be together for social or religious reasons.

The warning (and the tragedy) inside the dream is that many men have been in this position before and have also been duped by the 'faery child'. The men she has seduced all have high status – they are kings, princes and warriors; the latter are very much like the Knight. The tragedy of the poem is that the figures offer a precise warning about the future, yet the Knight finds himself living through and experiencing it.

Authorial method

This poem has quite a simple structure. It is composed of 12 stanzas, each with four lines. The rhyme scheme is an a-b-c-b pattern. This type of quatrain is often found in **ballads**.

The poem also has a cyclical structure. You will see that the final two lines are repetitions of lines 3 and 4 from the first stanza. The effect of this is to reinforce the fate of the Knight in this bleak landscape. The poem has a folkloric feel and is written in a style that is meant to be **archaic** and mysterious.

Key terms

Archaic. Having the features current in a much older period.

Ballad. A long poem that tells a story, and usually has a fast pace, with repetition a common feature.

'The Eve of St Agnes'

Many of the ideas above can be applied to the final poem in the selection by Keats – 'The Eve of St Agnes'. This poem is an unusual tragedy because the tragic events occur to more peripheral characters – the Beadsman and Angela. The poem is based on the superstition that a girl could foresee her future husband if she performed certain ceremonies on the eve of St Agnes.

The poem suggests that sometimes tragedy is brought upon us unwittingly by the actions of others. 'The Eve of St Agnes' has a clear narrative structure, so understanding the poem and its tragedy should be relatively easy for you.

Selected poems by Thomas Hardy (AS level)

As well as being a novelist who dealt with tragic themes, Thomas Hardy also wrote tragic poetry. He is interesting as a poet, since he approaches tragedy from a slightly different angle. Some general themes found in his work are:

- personal tragedies of regret and guilt over how things have worked out
- tragedies of love, where people are thwarted in relationships
- tragedies taking place in specific landscapes – often Dorset or Cornwall – where landscapes and spaces are used **metaphorically** to symbolize tragic events
- the tragedy of a worthless and unfulfilled life.

Hardy's personal tragedy

As you will see, many of Hardy's poems based on tragic themes involve personal relationships.

Although the *Poems of 1912–13*, or the 'Emma poems' as they are often called, mark a certain point in Hardy's own life, he also wrote a number of other works examining human tragedy from different angles. The more you read and engage with these poems, the more you will understand the way Hardy approaches tragic aspects within his writing. Sometimes, it appears that fate seals a tragic end to particular lives, and that this process is unstoppable.

Did you know?

Early in his life, when working in Cornwall in 1870, Hardy fell in love with Emma Gifford. They married in 1874. Later in life they became estranged, but her death in 1912 had a traumatic effect on Hardy. In the aftermath of her death, Hardy returned to Cornwall to revisit the places where their courtship took place. The poems written during this period convey the tragedy of missed opportunities and of deep regret. In 1914 Hardy married his secretary, Florence Emily Dugdale, but he was still haunted by his first wife's death and felt much remorse for all that had gone wrong in their relationship.

Activity

It is worth remembering that in your AS exam you will have to write about more than one poem. Choosing the most appropriate poems to write about, depending on the question, will be vital. To prepare for this, and to deepen your understanding of the range of poetry in this selection, make a list of the different ways in which various poems can be grouped. Below are some categories for you to start with. Suggest suitable poems for each of these and then add other categories/poems of your own.

- Poems apparently about personal experience
- Poems about more public events
- Poems with similar and different narrative voices
- Poems which tell quite-detailed stories
- Poems with little detail in their story
- Poems with a moral
- Nature poems
- Poems specific to certain time

Conclusion

Both Keats's and Hardy's poetry can be explored from the perspective of tragedy, with subtle differences and nuances in each poem. It is especially useful here to remember that this part of the specification is called 'Aspects of tragedy' – finding some tragic aspects and echoes can lead to interesting readings of the poems.

8 The poetry anthology: from Chaucer to Betjeman

In this chapter you will:

- explore a range of poetry from the medieval to the modern period
- consider how poets across different time periods and **genres** deal with aspects of tragedy
- examine how tragic **motifs** and ideas are developed in verse
- start to compare and connect with other tragedies you have read.

Did you know?

Geoffrey Chaucer (c.1343–1400) wrote *The Canterbury Tales* some time around 1387. This epic poem is about a group of pilgrims (people who travel to visit a significant religious site) undertaking a journey to Canterbury from Southwark in London. Along the way, the pilgrims tell each other stories.

Introduction to the poetry anthology

As you study the poems in this anthology, try to build a picture of how different poets have used the features of tragedy; how they have adapted, altered or reconfigured them, according to the needs of their age and its readers. You should also be actively trying to connect the poems studied here with other texts studied in the option 'Aspects of tragedy'. The requirements for AS and A level are slightly different, but the same basic skills are needed for you to be successful in each of the exams.

'The Monk's Tale' by Geoffrey Chaucer

The anthology contains a small section from the 'Prologue to the Monk's Tale' and an extract from 'The Monk's Tale'. Studying Chaucer can be quite daunting at first, because his English can seem so distant from our own. However, the answer is to start by reading the poetry aloud and gaining a general impression of what he is saying. You will soon find that you become more familiar with his language and enjoy working out its exact meaning.

Before each of the pilgrims tells their story, there is usually a connecting piece of text called the 'Prologue'. This often reflects on ideas in the previous tale, and sets up the context for the one that follows.

Activity

Read the 'Prologue to the Monk's Tale', then answer the following questions:

1. What does the Monk say about past tragedies?
2. How have they been written?
3. What does it mean when the Monk describes them as 'a certeyn storie'?
4. How do you interpret the final eight lines of the Prologue?

Commentary

The Monk seems to take a fairly jaunty line here, and argues that tragedies are just another form of story – outlining some of their characteristics. He explains that they are about men who have 'yfallen out of heigh degree / Into myserie'. The final eight lines here signal that he is about to begin speaking, while listing the type of men tragedy can affect. He explicitly mentions those at the top of the tree.

Lucifer and Adam

There are three main sections to the extract you are studying. The Monk begins by explaining what he is going to do. You may detect an almost comic **detachment** in the way he speaks. He explains that he is going to 'biwaille in manere of tragedie' and talks about the concept of Fortune. There is a sense that he does not care too much about tragedy and that he is speaking ironically.

The Monk then looks at two central tragic figures – Lucifer (sometimes known as Satan) and Adam. An eight-line stanza, rhyming *ababbcbc* is used here. The

Key term

Detachment. A lack of connection with the processes occurring around oneself.

rhyme in the middle of the stanza seems to tie the whole together. This is a slightly different kind of rhyme scheme from that found elsewhere in *The Canterbury Tales*, where rhyming couplets are used.

An illustration from a medieval illuminated manuscript of *The Canterbury Tales*

Activity

Tragedy is often said to be about the fall of illustrious men. Copy and complete the following table, trying to explain each character's fall in three stages. Find evidence in the poem to support your views.

Character	Why illustrious?	Fall caused by?	Implications of this?
Lucifer	1.	1.	1
	2.	2.	2.
	3.	3.	3.
Adam	1.	1.	1
	2.	2.	2.
	3.	3.	3.

Extract from *Paradise Lost*

You will probably have picked up on the idea that a fall from Paradise is often suggested in tragedies. At the beginning of *Othello*, the tragic hero is in a state of paradise, as a successful general and newly married, and yet he will shortly suffer. So, too, with Lear at the start of *King Lear*, where the island of Britain is in paradise-like order.

The idea of a fall from Paradise is a biblical one, described in the Book of Genesis, where the perfect Eden created by God is corrupted by Adam and Eve, who are tempted to eat the forbidden fruit and therefore introduce death into Paradise. This is expressed as a tragedy affecting all of humankind. In Christian theology, it is only the 'second Adam', Jesus Christ, who can end the tragedy and defeat death. The idea of a Paradise being lost is therefore particularly powerful.

The tragic expulsion of Adam and Eve from Paradise is a concept that dominated the Christian world-view for some time. It is such a powerful image that it is used over and over again in tragedies as a **metaphor** for the feeling of dislocation and disharmony caused by the chaos of tragedy: the original sin of Adam and Eve promoted the original chaos. You may also see the metaphor used in an ecocritical sense: a lot of literature now examines the way the environment has been corrupted and destroyed, denoting another tragic 'fall'.

The Fall of Man

In the anthology you will look at one short sequence from 'Book I' of *Paradise Lost*. The poem concerns the story of the Fall of Man: the temptation of Adam and Eve by the fallen angel Satan, and their expulsion from the Garden of Eden. Milton's purpose, as stated at the beginning of 'Book I', was to 'justify the ways of God to men'.

To understand this extract, it may be useful to know what happens before and after it. Milton explains his theme, humanity's disobedience, and then presents the defeated Archangel Satan. Satan questions the new environment he finds himself in, which is Hell (Milton calls this location Tartarus). Crucially, he says that it is better to reign in Hell than to serve in Heaven. It is Satan's over-ambition that has led him to these circumstances. At the same time, as Heaven is lost to him, there is a tone of regret in his voice.

Later in 'Book I', Satan addresses Beelzebub, his second-in-command, and the other rebellious angels who are lying on the burning lake of Hell. He then summons their support and forms a council. The palace of Satan, labelled Pandemonium by Milton, is then constructed.

In a sense, Satan's tragedy is determined by the fact that he is an Archangel (a highly esteemed angel) who rebels against God. He is therefore falling much further than a king or any other high-status character. His fall from the very top of the Christian order to the very bottom seems to be the ultimate tragedy.

Did you know?

The final version of *Paradise Lost* contains 12 Books, and the whole poem may be regarded as an epic. It is written in **blank verse**. This form is defined by lines that are of equal length but are unrhymed, and almost always in **iambic pentameter** (the most common **metre** for verse in English).

Activity

Complete the following activities with the extract from *Paradise Lost*.

1. Find examples of language and/or phrases that show Satan coming to terms with his new environment.
2. Which language and/or phrases do you think most represent his tragic fall?
3. How is Hell imagined?
4. Is there humour in Satan's account?
5. What connections can you make with other tragedies?
6. Do you consider this to be the ultimate tragedy?
7. How might Milton use Satan's fall to echo the fall of man?
8. Can Satan ever be regarded as a tragic hero, or will he always be regarded (by Christian readers at least) as an embodiment of evil?

Key terms

Blank verse. Unrhymed verse.

Iambic pentameter. Refers to the stress and length of a line of poetry. The 'iamb' part refers to pairs of syllables that are unstressed/stressed, and the 'pent' part refers to the fact that there are five pairs of syllables in each line. A classic line of iambic pentameter is the first line from Gray's *Elegy*: 'The curfew tolls the knell of

Metre. This is the basic rhythmic pattern in a particular piece of poetry.

Commentary

There are plenty of examples of Satan coming to terms with his new environment. Tartarus is presented almost like a newly discovered colony (this was, of course, a great age of imperialism and colonial discovery). Satan's fall is summarized by expressions such as 'make a Heav'n of Hell, a Hell of Heav'n' and 'We shall be free'. Hell itself is seen as a refreshing place of freedom, rather than the way it is presented in some other literature – as a kind of menacing torture chamber.

Satan is filled with confidence and is inclined to be humorous and witty – mainly at God's expense. Satan here could be connected to several other cunning tragic villains – such as Shakespeare's Iago and Edmund. It is possible, however, to see Satan as a tragic hero, and that it is not just humanity that defies God.

Mortals and the immortal: 'Tithonus'

Alfred Lord Tennyson's poem 'Tithonus', which was published in 1860, is a dramatic monologue written in blank verse, from Tithonus's point of view. Unlike the original Greek myth, Tennyson's Tithonus has asked for immortality, and Eos has granted this to him (in most versions before this one, it had been Zeus). In Tennyson's version, Tithonus is lamenting his longevity. His tragedy is to be separated from the world of mortals and also from the world of immortals. To add to his pain, he is also separated from Eos.

The opening four lines of the poem embody the tragedy Tithonus is already beginning to suffer.

> The woods decay, the woods decay and fall,
> The vapours weep their burthen to the ground,
> Man comes and tills the field and lies beneath,
> And after many a summer dies the swan.

The lines are filled with rich vowel sounds; their repetitive nature connects with the repetition of the seasons through which Tithonus has to linger. The fact that the woods decay emphasizes the fact that he will decay but not die – unlike the beautiful swan mentioned at the end of this opening sequence. Likewise, the normal agricultural year recurs, and other men work and then die, unlike Tithonus. His disempowerment through old age is therefore indicated at the start of the poem. There is already an indication of tragedy in the writing.

Did you know?

In Greek mythology, Tithonus was the lover of Eos, the Titan of the Dawn – known in Roman mythology as Aurora. A Trojan by birth, Tithonus was the son of King Laomedon and a water nymph named Strymo.

The tragedy of death removed

Initially, it might be difficult to take in all of the background to this poem, but once you realize that Tithonus's tragedy is that of someone who has been granted immortality, but has forgotten to ask for eternal youth alongside it, then the poem becomes much easier to understand.

As the poem shows, as time goes on, old age grows upon him. He becomes more and more withered, and yet cannot die. His tragedy is that he will simply continue to grow older. This is an unusual type of tragedy because tragedy most often culminates in death – especially for heroic characters such as Tithonus.

Activity

Tithonus is a narrative tragedy. A productive way to understand the poem is to 'bare-bone' the narrative. This means stripping back the narrative to its skeleton, so we understand the basic structure. You can create a flow diagram of the poem. Your first boxes might look like this:

Tithonus is speaking to Eos
at the 'quiet limit of the world'

↓

Mourns the fact that he is mortal

↓

To his great heart none other than a God!

You could add boxes coming off this structure to explain possible thoughts or ideas at certain points in the poem. Once you have completed this, you will have a useful map of the poem.

'Jessie Cameron'

Christina Rossetti was fascinated with the subject of 'fallen women', and ideas about sin and redemption. The phrase 'fallen women' referred to those who had become involved in difficult relationships, divorced, had children as single mothers, or who drifted into prostitution.

Did you know?

Christina Rossetti (1830–1894) was an English poet whose work celebrates and champions the power of women. Her writing sometimes has an **allegorical** quality, and she was much influenced by writers of the Romantic period.

Key term

Allegory. A sort of extended **metaphor**, where a story or meaning emerges under the surface of some other story. Famous examples are *The Pilgrim's Progress* and *The Faerie Queene*. Some critics have argued that J. R. R. Tolkien's *The Lord of the Rings* is an allegory of the First World War, in which Tolkien fought.

'Jessie Cameron' – which was first published in 1866 – is a narrative poem, and the first task is to sort through the narrative voices and dialogue in the poem. As a poem, it is dialogue heavy, and the speech within it has an important contribution to make to the tragic theme of the piece.

In the period in which Rossetti was writing, women were not supposed to be 'careless'. They needed to be careful and compliant – particularly in their relationships with men, and in issues such as sexuality. The implication here is that Jessie's flaws make her ripe for tragedy. Being outspoken was also regarded as an unexpected and unwanted habit in women.

Jessie is attractive to men, but she could bring both bliss and bane (bane means 'injury' or 'ruin'). She may remind you of characters such as Shakespeare's Desdemona, who is determined and unconventional, and Cordelia, who goes against the **patriarchal** order, and Hardy's Tess Durbeyfield, who is similar to Jessie Cameron.

Choice and marriage, sea and spell

As the poem continues, Jessie appears to think that she deserves better than the neighbour's son, and she recommends other girls to him. She appears to be making her own choices about marriage. While Jessie has 'gypsy blood' (further indicating her untamed nature), the neighbour's son has a witch for a grandmother.

The poem then shifts into tragic mode, when the sea appears to consume them and sweep them away together. One implication is that the grandmother cast some kind of spell to separate them, but tragically also involved her grandson. Perhaps, by this point, she stopped resisting his advances, but by now it is too late.

The sea is a tidy tragic device, since their bodies are never found. It is worth pointing out that early on in the poem the sea appears to be a place of play and freedom, where the couple may escape the restrictions of society. However, later in the poem it becomes their tragic adversary.

Activity

In your response to the poem, look at the following elements and consider their impact in tragedy:

- The importance of not lingering, and taking prompt action.
- The lack of a name for the neighbour's son – does this destroy any intimacy?
- The refusal of an offer of marriage – is this unexpected?

Commentary

The poem seems to say that it is important to take advantage of opportunities – otherwise your chance may disappear – and that it is tragic not to do so. Lingering in inactivity is therefore a kind of sin.

The fact that we do not know the name of the neighbour's son seems deliberate, since we find it harder to know him as a person.

It was perhaps unusual for a woman to resist an offer of marriage in this way – even though Jessie feels she may do better and elevate herself.

Epic poetic tragedy: 'The Death of Cuchulain'

Who was Cuchulain?

Cuchulain (pronounced *Ke-hulin*) is an Irish mythological hero who appears in the stories of the Ulster Cycle (known as *The Táin*) as well as in some Manx and Scottish folklore. He was supposedly the son of the god Lugh and Deichtine (a legendary mother figure). In his childhood he was known as Setanta, but gained his better-known name when he killed Culann's guard dog in self-defence. His name Cuchulain means 'Culann's hound'. He then offered to take the dog's place until a replacement could be found.

In the Cycle he defends Ulster single-handedly against the armies of Queen Medb of Conacht, when aged only 17. The Cycle explains how it is prophesied that his life would be amazing and that he would complete great deeds, although it would be short.

Cuchulain is famed for his terrifying battle fury, and he has been adopted in more recent times as a symbol of both modern Irish nationalism and Ulster unionism. A famous bronze sculpture of the dying Cuchulain stands in the Dublin General Post Office, in commemoration of the Easter Rising of 1916. He is also presented on a mural in Highfield Drive in Belfast. Here he is seen by unionists as an Ulsterman defending the province from enemies coming from the south.

Did you know?

W. B. Yeats was fascinated by Ireland's mythological and folkloric heritage, much of which stretched back to the Iron Age Celtic period. Yeats was a poet whose work often featured tragic storylines. The poem 'The Death of Cuchulain' was first published in 1892. It is an epic narrative poem.

Understanding the poem

It is often useful to read longer narrative poems in sections, understanding how the tragic narrative grows and develops, rather than trying to read the whole poem at once. This way you will come to understand how W. B. Yeats develops the tragedy in the poem.

There are many different versions of Cuchulain's ending, and this is Yeats's own retelling. Read the introductory section of the poem from 'A man came slowly from the setting sun' to 'Nor won the gold that now Cuchulain brings'. You will begin to understand the poem's theme when you know that Emer is Cuchulain's estranged wife. The poem is written in **iambic pentameter** and in what is termed rhyming or **heroic couplets**. This is a form often used for epic stories in poetry.

The jealousy of Emer

In the next sequence of the poem, Emer looks at her son Finmole and asks him to find her husband. It is her jealousy of her husband lying with a younger woman (not named here, but known in Irish folktales as Ethne Inguba) that makes Emer send her son to find him. Since it has been many years since Cuchulain has seen his wife, he does not know he has a son. When an individual comes to his camp and says he has the same bond as Cuchulain in not revealing his name until in the midst of battle, he does not believe him, and therefore challenges him to a fight. The hint that there is a family connection is only indicated when Cuchulain says:

> Your head a while seemed like a woman's head
> That I loved once.

In the next sequence of the poem, we see Cuchulain's famed battle rage at work. This rage is his most powerful ally, but it is also what will kill his son. This is part of his flaw as a noble tragic hero. Concobar is here seemingly presented as a possible ally of Queen Medb and in the poem later employs the druids to work magical incantations in his ear so that he will 'fight the waves of the loud sea'. The suggestion is that they are successful in getting Cuchulain to take his own life and surrender to the ocean.

There are clearly several tragic elements at work here: the estrangement between Emer and Cuchulain, Emer's jealousy, Cuchulain's affair, and his killing of his own son. The tragedy hinges around his family oath of not saying one's name. This is a flaw passing through the generations.

Yeats's efficient ending

Yeats builds up the subject matter in quite a lengthy – and sometimes puzzling – way, but the tragic moments of the poem happen very succinctly. In some respects, these moments are the most effective in the poem because they shock the reader. When he kills his son, Cuchulain's only words are 'I put you from your pain. I can no more'. Later on in the poem, when the druids have plied their magic, Yeats ends the poem with the following:

> In three days' time, Cuchulain with a moan
> Stood up, and came to the long sands alone:
> For four days warred he with the bitter tide;
> And the waves flowed above him, and he died.

Here, in this beautifully crafted ending, we see that Cuchulain is finally engulfed by the sea. Perhaps the tragic cycle is now ended.

Tragedy as satire: 'The Convergence of the Twain'

For Hardy, the important aspect of the tragedy is the inevitability of things – that human beings will always be brought back down to earth because of their excessive pride. The poem does suggest that there are bigger, supernatural forces at work, indifferent to human suffering. Even the largest ships in the world (created by skilled engineering) are subject to these unstoppable forces.

The ship and the iceberg are depicted as if they represent the 'consummation' of a marriage – that it is their destiny or will to be together. Marriage is usually a happy event, with the emphasis on the continuation or even procreation of life. Here, instead, it signifies a certain doom. The poem satirizes humanity's 'vaingloriousness' (Hardy's term for pride), and shows that sometimes we are too confident and too full of vanity.

Kismet lovers?

Although at first distant from each other, in the poem the ship and the iceberg grow to meet each other as lovers. The term 'Kismet' is useful here. It means 'fate', and Hardy shows us that the two were destined to meet. When they do finally meet, the jarring that occurs is on a global scale, affecting 'two hemispheres' of the earth.

Interestingly, Hardy begins the poem with the ship at the bottom of the ocean, among the sea creatures there, and then moves on to the 'convergence' that brought it to this place. Convergence usually means a happy or productive coming together of two parties (such as lovers or bride and groom), but here the convergence is tragic. The title of the poem uses this and the word 'Twain' – an archaic word meaning 'two' or 'pairing'.

Did you know?

When Thomas Hardy was asked to write a poem to be read at a charity concert to raise funds in aid of the *Titanic* disaster fund, he took a very unusual approach. Instead of seeking an emotive response, Hardy developed a detached, **satiric** tone that focuses on the ship and the iceberg and how the two were destined to meet.

Hardy's poem takes a very different approach to tragedy, since it is seemingly so lacking in emotion compared to many other texts. It also offers a **satirical** view. The poem starts from the aftermath of the tragedy, and goes backwards in time to explain how events happened. Most other tragedies work the other way – using a chronological structure and building to a tragic climax.

Intertextuality and tragedy: 'Out, Out...'

The title of Robert Frost's poem 'Out, Out...' (first published in 1916) is taken from *Macbeth*, written by Shakespeare in 1606.

It will be helpful for you to know that this poem was based on an incident that occurred on 15 April 1915, when Raymond Fitzgerald, the son of Frost's neighbour, lost his hand in an accident with a buzz saw. Raymond bled so profusely that he went into shock, and despite a doctor trying to save his life, he died.

Frost invites us to make an intertextual comparison between this poem and what Macbeth feels about his wife's death. To some extent, the Frost poem relies on his reader knowing this information and understanding the tragic context. Interestingly, although the incident is one of those ordinary accidents that sadly sometimes happen, Raymond's death is given a heroic status through the link to Lady Macbeth. In this way, Frost seems to be saying that the loss of ordinary lives is just as tragic as the loss of high-status ones.

Activity

In order to understand the poem, try answering the following questions:

1. In what way is the saw personified? What is the effect of this?
2. How are the boy's innocence and passivity presented?
3. What is tragic about what happens?
4. Look carefully at the last line of the poem. How does this compare to Macbeth's view? Why is it so blunt and detached?
5. Frost seems to argue that we have a disposable or even throwaway view of life. To what extent is this true here?

Commentary

Frost gives us perspective on tragedy that you may not have encountered before. Not only does he link tragic events of the present to those of another 'created' text, but he also seems to comment on the fact that human beings don't want to know about tragedy. They would rather get back to 'their affairs' and stay emotionally detached. There may also be an implication in the poem about the tragedy of wider events in the world.

Did you know?

Robert Frost (1874–1963) was an American poet most famous for his poetry about the natural world, and for the fact that his work contained a so-called 'woodland philosophy'.

Domestic deaths: 'Miss Gee' and 'Death in Leamington'

The final two poems in the anthology are placed together here because they have certain similarities and connections. W. H. Auden and John Betjeman wrote these poems about deaths in domestic, ordinary situations, involving non-heroic characters. Both poems are ironic and satirical, showing that society is content to move on without really dealing with the tragedy in these people's lives.

In some respects, Auden and Betjeman represent modern concerns relating to tragedy. Most of us do not have to deal with huge, epic tragedy; we usually only have to deal with smaller, more personal tragedy. These two poems explore this. Whenever you encounter these kinds of poems there is usually a darker side beneath what can seem quite a light-hearted approach to the topic. These poets create satire by undercutting the seriousness of events with humour.

The rhythm and rhyme of both of these poems counteract the subject matter. There is an apparent lightness, or even childishness, in the way they are structured. Perhaps the poets are arguing that this is how we would like things to be and really, we would rather not know about tragedy.

Auden's poem, in fact, uses an old blues tune called 'St James' Infirmary', around which it is written. In this sense, the poem is self-consciously a kind of folktale ('Let me tell you a story'). Betjeman's poem is a **ballad** too, but the rhythm and rhyme do not initially make it sound like tragedy. The perspective is that of someone who knows the woman and is observing her decline. The domestic setting is offered by the fact that we see the 'upstairs bedroom' and the fact that it takes place in Leamington Spa. Betjeman seems to have chosen this place as it is in the very centre of England. It is quintessentially English and perhaps, ironically, a place (a spa) where water with medicinal and life-preserving qualities is traditionally found.

Both poems show tragedy in normal life. Compared to, say, the extract from *Paradise Lost* or 'The Death of Cuchulain', these are not poems about epic, legendary scenarios. Auden's and Betjeman's poems might have more in common with Robert Frost's 'Out, Out...'.

The tragedy of repression

Miss Gee's tragedy is presented by Auden as one of sexual repression. It seems that the character wanted perhaps in her youth to be more adventurous and exciting, but life has forced her into a position where she is 'buttoned up'. A core idea in the poem is that her illness is a **metaphor** for cultural and moral illness in our society.

Activity

Think about the following questions relating to Miss Gee.

1. Is she a good woman only in God's eyes?
2. How is the poem about the 'tragic' lack of respect we have for people?
3. How does the poem change in the seventh quatrain?
4. Does anyone care for Miss Gee?

The tragedy of chintzy, chintzy cheeriness

In his poem, Betjeman shows how English people seem to deal with tragedy and death by covering it up and avoiding it. While the unnamed victim is dying, Betjeman presents her nurse fussing about her house, and being more concerned that the 'stucco is peeling' than with helping the sick woman. Betjeman depicts a cheeriness in the face of tragedy which is ironic and satirical about English manners. Chintz is a textile with a glazed finish, often used for drapes and curtains in middle-class homes in England during the middle years of the twentieth century.

Activity

Look at the following aspects of 'Death in Leamington'.

1. How does Betjeman use questions in the poem to progress the tragedy?
2. How does the poet show the shutting down of the house to be matched with a shutdown of the heart?
3. Why is middle-class pretence carried on in the face of domestic tragedy?
4. Does Betjeman present the nurse as taking pleasure in the tragedy?
5. How does the rhyme scheme reinforce tragic events?

Share your findings with the rest of your class.

Conclusion

Betjeman's poem may bring a kind of post-modern irony to our understanding of tragedy – and in his work we observe society giving a far different response to tragedy from that presented in earlier poetry.

The poetry studied in this unit shows the adaptable and changeable nature of tragedy. It appears to have shifted over time, as writers have responded to different contexts.

By now, you should be able to make connections across many of the poems and between the other tragic texts studied in this unit.

Further reading

Tragedy: A Very short introduction by Adrian Poole (2009). An easy-to-read guide to the major issues in tragedy

The Cambridge Introduction to Tragedy by Jennifer Wallace (2007). A book that examines in detail the core issues of tragedy

Shakespeare: Othello Casebook by John Wain (1994). A diverse collection of essays on many aspects of *Othello*

Shakespeare, Race and Colonialism by Ania Loomba (2002). A book debating some of the tragic consequences of race and colonialism issues

King Lear: Critical Essays by Linda Cookson and Bryan Loughrey (1989). A useful collection of commentaries on the tragedy of *King Lear*

King Lear: Shakespeare Handbook by John Russell Brown (1989). A book tracing the performance history of the play and looking at how different acting companies have interpreted the play over time

Richard II: Manhood, Youth and Politics 1377–99 by Christopher Hetcher (2010). A very readable account of Richard II's life and the events of his rule

Timebends: A Life by Arthur Miller (1987). An autobiography in which Miller offers many thoughts about tragedy and the influence of Ibsen and classical tragedy

Shakespeare: The Basics by Sean McEvoy (2000). See in particular the chapter 'Understanding Tragedy'

Component 1 Literary genres

Option 1B: Aspects of comedy

Comedy: an introduction

9

Aspects of comedy

As the Introduction to the Literature B course explained, you have to choose whether you will study 'Aspects of tragedy' or 'Aspects of comedy'. The following seven chapters are concerned with Option 1B: Aspects of comedy.

We begin in this chapter with an introduction to some of the core concepts within comedy, which should give you a vocabulary and some concepts for interpreting and understanding comedy. Chapter 10 considers further concepts and theories, while Chapter 11 covers two major Shakespearean comedies: *Twelfth Night* and *The Taming of the Shrew*. Chapter 12 examines three other dramatic comedies: *She Stoops to Conquer*, *The Importance of Being Earnest* and a modern domestic comedy, *Educating Rita*. Chapter 13 develops further aspects of comedy by exploring how two **prose** texts have developed the genre. The prose texts considered are two novels: *Emma* by Jane Austen, and *Small Island* by Andrea Levy. For AS level, you are also permitted to study *Wise Children* by Angela Carter. Chapter 14 then examines how poetry deals with this genre in the form of 'The Nun's Priest's Tale', and a set of selected poems by John Betjeman. The poetic investigation of comedy is continued in Chapter 15, where we explore a range of poetry from the anthology. The poetry selection begins with a Renaissance poem by John Donne, and ends with the 21st-century poet Carol Ann Duffy.

This chapter introduces you to the study of comedy within this specification. The course as a whole aims to encourage you to develop your interest in, and enjoyment of, literature and literary studies, and for the 'Aspects of comedy' option you will:

- read widely and independently set texts and others that you have selected for yourself
- engage critically and creatively with a substantial body of texts and ways of responding to them
- develop and effectively apply your knowledge of literary analysis and evaluation
- explore the contexts of the comedies you are reading and others' interpretations of them.

The literary genre of comedy

Comedy has a long tradition in literature, with its origins in the ancient world and with a special emphasis on drama. In this specification, texts have been selected and grouped together because they share some common features of traditional comedic work, while also offering some interesting variations. We will, therefore, be looking at a historical form and sometimes measuring later texts and their approaches to comedy against this long-established literary genre.

Aspects of comedy: some core concepts

At the centre of all the set texts are stories that primarily amuse, where the discomfort of characters generally excites laughter rather than concern, and where no great disaster occurs. All the texts contain a love interest for the **protagonist**, and marriage is often a focal point. In all cases, society itself (as represented in the texts) and the behaviour of the men and women in it are held up for our examination, and invite our laughter. There can be no exhaustive list of the aspects of comedy, but as detailed in the AS and A level specifications, the following areas might be considered:

- The type of comic text itself, whether it is a classic romantic drama, a **satire**, or a **comedy of manners**.
- The places and times in which comedies are set.
- The protagonists' journey towards knowledge and happiness (often in relation to their love interest), their mistakes and misunderstandings along their journey, their moments of unhappiness, and their ultimate sense of joy.

Key terms

Comedy of manners. A text which satirises the behaviour of a certain social group or groups.

Prose. Passages of text that are not in verse.

Protagonist. In dramatic terms, the first major character who offers a particular view. The protagonist is often seen in opposition to the **antagonist**.

- The role of the comic villain, or rival, who directly affects the fortune of the hero, and causes some disruption to the cheerful mood, but whose power is finally curtailed.
- The sense that all will be well and that fortune smiles.
- How the hero's behaviour affects primarily himself or herself, and perhaps one or two others, rather than countries and states, as in tragedy.
- The **significance** of human **folly**, trickery and gullibility.
- The inclusion of **clowns**, exaggeration, stereotypes, pompous attitudes and posturing.
- The use of disguise, escapes and discovery, and elements of the supernatural.
- The structural patterning of the text as it moves from **disorder** to order, incorporating rule and misrule; how competition between characters is set up and resolved; how opposites are contrasted and reconciled, leading to comic resolutions.
- The use of complex plotting and **sub-plots**.
- The way in which language is used to heighten the comedy, particularly wit and linguistic play.
- The way in which comedy draws attention to itself.
- How comedy stimulates growth in the central characters.
- Ultimately, how the comedy affects the audience, inviting laughter at the ridiculous behaviour of human beings and a sense of joy that positive resolutions are possible.

The absence of any one of these aspects might be as significant as its presence.

Key terms

Clown. A person who behaves comically, a buffoon.

Disorder. The inversion or destruction of the normal order in a society.

Folly. Foolishness.

Sub-plot. An additional or second plot that often parallels events of the main plot of the tragedy.

Connecting across the A level

The concepts described above make a good checklist for any student exploring aspects of comedy, but you will also make your own decisions and reach your own views about the texts. Later in the course, your views might be shaped by other aspects of your studies. For example, you may find that studying 'Elements of political and social protest writing' or 'Elements of crime writing' will inform your views about comedy. Likewise, your reading of the comedies you are studying might be informed by the critical methods and ideas from the 'NEA: Theory and independence' part of the A level. You may start to explore theories connected with narrative, feminism, Marxism, ecocriticism or post-colonialism, and literary value and the canon, as you proceed through the course. The important thing is always to be ready to make connections and examine your comedy from a new angle or perspective.

What is comedy?

An easy definition of comedy might say that it is a genre of literature that makes us laugh. However, we need to understand *why* comedic works make us laugh. Usually, it is because they are about people caught in difficult situations, which we find funny. We know that the situation they are in will most likely be resolved, but we enjoy seeing the way they cope with the difficulties. As an audience, we put ourselves in their places and wonder what we would do in the same situation.

In early and traditional dramatic comedy (such as that written by William Shakespeare), the play usually ends with a marriage or similar celebratory event; sometimes this is accompanied by music and dance. The resolutions of such plays show how the central characters have grown and developed. Marriage is important, because it suggests that a harmony has been reached and that the marriage might result in children for the future, so that society can continue to develop and grow.

Very often, there is disorder at the heart of the comedy. Disorder is an inversion of the normal order, so that everything in the society loses its harmony. Sometimes this disorder can be amusing, but it can also be threatening and dangerous. Only when it is overcome can things return to normality.

We may go further and argue that comedies are not just about laughter. At the centre is a key strand suggesting that human life and experience are really a **charade**, and that whenever civilization reaches a point of order, human beings seemingly have a natural ability to become foolish and act stupidly. This characteristic is called **folly**. You might be under the impression that writers create comedy to help human beings try to change their behaviour. Stand-up comedians often do this in live performances – they expose how silly people are. However, over time many dramatists have shown that the human race is unlikely to change, and that human weaknesses cannot be permanently overcome.

There are many different types of literary comedy to explore – among them: romantic comedy, the comedy of manners, black comedy, absurdist and **satirical** comedy. We will consider each of these in the following chapters. We will also explore some theories of comedy suggested by readers, observers and critics over the centuries. Indeed, comedy is one of the oldest forms of drama. You are probably aware of the two masks that traditionally represent drama: tragedy and comedy. While tragedies show over and over again that people can sometimes face insoluble problems, comedies remind us that human beings are often ridiculous and that basic human nature cannot change. Comedies often, therefore, confirm our view of the world.

Key terms

Caricature. An exaggerated portrayal of a person or type of person, often for comic effect.

Charade. An absurd pretence.

Pretentious. Claiming exaggerated merit or importance.

Characteristics of dramatic comedy

We might expect to see the following characteristics in dramatic comedy:

- Love is often a motivating force, and sometimes when people are in love or are infatuated with someone, they do foolish things.
- Comedy shows that people do face tricky and serious problems, but also that human beings sometimes take themselves too seriously.
- Some dramatic comedy intends to poke fun at the folly of human beings by using **caricature**.
- Human endeavour is often seen as being **pretentious** and ludicrous.
- Sometimes comedies expose the foolishness of society's customs and manners, or its rules and laws. Characters often say that they support these customs and rules, but then undermine them with their own behaviour.
- Exaggerations of character types are often used.
- Sometimes characters are placed in bizarre and absurd situations which they are unable to escape from. This reflects how we all feel sometimes – knowing that, in fact, the order of the world is a veneer that can easily be removed.
- The Seven Deadly Sins (in particular pride, lust and greed) are all prime targets for satire within comic writing.

Comedy and structure

Most comedies have the same basic structure. This is the tripartite structure of exposition, complication and resolution.

- The *exposition* prepares the audience for what will happen, probably by showing some alteration in the lives of the characters.
- The *complication* stage occurs when the writer develops the problems which the characters face. Usually as part of the complication, a sense of disorder and anarchy prevails – sometimes resulting in the lives of the characters being turned upside down. Occasionally, this can result in the wrong pair of lovers being placed together, confusions in identity or sexuality, and people generally getting the wrong end of the stick. Disguise, foreign or new locations, and mishearing key information all contribute to this disorder.
- At the end of the text comes the *resolution*. Usually, the complications and disorder are resolved and a new order is generated. The main characters usually come to realize their mistakes and then try to deal with the new situation.

This same pattern is found in most comedies, but what makes a comedy interesting is how the writer finds a new way of developing this structure. Thus, the huge complexities of human beings' experiences are considered within a tightly organized format. If you bear in mind this same order, you can more easily spot what makes a comedy individual and innovative.

No laughing matter: comedies in context

One important thing to say about comedy is that, in fact, it is often serious. There are moments in everyone's life where absurd or puzzling things happen, which we have to cope with. We know that sometimes events in life do not go according to plan. Comedy understands this and so is able to show us the folly of human beings, with their ambitious plans and their mistakes. This is its serious intent. By laughing at the misfortunes of characters on stage, we contemplate our own weaknesses and realize that we might do exactly the same thing.

One important way of thinking about comedies is to consider how they differ from tragedies. Generally, in comedies the complications are eventually resolved. In tragedies the complications are not resolved, and result in the death of one or more characters; the resolution can only come near to or after the death of key characters. Some comedies come very close to being tragedies but step back from the brink at the last moment. That is not to say that there are no casualties in comedies, but these tend to be individuals who appear to deserve to be the objects of satire or punishment.

Activity

Working with a partner, list all of the events, dramas, stories, films, songs, TV programmes and computer games which you can think of that involve aspects of comedy. Share some of these with your class. What common features can you identity? What makes the storylines particularly comic? What kinds of comedy appeal most to young people? You should be able to develop quite a long list.

Commentary

You and your partner have probably developed a long list of texts that involve aspects of comedy.

- Plays: You may have thought of plays you have read or heard of before, especially Shakespeare's comedies such as *A Midsummer Night's Dream*, *Twelfth Night*, *As You Like It*, *Much Ado About Nothing* and *The Comedy of Errors*. You may also have heard of some modern comedies, such as *The Importance of Being Earnest* by Oscar Wilde and Samuel Beckett's *Waiting for Godot*. The British playwrights Alan Ayckbourn and Alan Bennett have also written a number of comedies.
- Television programmes and computer games: Very likely, you will have thought of texts that feature mix-ups and confusion surrounding the main characters. Television soap operas such as *Coronation Street*, *EastEnders* and *Hollyoaks* often incorporate comic elements into their storylines. Also, a range of classic television comedy has been produced in Britain. Two popular TV comedies at the time of writing are *Miranda* and *Outnumbered*. Many computer games such as *The Sims*, *Monkey Island* and *Crash Bandicoot* use comic sequences. Several are also based on comic television programmes and films.
- Films: This is a particularly rich area to consider, since many plots use **motifs** and ideas from the comic genre. The early films of comedians such as Charlie Chaplin or Harold Lloyd may come to mind, but as film has developed through the 20th and 21st centuries, it has often borrowed **conventions** from dramatic comedy. Popular comedies of recent years have included *Hot Fuzz*, *Shaun of the Dead*, *The Hangover*, *Mr Bean*, *Ali G Indahouse*, *The Inbetweeners*, *Tropic Thunder* and *Bruce Almighty*. Although comic films are amusing to watch, they often convey a serious message about what it means to be human. They are often about a coming-of-age moment, where characters grow up or mature because of the things that happen to them.

The development of dramatic comedy

In order to write exam answers, you don't always need to refer back to older ideas about dramatic comedy, but it may be useful to have some awareness of the historical roots of the genre.

Greek writers of the 5th century BC wrote a number of comedies that seem to set down some of the rules for what comedies should be like – influencing their long-term development in European culture. Indeed, the Greek word *κομos* (*komos*) means a **revel** or celebration. This revel was often led through the countryside. Early plays by writers such as Aeschylus and Sophocles (usually regarded as writers of tragedies) often featured satyrs, who were pagan gods with long ears – often depicted as half-goat – who offered primitive stories, usually deceiving or outwitting a god. They were probably very **pantomime**-like, and their performances offered a contrast to the more serious tragic dramas. One of the surviving comedies from this period is *The Frogs* by Aristophanes, which contains plenty of dancing and satire. Aristophanes is considered the greatest of the Greek comic writers, and his dramas feature a number of high-and-mighty characters who are made to look unimportant. His plays have storylines that seem quite modern. Public figures were often ridiculed in such plays – a little like the way modern newspaper cartoonists draw politicians.

Key terms

Conventions. The accepted rules, structures and customs that we expect to see in a specific genre of writing.

Motifs. Repeated elements that usually have a symbolic function.

Pantomime. In modern culture, a play generally based on a folk-tale or fairy-tale, often performed around Christmas. In theatre, pantomime has a long tradition of a variety of styles.

Revel / Revelling. Lively enjoyment or merrymaking.

The critic F. L. Lucas (in *Greek Drama for the Modern Reader*) has summarized the features of these kinds of plays:

1. A character has a bright idea: a man thinks of stopping a war by flying to heaven on a dung-beetle, or a woman tries to stop it by organizing a sex strike among other women.
2. A **Chorus** – sympathetic or hostile – enters.
3. There follows a debate about the proposal.
4. The Chorus turns and addresses the audience directly.
5. A series of **farcical** episodes arise when the original idea is put into practice.
6. All ends in a scene of **revelling**, such as a feast or a wedding: this is a further relic of primitive merry-making.

Key terms

Chorus. In Greek drama, a group of performers who comment with a collective voice on the play's action; in later dramas, the chorus could be a solitary performer, who assists the audience by providing narration.

Farcical. Relating to farce, a type of entertainment that depicts improbable situations and ludicrous pretence.

Ritual. A repeated, traditional series of actions used for ceremonial or festive purposes.

Activity

Can any of the features listed above be applied to comedies you know well? What connections can you see? Discuss the above statements with a partner and consider whether they are still relevant.

Commentary

It is clear that these features are still highly relevant to comedy. Perhaps you thought of films or TV programmes where a character has a madcap idea to change the world and make it a better place. A second character usually either supports or disagrees with the idea – this is a bit like the Greek dramatic Chorus.

A debate is set up in a comedy, because we as the audience watch the development of events and have to decide whose side we are on. We are generally sympathetic to the madcap character, although we realize that his or her idea may be foolish. The Chorus might turn to the audience directly. In some modern comedies, this is in the form of direct address from characters (used to good effect in BBC television's *Miranda*). The farcical episodes are very characteristic of modern comedy (you may have thought of *Only Fools and Horses* or *Dad's Army*). It seems that dramas emerged from traditions such as **rituals** or celebrations, and plenty of modern dramatic comedy ends with a feast or wedding.

Aristotle on comedy

Aristotle wrote more extensively on tragedy, which he seemed to prefer, but he also understood comedy. In his main work on drama, *The Poetics*, he says that comedy is 'an imitation of inferior people', that 'the laughable is a species of what is disgraceful', and that comedy 'does not involve pain or destruction, for example a comic mask is ugly and distorted, but does not involve pain'. Aristotle also argues that comedies were initially not taken that seriously, but that they later became more popular.

By 'inferior' people, he seems to mean 'ordinary' people (that is, not the kings, gods or leaders who often feature in tragedy). He also argues that we laugh when we witness the disgraceful behaviour of others – perhaps behaviour that we ourselves would not engage in, but might like to. He also observes that watching comedy does not involve 'pain', whereas it would seem that watching tragedy causes much more mental anguish. These simple rules observed by Aristotle continue to have an effect on how comedies are structured and how they affect audiences.

Activity

1. How many of the following features do you observe in comedies that you are studying, and in other comedies that you know?
   - *Stereotypical characters* (such as young lovers, angry and/or grumpy old men). To what extent are these characters merely devices for comic rituals? Do they ever surprise you by being more than just stereotypes?
   - *A* **sub-plot**, *and interlocking plots*. What comic elements does the sub-plot have that are not present in the main plot? To what extent does the sub-plot contribute to the main plot by throwing light on its main concerns and issues? Interlocking plots offer comic ingenuity, especially if the author unravels this complexity by the end.
   - *A unity of place* (the action takes place in the same or a similar place). Consider the different ways that 'place' can be understood here, from a single room, to a city, to a region, to a country, to an empire, etc. Consider also the significance of such settings; how much of the social fabric of the place is shown; types who are mentioned but not seen, etc.
   - *Mistaken identity and disguise*. Think carefully about narrative knowledge surrounding mistaken identity and disguise. Who knows about the disguise and when do they know? Give particular thought to what the audience knows and when they know it. What significance lies behind identity and disguise, beyond visual humour? What is its significance, for example, in the moral and social issues that the comedy raises?
   - *Hidden characters, overhearing, eavesdropping,* **asides**. As with characters in disguise, you can ask who knows about the hiding, both inside the text and outside? What does the hidden character discover/uncover when eavesdropping? What use do they make of their secret knowledge? Does the hidden knowledge lead to positive or negative results? Is the knowledge shared with the reader through narrative asides?
   - *Games with language, the 'misuse' of words (***malapropisms***), language mannerisms, etc.* Comic characters can be quickly and easily identified through language use. Of course many single jokes rely on language for their effects, but consider some of the creative ways in which language is used to highlight, for example, social class and difference, intelligence, intelligence that goes beyond formal language use, pomposity, etc.
   - *Comic servants, and other signs of class differences*. As with language variation, servants offer the chance for social-class issues to be highlighted. The comic tradition of subverting social norms means that the 'lower' classes often have wisdom beyond that of their 'betters', but there are many variants of this.

Key terms

Aside. A brief **soliloquy**, where – within a longer sequence of dialogue – a character speaks a short line aside, as if privately, to the audience – revealing their true thoughts about events on stage.

Malapropism. A comical confusion of words, such as saying 'expedition' instead of 'exhibition'.

- *Siblings and rivals*. Although not all siblings are also rivals, comedy makes great use of family differences, usually – although not always – to present tension and conflict. Long-lost siblings and rivals can refresh comedy and introduce new elements.
- *Chance*, for example in encounters and meetings. In some literary contexts, chance is seen as a rather weak vehicle in narratives, but in comedy chance can be a positive and centrally significant addition to the plot overall. It can also contribute to the more physical and slapstick elements of comedy.
- *Structural divisions, such as scenes, chapters, stanzas, etc.* A truism of comedy is that it's not so much what you say but how you say it. Just as the successful telling of a joke relies on all of the parts working towards a conclusion, so all comic literature relies on its structures and sequences for its overall significance.

2. Which of the above elements do you recognize from any Shakespearean comedies that you know?

There is no commentary for this activity.

Comedy in literature

While the examples we have looked at overleaf incorporate comic elements, we have perhaps still used the term 'comedy' loosely. Comedy is a specific genre of literature, which operates within a set of **conventions**. As you will have gathered by now, comedy is one of the oldest literary traditions – although the conventions acquired in successive historical periods have helped to define what is expected on stage, and have influenced writers to construct comedies in certain ways.

One of the things that the audience should feel when watching a comedy is that the world is absurd and that we all do foolish things. As we continue through this unit, keep in mind popular and everyday ideas of comedy, but try to compare them with the literary genre of comedy. You will need to examine these conventions in your coursework (NEA), and comment on their use in the dramas you study.

Conclusion

This first chapter has introduced you to comedy as a literary genre; to some of the range of forms it can take; and to some of the conventions it involves. You have considered examples of comedy in other fields, such as television, films and computer games, and you have explored some of the historical development of comedy. This will stand you in good stead when analysing Shakespearean comedy and other comic literature.

Comedy: concepts and theories

10

Shakespeare and comedy

Many of Shakespeare's comedies could be labelled romantic comedies. These plays are light-hearted to an extent, but do have some darker and more disturbing elements. Most of them were written in the early to middle years of Shakespeare's career. Some of his later comedies, however, have very dark themes and almost become tragedies – seemingly stepping back from the brink before the end.

In Shakespeare's plays, the best kind of comedy is generated by a series of mix-ups, where **disorder** grows and life is turned upside down. All of his comedies depict the foolishness of human beings.

It is worth bearing in mind that watching or performing a play of this kind will give you much more insight into how the comedy is generated than you can gain from the printed page. As you proceed through this chapter, you will discover a set of further theories and readings of comedy which you should find useful.

There are several stages to understanding how a Shakespearean comedy works. To begin, it is often useful to consider the overarching structure of the play.

In this chapter you will:

- study further the concepts and theories behind comedy, so that you can make informed responses to texts
- begin to analyse the way in which established authorial methods shape meanings in comedies, and then apply these concepts and theories to your chosen exam texts
- consider the concepts and theories from the Renaissance period
- begin to apply these core concepts and theories.

Activity

Even if you don't know *The Taming of the Shrew*, consider the following stage directions at the start of each scene. With a partner, consider what they tell you about the comic structure.

Induction: Enter Christopher Sly and the Hostess.

Induction 2: Enter aloft Sly, with attendants; some with apparel, basin and ewer, and other appurtenances, and Lord.

1.1: Enter Lucentio and his man Tranio.

1.2: Enter Petruchio and his man Grumio.

2.1: Enter Katherina, and Bianca with her hands tied.

3.1: Enter Lucentio as Cambio, Hortensio as Licio.

3.2: Enter Baptista, Gremio, Tranio as Lucentio, Katherina, Bianca, Lucentio as Cambio, and attendants on Katherina.

4.1: Enter Grumio.

4.2: Enter Tranio as Lucentio and Hortensio as Licio.

4.3: Enter Katherina and Grumio.

4.4: Enter Tranio as Lucentio, and the Pedant, booted, and dressed like Vincentio.

4.5: Enter Petruchio, Katherina, Hortensio and Servants.

5.1: Enter Blondello, Lucentio as himself, and Bianca. Gremio as before.

5.2: Enter Bianca with Vincentio, Gremio with the Pedant, Lucentio with Baptista, Petruchio with Katherina, Hortensio with the Widow; followed by Francio, Blondello, and Grumio, with the Servingmen bringing in a banquet.

Commentary

Although by no means giving us a full picture of all of the comings and goings of various characters, the previous list does offer some useful ideas about the patterns and structure of the comedy. In the Induction (a kind of prologue to the main action of the play) we are first introduced to Christopher Sly, whose name gives us some indication of his function. He is deceived into thinking he is a lord, although we know from the pattern above that he is not likely to appear later in the play. We also note that it is a male-dominated world, which may therefore present problems for the female characters in the play.

When the female characters are mentioned, it seems that they are suffering from some oppression, and this is likely to relate to the title of the play. In the middle of the play we note a series of confusions and disguises, where characters pretend to be others. Resolution is indicated at the end with many of the cast on stage (most in pairs), and a celebratory banquet of some kind.

By focusing on the basic structure we can begin to understand the **significance** of some aspects of the comedy. However, our interpretation of the comedy has just begun. If you are not studying *The Taming of the Shrew*, try the same exercise with *Twelfth Night*.

Interpretations by other readers

As you proceed through your studies of English literature, you will come to understand that different readers offer different interpretations of texts. The ways in which texts have been interpreted are often influenced by the time in which the criticism was written, as well as the trends in literary criticism. You should aim to read and synthesize a number of different points of view to help you understand the text. It is often good to refer to these different readings in your answers; use other views to reflect on your own. You may also find new criticism and emerging interpretations, so it is always worth keeping an open mind on what different observers are saying.

Northrop Frye

The Canadian scholar Northrop Frye (1906–1991) has had a considerable influence on the way in which modern literary studies interpret comedy. In 1957, Frye wrote an influential book called *The Anatomy of Criticism*. One of the main ideas in his book is that Shakespearean comedy is written in harmony with the four seasons of the year: spring, summer, autumn and winter. You may think of the title of one of the two plays we will consider in Chapter 11 – *Twelfth Night*, a winter festival. Frye also discusses the patterns in Shakespearean comedies and comments that they:

> are usually divided up into four main phases, the four seasons of the year being the type for four periods of the day (morning, noon, evening, night), four aspects of the water cycle (rain, fountains, rivers, sea or snow), four periods of life (youth, maturity, old age, death).
>
> (Frye, *The Anatomy of Criticism*, page 160)

These patterns are not necessarily chronologically ordered across the play, but are part of the overall narrative of the drama.

Activity

Try applying some of Frye's ideas to either *Twelfth Night* or *The Taming of the Shrew*. You may want to think of spring occurring at the end of the play, as a kind of new beginning. Where do you find the four periods of life in a comedy like *The Taming of the Shrew*? Think about these ideas and design a table that illustrates your conclusions.

Commentary

Frye's theory is potentially useful, since it relies on the age-old concerns of human beings, and may be related back to the original functions of comedy in ancient Greece (see pages 71–73). Perhaps the idea of 'winter' applies when the characters suffer confusion and have to push through this to reach the 'spring' in their lives.

Comedies also often have a unity of time (a concept introduced by Aristotle) – working through 24 hours with darkness and night usually representing confusion. Dawn represents, like spring, a new era. Comedic plays are filled with **symbols** of these kinds.

Extension activity

1. Analyse the **metaphorical** language of either *Twelfth Night* or *The Taming of the Shrew*, and consider its connections with Frye's theory.

2. Connect the theories outlined in Chapter 9 with those described here. How might the theories here be considered an extension of those in the previous chapter?

Key term

Symbol / Symbolized / Symbolism. This involves suggestion or connection between things, rather than direct comparison. A symbol is often repeated, or part of a bigger scheme of suggestion. The meanings of symbols are not fixed.

Frye's 'Green World'

Frye also argued that Shakespearean comedy 'is the drama of the green-world, its plot being assimilated to the **ritual** themes of the triumph of life and love over the waste land' (*The Anatomy of Criticism*, page 182). By this, and his other arguments, he implies that in the rural world:

- urban and business concerns can be forgotten
- time is also forgotten: there are no clocks
- the older, restrictive generation can be dispensed with
- there is often gender confusion
- the mythical and real merge
- there is a temporary holiday atmosphere
- there is no social hierarchy.

Frye notes that this pattern can be seen again and again in Shakespearean comedy.

Old world, Green World, new world

One useful model for Shakespearean comedy draws on the theories of Frye. The central idea is that in any comedy by Shakespeare, three worlds are operating. The first is the so-called old world. This belongs to older people or parental figures. It is usually **repressive** and often urban. Most often, it is resisted by the young people, who find it unfair and unsympathetic to their needs. This is often the case in literature – stories are often about young people who resist expectations and are at odds with conventional standards. The old world may be seen only briefly in the play, but we can probably project backwards in time to understand its operation.

The 'Green World' is so called because it is often represented by a forest, wood or other non-urban environment. It is a world of freedom, but also of confusion. This is an environment most suited to fairies, and to mix-ups, disguise, and misinformation. The Green World represents **disorder**. As comedies developed over time, new ways of working with this Green World emerged.

The new world is that created out of the resolution in the play. This is a world that has learned from its past mistakes and resolved any serious problems. Usually, characters return from the Green World, often to an urban world, but a new order is established. This is **symbolized** by several elements – notably a marriage, and quite often multiple marriages. Multiple marriages are important because they usually cut across all classes of people, suggesting social harmony. Obviously, marriage not only signifies a union, but also the opportunity for children to be born, and therefore progress in the future. Although love is an uncontrolled and irrational force, marriage demonstrates that it can be productively controlled and managed in the new world.

Key terms

Repressive. Authoritarian, preventing people from finding fufilment.

Slapstick. Physical comedy (a term invented in the 20th century but applied to the past); it involves falling over, blows and collisions.

Trickster. A practical joker, sometimes clever at disguise, who may be a thief or liar.

Comic characters

Obviously the study of particular characters and their impact on a dramatic comedy is a significant area to investigate in your preparation for the exam. Often, comedic characters represent 'types' in European thought and culture.

Tricksters and clowns

Some characters might be described as **trickster** figures. They are unpredictable, somewhat manic, and delight in the chaos and disorder they create. They love making mischief. An example is Feste in *Twelfth Night* (see opposite).

Another classic type we might find in comedy is the **clown**. The comedy of clowns is usually played in a clumsy, **slapstick** style, and like the trickster, the clown usually has a number of structural functions in the drama. Such characters often speak in **prose**. Examples from *Twelfth Night* are Sir Toby Belch and Sir Andrew Aguecheek (also see opposite).

An RSC production of *Twelfth Night* from 2012, directed by David Farr. The characters portrayed in this scene (from left to right) are Sir Andrew Aguecheek (Bruce Mackinnon), Feste (Kevin McMonagle), Malvolio (Jonathan Slinger) and Sir Toby Belch (Nicholas Day).

Character as 'construction'

One of the errors which many students make in their written work is to present studies of comic characters as if they are 'real' persons – explaining their characteristics, personality and traits while forgetting that they are a fictional construct.

In order to counteract this, always think about the way in which the writer constructs the character – using language, form and structure. It will also be useful to consider the characters' dramatic function in the play. Keep checking your written work to be sure that you have not described them as if they were 'real' people.

Conclusion

This chapter has given you an understanding of some initial approaches to Shakespearean comedy. It has offered some development of the comic theories described in Chapter 9, and a number of pointers about ways forward with your exam answers – not least in ways to think about comedic characters and their construction.

The next chapter will explore in more detail the Shakespearean comedies *Twelfth Night* and *The Taming of the Shrew*.

11 Shakespearean comedy: *Twelfth Night* and *The Taming of the Shrew*

In this chapter you will:

- explore the connections between comedies (informed by the interpretations of other readers)
- further understand the **significance** of the context in which comedies are written and received
- start to apply the ideas of comedic characters to the texts you are studying
- focus on either *Twelfth Night* or *The Taming of the Shrew* as the Shakespearean comedy you will study.

In this chapter we will initially focus on *Twelfth Night*. As well as incorporating many of the elements discussed so far, the play has a number of additional components that you can usefully consider. Once some of these comedic **conventions** are established, we will turn to *The Taming of the Shrew*, perhaps a more controversial kind of comedy.

Twelfth Night

The dramatic comedy *Twelfth Night* was written around 1601. It was certainly performed at the Middle Temple in London in February 1603 – showing that it was in some ways a comedy devoted to the season of winter. The Middle Temple was a large indoor hall, unlike the traditional Globe-style theatre most associated with Shakespeare, although it is probable that the play was also performed at those outdoor theatres.

The Feast of Candlemas (2 February) was the official end of Christmas in the Church calendar, so this may have been the reason for the February performance.

Jesters, twins and cross-dressing

The main plot involves the separation of Viola and Sebastian. They are twin brother and sister who look alike, and after a shipwreck off the coast of the imagined country of Illyria, they cannot find each other. Alone in a strange country, for her safety Viola **cross-dresses** to look like a young man, giving herself the name Cesario. Disguising herself as a page, she takes service with Duke Orsino.

Key term

Cross-dress. To take on any form of disguise that presents one gender as another.

Orsino is in love with the Lady Olivia, but she rejects his offer of marriage. Orsino employs Viola (disguised as Cesario) as a go-between in his wooing of Olivia, but Olivia starts to fall in love with Cesario. Things are only resolved when Sebastian arrives, and is at first mistaken for Cesario. Eventually the mix-up over identity is resolved –- with Viola admitting she is a woman. She also admits that she has fallen in love with Duke Orsino.

There are several **sub-plots** in the comedy, and one involves the members of Olivia's household. Here, Sir Toby Belch (Olivia's uncle), Sir Andrew Aguecheek (a foolish suitor to Olivia), Maria (Olivia's waiting gentlewoman) and Feste (Olivia's jester) devise a plot to fool the pompous steward of the house, Malvolio. Malvolio is described by Maria as being 'sometimes … a kind of Puritan'; he disapproves of traditional celebrations involving dancing, singing and alcohol. Structurally, this makes for a conflict between the comic characters and Malvolio, who is a controlling figure. This is a pattern seen elsewhere in comedy.

Did you know?

Puritans were an important Protestant Christian group in the 16th and 17th centuries. They believed in a simpler kind of church ceremony and strictly disciplined behaviour. Broadly, they were anti-theatre, anti-festivals, anti-sports and anti-drinking.

The starting point for the analysis of any comedy you encounter can always be the list of characters at the start of the play – sometimes called the *dramatis personæ* ('people of the drama').

Activity

Look at the list below of the characters in *Twelfth Night*.

1. Consider issues of power and control, and who might be the confidante of other characters.

2. Try to identify three interlocking plots in the text.

3. Which characters do you think of as the most comic, and who might be the most serious?

Did you know?

The Globe Theatre was the most famous of the theatres on the South Bank in London during Shakespeare's day. It is characterized by its circular shape, thrust stage and three tiers of seating. A modern recreation of the theatre was built in 1997, and Shakespeare's dramas are performed there in original performance conditions.

Orsino, Duke of Illyria
Valentine }
Curio } gentlemen attending on the duke
1st Officer }
2nd Officer } in the service of the duke

Viola, a lady, later disguised as Cesario
Sebastian, Viola's twin brother
A Captain, of Viola's wrecked ship, who befriends her
Antonio, another sea captain, friend of Sebastian

Olivia, a countess
Maria, Olivia's waiting woman
Sir Toby Belch, Olivia's kinsman
Sir Andrew Aguecheek, companion to Sir Toby
Malvolio, Olivia's steward
Fabian, a member of Olivia's household
Feste, the clown, Olivia's jester
Servant to Olivia
Musicians, lords, sailors, attendants

Commentary

This is a good activity to try with any comedy. The presence of twins is likely to be of dramatic importance (you may note this in films, such as the *Star Wars IV*, *V* and *VI* trilogy and *Twins*).

A parallel is set up between Olivia with her waiting woman and Orsino with his gentlemen. The servant characters are likely to know all about the life and loves of their superiors. Feste will obviously be a humorous character, but we also note the surname of Sir Toby. We might already imagine him as rather rotund and a drinker. Sir Andrew's surname also sounds comic, in a contrasting way, simply because 'ague' (fever) is connected with weakness, and it suggests he is thin and unhealthy looking. Fabian and Antonio are more difficult to draw conclusions about, but they must be of importance to the plot since they are both named.

You may have noted the presence of musicians. In Shakespearean comedy, music and song have an important place. The songs often comment on the play's events.

Activity

Work your way through the character list and choose some short pieces of text that each character speaks (about ten lines). What do these pieces of text tell you about the characters?

Extension activity

Research the names given to the characters in your play. These can often indicate personality types or characteristics – a technique used to great effect in Restoration comedy, but also in modern **pantomime**.

Conventions and performance conditions

Shakespeare often took advantage of some of the restrictions around performance conditions that were in force when he was writing. The authorities in the city of London frowned upon plays that appeared to criticize people in power. Shakespeare sets *Twelfth Night* in the imagined country of Illyria, so that he cannot cause offence.

One of the major plot elements in *Twelfth Night* is the disguise of the young woman Viola as the boy Cesario. As you may know, women were not permitted to act on the stage in Shakespeare's time, so teenage boys training to be actors generally took the roles of women and girls – using voice, costuming and wigs to create their effects. Thus, the disguise of a female character as a boy would be relatively easy to achieve, and produce interesting effects.

Applying comic theory

Even if you know only a little about *Twelfth Night*, you will be able to apply some of the comic theory you have learned so far. There is obviously a connection with the theories of Northrop Frye, and although the model of 'old world, Green World, new world' (see page 78) may be slightly harder to spot, it certainly exists. The old world is defined by events before the shipwreck, while the Green World operates while the twins are separated and Viola is in disguise. The catastrophic event of the shipwreck is the ignition point for what follows.

The Green World need not necessarily always be a forest or wood, although most often the play is given a rural/pastoral setting; it can be the space created for confusion. The new world begins when the imprisoned Malvolio is released and the double wedding takes place between Viola and Duke Orsino, and Olivia and Sebastian. Sir Toby and Maria also marry.

Love is very much a motivating force in the play, and we understand that when people are in love they do foolish things. Caricature is used in the form of the clowns Sir Toby Belch and Sir Andrew Aguecheek. To some extent, the custom of Olivia's seven years of mourning for the death of her brother is made to look foolish, as is the tradition of duelling in the absurd fight that Viola is forced into with Sir Andrew.

The ritual year

In Britain, and most other European countries, a set of key dates and festivals were traditionally observed as cause for celebration. Some of these are now hidden by the demands of the modern world, but you may know Christmas, Easter, May Day, Midsummer Day, Harvest Festival, and Halloween. The origins of these festivals are not always obvious, but many are related to pre-Christian markers of the passing seasons, and some are associated with Christian beliefs about the life of Christ. The winter solstice marks a turn in the year when the days become longer again, and many of its pre-Christian traditions have been absorbed into Christmas (a major Christian festival).

Twelfth night is a festival in the **ritual** year in Britain. Traditionally, it was the culmination of the festival of Christmas, for in the Christian Church it is called Epiphany and commemorates the time when the Three Kings saw a new star indicating the birth of Christ. Epiphany means a 'showing forth'.

To celebrate twelfth night, tradition called for an individual to be randomly chosen to become the 'Lord of Misrule' who would oversee fun and games. Over time, twelfth night has become less significant as a festive point in the year, in Britain, but it is still known today as the date by which we are meant to take down our Christmas decorations.

Shakespeare was well aware of the significance of these ritual points in the year, and developed comedies inspired by or celebrating these key points.

Topsy-turvy day and *The Wicker Man*

To understand how the ritual year operates, you might want to watch a key sequence in the 1996 Walt Disney film *The Hunchback of Notre Dame* (directed by Kirk Wise and Gary Trousdale). It is set in Paris, and shows the 'Festival of Fools', which allows the working classes of the city to have a day of fun and rebellion in the streets, while singing a song called 'Topsy-Turvy Day'. This signifies that everything is turned upside down and back to front. Quasimodo is made 'King of the Fools'.

Clearly, in Shakespearean comedy there are moments when the key characters are experiencing their own topsy-turvy day, when the usual relationships and hierarchies are inverted.

The 1973 thriller-horror film *The Wicker Man* (directed by Robin Hardy) has a similar, if exaggerated connection with the ritual year. It is set on an imagined remote Hebridean island called Summerdale. Police Sergeant Neil Howie is sent to the island to investigate the disappearance of a girl. Howie discovers that the people of the island still follow the old Celtic ritual year, culminating in human sacrifice. Howie also finds that for the people there, old superstitions such as the celebration of May, and fears for crop failure, still persist. Although it has a fantastical plot, the film is a useful **representation** of the way in which seasonal traditions still underpin our lives in the modern era.

Festival in Britain

In some parts of Britain, during festivals local people become Mock Mayors and are paraded around town. Mock Mayors are comic figures – like Lords of Misrule – who tend to make popular and absurd declarations ('Free beer for everyone!' or 'Cabbages must be worn!'). Some observers believe that such traditional releases for working people, allowing them to be 'king for a day', discouraged revolt against their masters.

Activity

Read and perform the parts from Act 3 of *Twelfth Night* where Malvolio appears. He has been inspired by a false letter to dress and behave in a very different way from normal. How might this be an example of inverting relationships and hierarchies? Why is this sequence so comic?

Commentary

A recent Royal Shakespeare Company performance updated the look of Malvolio by dressing him in a set of yellow-and-black motorcycle leathers.

This sequence is a good example of comic inversion, because the 'Puritan' Malvolio is doing everything he should not be doing. He has been transformed into an unstoppable 'love machine', which of course offends Olivia, making her think him mad. As we know, love, or lust, makes people do crazy things. Note that Olivia labels it 'midsummer madness', referring to another time of year when people tend to do odd things outside their normal pattern of behaviour.

It is also an ironic parallel to the more traditional inversions performed by Feste, Sir Toby and Sir Andrew. It is at this point that these characters gain revenge on Malvolio. You may like to think about the value of revenge in comedies.

Different readings

C. L. Barber

Northrop Frye's reading of Shakespearean comedy was revised by the author C. L. Barber. Barber's contribution to Shakespearean scholarship was the idea that the comedies were constructed in direct relation to the range of holidays and festivities celebrated in Elizabethan society. He outlined these principles in his book *Shakespeare's Festive Comedies: A Study of Dramatic Form and its Relation to Social Custom* (1959). We might summarize Barber's arguments as follows:

- Shakespearean comedies have connections with village marriages, wassails or wakes.
- Holidays such as Candlemas, Shrove Tuesday, Hocktide, May Day, Whitsuntide, Midsummer Eve, Harvest Home, Halloween and Christmas are all starting points for comedy.
- Comedy is all about pleasure and merrymaking.
- Comedy offers a form of release.
- Comedy reacts against social conformity.

According to Barber, comedy also has a function to mock killjoy and authority figures who try to prevent merrymaking from happening. You can see this in the figure of Malvolio in *Twelfth Night*.

Activity

Examine the sequence from Act 2 Scene 3 of *Twelfth Night*, where Malvolio interrupts the activities of Sir Toby Belch, Feste, Maria and Sir Andrew Aguecheek. What elements of Barber's theory can be applied here? Does this make for a relevant reading of Shakespeare's comedy?

Commentary

We read this sequence in the light of the fact that twelfth night is a period of celebration in the ritual year. Feste, Sir Toby and Sir Andrew seek pleasure and merrymaking in part-songs ('catches'), this being a form of release from their day-to-day concerns about how Toby is to get money and how Andrew might woo Olivia. We also note that they rebel against social conformity and invert the normal order of things ('rouse the night-owl'). Maria is the first to note that they are 'caterwauling' and disrupting the household.

The dramatic build up to Malvolio's entry is made all the more powerful with the witty puns exchanged and the focus on the word 'peace': the one thing they will not do is 'Hold their peace'. Feste talks of Sir Toby's 'admirable fooling'. Malvolio's insistence that they are 'mad' shows his Puritan-like **ideology** but also, to the audience, it shows that he can be mocked as a killjoy. Taking him down a peg or two is part of the complication stage of the comedy. You may have noticed that Malvolio describes Sir Toby as having 'disorders' – a reference to his love of drinking, but also an insight into what is happening more generally.

Key term

Ideology. A view of the world held by a particular group of people at a particular time.

Mikhail Bakhtin

Another useful response to Shakespearean comedy is offered by the Russian critic Mikhail Bakhtin (1895–1975). In the 1930s Bakhtin formulated some of his ideas on the work of the French novelist François Rabelais (1494–1553), eventually published in English in 1968 as *Rabelais and his World*. In this book he makes observations about the contrast between the official culture of the state and religious organizations, and the culture of the marketplace and people. Bakhtin is a key figure in much contemporary work in English studies. His ideas have been used by linguists to support the idea that we all speak in many voices and adopt many roles in life. Such ideas are very relevant to comedy.

Bakhtin also notes that carnival is significant, because it allows freedom for people to get away from the official culture. Carnival allows indulgence in food and sexual activity, as well as a kind of misrule. Misrule permits a temporary suspension of the normal rules. In Christian countries, this happens during *Mardi Gras*, or Shrovetide, before the restrictions of Lent. Some bad and comic behaviour is thus traditionally tolerated. It has been argued that, today, events such as the Glastonbury Festival or the Reading/Leeds music festivals offer young people a temporary opportunity for 'controlled misrule'.

Comedy and celebration therefore have an extremely important social function. Bakhtin's theories tell us much about the issues of control and freedom as they relate to the genre of dramatic comedy. Dramatic comedy is one way for society and the Church to tolerate dissent and misbehaviour.

Is the Glastonbury Festival of Contemporary Performing Arts a modern-day example of a kind of controlled misrule?

When, in *Twelfth Night*, Olivia says 'There is no slander / In an allowed fool' (Act I Scene 5), she is commenting on the phenomenon of misrule, but in the case of Feste it is a more permanent feature, since 'fools' were expected to tell truths to their employers. One of the things we learn about the figure of the jester in *Twelfth Night* is that Olivia tolerates his insightful comments. In comedies, jesters operate as a kind of corrective to the irrational thoughts of other characters. They have insight because they see the world through comic and ironic eyes. Feste is allowed to call Olivia 'madonna' and she asks him for advice about relationships and life. Even though she is sometimes irritated by him ('Take the Fool away'), she realizes he is perceptive enough to be her counsellor. In this sense, he is a licensed or permitted fool.

Fools are usually more observant than other characters. It is Feste who first notices the attraction between Orsino and Cesario. While this attraction seems 'unnatural' (because homosexuality was regarded in that light), Feste also notices Cesario's lack of a beard.

Activity

Jesters are often presented in art and literature in a certain way. Discuss with a partner the characteristics of jesters. To what extent does Feste fulfil these? How do you imagine jesters to be dressed? You may also want to think about ways in which jesters may be re-thought and re-imagined.

Commentary

Jesters are primarily seen as being honest, witty and clever (especially with puns). Feste seems to fulfil these characteristics. Jesters are traditionally imagined as wearing brightly coloured clothes (often red and yellow) in a motley pattern. They wear hats with three long points, each with a bell at the end – supposedly a recreation of the ears and tail of a donkey. Jesters also often carry a mock sceptre, like a king.

In the 1996 film version of *Twelfth Night*, Ben Kingsley's interpretation of Feste imagines him as more of an itinerant storyteller or musician, effectively singing for his supper as he wanders through Illyria. Contemporary productions of *Twelfth Night* often seek to find alternative ways of presenting Feste from the stereotypical image outlined above.

Disguise and cross-dressing

Disguise and mistaken identity are crucial plot devices in *Twelfth Night* (and also in *The Taming of the Shrew*). What is significant is how the disguise delays the process of resolution. In *Twelfth Night*, when Sebastian and Viola first come to recognize each other, Sebastian's bewildered colleague Antonio asks 'How have you made division of yourself? An apple, cleft in two, is not more twin / Than these creatures'. It is the Duke who moves things forward with his declared intention to marry Viola: 'I shall have share in this most happy wreck'.

Disguise is also found in *Twelfth Night* in Feste's imitation of Sir Topaz at Malvolio's cell. This is a scene you may wish to consider further.

Today, disguise is still a much-used strand in comedy, allowing characters to move unnoticed in certain situations. Often, if the disguise is not very good, the comedy is enhanced because the audience knowingly suspend their disbelief in order to go along with it.

Misogyny, mask and marvel: *The Taming of the Shrew*

The Taming of the Shrew is a romantic comedy written by Shakespeare some time between 1590 and 1592. The play has an unusual structure, with a **framing device** known as the Induction. The Induction tells the story of a drunken tinker from Warwickshire, called Christopher Sly, who is tricked into thinking he is a nobleman. The play is then performed as if it is for Sly. The frame perhaps shows us how easily we can be duped; it is also not really closed at the end of the play.

The play is set, like other Shakespearean comedies, in an exotic location: this time the Italian town of Padua. The play's plot is centred on Petruchio's courtship of Katherina, a headstrong young woman who is the 'shrew' of the title. At the start of the play Katherina is not interested in him, but Petruchio uses various psychological ploys to 'tame' her until she becomes – outwardly, at least – an obedient bride. The **sub-plot** to the play involves various suitors competing for the affections of Katherina's more conventional sister, the beautiful Bianca.

Key terms

Framing device. A structure that helps introduce and/or conclude a play, offering a context for its performance.

Misogynistic. Showing a hatred or distrust of women.

The Bianca sub-plot

Bianca has two suitors who are comedic stereotypes – the old fool Gremio and the young fool Hortensio. It is they who persuade Petruchio to tame Katherina, in order to clear their way to Bianca. At the same time as this plot develops, a handsome young man named Lucentio is also preparing to court Bianca. He disguises himself as Cambio, a teacher of Latin, and begins to flirt with her. The disguise aspect of the play becomes even more complex when we learn that Hortensio is also in Bianca's house – disguised as a music teacher – and that Tranio (a servant of Lucentio) is also there, disguised as his master. He pretends to be Gremio's rival. The complex use of disguise and deceit in this part of the play makes for an expansive 'Green World', which stays in place until Lucentio's father Vincentio turns up and clarifies who is who. Lucentio and Bianca, meanwhile, have been secretly married. This forms the climax of the Bianca plot of the play.

Resolution in *The Taming of the Shrew*

Katherina's plot is resolved at the banquet scene in Act 5, where she demonstrates that she will be a more obedient wife than Bianca, or the rich but shrewish widow who Hortensio has found for himself. The bridegrooms bet on whose wife will be the most docile. Because of the way in which the women in the comedy are treated, the play is sometimes uncomfortable for modern audiences to watch, and has thus been labelled **misogynistic**.

Comedic elements of *The Taming of the Shrew*

Shakespeare employs a number of comedic elements in this play. As you read and respond to the text, find examples of:

- disguise and fluid (or changing) identity
- complicated relationships and differences between men and women
- shrews and gossipy wives
- cruelty
- issues to do with money
- female submissiveness and **patriarchal** society
- marriage and economics
- parents in conflict with their children.

Key term

Patriarchy. A social system run by men for the benefit of men.

Often, Shakespearean comedies end with a wedding, which symbolizes the beginning of a new life. Here it is interesting that Shakespeare devotes some attention to the characters after the ceremony itself. This focus on marriage may have been a direct result of public interest in Henry VIII's separation from the Catholic Church after the Pope refused to grant him a divorce.

Different readings

Some feminist observers have criticized the play for the way in which it apparently supports a patriarchal system and denigrates women. Other critics have argued that such a view takes the play too seriously. They argue that the Induction sets up the play as a farce from the outset, and that the view of women within the comedy should not be taken at face value. *The Taming of the Shrew* is one of Shakespeare's earliest comedies and he may not have been working with the seriousness that is evident at the height of his powers. It remains unclear whether the behaviour of the male characters in the play is being celebrated or parodied.

The critic Neville Coghill (1899–1980) wrote about *The Taming of the Shrew* in his classic essay, 'The Basis of Shakespearean Comedy'. Coghill takes a different approach to the play, arguing that:

> *The Taming of the Shrew* has often been read and acted as a wife-humiliating farce in which a brave fortune-hunter carries all, including his wife's spirit, before him. But it is not so at all. True, it is based on the medieval conception of obedience owed by a wife to her wedded lord, a conception generously and charmingly asserted by Katerina at the end. But it is a total misconception to suppose she has been bludgeoned into defeat. Indeed if either of them has triumphed in the art and practice of happy marriage, it is she.
>
> 'The Basis of Shakespearean Comedy' in Anne Ridler (ed.), *Shakespeare Criticism 1935–60*, page 207

Meanwhile Christopher Hicks, in his book *English Drama to 1710* (page 188), argues that what is noticeable in *The Taming of the Shrew* is how the play embraces 'popular festivities such as the May Games and Lord of Misrule (in which servants changed roles with their masters)'. This is similar to some of the characteristics we see in *Twelfth Night*, at the winter equivalent of the May Games.

You may like to read how modern observers have interpreted this comedy. The following is an extract of a review by Michael Billington of a production of *The Taming of the Shrew* at the Globe Theatre, London in 2012:

> In short, this is a broad, knockabout *Shrew* that doesn't go in much for psychological depth and presents Katherina's final speech of submission without irony. But it goes down well with its audience and yields two very good supporting performances. Pearce Quigley turns Petruchio's servant, Grumio, into a faintly subversive figure who punctuates his master's obsessive references to his father's death by ostentatiously kicking a bucket. And Sarah MacRae suggests that Bianca is not just a spoilt brat, but potentially as violent a virago as her older sister. That aside, this is a conventionally jolly evening that never troubles to dig far below the play's disturbing surface.
>
> The *Guardian*, 5 July 2012

Activity

Discuss with members of your class these various interpretations of *The Taming of the Shrew*. In particular, consider the elements of inversion in the play, and how it comes to a problematical resolution.

Conclusion

In the course of your studies so far, you have started to develop an informed response to Shakespearean comedy and have understood how authorial method shapes meaning for audiences and readers. Also, you have explored connections to other comic texts, comparing them, and interpreting other readers' commentaries on them. The significance of the contexts of production and reception of comedic texts has also been introduced.

The next chapter will consider other dramatic comedies.

12 Dramatic comedy: *She Stoops to Conquer, The Importance of Being Earnest* and *Educating Rita*

In this chapter you will be introduced to:

- further drama choices – *She Stoops to Conquer* or *The Importance of Being Earnest*
- the additional choice of *Educating Rita* if you are taking AS level
- alternative ways in which dramatists have explored comedy in other settings
- ways of connecting this drama to other comedies.

Introduction: choosing plays

So far on your AS- or A-level course you will have studied one of two dramatic comedies by William Shakespeare. Now, by selecting either *She Stoops to Conquer* or *The Importance of Being Earnest*, you will also cover the requirement to study a pre-1900 text at A level.

If your centre is following an AS route through this course, you also have the option of studying *Educating Rita*. Clearly, these choices are quite different. While *She Stoops to Conquer* is an 18th-century comedy, *The Importance of Being Earnest* is a late 19th-century **comedy of manners**, and *Educating Rita* is a modern comedy, set in a working-class Liverpool of the early 1980s.

She Stoops to Conquer

She Stoops to Conquer, written by the Irish playwright Oliver Goldsmith (1720–1774), was first performed in 1773. Originally, the play was entitled *The Mistakes of a Night*, and this was apt because all the events of the play take place in one night. The title was later revised to *She Stoops to Conquer*. The play has been called both a **laughing comedy** and a **sentimental comedy**. In general, sentimental comedy is seen as a slightly less humorous form, while laughing comedy is more of a direct successor to Shakespearean comedy.

The play is also a **comedy of manners**. This term is used for comedies that depict characters who try to adhere to the conventions of their society, particularly its rules of polite behaviour, but who sometimes behave in outrageous or shocking ways. In this sense, the play is a **satire** because we know that some characters (for example, Mrs Hardcastle) will never reform or change.

There are also traces of romantic comedy, which shows young people falling in love and sometimes behaving foolishly as a result. In *She Stoops to Conquer* this can be seen in Marlow's nervousness and in Kate's 'stooping'. Having studied a Shakespearean comedy, you will doubtless see many similarities between that text and what is constructed in *She Stoops to Conquer*.

The title of the play refers to the actions of Kate. She realizes that in order to get close to Marlow (who is more confident with lower-class women) she will need to pretend to be a servant. She thus 'stoops' socially, in order to get what she wants.

For a discussion about different kinds of comedy, re-read Goldsmith's prologue to the play. Goldsmith was concerned about 'the impending death of comedy' – though perhaps he had no need to worry.

The mistakes of a night

As you read *She Stoops to Conquer*, you will become familiar with the plot, which is based on a series of mistakes. For the audience, these mistakes lead to comedy. In a sense, the whole of the comedy turns the traditional order upside down, so we are watching a topsy-turvy world.

Key terms

Laughing comedy. This is often compared to sentimental comedy, which was seen as socially mild and inoffensive. Laughing comedy claims to show life as it is, with human follies shown up for what they are.

Sentimental comedy. This is often compared to laughing comedy and is usually seen as socially mild and inoffensive. Laughing comedy claims to show life as it is, with human follies shown up for what they are.

Activity

With a partner, look at the following elements and try to map the ways in which they lead to further comedy:

- The mistaking of Hardcastle's house for an inn.
- Contrasting characters who misunderstand one another.
- Marlow treating Hardcastle as the landlord.
- Mrs Hardcastle's mistake, at the end of the play, about her location.

The three unities

In his theories on comedy and tragedy, the ancient Greek writer Aristotle developed the idea of the 'three unities' as rules for making a play coherent. They are: unity of action, unity of time and unity of place. Unity of action is achieved when all of the events and relationships in the play are part of the same general theme or story. Unity of time means the compactness of time in which actions of the play take place: ideally, the action covers 24 hours. Unity of place means that events take place in one or two related locations only. When we review the structure of *She Stoops to Conquer*, there is a good argument for suggesting that these unities have been observed in Goldsmith's play.

Activity

Discuss how the three unities are observed in the play.

Commentary

The play achieves unity of action, because the central theme of the play is relationships. They are important to the main plot but also to the **sub-plot** between Constance and Hastings.

Unity of time is demonstrated, because of the compactness of events in the play. Most of the action takes place in the darkness of night, which is related to misunderstanding and subterfuge. In the night-time, many unhelpful coincidences take effect.

Most of the action in the play takes place in the Hardcastles' house, so this achieves the unity of place. However, a couple of scenes take place elsewhere. These are at the nearby Three Pigeons inn and (possibly) on 'Crackskull Common', but the latter is shown to be really the Hardcastles' own garden.

Comic characters

Activity

Consider the following characters and, with a partner, explain how they are constructed for comedic purposes. In your discussions, also think about the characters' names.

- Mrs Hardcastle
- Tony Lumpkin
- Sir Charles Marlow
- Diggory

Goldsmith's authorial method

Goldsmith takes the established models of comedy and gives them a new direction. Although the language of the play might be tricky to grasp at first, you will soon begin to appreciate Goldsmith's authorial methods in the following areas:

- His assured handling of the ludicrous plot.
- The way in which all the characters are interested in the pursuit of pleasure.
- The interplay of characters from different parts of society.
- The approach towards morality.
- Aspects of gender roles.
- His use of dialogue.

Activity

Plays during this period were often accompanied by a Prologue and an Epilogue. Re-read the Epilogue for this play. What bearing do the words of the Epilogue have on the comic events of the play?

Commentary

Such Epilogues usually offer a pithy and taut summary of the action of the play, and also advice for the audience about their own actions and behaviour. They usually encourage the audience not to make the same mistakes as the characters.

Different readings

She Stoops to Conquer has been viewed by successive generations as a classic dramatic comedy. In general, much of the focus has been on Tony Lumpkin, who has been described as a 'rural genius' who is distrustful of all pretension and feigned politeness. Audiences greatly empathize with him. Given the ludicrous plot of the play, some observers regard it as one of the first successful **farces**.

The Importance of Being Earnest

First performed in 1895, *The Importance of Being Earnest* was written by Oscar Wilde (1854–1900). The play has been described as a farce and a comedy of manners. It considers the conventions of late 19th-century London life, and satirizes them through poking fun at various institutions (such as marriage and inheritance) and showing them to be a sham. One of the basic acts in the comedy is the hero's maintenance of a fictional persona in order to fulfil society's obligations and expectations – thus the importance of *being* earnest. The pun in the title points up the importance of honesty in one's social behaviour, the central concern of the play.

Did you know?

The play has a sub-title – 'A Trivial Comedy for Serious People', which neatly summarizes its content.

Comic structure

Wilde is indebted to earlier comic structure for the basis of his play. The main plot involves two 'men about town', John (Jack) Worthing and Algernon (Algy) Moncrieff. They are romantically interested, respectively, in Gwendolen Fairfax and Cecily Cardew. The play is dependent on disguise, because both men have doubles: Jack is Ernest, while Algy creates a false relative called Bunbury as an excuse for his absences, and also at one point claims to be Ernest. This doubling instantly sets up comic confusion in the play, which is only resolved at the end.

Lady Bracknell is the epitome of Victorian ethics and values. Her function in the drama is to act as comic judge of people and events. A back-story is also provided in the form of a governess, who mislaid Jack as a baby in a handbag at Victoria station; there follows the revelation that Jack and Algy are, in fact, brothers. This revelatory structure is crucial to the development of the comedy.

Additional comedy is created by the servants Lane and Merriman sometimes appearing to know more about events than the main characters. This comic master–servant relationship is one that is seen time and again in comedy.

A performance of *The Importance of Being Ernest* at the Vauderville Theatre, London, in 2008. The characters portrayed in this drawing room scene are (from left to right): Jack Worthing (Harry Hadden-Paton), Lady Bracknell (Penelope Keith) and Cecily Cardew (Rebecca Night).

The Importance of Being Earnest also observes the unities of action, time and place (see page 91). Much of the play takes place in the Manor House, Woolton, with Act I in Algy's West London flat.

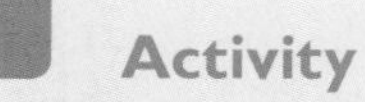

Activity

Read the short section of dialogue between Cecily ('Whatever unfortunate entanglement...') and Gwendolen ('...have been wildly different') in Act 2. Comment on its use of language.

Commentary

In this short sequence, we see Wilde's crystal-clear, satirical language and how the mask of manners is evaded and ridiculed. Such a sequence neatly summarizes Wilde's dramatic technique, which is to combine colloquial speech with precise plotting.

Satire

In the play, Wilde directs his satire at:

- the upper classes
- trivial ideas about marriage
- people who live lives of leisure
- Victorian manners and morals.

Activity

How do these strands of satire compare with other comedic texts that you have read? Discuss the similarities with a partner.

Different readings

Some observers have criticized the play for not having any underlying social message – claiming that it represents the **decadence** of Wilde's own life. Other critics have praised its witty engagement with the society of the period, and the way it exposes the double standards of the time. It has also been viewed as one of the first modern social comedies.

Key term

Decadence. A process of decay in moral standards, revealed in undignified and wasteful behaviour.

Educating Rita

If you are studying for AS level, you may study *Educating Rita* – a comedy written by Willy Russell (born in 1947), and first performed in 1980.

The play is set in the office of an Open University lecturer, and is a 'two-hander' (meaning the piece is played by only two actors). This should already make you think about the different comedic structure created here. Because there are only two actors, the play is likely to be more intense, and also to compromise on some of the comedic elements established in other dramas. It is likely that the comedy will be more modern, satiric and educative – that is, the audience will learn something about themselves and society.

The play depicts the relationship between a young working-class woman from Liverpool and a middle-aged university lecturer over the course of a year. We learn that the woman is a hairdresser who is dissatisfied with her life and seeks to expand her education by signing up for an Open University course in English Literature. The play opens as Susan (who initially calls herself Rita) meets her tutor, Frank, for the first time.

Frank is an academic and an alcoholic. He has taken on the Open University job to pay for his drinking. The play examines their relationship and growth. Much of the humour is generated by the collision of classes, and the way that one culture is swapped for another. Susan, for example, takes on all the pretensions of academic life that Frank so despises. In this way, the play also reflects the topsy-turvy culture often found in comedy.

Although much of the play is light-hearted, there are some darker moments. One of Susan's friends attempts suicide, and this makes her rethink her direction. Frank has offered her much guidance but, at the end, he is sent to Australia on a sabbatical and the two are separated. Unlike other comedies, the plot ends in disharmony. This may be a more modern and realistic take on the comic scenario. Susan also realizes that whatever class you are a part of, the same duplicity exists.

Claire Sweeney as Rita and Mathew Kelly as Frank in a production of Willy Russell's *Educating Rita* at the George Square Theatre, Edinburgh in 2012 ▶

A new *Pygmalion*?

In 1912, George Bernard Shaw wrote a social comedy called *Pygmalion*, later adapted into the film *My Fair Lady*. The play depicts a working-class woman who is taken out of her usual environment and educated. It shows a Professor of Phonetics, Henry Higgins, trying to educate a Cockney flower-seller named Eliza Doolittle. There are obvious similarities to Russell's drama.

Scouse humour

One of the ways in which comedy is created in *Educating Rita* is in the juxtaposition between Susan's working-class Scouse (or Liverpudlian) dialect, and Frank's more educated style of speaking. He is able to see humour in what she says, but likewise Susan uses her language to undercut and satirize Frank's pretensions.

There is a long history in the comic genre of working-class people moving up the social ladder, while those who are **pretentious** are brought down a peg or two. The comedy here is often described as 'bittersweet'.

Activity

Choose a section of the play that you are familiar with and examine how Russell creates comedy from differences in social class. Create a table showing the authorial methods that Russell uses to show elements of both Frank's and Susan's comedic nature.

Different readings

Both characters have regrets at the end of the play. Some critics have viewed this as important – and as indicating that social mobility is much harder than just gaining an education.

More recently, some readers of the play have seen it as dated, because such social mobility is more possible in 21st-century Britain. Other observers see the play as a love story in which the main characters never kiss.

Conclusion

This chapter has shown your choices about the kinds of comedy you can study. It has also outlined some further concepts and ideas about comedy – focused primarily on sentimental comedy and the comedy of manners. *Educating Rita* allows you, as an AS candidate, to look at a modern stage comedy.

In the next chapter are further options for your studies, relating to how comedy has been constructed in prose – and, in particular, in fiction.

13 Prose comedy: *Emma*, *Small Island* and *Wise Children*

In this chapter you will:

- examine the aspect of comedy in prose fiction
- explore the ways in which Jane Austen, Andrea Levy and Angela Carter present comic figures within their work.

Link

See the Introducing Narrative chapter in the NEA Component (Chapter 29).

The comic novel

Comic novels, whether set in the past or more contemporarily, are primarily intended to make us laugh at and rethink the world. Compared to realist or tragic novels, they can sometimes seem slight or lightweight, as if they present a less-substantial view of human experience. However, this can be misleading, because comedic moments are part of life. Some critics have argued that comic novels are a way of reworking social criticism to make it entertaining. Although that may be part of the comic novel's purpose, it is not its only function.

The important thing to remember about comic novels is that comedy itself is usually central to their structure and plot. Whereas novels are generally about individuals who are at odds in some way with the complex society they find themselves in, the characters in comic novels find themselves caught up in tricky situations which prove amusing for the reader.

Comic novelists usually write from a detached point of view, in which a comprehensive view of things can be observed, while in more realist or tragic novels the point of view is more central and is often involved in the action. However, there are exceptions to this rule.

One other thing to note about comic novels is that we see people repeating familiar actions in familiar situations. Often, as in dramatic comedy, the characters are instantly recognizable types, and they are usually subject to the human weaknesses (such as lust or greed) found elsewhere in the genre of comedy; their evident faults are designed to mock the human condition. The comic novelist usually examines the world from this perspective, and on some level this might be deemed gloomy, but the emphasis is usually on the absurdity of being human.

Types of comic novel

There are several different types of comic novel. Novels may be a combination of two or three of these types:

- Novels of cruelty. These are less common now, but involve laughing at the misfortunes of others. The more-sophisticated versions allow novelists to explore how seriously people take themselves. There are traces of this in Jane Austen's *Emma*.
- Romantic comic novels. These poke fun at youthful naivety and **folly** – often when people are in love. You will see aspects of this in *Emma* and *Small Island*.
- Satiric novels. These mock pretension and affection – attempting to laugh people out of their folly. *Small Island* also shows aspects of this.
- Novels that present the world as crazy or absurd. Novels of this kind were among the earliest types of fiction; they demonstrate how fickle and ultimately disturbing the world can be. Such novels often show that a strange world lurks under established social façades. *Wise Children* has many of these characteristics.

All of these types suggest that comic novels present a vision of life as an elaborate **charade**, and that human beings tend to be stupid and/or filled with self-interest. They can therefore be viewed as serious works addressing difficult social issues. This is certainly the case with the two novels you can study at A level: Jane Austen's *Emma* (published in 1815) and Andrea Levy's *Small Island* (written in 2004). Although the two novels were written almost 200 years apart, they share many similarities. At AS level you can also study *Wise Children* by Angela Carter, a **post-modern** novel about how crazy and absurd the world can be.

Emma by Jane Austen

To an extent, Jane Austen's novels are both realist and comic in their intention; they are intended to be a realistic interpretation of the society depicted, but they do this in a comedic way.

Generally, Austen's narratives centre on young women who are living in a society that places great emphasis on their duty to make a good marriage. Austen is able to examine all of the issues connected with this social phenomenon that affect the heroine. In this sense, the search for a good marriage is as important as that found in Shakespearean comedies. One of Austen's achievements is to present a **satire** of Regency England, as well as presenting a **comedy of manners**.

Emma, written in 1814 and published in 1815, is about Emma Woodhouse, a significant comic character because of the way Austen has shaped her. She is presented as well-intentioned but sometimes lacking in wisdom, and therefore making bad (and inevitably comic) decisions. Her comic flaws are a tendency to arrogance and a refusal to listen to warning voices. She also tries to interfere in other people's affairs – thinking she knows what's best for them.

However, Emma's faults are seen through the eyes of a kindly and benevolent narrator, who sympathizes with the character because of her basic good nature and the society in which she is forced to operate. The novel's comic premise is simple: Emma finds her way through a series of blunders and misadventures to self-knowledge and personal growth. In a way, this follows a much older model for the development of comedy.

Comedy in *Emma*

At the core of the comedy in *Emma* is the fact that the heroine believes she could love Frank Churchill, but she also believes that she will never marry – preferring to continue looking after her elderly father. Seemingly in order to compensate for this, she tries to pair up other people for love affairs and marriage. Much of the comedy in the novel is a result of Emma feeling she must remain a pillar of Highbury society, and it soon becomes clear that she cannot understand her own feelings. To achieve fulfilment in love, characters have to overcome their faults.

Activity

When you have completed your first reading of *Emma*, try one or more of the following activities:

1. Write a 50-word narrative summary of the plot of the novel. Do not exceed this word count. Try to include some indication of the novel's comic power.
2. Write a voice-over for a two-minute trailer for a new film adaptation of the text. Include key information, teaser sequences and core dialogue. What will the final words of the trailer be?

Key term

Post-modernism. A movement in art and literature away from modernism, and characterized by a new understanding of historical events.

3. Choose a section of the dialogue that you think is particularly witty or comic. Adapt it into a short radio script. Test out different voices, rhythms and speeds, and record the final work. Replay it and evaluate its success.

Comic structure

Emma has a classic comic structure, matching the pattern found in Shakespearean comedy. This might be seen as the 'old world, Green World and new world' structure (see page 78) or possibly as exposition, complication, and resolution (see page 70). What makes this basic pattern more complex in *Emma* is the wide range of characters depicted, but if you keep these basic models in mind, you will be able to see them in operation.

Activity

Explore how the structure of old world (exposition), Green World (complication) and new world (resolution) is handled by Austen in *Emma*. For each phase of the text, write a list of the factors that contribute to it. This will help you better understand the comedic structure of *Emma*.

Although we have established that the comic structure of *Emma* is quite simple, it is the way in which Austen adds layers to this structure which really develops the comedy in the text. Some useful areas for you to focus your attention on could be:

- how Austen depicts snobbery
- the obsession with trivial matters
- Emma's growing self-knowledge, and the way this is presented
- social manners and codes of behaviour
- the differences between men and women
- ironic situations and observations.

Comic characterization

Activity

Look at the following and try to identify why they are comedic:

1. Vulgar Mrs Elton, with her 'caro sposo' and her brother-in-law's seat at Maple Grove.
2. The unmarried Miss Bates, who lives with her widowed mother and who enjoys 'a most uncommon degree of popularity for a woman neither young, handsome, rich, nor married'.
3. The scene in which Emma is reprimanded by Mr Knightley for making a joke at Miss Bates's expense.

Commentary

Mrs Elton is an important comic character. Everything about the way she is presented depicts her as ridiculous. She is vulgar, because her family has recently made money, and she has no idea how to behave or what to do with it. She speaks **pretentiously** of her 'caro sposo' (Italian for 'dear husband') and has many other comedic qualities – such as wearing too much lace. Her mentions of her brother-in-law's seat (large house) are all part of trying to present a false image of herself. Such figures are always ripe as comic targets because of their social pretensions.

Miss Bates, meanwhile, is a gossip and a classic spinster figure. She is quite a tragic character, because she was used to a certain lifestyle which has now been compromised. However, even Emma satirizes her tendency to chatter.

The scene with Mr Knightley is important, because he has good judgement about how to behave in social situations, so his reasons for criticizing Emma need to be examined carefully.

Different readings

Many observers have praised the way in which Austen creates the intense comedy of this small social world, and the way she satirizes the lives of people in the wealthy home counties of England. Other critics have found the subject matter of the novel quite narrow and perhaps wish for a more diverse range of characters.

Marxist critics (see pages 219–220) generally observe that there is relatively little social conscience in Austen's comedic world, and that essentially it is 'genteel' comedy. The novel also tends to ignore the wider political events of the period in which it is set. For example, Britain was fighting in the Napoleonic Wars, and very little of this is mentioned.

Feminist criticism (see pages 220–223) would offer a different perspective – outlining the refreshing way in which Austen presents a non-marginalized, complex female character, who shows none of the female 'hysteria' found in some 19th-century novels. They also note that Emma is rich, and has no brothers, so in this sense she is freed from the usual **patriarchal** order.

Conclusion

Emma may appear to be a relatively simple comic novel, but its complexity of characterization makes it much more than that. Although set in a tight social world and a particular period of English history, the characters are presented as types which we can still recognize today. We are therefore easily able to relate to them, and to the mistakes that Emma makes.

Emma also gives pointers to the way in which comic novels would evolve in the future – particularly in their use of ironic observation, satire and the comedy of manners.

Small Island: small or great comedy?

Small Island (2004) was written by Andrea Levy (born in 1956). It can be regarded as a contemporary comic novel, although one which carries much social criticism. The novel has **post-modern** characteristics, including four main characters who all narrate the text. These are Hortense, Queenie, Gilbert and Bernard.

The main plot begins after World War II, around the year 1948, when a number of immigrants escape hardship on their own 'small island' of Jamaica and move to another 'small island' – Britain. The novel follows their experiences as part of the Jamaican **diaspora**, showing how they go about making a new life in post-war England.

Key term

Diaspora. The scattering of a population whose origins lie in a particular geographical area.

Ironically, although some of the men fought for Britain during World War II, they become victims of racism when they move there. Gilbert and Hortense hope for an embrace from the country they have moved to, but that is not quite the case. However, Levy manages to present all of this with a comic edge.

One of the core relationships in the novel is that between Queenie and Michael, but there are connections between all of the characters. In this way, Levy seems to be arguing that despite colour and background, we are in some ways all connected. The novel is non-linear and non-chronological, with readers having to work out the connections as they proceed through the text.

Comic characterization

One of Levy's achievements in the novel is to create some very diverse and appealing comic characters.

Activity

Write the names of the four characters Queenie, Michael, Gilbert and Hortense in four corners of a piece of paper. Identify the comic features of each of them, including any dialogues or descriptions that you think contribute to the comic effects. In a different colour, draw connections between these characteristics, but also identify their individual comic natures in the text. Share your results.

Commentary

This activity should show you the foundations of the comedic characterizations of the main characters. You will have started to explore how they interact and create comedy.

Sidelong style

Levy's style of writing has been described as 'sidelong', because she normally does not depict events straightforwardly. Instead, she seems to slide into them gently – almost unfolding them, the way they appear to unfold in real life. Think about the impact of this style on the comedic intention of the novel.

If you re-read Gilbert's narrative in Chapter 2 from 'Is this the way the English live?' to 'You are lucky', you will see how Levy gently slides in some of the issues that have affected Gilbert. The style is chatty and confessional, but underpinning this are the bigger issues.

Activity

1. Much of the humour and comedy in *Small Island* comes from misreadings, mishearings and misinterpretations. Can you find some good examples of these in the novel? How do these comedic moments contribute to the progression of the plot?
2. To help you better understand the novel, find examples of the following elements in the text. Try to explain how Levy views each of these aspects with a comedic eye:
   - young friendship
   - casual racism
   - middle-class romance
   - relentless warfare.
   - the collision of different cultures

There is no commentary for this activity.

Is the small island Jamaica or Britain?

This is the comic question at the heart of this novel. Throughout, we are encouraged to rethink our understanding of both of these small islands, and also question their inter-relationship. The eventual conclusion seems to be that although some people are open-minded and accepting, others are small-minded. You may like to discuss this issue in the light of current political debates about immigration to the UK.

Different readings

Some readers comment on the way in which the novel comically details the Caribbean experience of post-war Britain, but others have observed that the text has a much wider remit than this, and depicts much wider change and **transition**.

In some senses, the novel is a 'family saga', but on another level it is the saga of modern Britain. Gary Younge, a recent critic of Levy, writes that Levy shows how 'porous' historical labels are. Younge is referring to the fact that when we try to categorize individuals within an historical approach, they constantly defy this categorization.

Conclusion

Levy's novel is particularly interesting for the way in which it shapes its comedy through very specific narrative methods. It also uses the genre of comedy to explore the cultural diversity of post-war Britain.

Wise Children (AS level)

If you are a candidate for AS level, you can also choose to study *Wise Children*. Angela Carter (1940–1992) was an English comedic novelist famed for her short stories, which often have a feminist and **magical realist** approach. *Wise Children* was her last novel, published in 1991.

The first 'wise children' of the title are Dora and Nora Chance. They are twin chorus girls and have emerged from a bizarre and absurd theatrical family, which they reminisce about. Within the context of the **carnivalesque** feel of the novel, we learn much about their father and how his 'free' sexual behaviour has impacted on the twins' lives. They are thus led into a life of lechery and **decadence**.

Under the surface of the novel you may be able to detect many similarities with Shakespearean comedy. The narrative also contains many aspects of fairy tale, which is one of Carter's main concerns as a writer.

Activity

Read Chapter 1 of the novel, making notes about the lives and histories of the characters. What do we discover as readers at this point? What are the significant comedic components of the novel?

Key terms

Magical realist. A **genre** of writing in which magical and strange elements are part of what is otherwise realist writing.

Carnivalesque. Related to a literary form that subverts dominant forms by using humour and chaos; it has its origins in festival culture, which itself subverts the normal order of things.

Transition. A process of change or development.

Commentary

We learn that the story centres on identical twin sisters, Dora and Nora. It is their 75th birthday, and by coincidence it is also the 100th birthday of their natural father, Melchior Hazard, and his twin brother, Peregrine Hazard, who at this point in the story is believed to be dead. The date here is significant, because 23 April is assumed to be Shakespeare's birthday. As readers we are surely making connections with early Shakespearean comedies, where identical twins often formed part of the plot.

The comedy is derived from Dora's narration about her own and her sister's lives so far, and by the fact that we encounter such a bizarre set of characters and coincidences. The magical-realist style means that the reader is forced to suspend disbelief and go along with the strange world that Carter has constructed.

The novel steps through several different genres of fiction. At first, it seems to be an autobiographical novel, but then it also has hints of a detective or mystery text when Tristram Hazard appears.

Activity

What is the function and purpose of Tristram Hazard in the novel at this point?

Commentary

Tristram is another bizarre character. He believes himself to be a nephew of the twins. He announces that his partner, and the goddaughter of the twins, Tiffany, is missing. We also learn that she is pregnant with Tristram's baby, and when it emerges that a body has been found, it is believed to be that of Tiffany. The comedy here comes from the speed at which events happen and how such a character as Tristram can become so quickly embroiled in such an absurd set of circumstances. Alongside the bizarre nature of all of this, there is also a deeply **Gothic** thread to the story.

Key term

Gothic. A **sub-genre** of literature devoted to horror and the supernatural.

Dora's account

Part of the purpose of Dora's account is to allow the reader an insight into the life of her father, Melchior, and the complex relationship between him and their legal father Peregrine and their guardian, Grandma Chance. Another important purpose of her narrative is to explain her own and her sister's experiences in the theatre and in the development of cinema. Here, another Shakespearean reference is dropped into the text, because the twins were involved in the production of a film version of *A Midsummer Night's Dream*. This seems to further emphasize the dream-like quality of the text.

Along the way, Dora also drops hints that she was involved in an incestuous relationship with Peregrine, although this is only confirmed towards the end. The creation of such doubt is part of Carter's comic purpose as a novelist: she wants us to be insecure as readers and never know the full truth about her characters.

Mapping relationships

On first reading the novel, there seems to be a bewildering range of characters and relationships. It may be useful for you to represent these diagrammatically as you proceed through the text. Some of the minor characters are also extremely well-drawn comic portraits of characters from the theatrical and film world. All the time, Carter seems to be pushing the boundaries of what is possible with these characters and their previous relationships.

Comic resolution

The way the novel works toward a resolution seems to have its roots in dramatic comedy. Gradually, the confusion of the 'Green World' is cleared up and a new era can begin. In an echo of the start of the novel, Dora and Nora attend Melchior's 100th birthday party, where he finally acknowledges them as his own children. Doubts about the lives of Peregrine and Tiffany are also resolved. They are alive.

Peregrine then presents the twins with twin babies to look after – which means that they must try to live for another 20 years or so, since they want to see these new 'wise children' grow up. The final line of the novel is celebratory and very much in the tradition of comedic drama: 'What a joy it is to dance and sing!' All of these events are bizarre and almost unbelievable, but the magical-realist format of the novel encourages us to believe in them.

Different readings

Some readers have highlighted the importance of the carnivalesque aspects of the novel in the way its comedy is developed. You may wish to look, for example, at the 'orgiastic' scenes that precede the fire. Carnival was always a lowbrow form of artistic expression, but when Dora and Peregrine have sex, highbrow culture and lowbrow culture seem to merge. You may also notice the carnivalesque background of London.

Other observers feel that the central comic story of *Wise Children* is based around issues of illegitimacy and legitimacy. The title of the novel is therefore deeply ironic. We really are not 'wise' about such matters.

Conclusion

Austen, Levy and Carter offer readers a new understanding of comedy in these three texts. They show that the novel is a very productive form in which to locate comedy, and build on **conventions** established in drama over a number of centuries. In the next chapters we will see how, over time, poets have also used comedy in their work.

14 Poetic comedy: 'The Nun's Priest's Tale' and poems by John Betjeman

In this chapter you will:

- examine poems with comedic themes, written by Geoffrey Chaucer and John Betjeman
- consider both medieval and modern poetry
- explore Chaucer and Betjeman's authorial methods in shaping these comedies
- make connections to other comedies you have read in this unit.

'The Nun's Priest's Tale'

Geoffrey Chaucer (c.1343–1400) wrote *The Canterbury Tales* some time around 1387. This poem of 17,000 lines is about a group of pilgrims (people who travel to visit a significant religious site) travelling to Canterbury from Southwark in London. Along the way, the pilgrims tell stories to each other. Chaucer mainly wrote their tales in rhyming couplets, although he does use other forms of verse as well. They are often comic and **satiric**, reinforcing the points Chaucer wishes to make about his society.

At first, studying Chaucer can seem quite daunting, because his medieval English can seem so distant from our own. However, if you read the poetry aloud, you will soon gain an impression of Chaucer's meaning. You will find that you become more familiar with his language and enjoy working out its exact meaning.

Note that you are not required to look at the way the Nun's Priest is presented in what is known as 'The General Prologue' (the main introduction to the poem).

In the surviving order of *The Canterbury Tales*, 'The Nun's Priest's Tale' comes shortly after 'The Monk's Tale'. 'The Monk's Tale' tells of the tragedies of several people, and the Knight requests a tale that is somewhat lighter in content. This is why the Host asks the Nun's Priest to speak. We know very little about the storyteller himself – but something of his personality is revealed through the story he tells.

Activity

With a partner, read the opening of 'The Nun's Priest's Tale' from 'A povre wydwe, somdeel stape in age' to 'For she was, as it were, a maner dey'. Don't worry too much about an exact 'translation' of the text into modern English, but see whether you can work out the general meaning. Share your interpretations.

Commentary

The context of the poor widow and her farmyard sets up the comedic narrative here. You will have been able to understand a lot of Chaucer's poetry even though some of the language is tricky. When you have completed an initial account of its meaning, go back over your text and add in any missing information gained from your classmates or teacher. Use this technique again as you steadily work through the poem. You will find that you quickly become familiar with the way in which the language is used.

Key terms

Anthropomorphic. With imagined human qualities.

Beast fable. A story involving beasts or animals, usually with a moral applicable to human beings.

Mock-heroic. Parodying heroic verse.

Reynard Cycle. A series of medieval stories centred on a fox, Reynard.

Beast fables

The Nun's Priest tells his audience a **beast fable** or **mock-heroic** story, based on the ancient **Reynard Cycle** (or Fox Cycle), which was a common **motif** across medieval Europe. The story here involves a proud cockerel, called Chanticleer, and a Fox. The world constructed in the tale is one in which **anthropomorphic** animals can talk, and often behave like human beings. This pokes fun at the chivalric narratives that were traditional at the time. Naturally, encounters between foxes and chickens would have been a common sight throughout medieval Britain, as many people kept domestic fowl.

The comedic plot

The plot of the tale is based on pride and deception. Chanticleer is a proud cockerel with seven wives. Asleep one night, he dreams of his own doom in the form of a fox. Scared by this, he informs Pertelote, his favourite wife, of what he has foreseen, but she tells him the dream was caused by indigestion. He tells her of the prophets in the Bible whose dreams did come true, but is still comforted by her.

The next day, a fox lies in wait for Chanticleer (the same fox, we learn, also deceived Chanticleer's mother and father). The fox cunningly asks if he might hear Chanticleer crow, just as his amazing father used to do. When Chanticleer crows in his egotistical manner, the fox takes advantage of his unguardedness by pouncing on him.

The fox runs to the forest, carrying Chanticleer in his mouth, with the entire farmyard in pursuit. Chanticleer saves himself and takes revenge on the fox by suggesting that he should taunt his pursuers. The fox, in his pride, opens his mouth to speak and lets go of Chanticleer. Chanticleer flies to the nearest tree and, in spite of the fox's repentance, refuses to fall for the trick a second time.

The tale, as you can see, is quite simple, but the Nun's Priest adds plenty of diversions and draws parallels from history. In this way, he displays all of his learning – but the tale is about a farmyard, so all of this is deeply ironic. The comedy of the piece is principally about displaying learning, and about being full of pride.

Activity

Read and discuss the sequence in the poem from 'The verray preeve sheweth it in dede' to 'And were anhanged by the nekke-bon.' How does Chaucer use dreams to enhance the comedic plot of the tale?

Commentary

This is one of the diversions in the poem where the Nun's Priest deviates from the central narrative thrust of the story and offers justifications for the importance of dreams. This diversion delays the narrative but also enhances its comic meaning when it reaches full development.

The importance of Fortune

Although the Wheel of Fortune is often a tragic concept, in this poem Fortune works as a remedy for the misfortunes of Chanticleer. It is fortunate that the Fox's pride means he will open his mouth and let the cockerel go. After the **disorder** of the attack by the fox, order is brought back to the farmyard by Fortune.

Link

See page 23 for more about the Wheel of Fortune.

Activity

Examine Chaucer's initial presentation of the fox, from 'A col-fox, ful of sly iniquitee' to 'That thilke day was perilous to thee'. Does this confirm the picture of a fox that you have?

Commentary

Chaucer carefully builds up the picture of the fox, who has all the characteristics we traditionally associate with the creature. Plenty of warning signs are given, but a comic situation is still likely to develop, given what we know about Chanticleer not wishing to listen to advice. In this way, he is similar to Emma Woodhouse from Jane Austen's *Emma*.

Different readings

Some commentators have suggested that the origin of the story might be in Aesop's *Fables*, where a fox and a crow try to outwit each other.

One of the key aspects of Chaucer's story is the issue of women's advice. Should Chanticleer have paid more attention to Pertelote? There might be an indication in the story that the Nun's Priest is a man ruled by women, as he tells a story about women trying to offer guidance. Perhaps Chanticleer should not have listened to her advice about his dreams.

Conclusion

However the tale is read, it is a satiric comedy based on the foibles of human beings. Here, comedy is full of instruction about how we should behave.

Selected poems by John Betjeman

If you are an AS candidate, you have the option to study selected poems by John Betjeman. Betjeman (1906–1984) is famed for the humour in his poems, which often examine the nature of Englishness in the 20th century. He is interested in the provincial and the ordinary; sometimes he laments the loss of a traditional England that was rapidly changing and disappearing.

Betjeman's comedic poetry often takes an interest in place and setting, which form a starting point for his reflections. The comedy is gentle and mocking, rather than consistently satirical. There is, however, an undertone of dark humour within the pieces, suggesting that English civility needs to be questioned and examined. Given the range of his work, this chapter can give only brief indications of how to approach the poems.

Comedic poems of place

'Upper Lambourne', 'Slough' and 'The Licorice Fields at Pontefract' can be called poems of place.

'Upper Lambourne'

The first of these poems of place was published in 1940. Upper Lambourne is a village in Berkshire, which Betjeman seems to argue is the epitome of Englishness. From the village can be seen the counties of Berkshire, Oxfordshire and Wiltshire. In the poem he initially describes the landscape, but in the third stanza focuses on one of its famous activities – horse-racing and training.

Activity

1. Consider how the adjective 'leathery' is used in the poem at this point.
2. Examine how the image of the sarsen stone is used.

Commentary

The 'leathery' nature of the landscape and people suggests both resilience and survival, but it perhaps mocks the tenacity of this corner of England and the horse-racing fraternity. The sarsen stone alludes to the fact that humans have been active in this part of England for thousands of years – this is comically contrasted with the newer and more desirable Edwardian plantations.

'Come, friendly bombs'

'Slough' is another poem about unremitting change in England in the early part of the 20th century. Until the mid-1930s, Slough had been a rural area, but by 1937 it had gained over 800 factories and witnessed rapid population growth. This process was therefore ripe for mockery, which is why Betjeman suggested bombs should fall on it. The poem almost seemed to operate as a prophecy, because from the outbreak of World War II many German bombs landed on the town. The poem is comedic, because the persona it creates explicitly asks for bombs to be dropped on it.

Activity

Look at the middle stanzas of 'Slough'. What faults does Betjeman note in the design of the new town? What do you notice about the rhyme scheme he uses here?

Commentary

Betjeman's poem expresses direct criticism of the architecture and economy being developed in the new town. He reinforces this by use of *aaa* rhymes in each quatrain. The final *b* rhyme is echoed in the *b* rhyme of the next stanza, reinforcing what in his view was an unwelcome development. In the final stanza, he comically wants to return Slough to a more 'Medieval' lifestyle of the plough and cabbage.

'The Licorice Fields at Pontefract'

This is quite an unusual comedic poem. Most of the poem relates a memory of when the speaker was young, and recalls an encounter (or imagined encounter) with a girl in the licorice fields at Pontefract, a town in West Yorkshire. Betjeman is initially concerned with sexual thoughts about the girl, but his memory fuses the licorice and the girl together because of their colours. The comedy is created by the speaker's almost perverted interest in the girl and by the outrageous, daring rhymes.

Key term

Vignette. A short, impressionistic scene, providing insight.

Comedic love poetry

'A Subaltern's Love Song', 'Late Flowering Lust' and 'Senex' are love poems.

'A Subaltern's Love Song' dates from 1945 and is a **vignette** about the persona's love for a middle-class siren named Joan Hunter Dunn. A subaltern was a junior military officer, and this was Betjeman's rank at this point. The crush on Dunn is described through the speaker's feelings while he plays a game of tennis with her.

'Late Flowering Lust' is a poem about the process of ageing, but also shows that sexual feeling (or, as Betjeman puts it, lust) survives. The poem has a **Gothic** tone to it, as Betjeman imagines his partner and himself as skeletons and ponders how much time they have left on earth. The comedy comes from the way in which Betjeman presents himself as he ages, and from the way the two lovers cling together.

The title of the poem 'Senex' is intriguing. It was published in 1940, when Betjeman was aged 34. Traditionally, a senex (Latin for 'old man') is a wise and kindly father figure. The poem is given this ironic title because the speaker is thinking lustful thoughts about the young girls he observes. In the end, it is the dogs barking that jolt him back to reality and the process of growing older.

In all three poems, Betjeman creates personas who have a perverted kind of interest in the opposite sex. This 'weakness' in otherwise decorous middle-class behaviour is the source of much of the comedy.

Religion and comedy

'Diary of a Church Mouse' is a comedy in which Betjeman steps into the mind of a church mouse, who narrates his experiences of Christian life. As we might expect, the mouse notes the drudgery of events and how, in fact, people are less keen on religion in the modern era. However, the Harvest festival (when the church is filled with the products of harvest) brings him hope, for he will at least have plenty of good things to eat then.

'In Westminster Abbey' was written in 1940 during World War II. While Westminster Abbey remained the Christian centre of Britain during the bombing of London, Betjeman seems to be satirizing this blind faith that Christianity could save the world. Interestingly, the female persona notes the contribution of colonized communities to the British war effort, as well as explaining what we all ought to be doing. In the end, however, real life intervenes – for she has a lunch date, which comically undercuts the persona's higher thoughts.

'Lenten Thoughts of a High Anglican' is a poem in which Betjeman sees traces of God in a woman who is known as the Mistress. The poem is set around Lent (a period of abstinence and an important marker in the **ritual** year) and the persona recalls a childhood memory, but the holiness of the Lent period is undercut by his fantasies about this woman. There is something fascinating about her which makes the young persona stare. A key aspect of the comedy comes at the end, where the persona hopes 'the preacher will not think / It unorthodox and odd / If I add that I glimpse in 'the Mistress' / A hint of the Unknown God'.

'On a Portrait of a Deaf Man' is a poem implicitly about Christianity and the afterlife, but outwardly it simply details the existence of a hearing-impaired individual whom Betjeman knew as a child. When Betjeman thinks of him he remembers him being wise, but now that the deaf man is dead he can only think of the 'maggots in his eyes'. The man is buried at Highgate cemetery in North London, and Betjeman questions whether his soul will be saved.

Comedies of class and culture

The Cadogan Hotel is on Sloane Street in Knightsbridge, London, and shortly after it opened, it became infamous as the location of the arrest of the playwright and essayist Oscar Wilde. He was arrested on 6 April 1895, in room number 118, and charged with 'committing acts of gross indecency with other male persons'. The era was intolerant of homosexuality.

What Betjeman does in the poem 'The Arrest of Oscar Wilde at the Cadogan Hotel' is not only celebrate Wilde's flamboyant lifestyle at the Cadogan Hotel, but effectively to contrast the voice of Wilde with that of the police officers who have come to arrest him.

The poem makes mention of 'The Yellow Book'. This was a radical journal devoted to literary activity. A key moment of comedy comes with the dialogue of the arresting officers, who say:

Betjeman has manipulated the language of the policeman to make him sound Cockney.

'Mr Woilde, we 'ave come for tew take yew
Where felons and criminals dwell:
We must ask yew tew leave with us quoietly
For this *is* the Cadogan Hotel.'

This connects the comedy of Wilde's life, career and plays within this moment.

High and low culture are contrasted in this line, and specifically in the italicization of the word 'is'.

'Ireland with Emily' is a celebration of Irish history, culture and identity, though along the way it pokes fun at some aspects of that country's legacy. Two central **metaphors** are important in the poem; the first is the notion of Ireland being a very ancient country; the second is its Catholicism. The poem reveals Betjeman's comedic evaluation of the environment and its people as he witnesses mass. An important comedic moment is where the landscape is described as 'Bog-surrounded bramble-skirted – / Townlands rich or townlands mean as / These, oh, counties of them screen us / In the Kingdom of the West.'

'Executive' is a poem that satirizes social change in Britain. Betjeman creates a dramatic monologue spoken by a senior executive in a company. He explains his lifestyle and the material assets he has gained. There is a seediness in what he does – mingling with those who are development gatekeepers. Betjeman himself is the likely 'preservationist' in the poem, whereas the executive seeks a more modern future.

Comedic poems of English life

'The Village Inn' sees Betjeman doubting his own experiences. He finds himself in a village inn which is full of rusticity and tradition, but then after listening to a local and reading about its history, he begins to doubt the validity of such places, partly because of their growing modernity and tendency to change, and this throws doubt on his perception of English life. He concludes the poem by explaining that he must be wrong, but even then there is a sense that he may, in fact, be completely right.

'Hunter Trials' is a comedic poem satirizing the world of equestrian events. Betjeman seems to be poking fun at the competitive world of horse-riding and dressage (known as 'hunter trials'). Many of the riders are young middle-class women who seemingly have nothing better to do than ride in such events and be unpleasant to each other. The response to observing other riders in the trials is very childish.

Broomhill is a district of Sheffield, with clear views over the city. Once a posh suburb (although now more of a student area) its fine houses overlooked the steel works and other heavy industry of Sheffield. 'An Edwardian Sunday, Broomhill, Sheffield' is a satire on the contrast between the lives of those who lived in Broomhill, and those who lived and worked in the city's industrial areas. Something darker is indicated with its final lines about the city's manufacturing heritage of 'razors and knives'.

Key term

Adage. A frequently used saying that sets out a general truth.

Betjeman approaches the subject matter of 'Advertising Pays' in a slightly different way. He assumes the persona of an advertising executive sitting in Claridges, a sophisticated hotel in Mayfair in London, frequented by royalty and other important people in society, such as politicians and opinion-makers. The normal **adage** that 'advertising pays' is subverted here, with Betjeman saying it pays to influence key people who will then inspire other people to buy one's products. The persona indicates that he can work both sides of the political divide: he can be nice to anyone if need be. The second half of the poem explores more of the 'writing lies' that advertising involves, giving some examples from his portfolio of clients.

Conclusion

Betjeman's poems may bring a kind of **post-modern** irony to our understanding of comedy – and in his work we observe society from a different comic perspective.

The poetry studied in this option also shows how adaptable and changeable comedy is. Its features appear to have adapted to suit the focus of different ages, as writers have responded to the needs of their readers. By now, you should be able to make connections across plenty of poems, and with the other comic texts studied in this option.

The poetry anthology: from Donne to Duffy 15

Introduction to the poetry anthology

If you have chosen to study this option, you will need to read and study the nine poems included in the Comedy section of the poetry anthology. Although it is unlikely that you will need to write about all of the poems in your final AS- or A-level exam, you need to familiarize yourself with all of the poetry here.

The poems exemplify different aspects of comedy, and eventually you will need to carefully select from them to write your answers. As you study the poems, try to build a picture of how different poets have used the vehicle of comedy; how they have adapted, altered or reconfigured it, according to the needs of their age and their readers. You should also be actively trying to connect the poems studied here with other texts studied in the option 'Aspects of comedy'. The requirements for AS and A level are slightly different, but you need the same basic skills in order to be successful in each of the exams.

In this chapter you will:

- explore a range of poetry from the Renaissance to the post-modern period
- consider how poets across different time periods and genres deal with aspects of comedy
- examine how comedic **motifs** and ideas are developed in verse
- start to compare and connect with other comedies you have read.

Studying poetry

Many students at AS and at A level make the mistake of thinking that in order to understand poetry at this level, you always have to know about a complex range of poetic techniques. The implication is that you have to pick through and understand these first before you can write intelligently about poetry. While poetic technique is important, this course wants you to evaluate how comedy is explored within the poetic medium, so it is to that central issue that we shall always be returning. Along the way, however, some of the more significant poetic techniques will be explained. The core thing you need to do is to write about the poems as comedies and explain how they reveal aspects of the genre.

Comedy in poetry

It may be useful to define two main kinds of poetry here. Some poems are narratives – they tell a story. We would expect a comic poem to tell an amusing story, which may sometimes be epic in nature; as an example, consider 'Tam o' Shanter' by Robert Burns. Other poems are a direct response to human experience, and have come to be known as **lyric poems**. The kinds of comedy explored in say, 'Sunny Prestatyn' by Philip Larkin, or 'My Rival's House' by Liz Lochhead, are not epic, but are responses to real-life comic events and feelings. They are therefore observational lyrics. If you understand this basic division, it will help you to work out how a poem is operating and what it is trying to do.

Key term

Lyric poetry. The medium in which classical drama is written.

One of the intriguing aspects of poetry is that it is a highly ordered and sometimes highly structured form. In this sense, poets' decisions about their authorial methods are dependent on that order. However, as we know, comedy often involves a disruption of order and takes us to where chaos and anarchy reign. Therefore, in comic poetry we may expect to see dislocations and new structures created by the author's methods. However, some poets use the rigorous nature of poetic structure to 'control' the comedy. This is seen best in, say, 'The Flea' by John Donne or 'A Satirical Elegy on the Death of a Late Famous General' by Jonathan Swift, where irony is central in terms of how the comedy is communicated.

'The Flea'

On the face of it, writing a poem about a flea already seems quite a comedic thing to do. Fleas are not normally the topic of poetry, and yet as we read this poem we see that its author, John Donne (1572–1631), weaves plenty of comedic elements into his work – notably strands that we already associate with comedy: marriage, love, lust and parental opposition.

When Donne was writing, fleas were common pests in Britain and people of all classes would have had to deal with them. Donne's trick here is to use the flea to **symbolize** love and sex, for inside the flea, the lovers' blood is mixed. The idea of love is given attention, but at the end of it, there is a clever change in the argument. Donne argues that because the woman he is addressing has killed the flea, she has justified his wish to have sex with her.

Key terms

Conceit. An extended and ingenious simile.

Paradox. An apparent contradiction that holds some unexpected truth.

Activity

The poem might be characterized as containing the following elements. Look over the list below, and note where you can find evidence of each in the poem:

- a strong speaking voice
- the use of a **conceit**
- the display of wit
- the use of **paradox**
- a powerful sense of persuasion
- a concentrated argument.

Commentary

You should be able to spot all of the above ingredients at work here. You may, for example, be able to see the connection made in the argument between the intimacy of the marriage bed and the blood inside the flea. You may be persuaded by the use of the conceit of the flea to put across this point. The poem has paradoxical moments that complicate and progress the argument. The speaker's wit is somewhat 'tongue-in-cheek' as he pursues his efforts at persuasion.

Extension activity

Donne's poetry is often called 'metaphysical'. This label is applied to a selection of poets from around Donne's time, whose work often had comedy and elaborate conceits at its heart. Research other metaphysical poets and compare their use of comedy with the way Donne writes here.

Different readings

Some critics have found much erotic imagery within the comedy of 'The Flea'. It may also hint at **representations** of the Holy Trinity of Christianity: the Father, the Son and the Holy Spirit.

'A Satirical Elegy on the Death of a Late Famous General'

We have already learned that the tool of satire is an effective comedic device. Jonathan Swift (1667–1745) was a noted satirist who ridiculed the politicians and events of his era. You will probably have heard of him as the author of *Gulliver's Travels* (1725), which in itself is a satire.

The term 'satirical elegy' is a contradiction, because usually an elegy is offered in praise of someone who has recently died, while a satire generally makes the subject matter of the writing look foolish or misguided. We can therefore guess that very likely, Swift would not have a kind view of the 'General' he was thinking of here.

The poem might be about John Churchill, the first Duke of Marlborough, who died on 16 June 1722. Swift, an Irishman himself, was pro-Irish, whereas Churchill had promoted the suppression and colonization of Ireland.

Activity

1. Read the poem a couple of times and then respond to the following questions.

- How does the 'gossipy' feel of the poem contribute to the satire?
- What is the effect of the mock-heroic couplets?
- How does Swift develop the satire of the piece?
- Swift seems to suggest that the General's honours were 'ill-got'. Why do you think he feels this way?
- How precisely is comedy achieved in the poem?

2. Try reading the poem aloud to hear its satiric tone. Experiment with different tones of voice to see which is most effective. Discuss with members of your class whether you think the poem could be as relevant in the modern era as when it was written (around 1722).

Commentary

The 'gossipy' feel of the poem gives it an urgent and contemporary note, as if everyone in society is talking about the General's death. The mock-heroic couplets are associated with high-status, epic poetry, but here Swift undercuts them and makes a mockery of them. He uses simple one-syllable end rhymes to reinforce this.

The satire is developed through imagery such as the 'loud trump', the candle and the orphans and widows who will supposedly mourn him. Politically, Swift and the General were probably opposed, and the poet believes the General gained his honours not through valour but by flattery and deceit. Comedy is achieved by drawing attention to an important figure and satirizing his achievements.

Different readings

You may wish to complete some background research on Marlborough's campaigns in Ireland, which so incensed Swift. Swift also seems to indicate that the General would prefer to sleep through the Last Judgement.

'Tam o' Shanter'

The comic narrative poem 'Tam o' Shanter' was written by Robert Burns (1759–1796) in 1790. It is in English and **Scots**, and shows how poetry can take a comedic direction but still contain subject matter that is quite dark and disturbing.

Key term

Scots. The dialect spoken in lowland Scotland.

Reading a poem such as 'Tam o' Shanter' can be quite daunting if you have not read such a text before, so it will help if you read the poem aloud a few times. Your initial task will be to understand the narrative of the poem.

Activity

Try answering the following questions:

1. Who is Tam most thoughtless towards, because of his drunken ways?

2. What does he encounter at the old church?

3. What are the gruesome things he sees?

4. What happens when he sees one of the witches wearing a short dress?

5. What happens at the River Doon?

Commentary

If you can answer the questions, you will start to see the comedy in the poem. You may find it useful to know that in Scots, *mishanter* means 'ill-luck' or 'misfortune', hence the title of the poem. Importantly, the term *cutty-sark* means a short shirt or dress.

Obviously, Tam falls foul of two comedic weaknesses: first, alcohol, which often causes people to behave badly; secondly, lust for the witch Nannie wearing the 'cutty-sark', which makes him weak. We also note that he has already flirted with the landlady of the public house he visited. The poem is therefore a comedy about men's weaknesses, and how these cause them to make the wrong decisions.

Activity

When you know the poem well, look again at its ending, below. Many comedic poems have a moral. What moral do you think Burns is trying to outline here?

> Now, wha this tale o' truth shall read,
> Ilk man and mother's son, take heed:
> Whene'er to Drink you are inclin'd,
> Or Cutty-sarks rin in your mind,
> Think ye may buy the joys o'er dear;
> Remember Tam o' Shanter's mare.

Commentary

The poem playfully ends with the advice that we should not take too much alcohol or think too much about 'cutty-sarks'. You may want to compare this poem with other works where advice is given but ignored, which results in comedic effects.

Different readings

Many critics believe that 'Tam o' Shanter' is Burns's greatest poem. They note that its use of Scots and English rhymes makes the poem very vibrant. Other readers think that it is the creation of superstitious terror that makes it such a lively piece of writing.

'Sunny Prestatyn'

Philip Larkin (1922–1985) was a 20th-century poet whose poems are noted for their comedic interpretation of life in provincial Britain. Often, Larkin presents lives and events that are in many ways frustrated, melancholic and inglorious. These are looked at through a comic lens that is always witty, and often satirical.

Prestatyn is a small and somewhat neglected seaside resort in North Wales, where many English tourists would spend their summer holidays. Here, Larkin details an advertising poster that makes the town seem more exciting than it really is. The poster is gradually defaced with vulgar graffiti. Eventually, it is replaced by the more realistic 'Fight Cancer' poster. This is a good example of **bathos** in comedic poetry.

Key term

Bathos. An abrupt transition in style from high to low, intended for ludicrous effect.

Although the poem seems simple and amusing, there are deeper meanings in the work.

Activity

Consider the following.

1. What connection is made between the poster girl's body and cancer?
2. Is the poem sexist?
3. Some of the language seems to hint that the girl is a 'slapper'. What is the effect of this?
4. Does the mention of the knife prompt a darker image?
5. Does Prestatyn sound attractive?

Commentary

The poem can also be read as exploring the illusory nature of desire, of making the world a beautiful place. The rapid deterioration of the model's image, and its final replacement, suggest a much harsher reality. The comedy here is therefore sharp and acerbic.

Different readings

The poem is often read as a comic satire on advertising and marketing. The vandalism of the poster may represent how the town itself has been altered and vandalized for and by the tourists. Frustration with the state of the town may make the local population vandalize the poster.

'Not My Best Side'

U. A. Fanthorpe (1929–2009) was an English 20th-century poet. This comedic poem is based on a painting by Paolo Uccello, completed in about 1470, which features St George and the Dragon (see overleaf).

The poem is comical because we hear three voices: the first is that of the dragon, commenting on his depiction; the second is that of the damsel (who is in the front left of the painting), complaining about the fact that she is being 'rescued', because she quite likes the dragon; and the third is St George, who explains that he is trained and technologically equipped for the job of saving her and killing the dragon, though he has concerns about her not appreciating his efforts. The poem is therefore a satire on the usual narrative of a damsel in distress who is grateful for the knight's efforts in delivering her from a dragon.

***St George and the Dragon* by Paolo Uccello, now in the National Gallery, London**

Activity

Re-read the poem a few times. On your own, write down a list of the damsel's central concerns. Compare these with a friend's list. Do you come to the same conclusions?

Then, together, look at the knight's monologue in the final stanza of the poem. What are his central concerns? Try to work out what is comedic about these worries.

Commentary

Whatever you note about the damsel and the knight's concerns you will surely have realized that the comedy is derived from:

- their realistic and down-to-earth assessment of their situation
- the damsel's view of the dragon
- the use of technical and legalistic language
- the fact that they are in a heroic/epic situation but are behaving in a very modern way
- the implied sexuality and prowess of the dragon
- the implied inability of the artist to paint them in the way they wish.

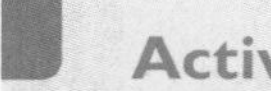

Activity

Prepare recordings of the poem, using tones of voice to exaggerate the concerns of the damsel and the knight.

Extension activity

Search for other paintings of this subject and apply the same technique to them.

Different readings

Some observers have described this as a feminist poem in that it subverts the normal narrative of the dragon-slaying St George and the damsel in distress. Other readings contend that it is a perfectly realistic and natural response to the situation the mythological characters are facing.

'My Rival's House'

Liz Lochhead (born in 1947) is a Scottish poet. 'My Rival's House' is a comic, satirical poem about the relationships between women. In the poem, the poet visits another woman (who is her rival in some capacity – perhaps her mother-in-law?) – and Lochhead initially explains how they go into combat. However, as the poem progresses, their relationship is shown to be more complex, and in fact there are connections between them. The poem is not conventionally funny, but underneath it has the sharp comedy of observation about human life.

Activity

Read the poem aloud several times. Ask a partner to coach you in a reading of the text – trying differences of emphasis on particular words and phrases. Settle on a version you like, and perform it to your class. When you have completed this, answer the following questions:

1. Why are the two women rivals?
2. What does the poet note about the other woman?
3. What connections are there between them?
4. What is important about the son?
5. Why are they so alike?

Commentary

Lochhead is deliberately ambiguous in the poem so there are no right or wrong answers to these questions. The comedy comes from the way in which Lochhead's persona responds to the environment around her.

Different readings

The poem contains no rhyme, and the structure of the poem is very ragged, perhaps representing a **post-modern** breakdown of relationships. However the 'She' at the end of the poem could represent both of the women who are battling here.

'Mrs Sisyphus'

To understand this poem by Carol Ann Duffy (born in 1955), you need to know that Sisyphus was a figure in Greek mythology, doomed to repeatedly roll a large stone up a hill after betraying a secret of Zeus's. In the poem the persona (Mrs Sisyphus) is comically complaining about her husband, and the fact that he is pushing a huge stone up a hill. She believes that his actions are a waste of time and energy, and this is reinforced by comic rhymes and half-rhymes.

Duffy achieves comic effect here by reducing the mythical to the level of the domestic and everyday, and by showing that Mrs Sisyphus is disgruntled.

Activity

1. With a partner, discuss the second stanza of the poem. Apparently, Duffy constructed the poem here by writing lists of words that rhymed or half-rhymed. Do you regard this as successfully achieving a comic effect?
2. Consider the final stanza. Why do you think comparisons are made to Noah and Bach?

Commentary

The rhymes and half-rhymes used to describe her husband are comically successful, because they are very earthy in comparison with the classical origins of the poem. Noah and Bach are included because they also had to complete large-scale and seemingly endless projects. Some observers have commented that this shows the difference between men and women – that men are much more goal-orientated in their completion of tasks, whereas women can multi-task.

Different readings

This poem is from a collection called *The World's Wife* (1999), where Duffy imagines the feelings of the wives of many famous figures. It may be regarded as a piece of feminist writing, taking an alternative and comic look at history. Duffy's poem may give a kind of post-modern irony to our understanding of comedy.

Conclusion

The poetry studied in this option shows the adaptable and changeable nature of comedy. By now, you should be able to make connections across many of the poems and between these and the other comic texts studied in this option.

Further reading

The Elizabethan World Picture by E. M. W. Tillyard (1943). This book explains how Elizabethan people imagined the world to be ordered. Shakespeare's comedies involve an interaction with that order.

A National Joke: Popular Comedies and English Cultural Identities by Andy Medhurst (2007). This book explains the tradition of popular comedy in England from theatre, television and film, and how it has shaped identity.

The Place of the Stage: Licence, Play and Power in Renaissance England by Stephen Mullaney (1988). Mullaney examines the legality of performances of dramatic comedy in the Renaissance.

English Stage Comedy 1490-1990 by Alexander Leggatt (1998). This is a comprehensive guide to comic theatre, with a useful section on Shakespeare.

The Rise and Fall of Merry England: The Ritual Year 1400–1700 by Ronald Hutton (1994). This explains how comedy in England connects to the ritual year, and demonstrates the seasonal impact of folkloric traditions upon drama. It looks at whether disorder can be found in celebration.

Fools and Jesters at the English Court by John Southworth (1998). This easy-to-read volume examines the functions and place of jesters in relation to the kings and queens of England.

Literature, Politics and Culture in Post-War Britain by Alan Sinfield (1989). A really useful volume which locates dramatic comedy and other literature in the context of the post-war period.

Writing Englishness 1900–1950 edited by Judy Giles and Tim Middleton (1995). This is an anthology of how different comic writers have imagined classic ideas about English identity.

State of the Nation: British Theatre Since 1945 by Michael Billington (2009). This is a very readable book about the theatre in this period, considering many dramatic comedies.

Component 2 Texts and genres

Option 2A: Elements of crime writing

An introduction to the genre

16

What is crime writing?

This chapter will:

- consider the nature and variety of crime writing
- introduce some of the key elements of the genre.

People have been fascinated by stories about crime for a long time. The history of crime writing goes back as far as the earliest forms of storytelling, and crime fiction today is an international phenomenon. 'Nordic Noir', for instance, from Henning Mankell's *Wallender* and Stieg Larsson's *The Girl with the Dragon Tattoo* to the television productions of *The Killing* and *The Bridge*, is merely the most recent manifestation of a genre whose enduring popularity can be judged by a quick skim through any week's television schedules.

The appeal of crime writing can be attributed to several factors:

- Crime stories have the capacity to thrill and excite, which they share with tragedy and the **gothic**.
- Many stories offer the consolation of seeing villainy unmasked and virtue rewarded, and this sort of moral reassurance characterizes the more conservative forms of the genre.
- Psychoanalytic readings might see crime stories as offering something more unsettling – either a dream or nightmare world from which the reader can awake, or the opportunity to indulge in vicarious and guilty pleasures which can then be safely put aside. Perhaps this is what W. H. Auden had in mind when he spoke of crime fiction as being 'an addiction like tobacco or alcohol'.
- All crime writing involves a puzzle of some sort, whether it is largely a question of 'whodunit', or an unravelling of the mysteries of the human mind. The attempt to solve this puzzle is a sort of intellectual challenge. For many readers this is what makes the genre so attractive. In some ways, the attentive reader has a similar role to that of the detective: both sift information and make deductions, creating 'readings' of the text.

Did you know?

George Orwell, the author of *Animal Farm* and *1984*, wrote an essay entitled 'Decline of the English Murder', published in 1946. In this essay he considers the nature of those murders which 'have given the greatest amount of pleasure to the British public'. Orwell uses the term 'pleasure' in the sense of providing appealing reading matter in popular newspapers. He concludes that the 'perfect' murder should involve a murderer from the professional class, and the crime should have 'dramatic and even tragic qualities which make it memorable and excite pity for both victim and murderer'.

What are the characteristic features of crime writing? Below are two short stories with crime as their main subject. The first is an extract from the King James Bible, Genesis 4:1–12. This is an account of what is sometimes described in Judaeo-Christian contexts as the first recorded murder – that of Abel by his brother Cain.

> And Adam knew Eve his wife; and she conceived, and bare Cain, and said, I have gotten a man from the Lord. And she again bare his brother Abel. And Abel was a keeper of sheep, but Cain was a tiller of the ground. And in process of time it came to pass, that Cain brought of the fruit of the ground an offering unto the Lord. And Abel, he also brought of the firstlings of his flock and of the fat thereof. And the Lord had respect unto Abel and to his offering: but unto Cain and to his offering he had not respect. And Cain was very wroth, and his countenance fell. [...] And Cain talked with Abel his brother: and it came to pass, when they were in the field, that Cain rose up against Abel his brother, and slew him.
>
> And the Lord said unto Cain, Where is Abel thy brother? And he said, I know not: Am I my brother's keeper? And he said, What hast thou done? the voice of thy brother's blood crieth unto me from the ground. And now art thou cursed from the earth, which hath opened her mouth to receive thy brother's blood from thy hand; when thou tillest the ground, it shall not henceforth yield unto thee her strength; a fugitive and a vagabond shalt thou be in the earth.

Did you know?

The phrase 'the mark of Cain' comes from this biblical story. It is often used to describe the visible sign of guilt on the face of a murderer. In Genesis, God condemns the murderer to a life of toil and vagrancy, but 'set a mark upon Cain' so that he would not be killed or harmed.

Did you know?

The crime novel *The Daughter of Time*, by Josephine Tey, deals with Richard's supposed murder of his nephews. In the story, the hospitalized police officer Inspector Adam Grant sees a portrait of Richard III in a history book. Drawing on his experience of reading faces in identification parades, he is struck by the king's expression and undertakes his own investigation of the crime.

A portrait of Richard III by an unknown artist. In the portrait, the king's gaze seems unfocused, distant, deep in thought. He seems to be playing abstractedly with the little finger on his right hand. This portrait reveals a contemplative man rather than an obviously malevolent one.

The second extract is from a tourist information sheet about the English king, Richard III.

The Mystery of Richard of York

The year is 1485. These are unforgiving times. Men need to be ruthless to survive. Richard Plantagenet, King Richard III, sits in his tent before the Battle of Bosworth. He has been an efficient king, in some ways a good one. The legal system has been reformed; government made more efficient. But his short reign has been constantly disrupted by plots and rebellions. There have also been dark rumours. Richard gained the throne only after his nephews, the heirs to King Edward IV, were declared illegitimate. The boys were sent to the Tower of London and have not been seen since.

Nearby are the armies of Henry Richmond. He is a man with no hereditary right to the throne, but claims he has come to remove a tyrant. He says he will make Richard pay for his many crimes.

The night draws on. Darkness gathers. Ghosts and memories circle Richard's tent. Richard has the larger army, but can he trust his followers? Lord Stanley has been acting suspiciously. Tomorrow will tell.

***

It is the end of the next day. Richard has been defeated and killed. His naked body has been slung on the back of a horse and carried off into the night. Henry Richmond will be crowned Henry Tudor. He will base his right to the throne on having overthrown a usurper. But still there are no signs of the young sons of Edward, living or dead. And some say that Henry himself now has a very good reason to wish them out of the way. If they are not already dead, of course…

Activity

What familiar elements of crime writing can you find in each of these two extracts?

Commentary

1. In both stories there is a possible *motive* for the crime. In the case of Cain it is jealousy and fraternal rivalry; in the case of Richard, it is the lust for power.
2. There is a *victim* of the crime.
3. Both stories take place in a *specific social context*, which has an influence on the crime.
4. There is an attempt to *conceal* the crime. In the case of Richard III, there is an assumed murder of the two boys.
5. A process of *detection* takes place, leading to an accusation of guilt. In the case of Richard, this detection process leaves the crime still unsolved.
6. The criminal is then *punished*. In the case of Richard, this is based on the assumption that he is the guilty party.
7. There is therefore a *moral dimension* to the story. Questions of guilt and justice come into play.

What you may also have noticed are the significant differences between the two narratives. Both involve disputes within families – very often the background to murder stories – but in the second example, family rivalries impact on the whole country. The victims occupy rather different places in the narrative. Little attention is paid to Abel once he has been killed, but the fate of the two young boys hangs over the second story.

There is also a difference in terms of proven guilt. Cain is undeniably guilty, but Richard's case is less certain. There is even a suggestion that the figure who claims to represent avenging justice may himself have been responsible for the murders.

In the first story, the narrative voice is distanced and authoritative. The only direct speech we hear is that of God, the voice of the law, which admits of no doubt or uncertainty. In the second story, there are moments when we are able to view events from Richard's perspective, which may encourage us to identify with him.

In the first story, the murder is placed in the middle of the chronological narrative – so there is a straightforward temporal sequence of motive, crime, and detection. In the second story, the timing of the murder is less straightforward. Because of the final hint of mystery, it is not certain whether the murder has already occurred when the narrative opens, or whether it is still to come after it ends.

What you will find in your studies of crime writing is that the differences between stories are at least as interesting and significant as the basic similarities.

Crime writing and other genres

One of the factors that make crime writing so varied in content and form is the way it overlaps with other **genres**. In this sense, crime writing is an excellent example of the ways in which genres tend to reinvent themselves over time. In some ways any genre only exists in relation to other genres against which it identifies itself, and with which it overlaps.

Some reviews of Kate Atkinson's *When Will There Be Good News?* drew attention to the fact that the story is difficult to pin down in terms of genre. *The Sunday Times* described it as 'one of those rare fictions that defies categorization', and the *Independent* argued that the author 'subverts the genre by refusing to neatly tie up every thread'. What this novel also illustrates is the tendency of some crime writing to assert its literary qualities. At different times *When Will There Be Good News?* makes allusions to (among many others) ballad literature, a novel by Alan Sillitoe, Robert Browning's poem 'My Last Duchess', nursery rhymes, *Twelfth Night*, and the *Odyssey*.

This **intertextuality**, this connection with mainstream fiction, may be a consequence of the sometimes disparaging attitude shown to crime writing; in fact the term 'genre fiction' is often used to refer specifically to 'popular' genres such as science fiction and crime writing. Two of the staple features of crime writing – the existence of secrets and the ultimate disclosure of the importance of apparently insignificant details – are also central to the narratives of such 'canonical' texts as Charlotte Bronte's *Jane Eyre* and George Eliot's *Middlemarch*.

Key term

Intertextuality. The relationship that a text may have with other texts. In structural and post-structural theory, texts are often regarded as referring to other texts or to themselves, rather than to any external reality.

Activity

To what extent are your texts shaped by the features of other genres? For example:

- *Hamlet* can clearly also be seen as a tragedy
- Agatha Christie's *The Murder of Roger Ackroyd* has many elements of romance and pastoral

- *Oliver Twist* is like many gothic tales, in that it deals with a family with a guilty secret and operates within what is often a dream-like, nightmare world.

Extension activity

Crime writing is also a popular form for film or television narrative. Consider aspects of your set text which might make it suitable for adaptation into film (or which have already contributed to its success as a film adaptation).

The significance of place

You may have identified another important element within the genre of crime writing: the significant use of place. Crime writers frequently place their stories in a recognizable setting (local, national or universal), and this seems to add to their appeal. The settings of crime stories can also operate metaphorically, where they can come to represent some particular human feeling or experience.

Consider these examples:

- The Brighton of *Brighton Rock* – a seedy, often vulgar, decaying seaside town – seems ideally suited to a tale of sordid crime, placed within a very physical world of both pain and sensual pleasure.
- The cottage of Robert Browning's 'Porphyria's Lover' could be seen as a place of refuge from a stormy outside world, but it is also enclosed and claustrophobic, very much the lair of the lover.
- In Coleridge's 'The Rime of the Ancient Mariner' the central stage is the huge expanse of the sea, where the Mariner commits his crime and where he suffers his punishment. The immensity of the ocean helps to emphasize the Mariner's isolation and guilt, 'Alone on a wide, wide sea'.

Activity

Read the following passage from Dickens's *Oliver Twist*, in which Fagin, here referred to as 'the Jew', goes to meet Bill Sikes, the house-breaker. How does Dickens use the setting to convey important impressions about the characters and moral world of the novel?

> It was a chill, damp, windy night, when the Jew, buttoning his great-coat tight round his shrivelled body, and pulling the collar up over his ears so as completely to obscure the lower part of his face, emerged from his den. He paused on the step as the door was locked and chained behind him; and having listened while the boy made all secure, and until their retreating footsteps were no longer audible, slunk down the street as quickly as he could.
>
> The house to which Oliver had been conveyed, was in the neighbourhood of Whitechapel. The Jew stopped for an instant at the corner of the street; and, glancing surreptitiously round, crossed the road, and struck off in the direction of Spitalfields.
>
> The mud lay thick upon the stones, and a black mist hung over the streets; the rain fell sluggishly down, and everything felt cold and clammy to the touch. It seemed just the night when it befell such a being as the Jew

> to be abroad. As he glided stealthily along, creeping beneath the shelter of the walls and doorways, the hideous old man seemed like some loathsome reptile engendered in the slime and darkness through which he moved: crawling forth, by night, in search of some rich offal for a meal.

Commentary

Although Dickens has identified clearly the district of London in which the action occurs, the effect of this passage is rather to convey an imaginary setting inhabited by beasts and demons in human form. Fagin's movements are described in terms that suggest a predatory animal: he emerges 'from his den', he 'slunk down the street', 'he glided stealthily', he is seen 'crawling forth, by night'. Dickens uses a simile to drive home the bestial association: 'like some loathsome reptile'.

Twenty-first century readers might well find Dickens's presentation of Fagin problematic, or even anti-Semitic, particularly in relation to his use of the term 'the Jew'. Dickens was made aware of the hostility of some members of the Jewish community to his portrait of Fagin. His creation of Riah, a worthy Jewish character, in *Our Mutual Friend*, seems to have resulted from his wish to make amends.

Extension activity

Read what George Orwell has to say in his essay 'Charles Dickens' about the charge of anti-Semitic elements in Dickens's work. You might also look at Alec Guinness's portrayal of Fagin in David Lean's 1948 film adaptation. The performance provoked riotous opposition in some parts of the United States and Palestine.

Fagin is significantly seen as very much a creature of his surroundings. He has seemingly been 'engendered in the slime and darkness through which he moved'. This is almost a prehistoric, underwater world: thick with mud, heavy with mist, a place where 'everything felt cold and clammy'. There are none of the features of elegance, wealth or modernity that we might expect to find in the capital city of Great Britain.

But the environment we are shown is not merely physically uncomfortable. This breeding ground for crime is presented as a **representation** of hell. The word 'night' is repeated; Fagin moves through 'darkness'; he is by implication presented as something satanic: a reptile, a serpent. London here is revealed as a diabolic world from which light and decency have been banished. Criminal and setting are inextricably associated, thus inviting a reading of the text which questions how far the material conditions in which criminals live can be held responsible for their crimes. Throughout his life Dickens insisted on the relationship between crime and the poverty and ignorance that fuelled it.

Link

The moral questions that crime writing invites will be further considered in a later chapter.

Summary

In this chapter you have been introduced to:

- some of the main components of crime writing
- the ways in which crime stories can incorporate features of other genres, which lead to different readings of the text
- the ways in which the settings that crime writers use can play a significant role within the narratives.

17 The criminal

This chapter will:

- consider the fascination with the figure of the criminal in crime writing
- analyse some ways in which the criminal is represented
- explore the significance of the crime.

Link

To learn more about narrative methods, look at the coursework chapter on narrative points of view, page 226.

In the world of crime writing, the figure of the criminal has always fascinated readers and audiences. There are many possible reasons for this:

- We may see in the figure of the criminal a representation of some aspects of ourselves – but twisted and corrupted. The degree of empathy or identification may be increased if the criminal is also one of the significant narrative voices within the novel.
- The actions and motives of the criminal may generate some sympathy, especially if the world in which the criminal operates is presented as flawed or corrupt. You may be able to think of several examples of such fictional characters, operating in a society where the forces of law and order seem deeply compromised. The legendary figure of Robin Hood is a famous example of such a character.
- In witnessing the actions of the criminal, we may feel a degree of guilty pleasure, a frisson of excitement. We can enjoy the experience of safely witnessing violence and danger, and immerse ourselves in the world of the criminal, while feeling confident that in the end crime will be punished.

These very different responses suggest that we may have a complex moral engagement with the figure of the criminal in crime stories. There may well be an ambiguity in our response, and this ambiguity may significantly contribute to the impact of the text. The moral questions raised by crime writing will be explored further in a later chapter.

It is important at this point to emphasize that the texts you will study take a very broad view of 'crime' and 'criminals'. Criminal activity in your texts is not confined to something that is punishable by law. In fact, you may feel in your reading of the stories that actions which are not strictly 'illegal' are presented as more morally repellent than those the law can punish.

The criminal and the narrative voice

Key terms

Extradiegetic. Extradiegetic narration is when the narrator occupies a position above and apparently superior to the story they narrate.

Heterodiegetic. A heterodiegetic narrator does not take part in the narrated action.

Intradiegetic. An intradiegetic narrator operates on the same level as characters in the story, so is different from the extradiegetic narrator who occupies a position above the story.

The positions that criminals take within the narrative have considerable significance in terms of the ways in which we read the text. These narrative positions include the degree of their participation in the story, the level at which they operate, and the extent to which they can be considered 'reliable'.

In some crime writing the narrators occupy a position above or apparently superior to the story they narrate. This is often called **extradiegetic** narration. *Oliver Twist* is an example of such a narrative, where the narrator seems to have a sort of omniscience – access to characters' thoughts and an ability to know what is happening in different places at exactly the same time. In the case of this text, the narrator can also be called **heterodiegetic**, in that he does not take part in the action. George Crabbe's *Peter Grimes* is another example of a narrative that is both extradiegetic and heterodiegetic.

How does this sort of narrative position affect your response as a reader? Do you find yourself also placed as an objective observer, 'above' the events of the story?

In other texts, such as Emily Bronte's *Wuthering Heights*, the narrators are **intradiegetic**, meaning that they are involved in the telling of the tale and identified as the narrator, but also as **homodiegetic**, meaning that they take part in the story that is being told. Coleridge's 'Ancient Mariner' is another example of this sort of narration, where the criminal is the narrator.

Does this narrative position create a different effect? Does the degree of involvement of the narrator in the story tend to affect your response? Does, for instance, the Mariner's direct and personal account of what happened to him tend to engage us more fully in his experience?

In some crime writing, the nature of the narrator's participation in the story is complex. In Chaucer's 'The Pardoner's Tale' (a gothic crime story from *The Canterbury Tales*), the figure of the Pardoner occupies a series of different positions. In one sense he is just another character in the over-arching narrative of *The Canterbury Tales*. He is also, however, a narrator of his own tale in which he does not participate (therefore intradiegetic and heterodiegetic), but during the prologue to his tale he tells another story in which he *is* a participant (therefore intradiegetic and homodiegetic).

The character of Briony in *Atonement* also emerges as both participant and narrator at different times in the story. The ways in which we read *Atonement* are significantly affected by these changes in narrative position. In some places Briony seems to be just another character in a tale told by an external, extradiegetic narrator. At the end of the novel, she is clearly telling her own story. One position overlaps with and slides into the other, and this playing with narrative positions is central to how we read the story, and how we react to Briony herself.

Remember that in order to talk about the narratives in your texts, you do not necessarily have to use any specific literary terms. What you do need to do is find ways in which you can describe accurately how the narratives work, and how the different narrative voices operate.

Another distinction you might make is between first- and third-person narrators, and the degree to which the narrators seem to be reliable. It is certainly possible to respond to the tale narrated by the Duke in Browning's 'My Last Duchess' as being a story told by a criminal narrator whose point of view we might reasonably doubt. The Duke tells his story directly to the envoy of a count. The envoy listens, but says nothing that we hear, and in some ways might seem to represent us as readers. The Duke seems to have it all his own way, but the evidence he offers of the Duchess's 'guilt' is double-edged, and reveals his own debased value system: a 'spot of joy' called into her cheek by someone other than him; the fact that she thanked people who brought her a 'bough of cherries' and smiled at almost everyone who passed her. These, it seems, were crimes enough to warrant his fatal 'commands'. It might be argued that even the form of the narrative is to the Duke's ultimate disadvantage. By definition, a first-person narrative will employ a lot of first-person pronouns, but the Duke refers to himself so many times that this might be significant in itself in showing his self-obsession.

If the criminal is not the narrator, they may be a significant **focalizer** within the text, the person whose perspective shapes how we see events. In *Brighton Rock*, much of the narrative is focalized through the murderer, Pinkie. Pinkie is not the only focalizer that Graham Greene uses in the novel, but we are taken more often into his past than in the case of any other character.

Key terms

Focus / Focalizer / Focalization. A narrative point of view through which the text is mediated. We see the events of the story from the perspective of the focalizer.

Homodiegetic. A homodiegetic narrator takes part in the narrated action.

In this extract Pinkie bitterly reflects on Rose's love for him:

> All his pride coiled like a watch spring round the thought that *he* wasn't deceived, that *he* wasn't going to give himself up to marriage and the birth of children [...] He knew everything, he had watched every detail of the act of sex, you couldn't deceive him with lovely words, there was nothing to be excited about, no gain to recompense you for what you lost; but when Rose turned to him again, with the expectation of a kiss, he was aware all the same of a horrifying ignorance. His mouth missed hers and recoiled. He'd never yet kissed a girl.

This insight into his mind, however, does not necessarily make it easier for the reader to empathize with him. Pinkie regards himself as knowing, free from the illusions and weaknesses of other people, but his knowledge is a narrow, bitter thing, regularly revealed as a sort of corrupted ignorance.

Activity

Identify in your text any criminals who play a significant part in the story, and analyse their function and position within the narrative. What elements of their narrative position most influence your response to their character?

Narrative structure

Another important way in which the criminal is revealed is through their place in the structure of the narrative. The pattern of the appearances of the criminal will significantly shape the response to the plot by the reader or audience. In *When Will There Be Good News?*, for instance, the narrative focus tends to be on the victims of the crime or the actions of the detectives. The lives, thoughts and emotions of the criminals are kept firmly in the background, inevitably influencing reader response. They are often only shadowy figures; their existence is largely filtered through the consciousness of those set in opposition to them. We seldom get more than a hint of the motives behind their actions or the nature of their inner experience.

In *Atonement*, on the other hand, Briony dominates the narrative, both as an actor and a focalizer, for much of the text. The figure of Peter Grimes is a constant presence in the story that bears his name. In these cases, our constant exposure to the consciousness of the criminal must affect the degree to which we can identify with their experience.

Narrative language

Language is likewise a significant method by which the criminals are presented. Their language may take many different forms and will help to characterize the nature of the narrative. For instance:

- 'The Rime of The Ancient Mariner' and 'Peter Grimes' are dominated by confessions.
- By contrast, Browning's 'My Last Duchess' and 'Porphyria's Lover' are statements of self-justification, and the protagonists never seem to see their actions as crimes.
- *The Murder of Roger Ackroyd*, dominated by the investigations of the detective Poirot, is structured around a series of interviews.

There are other aspects of narrative language that may help to convey the experience of the criminal. The use of underworld jargon can help to create the impression of a sharply distinguished 'other' world, from which we are excluded. The housebreaker Bill Sikes's entrance in *Oliver Twist* is accompanied by a detailed description of his imposing physical appearance, but also by the narrator's observations about his language: 'He then, in cant terms, with which his whole conversation was plentifully besprinkled, but which would be quite unintelligible if they were recorded here, demanded a glass of liquor.'

Activity

Read the following extracts from *Oliver Twist*, and compare the ways in which the thoughts and feelings of the two criminals are expressed. In the first extract, Sikes is in flight after the death of Nancy, but he is pursued by visions of the murdered girl. In the second extract, Fagin is waiting in the condemned cell.

> For now, a vision came before him, as constant and more terrible than that from which he had escaped. Those wildly staring eyes, so lustreless and so glassy, that he had better borne to see them than think upon them, appeared in the midst of the darkness: light in themselves, but giving light to nothing. There were but two, but they were everywhere. If he shut out the light, there came the room with every well-known object – some, indeed, that he would have forgotten, if he had gone over its contents from memory – each in its accustomed place. The body was in its place, and its eyes were as he saw them when he stole away. He got up, and rushed into the field without. The figure was behind him. He re-entered the shed, and shrank down once more. The eyes were there, before he had laid himself along.

> As it came on very dark, he began to think of all the men he had known who had died upon the scaffold; some of them through his means. They rose up, in such quick succession, that he could hardly count them. He had seen some of them die – and had joked too, because they died with prayers upon their lips. With what a rattling noise the drop went down; and how suddenly they changed, from strong and vigorous men to dangling heaps of clothes!
>
> Some of them might have inhabited that very cell – sat upon that very spot. It was very dark; why didn't they bring a light? The cell had been built for many years. Scores of men must have passed their last hours there. It was like sitting in a vault strewn with dead bodies – the cap, the noose, the pinioned arms, the faces that he knew, even beneath that hideous veil. – Light, light!

Commentary

The first extract is dominated by the **motif** of eyes, the eyes that Nancy turned upon Sikes as he struck her down. This is a world of nightmare, where Sikes is constantly and involuntarily taken back to the scene of the crime. In the darkness the eyes are 'light', but give out no light to relieve his suffering. The short, emphatic sentences at the end of the passage reflect the trapped hopelessness of the murderer's attempt to escape.

Did you know?

Dickens gave public and private readings from his novels throughout his life. One of the most popular of these, and one of the most intensely dramatic of his performances, was his reading of the scene where Nancy is killed by Bill Sikes. During these readings members of the audience are recorded as having fainted, and there is a theory that, because of the physical effort the performances required, they helped to accelerate Dickens's own death.

George Cruikshank's portrait of Fagin in the condemned cell. Fagin is shown here as a shrunken, beaten figure. His hat lies on the bed beside him, exposing his face with its dark staring eyes and his hand clawing at his mouth. His whole body seems drawn into itself, a small, shrivelled thing within the cell that encloses him.

> **Key term**
>
> **Free indirect speech.** This refers to speech that is embedded in a narrative, so it is unattributed (free) and a report of the speech rather than the actual words (indirect).

The second extract also opens with darkness. Again the criminal is forced to revisit the scenes and victims of his crimes. The constant presence of these anonymous men in Fagin's thoughts is signified by the number of references to them by noun and pronoun, at least twice in every sentence. The wider inhumanity of the scene is represented by the ways in which humans are reduced to inanimate things: 'dangling heaps of clothes', and 'dead bodies'. In places the narrative presents Fagin's thoughts as if from his point of view: 'why didn't they bring a light?' This narrative technique is sometimes called **free indirect speech**. As in the previous passage, light (both literal and metaphorical) is absent in a world of darkness.

Representation in drama

Dramatists use language and structure in different ways to prose writers. In drama, the presentation of character and consciousness largely emerges from the interplay of the voices of characters on stage. In *Hamlet*, Shakespeare presents Claudius through his dialogue with others, through what others say to and about him, and through **soliloquy**, his own words when alone on stage.

> **Activity**
>
> Compare the following three extracts from *Hamlet*. In the first extract, his father's ghost appears to Hamlet at the beginning of the play and tells of his murder at the hands of his brother, Hamlet's uncle. In the second extract, Claudius has just arranged for Hamlet to be sent away to England and for Polonius to spy on the prince during his visit to his mother's room. The king is now left alone on stage. In the final extract, Laertes has returned from France, furious to hear of the murder of his father, Polonius. The king has persuaded him that Hamlet was responsible, and together they plot revenge.

GHOST: Now, Hamlet, hear:
'Tis given out that, sleeping in my orchard,
A serpent stung me; so the whole ear of Denmark
Is by a forged process of my death
Rankly abused. But know, thou noble youth,
The serpent that did sting thy father's life
Now wears his crown.

HAMLET: O my prophetic soul!
My uncle!

GHOST: Ay, that incestuous, that adulterate beast,
With witchcraft of his wit, with traitorous gifts –
O wicked wit and gifts, that have the power
So to seduce! – won to his shameful lust
The will of my most seeming-virtuous queen.

Hamlet I.v.34–46

KING: O, my offence is rank, it smells to heaven;
It hath the primal, eldest curse upon't –
A brother's murder! – Pray can I not,
Though inclination be as sharp as will.
My stronger guilt defeats my strong intent;
And like a man in double business bound,
I stand in pause where I shall first begin
And both neglect.

Hamlet III.iii.36–43

KING: What would you undertake,
To show yourself your father's son indeed
More than in words?

LAERTES: To cut his throat in the church.

KING: No place, indeed, should murder sanctuarize;
Revenge should have no bounds. But, good Laertes,
Will you do this, keep close within your chamber.
Hamlet returned shall know you are come home.
We'll put on those shall praise your excellence,
And set a double varnish on the fame
The Frenchman gave you; bring you, in fine, together
And wager on your heads.

Hamlet IV.vii.125–135

Commentary

Before the first extract we have been briefly introduced to the king in council. He has efficiently dealt with state business and politely, but firmly, refused Hamlet's request to return to university. Hamlet is seemingly isolated in his state of depression. The appearance of the Ghost changes everything. The Ghost claims that he was murdered and exposes the version of events that was used to cover up the crime. The false claim that a serpent 'stung' him is ironic. The Ghost names the king as the real serpent, with clear allusions to the temptation of Eve in the Garden of Eden. This analogy is developed with the account of the second crime, the seduction of the queen.

We see a very different Claudius in the second extract. Again there is a biblical reference, here to the murder of Abel by Cain, another brother by a brother (see Chapter 16, page 121). The king thus sees himself as cursed; his crime offends God as well as man. Like Macbeth before the murder of Duncan, he tries to pray, but cannot do so. He is bound to 'double business'. This image reveals the consequences of murder: a man becomes divided against himself, as in a wider sense the kingdom is also divided.

The third extract shows Claudius in a different role again – the calculating, desperate criminal seeking to draw others into his corrupt world. The passage is full of ironies. Claudius makes a hypocritical appeal to the ties of blood. He applauds his victim's wild declaration that he would 'cut his throat in the church' and – a murderer himself – claims that no place should be shelter to a murderer. He calls on the spirit of revenge, but he will be its victim. He creates a careful plot, and Laertes is coached in the part he has to play. Hamlet has previously created a play to 'catch the conscience of the king'; Claudius now attempts to create a counter-narrative in which Hamlet will be destroyed.

Extension activity

Look at the sequence of the king's appearances in Hamlet. In which scenes does he appear? With which characters is he normally seen on stage? How often do he and Hamlet speak together before the final scene? What **significance** can you find in these patterns of appearance?

The criminal as victim

Our responses to the ways in which criminals operate within crime writing may be affected by the degree to which they can also be seen as victims. Marxist or feminist readings may suggest that any interpretation or judgement of criminals cannot be separated from an understanding of the social or economic conditions in which they operate. In this context, the figure of the female criminal can occupy a very significant place.

Below are four examples of female characters in crime stories, who might be regarded to a different extent as both victims and victimizers.

Nancy in *Oliver Twist*

The character of Nancy has generated some critical debate. It has been argued that Dickens over-sanitized his presentation of a woman who worked as both thief and prostitute, to avoid offending the sensibilities of his readers.

Dickens, however, in the preface to the third edition, defended his portrait against charges of indelicacy and fantasy:

> It is useless to discuss whether the conduct and character of the girl seems natural or unnatural, probable or improbable, right or wrong. IT IS TRUE. Every man who has watched these melancholy shades of life knows it to be so [...] It involves the best and worst shades of our common nature; much of its ugliest hues, and something of its most beautiful; it is a contradiction, an anomaly, an apparent impossibility, but it is a truth. I am glad to have had it doubted, for in that circumstance I find a sufficient assurance that it needed to be told.

The speaker in 'The Laboratory'

In many ways, Robert Browning's poem is a chilling portrait of a murderous woman who has come to a laboratory to purchase the poison with which she intends to destroy a hated rival. The second stanza of the poem, however, with its rapidly switching personal pronouns, urgent run-on lines, and the nervous, emphatic breaks in the rhythm of the verse, offers another possible reading of the character: a desperate, isolated and abandoned victim of a callous pair of lovers.

> He is with her, and they know that I know
> Where they are, what they do: they believe my tears flow
> While they laugh, laugh at me, at me fled to the drear
> Empty church, to pray God in, for them! – I am here.

Gertrude in *Hamlet*

It is never made absolutely clear, in *Hamlet*, exactly how guilty Gertrude is of the murder of her former husband. The Ghost orders Hamlet not to 'contrive / Against thy mother aught', but to 'Leave her to heaven / And to those thorns that in her bosom lodge / To prick and sting her'. It seems at times, however, that the crime that causes both Hamlet and the Ghost most outrage is that of lustful adultery rather than murder. For much of the play, Gertrude is presented rather as a victim of the personal and power struggles in Denmark, than as a coolly calculating murderer.

Rose in *Brighton Rock*

In *Brighton Rock*, Rose is another character caught up in a complex web of crime created by other people. She defiantly allies herself with Pinkie, even at the risk of her own damnation, but is seldom in a position to influence events. Ironically, the character who is most determined to view her as a victim, Ida Arnold, is treated by Rose as a threat to her safety and happiness: 'Why don't you give it up? [...] It's over and done, isn't it? Why not let us all be?'

Activity

In the crime stories you are studying, to what extent are the female characters presented as victims?

The isolation of the criminal

You may have noticed a characteristic feature of many criminals within the world of crime fiction: their isolation. In Agatha Christie's novels, the criminal is often presented as an aberrant threat to normal society, an infection that needs to be diagnosed and removed. It is the isolation of many fictional criminals (such as Raskolnikov in Dostoyevsky's *Crime and Punishment*, Peter Grimes, the Mariner, Macbeth, Pinkie, Bill Sikes and Porphyria's lover) that is presented as both a basic condition of their existence and as a punishment for their crime.

The crime

Inextricably associated with the criminal is the crime that they commit. Look carefully at the structural positioning of the main crime within your crime stories. In some texts (such as 'The Ancient Mariner') the crime has occurred before the narrative begins; in others (such as 'Porphyria's Lover') the narrative builds towards the crime; in *Atonement* the crucial crime occurs early in the narrative and its consequences drive the rest of the novel.

The nature of the crime will also be important. Murder is by far the most frequent form of crime in crime stories, and its popularity within the genre can lead to some rather strange consequences, such as those television series where a small village or city seems to be constantly afflicted by a succession of grisly murders. By contrast, in the stories of Sherlock Holmes, only occasionally was murder the crime under investigation. You may wish to consider the impact that the nature of the crime has on your reading of the narrative, and whether the taking of a life is always presented as the most serious of crimes. The writer Colin Wilson, in *A Casebook of Murder* (1968), claimed that:

> Murder interests me (as a writer) because it is the most extreme form of the denial of the human potentiality for freedom' and that a murder case arouses in us a sick curiosity 'because we instinctively recognise it as a denial of these secret potentialities of freedom.

The motivation for the crime is also a significant factor in how we read the story. The degree to which the motive is personal, financial, or derived from more complex social issues will allow for different interpretations of the text. The extent to which the motivation for crime is explored within your crime stories will tell you a great deal about the ideology of the text.

Link

This wider moral context of crime writing will be further explored in the next chapter.

Extension activity

If you wish to explore the world of crime writing further, an interesting writer to look at is Patrick Hamilton (1904–62). Now rather neglected, Hamilton gained his reputation largely through his two plays about murder, *Gas Light* and *Rope*, both later made into successful films. He was also a prolific novelist, and two of his novels, *Hangover Square* and *The West Pier* have as their theme the predicament of the helpless innocent when confronted by malevolent evil.

Summary

In this chapter you have:

- identified some of the different ways in which authors represent criminals in crime writing
- considered the appeal of the criminal in fiction
- explored ideas of victimhood and isolation within crime writing
- looked at the significance of the crime.

Detection

18

As crime writing requires a crime, so it requires in one way or another the detection of that crime. In this chapter we will use the term 'detective' to refer to anyone centrally involved in the process of solving a crime. The process of detection can take many forms and involve a wide range of types of characters. It is likely that your text contains a character who performs some of the functions or has some of the characteristic features of the detective.

This chapter will:

- explore the roles and functions of the detective
- illustrate the range of ways in which the detective is represented
- consider the significance of the detective figure.

The role and function of detectives

In many ways, the detective's role within the narrative can be seen as being very similar to that of the writer or the reader of the text.

The detective may take on any of the following roles.

A source of knowledge, talent or wisdom

As a source of wisdom, the detective in some ways adopts the position of the **omniscient** narrator.

Many detectives are presented as having powers that separate them from ordinary men and women, and therefore by implication from the reader. In Edgar Allan Poe's *The Murders in the Rue Morgue*, the narrator begins with a lengthy discussion about the nature and operation of analysis. This faculty is then illustrated through a description of the narrator's friend, Auguste Dupin, and his apparently miraculous ability to read people's thoughts.

In Sir Arthur Conan Doyle's *A Study in Scarlet*, the first Sherlock Holmes story, Holmes claims to be 'a special one': 'I suppose I am the only one in the world. I'm a consulting detective, if you can understand what that is.' Shortly afterwards he immodestly asserts: 'No man lives or has ever lived who has brought the same amount of study and of natural talent to the detection of crime which I have done.'

In this first Sherlock Holmes novel, Watson makes reference to Poe's Dupin, whom Holmes dismisses as 'a very inferior fellow'. You may find further reading about the two detectives useful in providing a wider context to your own examples of crime writing.

Agatha Christie's Hercule Poirot also seldom hesitates to proclaim his own genius – frequently referring to himself in the third person as a means of asserting his eminence. Towards the end of *The Murder of Roger Ackroyd*, Poirot warns the unmasked murderer: 'It would be most unwise on your part to attempt to silence me as you silenced M. Ackroyd. That kind of business does not succeed against Hercule Poirot, you understand.'

Some detective figures, however, are presented as being far less enamoured of the role they have to play. In *Farewell, My Lovely*, Raymond Chandler's Philip Marlowe reflects sardonically on the role he has had to play while interrogating a pitiful wreck of a woman:

> A lovely old woman. I liked being with her. I liked getting her drunk for my own sordid purposes. I was a swell guy. I enjoyed being me. You find almost anything under your hand in my business, but I was beginning to be a little sick at my stomach.

Key term

Omniscient. An omniscient narrator operates from 'above' the story and seems to have a higher narratorial authority in relation to it. There is a sense that such a narrator knows 'everything' about the story (the word 'omniscient' comes from the Latin for 'all-knowing'). The narrator of Dickens's *Oliver Twist* falls into this category.

Did you know?

Neither Holmes nor Dupin get to narrate their own stories. Their 'genius' is conveyed to us through the narratives of their friends – in Holmes's case, Dr Watson. This choice of narrative voice allows the narrator to share with the reader an awed appreciation of the detective's gifts.

Activity

To what extent does any character who operates as a detective in your texts seem to represent a source of wisdom and authority?

A focalizer within the narrative

In many crime stories, detectives (such as Raymond Chandler's Philip Marlowe) act as the narrators of their own stories. Very frequently, the detective acts as a **focalizer**. This focalization is almost always internal; the detective is actively involved with the events of the story. In some texts, such as Graham Greene's *Brighton Rock*, the detective figure (here, Ida Arnold) alternates as focalizer with the criminal; in other texts, such as Kate Atkinson's *When Will There Be Good News?*, a number of detectives provide alternating and even overlapping points of view. In all of these examples, the focalization may help to create a sympathetic bond of engagement between the detective and the reader.

In Book II of *When Will There Be Good News?*, the chapters alternate between the points of view of Jackson Brodie, Reggie (a young girl), and DCI Louise Monroe – all apparently living separate existences. The chapters that focus on Brodie tend to be shorter, perhaps to allow more space to develop the other two characters, but in the final three chapters all three viewpoints converge on the same experience – a horrific train crash.

Activity

Is there any significance in the structural patterns created by different narrative points of view in the texts you are studying?

An interpreter or reader of stories

One aspect of this engagement is that the detective is often placed in a position where he or she deconstructs other people's stories on behalf of, and at the same time as, the reader. In Agatha Christie's story *Five Little Pigs*, Poirot gets the five suspects (the 'little pigs' of the title) to write their own accounts of the murder, presented in five chapters of the text as the separate 'narratives' of the different characters. 'I am going to visit these five people', says Poirot, 'and from each one I am going to get his or her own story'. Rather in the manner of a literary critic, Poirot then goes on to consider the meanings of these stories, even to the extent of arguing that all narratives are slippery things which allow for multiple readings: 'You are at least right in this – not to take what has been written down as necessarily a true narrative. What has been written may have been written deliberately to mislead.'

Link

See later in this chapter (page 141) for some comments about the detective as an unreliable narrator.

A maker of stories and creator of plots

As detectives decipher plots and stories, so they also create and narrate them. In the final scene of many crime narratives, the detective offers a new version of the story that has previously unfolded, one in which earlier confusions are removed and uncertainties clarified. This story-telling sometimes takes place in the rather theatrical context of a gathering where all the main suspects are present to hear the final version of the tale.

The significance of detectives

You have already been introduced to the importance of the idea of signification within a text. The character within a text who acts as a detective, a solver of crimes, may signify very different things:

1 Representing conventional society

The detective can appear to represent the conventional society of the world within which he or she operates. In this sense, the detective acts as an authority figure who protects the property-owning community and so preserves the status quo in terms of socio-economic power.

Many detectives from the so-called 'golden age' period of crime writing (such as authors Agatha Christie, Ngaio Marsh, Margery Allingham, Dorothy L. Sayers) seem to act in this way. Later in this section you will look at some of the features of the 'golden age'.

Link

For more about Marxist critical theory, see Chapter 28 in the NEA section of this book.

2 Teamwork

Detectives often demonstrate the ability to work with others, either as one of a pair or as part of a wider workforce. This may implicitly contrast their position with that of the more socially displaced, isolated criminal.

A sub-genre of the genre of crime writing, called the **police procedural**, deals with the day-to-day work of police officers, focusing on their work as a team.

When detectives work as a pair, the relationship between the two and the differences in their character and methods are often important to the narrative. Examples of such pairings include Holmes and Watson, Poirot and Hastings, and Morse and Lewis (in the novels of Colin Dexter).

Key term

Police procedural. A crime **sub-genre** in which the narrative involves the solving of the crime and the identification of the perpetrator.

Activity

Consider the operation of any pairs or groups of detective figures who operate in your texts. What is the dynamic of their relationship? How is it used to further the plot?

3 An uneasy relationship with society

At other times detectives are portrayed as having a rather uneasy relationship with the society within which they work.

The 'private eye', as shown in the works of Raymond Chandler and Dashiell Hammett, is a good example of this. These detectives may be loners, flawed or vulnerable personalities with troubled pasts (and presents). Their presence is often characteristic of more modern texts, where the society in which the detectives work has itself lost many of the moral certainties of previous times. In *Hamlet*, however, Hamlet also searches after the truth of his father's murder in a corrupt court and country. From the beginning of the play, it seems unlikely that the process of detection will leave the investigator unscathed.

4 Representing a profession or point of view

The detective may represent a profession, or a body with recognizable principles and practices. Police procedural crime stories, for instance, describe how members of a particular police force work together. The '87th Precinct' novels of Ed McBain are an example of this sub-genre. Other detectives, however, remain very firmly private operators, acting without the resources of professional organizations. In these cases, the interaction between the private investigator and the official police force may be presented as problematic or productive. At times, this relationship is further complicated by personal issues, as with Jackson Brodie and DCI Monroe in Kate Atkinson's *When Will There Be Good News?*

Some detectives represent a particular group within the community, or a particular point of view. Minority ethnic, gay and lesbian groups have all been represented in recent crime fiction.

Extension activity

Research some of the works of Chester Himes, Walter Mosley, Sara Paretsky, and Katherine V. Forrest. These challenge the dominant ideology of white heterosexual males that characterizes much crime writing.

What all of the detectives described above have in common, however, is that detection, one way or another, is a significant part of their life. This is even the case with 'amateur' detectives. Agatha Christie's Miss Marple is an apparently unremarkable spinster living in a small English village, but she nevertheless finds herself regularly involved in solving a series of baffling murders. In your texts, there may be characters who through chance or circumstance find themselves for the only time in their lives required to act the part of a detective – or believe that they are required to do so. Examples of such characters are: Tom Crick, in Graham Swift's *Waterland*; Joe Rose, in Ian McEwan's *Enduring Love*; Briony in the same author's *Atonement*; and Hamlet. The narrative may well reveal a conflict within the character between the imperatives of detection and what might be seen as the character's everyday life, with its own claims and priorities. In these cases, you might consider exactly how and to what degree the characters are presented as being affected by this unaccustomed role, either positively or negatively.

Activity

Read the extract below from Graham Greene's *Brighton Rock*. Charles Hale has been killed by a mob in Brighton. Shortly before he died, he briefly met Ida Arnold in a pub. She knows very little about him, but is suspicious when she is given the official account of his death in the local newspaper. What significance is there in the character and role of Ida Arnold as presented in this passage?

> 'The bitches,' Ida said, 'what would they go and tell a lie like that for?'
>
> 'What lie? Have another Guinness. You don't want to fuss about that.'
>
> 'I don't mind if I do,' Ida said, but when she had taken a long draught she returned to the paper. She had instincts, and now her instincts told her there was something odd, something which didn't smell right. 'These girls,' she said, 'he tried to pick up, they say a man came along who called him "Fred", and he said he wasn't Fred and he didn't know the man.'
>
> 'What about it? Listen, Ida, let's go to the pictures.'
>
> 'But he *was* Fred. He told me he was Fred.'

'He was Charles. You can read it here. Charles Hale.'

'That don't signify,' Ida said. 'A man always has a different name for strangers. You aren't telling me your real name's Clarence. And a man don't have a different name for every girl. He'd get confused. You know you always stick to Clarence. You can't tell me much about men I don't know.'

'It don't mean anything. You can read how it was. They just happened to mention it. Nobody took any notice of that.'

She said sadly, 'Nobody's taken any notice of anything. You can read it here. He hadn't got any folks to make a fuss. "The Coroner asked if any relation of the deceased was present, and the police witness stated that they could trace no relations other than a second cousin in Middlesbrough." It sounds sort of lonely,' she said. 'Nobody there to ask questions.'

'I know what loneliness is, Ida,' the sombre man said. 'I've been alone a month now.'

She took no notice of him: she was back at Brighton on Whit Monday, thinking of how while she waited there, he must have been dying, walking along the front to Hove, dying, and the cheap drama and pathos of the thought weakened her heart towards him. She was of the people, she cried in cinemas at *David Copperfield*, when she was drunk all the old ballads her mother had known came easily to her lips, her homely heart was touched by the word 'tragedy'. 'The second cousin in Middlesbrough – he was represented by counsel,' she said. 'What does that mean?'

Commentary

In this passage, Ida performs many of the functions of the detective. She is presented as being unconvinced by, even suspicious of, the official version of events. She seeks for meaning – 'What does that mean?' – where other individuals or public bodies are indifferent, or only concerned about their own immediate needs. Her qualities emerge in part through the contrast with the person she is talking to. She pays close attention to details such as the dead man's name, and the implications of those details. In this sense, she is attempting a reading of a text. Ida is far removed from the god-like figure of the all-seeing master-detective; she is 'of the people', an earthy, physical being, driven by 'her instincts'. But she is knowledgeable about her own world – 'You can't tell me much about men I don't know'; she seems to represent a very female point of view. Although no cerebral Poirot-figure, she seems well suited to exploring the grubby environment of 1930s Brighton. She gives the impression of one who will stick to her task. At the inquest there was 'Nobody there to ask questions', but asking questions, the characteristic method of the detective, is what Ida does, and will continue to do.

The representation of the detective

The role that the detective plays within the text emerges through the ways in which he or she is presented. An important distinction that you will have to make is between character and characterization; that is, the features of personality attributed to the character and the narrative methods whereby that character is revealed to us. Some important methods of **representation** include the following.

Sidney Paget's illustration of Holmes and Watson travelling to Dartmoor in the story 'Silver Blaze'. Note the physical appearance of Holmes here: he is drawn in sharp profile; he leans urgently towards the more passively positioned figure of Dr Watson; his long fingers jab at the palm of his other hand, apparently emphasizing a point. Everything about him suggests focus and intensity.

1 Description of the detective's physical appearance

The physical appearance of some detectives is designed by the author to reflect the degree to which they represent energy and power.

In the extract below from *A Study in Scarlet*, Watson describes his early impressions of Holmes.

> His very person and appearance were such as to strike the attention of the most casual observer. In height he was rather over six feet, and so excessively lean that he seemed to be considerably taller. His eyes were sharp and piercing, save during those intervals of torpor to which I have alluded; and his thin, hawklike nose gave his whole expression an air of alertness and decision.

Physical appearance is not always used for this effect, however. Relatively little is said about the appearance of Jackson Brodie in *When Will There Be Good News?*, although his physical strength can be deduced from his actions.

Activity

Consider the very different effects achieved in the following two descriptions of detectives.

> 'Really a most impossible person – the wrong clothes – button boots! – an incredible moustache! Not his – Meredith Blake's – kind of fellow at all. Didn't look as though he'd ever hunted or shot – or even played a decent game. A foreigner.'

Poirot, in *Five Little Pigs* by Agatha Christie

> She wasn't old, somewhere in the late thirties or the early forties, and she was only a little drunk in a friendly accommodating way. You thought of sucking babies when you looked at her, but if she'd borne them she hadn't let them pull her down: she took care of herself. Her lipstick told you that, the confidence of her big body. She was well-covered, but she wasn't careless; she kept her lines for those who cared for lines.

Ida Arnold, in *Brighton Rock by* Graham Greene

Commentary

In the first of these extracts, a suspect in the case reacts negatively to the dress and appearance of Hercule Poirot. The provincial prejudices of Little England are revealed here, and a characteristic failure to recognize the threat that the detective poses. In *The Murder of Roger Ackroyd*, one of the characters refers to Poirot as 'This ridiculous little man'. Poirot is presented as a sort of walking brain – even his head is 'egg-shaped'. His appearance distracts attention from his intellectual powers.

In the second extract, Ida Arnold seems to represent none of the physical attributes normally associated with powers of deduction and detection. In fact, she is at first rather dismissed by those she pursues and those she attempts to enlist on her side. Unlike Poirot, however, she is all body. Both motherly and sexual, she represents a sort of instinctive lust for life that stands in opposition to the dark and destructive impulses that drive other characters in the story.

Did you know?

G. K. Chesterton's Father Brown is presented – like Poirot – as being physically unimpressive. In *The Hammer of God*, we are told he had 'a small and colourless voice' and 'was not an interesting man to look at, having stubbly brown hair and a round and stolid face'. Nevertheless, he also emerges as the dominant figure within the story.

2 Characteristic uses of language or idiolects

Poirot is given a very distinctive idiolect, a strange mixture of French words and clumsily constructed English:

> 'I thank you, my friend. The word exact, you are zealous for it. *Eh bien*, what about our friend Parker now? With twenty thousand pounds in hand, would he have continued being a butler? *Je ne pense pas*' (*The Murder of Roger Ackroyd*).

The effect, again, is to establish Poirot as a faintly ridiculous outsider, the parody of a comic Frenchman (even though he is Belgian), which makes his ultimate triumph all the more telling.

In Robert Browning's 'My Last Duchess', the Duke presents himself as a type of detective figure in that he claims to have uncovered evidence of his Duchess's inappropriate behaviour, a 'sort of trifling'. He has accordingly 'given commands'. The Duke's narrative is delivered in the form of a dramatic monologue, and the controlled, understated rhyming couplets reflect the cool objectivity of the Duke, which is even chilling in its reserved formality:

> Oh, sir, she smiled, no doubt,
> Whene'er I passed her; but who passed without
> Much the same smile? This grew; I gave commands;
> Then all smiles stopped together. There she stands
> As if alive.

3 Allegorical representation

The descriptions of some fictional detectives suggest some form of **allegorical** significance within the text.

In his essay *The Simple Art of Murder*, Raymond Chandler characterized his most famous detective, Philip Marlowe, as a rather heroic, even chivalric figure:

> down these mean streets a man must go who is not himself mean, who is neither tarnished nor afraid. The detective in this kind of story must be such a man. He is the hero, he is everything. [...] He must be, to use a rather weathered phrase, a man of honour.

Kate Atkinson presents Jackson Brodie as a similar kind of hero. We are told that 'Jackson had never been one to say no, either to goddesses or to requests for help'. In the penultimate chapter, Brodie himself reflects on the nature of the detective's job: 'you should try and clear everything up as much as you could while you were still alive. Find the answers, solve the mysteries, be a good detective. Be a crusader.'

Key term

Allegory. A sort of extended **metaphor**, where a story or meaning emerges under the surface of some other story. Famous examples are *The Pilgrim's Progress* and *The Faerie Queene*. Some critics have argued that J. R. R. Tolkien's *The Lord of the Rings* is an allegory of the First World War, in which Tolkien fought.

4 Operating as a narrative voice

See the comments in the section on the detective's role and function (pages 135–136). You might also consider here to what extent the main narrative voice can be considered reliable. In Robert Browning's 'My Last Duchess', for instance, the protagonist and first-person narrator considers himself justified in handing out punishment for a 'crime' that he feels has been committed by someone close to him and that he alone has detected. You may feel that there is plenty of evidence within the texts that suggests his conclusions are seriously flawed, and in fact we as readers are positioned as detectives sifting the Duke's account for evidence of his guilt. Briony, in *Atonement*, acts as a **focalizer** for much of the novel. Again, she is presented as a very dubious judge of other people's motives and actions.

Key term

Soliloquy. A speech where a character tells or confesses thoughts to the audience, unheard by other characters. Soliloquies are often used in tragedies because they tell us why particular characters are doing something. In films, this is often presented as a voice-over to imitate the thoughts inside a character's mind.

Activity

Read carefully the sequence of Hamlet's **soliloquies** in *Hamlet*. To what extent do you feel that these represent the developing thoughts of a man whose deductions and intentions an audience can have confidence in, or even feel admiration for?

Commentary

Two extracts from early soliloquies are given below, as an example.

In the first, Hamlet has just encountered the ghost of his father, the late King of Denmark. He encourages Hamlet to remember him, and take revenge on his murderer, Hamlet's uncle. Hamlet's mother, the queen, has recently married Hamlet's uncle, but the ghost instructs him to leave her to the justice of heaven.

> Remember thee!
> Ay, thou poor ghost, while memory holds a seat
> In this distracted globe. Remember thee!
> Yea, from the table of my memory
> I'll wipe away all trivial fond records,
> All saws of books, all forms, all pressures past,
> That youth and observation copied there;
> And thy commandment all alone shall live
> Within the book and volume of my brain,
> Unmixed with baser matter. Yes, by heaven!
> O most pernicious woman!
> O villain, villain; smiling, damned villain!
> My tables – meet it is I set it down,
> That one may smile, and smile, and be a villain.
>
> (*Hamlet* I.v.95–108)

In this rather hyperbolic speech, Hamlet seems to commit himself to immediate and resolute action. His dismissive references to books and forms suggest that he is now going to put his student past firmly behind him and focus all his energies on bringing his father's murderer to justice. He does, however, feel the immediate need to write down a 'saw' (a general truth about life). We may feel he is less in command of himself than he believes. It is also interesting that, despite the fact that his father has specifically ordered him to focus his revenge on his uncle, the first focus of his outrage is his mother.

In the second extract, Hamlet has met a band of travelling actors, come to entertain the court. He has watched them rehearse a tragedy, and bitterly contrasts what he sees as his own weak-willed delay with the energy and resolution displayed by mere actors.

> I'll have these players
> Play something like the murder of my father
> Before mine uncle. I'll observe his looks;
> I'll tent him to the quick. If he but blench,
> I know my course. The spirit that I have seen
> May be the devil. And the devil hath power
> To assume a pleasing shape; yea, and perhaps
> Out of my weakness and my melancholy

> As he is very potent with such spirits
> Abuses me to damn me. I'll have grounds
> More relative than this. – The play's the thing
> Wherein I'll catch the conscience of the king.
>
> (*Hamlet* II.ii.569–580)

Clearly Hamlet has still not translated intentions into action. He speaks here as if he has just thought of the plan, but in fact he has already given the players their instructions. The speech, then, is a form of self-justification, and an anticipation of future events, partly for the benefit of the audience. During this future 'play within a play', Hamlet intends to position himself as an audience at a play that he has created. Ideas of concealment, guilt and interpretation are here foregrounded – the stuff of crime fiction. The final line, with its confident use of the future tense, suggests that Hamlet feels he is once again in control of events.

5 Contrasts between the detective and other characters

Here, again, the Watson figure provides a familiar model, whereby the acuity of the detective is brought into sharper relief by contrast with the puzzled sidekick. (This is a very old literary pairing, not confined to crime writing, going back at least as far as Don Quixote and Sancho Panza). For the general air of mystery to establish itself within the story, it is often necessary for one person to perceive more than the rest. In Shakespeare's *Macbeth*, if we regard Macduff as fulfilling some of the functions of a detective, then his meeting with Malcolm parallels many such fictional interviews where the seeker after truth faces considerable difficulty in persuading others of the justice of his suspicions. Some pairings or collaborations are, of course, productive. It could be argued that Hamlet and Horatio operate as a significant pairing in this context, and that the presence of the one is needed to draw out and justify the observations and conclusions of the other.

6 A detective who changes

The degree to which the detective does or does not change during the process of the narrative is always noteworthy. If Hamlet is seen as a sort of detective, then he is clearly an example of one who does change, and the changes that he undergoes are central to the wider significance of the play. Detectives from the 'golden age' of crime fiction tend to be largely untouched by the crimes they witness. Investigators in 'hard-boiled' crime stories may suffer, and at times may even undergo life-changing experiences, but the general sum of their rather bitter understanding of life does not significantly alter.

Detectives may or may not be presented as having learned something about themselves through their pursuit of the criminal. In *Brighton Rock*, it is doubtful how much Ida has learned about the complex psychological and spiritual conflicts that motivate Pinkie and Rose. 'Don't ask me', she says at the end. 'Anyway she's got me to thank she isn't dead.' In fact, and ironically, Rose does not seem to be at all thankful: 'She said with breaking voice, "That woman. *She* ought to be damned. Saying he wanted to get rid of me. She doesn't know about love."'

Activity

In what ways, or to what extent, can any detective figure in your text be seen to have changed by the end of the narrative?

7 Connections between detective and criminal

It has been suggested that in some ways the detective only exists in relation to the criminal; that they have a complex relationship in which the one is presented as almost being necessary to the other – a means of giving significance to their lives. Famously, in 'The Final Problem', Sherlock Holmes argues that the success of his career might be judged by the degree to which he is able to destroy his enemy, Moriarty. During the process of combat in which the two are engaged, however, it becomes apparent that they have much in common, even in terms of their physical appearance. Holmes's praise of his adversary seems to acknowledge a bond between them in terms of their abilities:

> He is a genius, a philosopher, an abstract thinker. He has a brain of the first order [...] You know my powers, my dear Watson, and yet at the end of three months I was forced to confess that I had at last met an antagonist who was my intellectual equal. My horror at his crimes was lost in my admiration at his skill.

This ambiguity of response is a common feature of crime writing. At the conclusion of *The Murder of Roger Ackroyd*, Poirot twice compliments the murderer on the clever touches that had been used to disguise the crime. In doing so, of course, the detective implicitly draws attention to his own superior intelligence in uncovering the truth.

In Ian McEwan's *Enduring Love*, Joe's attempt to bring Jed Parry to justice leads to an obsession that nearly destroys both him and those he loves, but the reader is at least offered a final hope that love of a positive kind will endure. In *Atonement*, the person who exposes the crime and helps to convict the accused is permanently damaged by this action, with a future life tied to the fate of the individual wrongly convicted.

Hamlet's relentless determination to discover the truth about his father's murder and punish the murderers seems increasingly to become the only purpose of his existence. In his increasing obsession, he is forced to confront not only the flaws in his own character, but also the inescapable temporality of all human life. Contemplating his own death, he says: 'If it be now, 'tis not to come; if it be not to come, it will be now; if it be not now, yet it will come. The readiness is all' (V.ii.203–5)

In these ways, as the criminal is often portrayed as being unable to escape the pursuing detective, so the detective is bound to the criminal, both in terms of their shared experience, but also through the patterns of the plot which constantly draw them together, apart and together again.

Summary

In this chapter you have learned:

- that crime writing often involves a figure who seeks to solve or expose a crime
- that a figure can operate within the text in many different ways and represent many different ideas
- that there are many different ways in which writers represent those characters who carry out the process of detection.

Crime and punishment: crime writing as a moral genre

19

Crime is inseparable from its environment, and in crime writing the relationship of crime to the moral and social structures of the environment in which it occurs is central to any reading of the text. In this context, concepts such as guilt, confession, suffering, law and justice, punishment, and the consequences of crime are all areas that you may wish to explore.

Some crime writers are explicit about their purpose in creating their stories. Charles Dickens, writing about *Oliver Twist*, claimed:

> It appeared to me that to draw a knot of such associates in crime as really do exist; to paint them in all their deformity, in all their wretchedness, in all the squalid poverty of their lives [...] it appeared to me that to do this, would be to attempt a something which was greatly needed, and which would be a service to society. And therefore I did it as I best could.

Dickens here sets out his determination to avoid any of the romanticizing of crime which he felt occurred in such texts as John Gay's *The Beggar's Opera*. In a previous chapter you looked at some of the ways in which the reader might be drawn to identify with the criminal. Dickens suggests that such identification is morally unsound and results from a failure to confront the reality of crime.

In this chapter you will look at:

- the influence of other genres on crime writing
- some of the moral issues raised by crime writing
- the ways in which crime writing deals with the idea of punishment
- the significance of the motivation behind the crime
- the significance of the presentation of the victim.

Crime writing and other literary genres

As has been explained earlier, no literary genre operates in isolation, and it will not be surprising if you find elements of other genres in your crime-writing texts. Two genres, **gothic** and revenge tragedy, both have features in common with crime writing, and incorporate a strong moral element within their narratives.

Key term

Gothic. A **sub-genre** of literature devoted to horror and the supernatural.

Gothic literature

Gothic writing characteristically depicts a world in which:

- transgression, whether political, religious or moral, threatens society
- the boundaries between good and evil become blurred
- passion and emotion threaten to overcome reason
- horror and terror exercise a disturbing fascination
- the protagonists are tortured by guilt and self-doubt.

Many texts can be categorized as both gothic tales and crime stories. Robert Louis Stevenson's *The Strange Case of Dr Jekyll and Mr Hyde* (1886) is a good example. The story includes all of the gothic features listed above, but also contains such familiar elements of crime writing as a guilt-stricken criminal (Jekyll), a detective figure (Mr Utterson), and the slow unravelling of a mystery (eight of the story's ten chapters are about the process of solving the case).

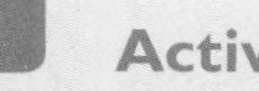

Activity

Read the following passage from the beginning of Chapter 4 of *Dr Jekyll and Mr Hyde*. What familiar features of crime writing are present here?

The Carew Murder Case

Nearly a year later, in the month of October, 18–, London was startled by a crime of singular ferocity and rendered all the more notable by the high position of the victim. The details were few and startling. A maid servant living alone in a house not far from the river, had gone up-stairs to bed about eleven. Although a fog rolled over the city in the small hours, the early part of the night was cloudless, and the lane, which the maid's window overlooked, was brilliantly lit by the full moon. [...] And as she so sat she became aware of an aged and beautiful gentleman with white hair, drawing near along the lane; and advancing to meet him, another and very small gentleman, to whom at first she paid less attention. When they had come within speech (which was just under the maid's eyes) the older man bowed and accosted the other with a very pretty manner of politeness. [...] Presently her eye wandered to the other, and she was surprised to recognise in him a certain Mr Hyde, who had once visited her master and for whom she had conceived a dislike. He had in his hand a heavy cane, with which he was trifling; but he answered never a word, and seemed to listen with an ill-contained impatience. And then all of a sudden he broke out in a great flame of anger, stamping with his foot, brandishing the cane, and carrying on (as the maid described it) like a madman. The old gentleman took a step back, with the air of one very much surprised and a trifle hurt; and at that Mr Hyde broke out of all bounds and clubbed him to the earth. And next moment, with ape-like fury, he was trampling his victim under foot and hailing down a storm of blows, under which the bones were audibly shattered and the body jumped upon the roadway. At the horror of these sights and sounds, the maid fainted.

Commentary

You may have noticed some of the following aspects of the story:

- The title of the chapter, 'The Carew Murder Case', uses the register of police work.
- There is the familiar temporary use of a different focalizer, here a witness to the crime. Her final reaction, 'the maid fainted', testifies to the horror of the deed.
- Intensifying adjectives such as 'singular' and 'startling' help to increase the impact of the narrative.
- Stevenson is imprecise about location for much of the story, but this scene takes place in what was probably a lower-class district of London, 'not far from the river', and open to criminal activity. The passage is also set during a foggy night, but the moon comes out for just enough time to allow the crime to be observed.
- The location is also significant in another way: the tale is built around the idea that the line between good and evil is easily crossed, and that a moral ambiguity lies at the heart of human affairs. What is this apparently respectable gentleman doing at night in such an unsavoury district? Some readings of the text argue that Jekyll's double life is driven by homosexual activity – behaviour that would have been illegal at the time – and this interpretation also offers a possible solution to this particular problem.

Revenge tragedy

Revenge tragedy is often included within the broader genre of gothic literature. As its name suggests, it is a form of dramatic tragedy, with the characteristic elements of violent death, a flawed central protagonist, and a sense that forces beyond human control are operating within the plot. The flaw within the protagonist is often balanced against the idea that the world of the play is also deeply corrupt. At the centre of the story is the motive of revenge, a motive that plays a prominent part in much crime fiction.

Activity

Look at the extract below from a soliloquy in *Hamlet*, the most famous of revenge tragedies. Hamlet has been given what seems to be a perfect opportunity to kill the king. He agonizes over what to do. What moral issues arise from this speech?

Now might I do it pat, now he is praying;
And now I'll do't – and now he goes to heaven
And so am I revenged – that would be scanned.
A villain kills my father, and for that,
I, his sole son do this same villain send
To heaven.
O, this is hire and salary, not revenge.
He took my father grossly, full of bread,
With all his crimes full blown, as flush as May;
[...]   And am I, then, revenged,
To take him in the purging of his soul,
When he is fit and seasoned for his passage?
No.

Hamlet (III.iii.73–86)

Commentary

The passage is full of religious allusions (the phrase 'full of bread' comes from the Bible, Ezekiel 16:49, and refers to a preoccupation with worldly desires). Hamlet's decision is finally driven by his belief in what will happen in an afterlife. His father was killed without the chance to repent of his sins; he decides against killing Claudius while he is at prayer, and thus temporarily in a state of grace. Remember also that revenge tragedy insists on the double-edged nature of revenge. When Shakespeare was writing, revenge would have been considered a crime against both secular and religious law. Characteristically, in revenge tragedies, the revenger is successful in carrying out his plan – but destroys himself in the process.

Extension activity

Read the whole of the speech shown above in the wider context of the scene in which it occurs, and explore the nature of the debate which Hamlet has with himself. Reading other revenge tragedies, such as Middleton's *The Revenger's Tragedy* and Webster's *The White Devil*, will allow you to compare their treatment of revenge with that of *Hamlet*, and perhaps give you a sense of what makes Shakespeare's play special.

Did you know?

An interesting example of the revenge tragedy genre is *Get Carter* (1971), one of the most famous British crime films, starring Michael Caine. Set in Newcastle, the film follows the gangster Jack Carter in his search for the murderers of his brother. The character of Carter, in his dual role of both criminal and detective, resists any comfortable moral judgement from the audience.

Other motives in crime stories

Your reaction to the criminal within the story and your wider response to the text are likely to be influenced by your judgement about the motive for the crime. These motives are as varied as the stories themselves.

Activity

Read and assess the motives of the four fictional criminals below.

1. The Duke in Robert Browning's 'My Last Duchess', is speaking about the behaviour of his late duchess:

> Oh sir, she smiled, no doubt,
> Whene'er I passed her; but who passed without
> Much the same smile? This grew; I gave commands;
> Then all smiles stopped together.

2. Pinkie, in *Brighton Rock*, discusses with other members of his gang the vital necessity of silencing Rose, the girl he is going to marry:

> 'The trouble with you is,' the Boy said, 'you don't look ahead. There's years… And any day she might fall for a new face or get vexed or something… if I don't keep her smooth… there's no security,' he said. The door opened and there she was back again: he bit his words short and smirked a welcome.

3. Fagin, in *Oliver Twist*, plots the downfall of Nancy:

> Mortification at the overthrow of his notable scheme; hatred of the girl who had dared to palter with strangers; an utter distrust of the sincerity of her refusal to yield him up; bitter disappointment at the loss of his revenge on Sikes; the fear of detection, and ruin, and death; and a fierce and deadly rage kindled by all; these were the passionate considerations which, following close upon each other with rapid and ceaseless whirl, shot through the brain of Fagin, as every evil thought and blackest purpose lay working at his heart.

4. Briony in *Atonement*: Towards the end of Part One of the novel, two young boys have gone missing from the house where they are staying. During the search, Briony has come upon their sister, Lola. She is in some distress, apparently having been attacked. Briony is convinced that she knows the identity of the person who has assaulted her.

> Suddenly, Briony wanted her to say his name. To seal the crime, frame it with the victim's curse, close his fate with the magic of naming.
>
> 'Lola,' she whispered, and could not deny the strange elation she felt. 'Lola. Who was it?'
>
> […] She may have been about to speak, she may have been about to embark upon a long confession in which she would find her feelings as she spoke them […] Perhaps she had already drawn breath and parted her lips. But it did not matter because Briony was about to cut her off and the opportunity would be lost. So many seconds had passed – thirty? forty-five? – and the younger girl could no longer hold herself back. Everything connected. It was her own discovery. It was her story, the one that was writing itself around her.'

Did you know?

The Go-Between by L. P. Hartley (1953) has many features in common with *Atonement*. Both novels are largely set in an English country house. In *The Go-Between*, the narrator in later life recalls his boyhood and his disastrous involvement in – and, as he sees it, betrayal of – a love affair between grown-up people. He describes himself as 'a foreigner in the world of the emotions' and the past as 'a foreign country: they do things differently there'.

Commentary

The first of these extracts reveals the Duke as almost psychopathic in his icy justification of his decision to have the Duchess removed. We assume that the motive was a sort of jealousy, but the Duke will not 'stoop' to acknowledge this feeling. You might think about the historical context of the poem – the Italian Renaissance – when considering the Duke's attitude and motivation. Is it more explicable when you bear in mind social attitudes of the time? Or, on the other hand, are we dealing here with a form of moral corruption that is simply inexcusable in any context of time or place?

Pinkie's comments might at first seem simply to indicate a different type of jealousy, but here also we find a failure to engage in any empathetic understanding of another human being. Rose is a threat and that threat must be eliminated.

Fagin's motives are presented as far more furiously intense. As with Pinkie, the main impulse seems to be self-preservation, and again a young woman is the victim. Dickens presents Fagin's thoughts as a whirlpool of different kinds of malice. Ironically, his own thwarted plans for revenge spur on another act of revenge; again ironically, he is too corrupt to believe in Nancy's basic loyalty, and so sets in motion a series of actions that will lead to his ruin.

The motives of Briony are complex and at this stage in the narrative imperfectly understood or acknowledged. They are inextricably connected with her desire to create, control and act in a narrative. The problem is that she has constructed a narrative about her sister, Cecilia, and her sister's lover, Robbie, that is based on a total misinterpretation of the facts. Once more, the debased motives of the 'criminal' are shown to derive in part from a failure of the imagination.

Judging motives

In some texts, we may have great difficulty in coming to a confident moral judgement about the crime and the motives that lie behind it – largely because of the inexplicable nature of those motives. In the preface to the 1841 edition of *Oliver Twist*, Dickens describes Bill Sikes as one of those 'insensible and callous natures that do become, at last, utterly and irredeemably bad'. In trying to deduce the motives behind the actions of such characters as Sikes, the Ancient Mariner and Peter Grimes, we may ultimately be left bewildered at the seemingly impenetrable darkness that can exist within the human consciousness.

At other times, the criminal's motives may be difficult to judge, simply because there are so many alternative possibilities. In *Hamlet*, for example, the motives that led Claudius to murder his brother might include the following:

- Political ambition. Hamlet's father is well spoken of as a king; Horatio refers to him as 'valiant. The Ghost – who may admittedly be somewhat biased – claims that Claudius's 'natural gifts were poor' compared to those of his predecessor. Nevertheless, the play shows Claudius carrying out affairs of state efficiently and well, and this may influence our opinion of him.
- Sexual desire. Both the Ghost and Hamlet stress the motive of lust in reference to Claudius and the queen. If they are regarded as genuinely in love with each other, they are a unique couple in the play and form an interesting contrast with Hamlet and Ophelia.
- Fraternal rivalry. Shakespeare's history plays are full of examples of power struggles between family members. The jealousy of a younger brother drives the plots of both *Richard III* and *King Lear*.

Whichever of these motives we regard as most significant will inevitably affect our reading of the moral issues of the play.

As has been suggested earlier, it is possible at different points in the story to regard Hamlet as taking on the role of victim, criminal or detective. If we think of him as a criminal in the sense that, like Claudius, he plots regicide (the murder of a king), then his motives can also be seen as complex. Several possible motives might be ascribed to Hamlet, some of which are interestingly similar to those of Claudius:

- Political ambition. Rosencrantz and Guildenstern suggest to Hamlet that he believes Denmark is a prison, because his 'ambition makes it one'. In terms of **primogeniture**, he is the rightful heir to the throne.
- A complex and intense emotional involvement with his mother. It can be said that Hamlet seems to see Claudius as a sort of love-rival. He pleads with his mother at one point to 'go not to my uncle's bed'. Some readings of the play have stressed the **Oedipal** nature of Hamlet's feelings.
- Loyalty to the memory of his father. At the beginning of the play he is mourning his father's death, and the appearance of his father's ghost is what first activates his desire for revenge.
- Emotional instability brought about by the collapse of his relationship with Ophelia. This could be seen as the source of a general rage against the world. But Claudius is not convinced by this argument – 'Love! His affections do not that way tend' – and suspects some other motive.

The judgements we make about the justice of Hamlet's revenge will be influenced by which of these, or other, motives we ascribe to him.

Key terms

Oedipal. An adjective deriving from the Greek legend of Oedipus, who unknowingly murdered his father and married his mother. It refers to the repressed desire of a son for his mother and thus rivalry with his father.

Primogeniture. The right of the first-born son of the monarch to succeed to the throne.

Activity

Explore the motivations represented in your texts, and consider the degree to which they invite your sympathy.

The victim

As every crime story will have a character who commits a crime, so it will have a victim of that crime, although at times the boundaries between criminal and victim can become blurred. Who is the victim in *Hamlet*, for instance? One view might be that Hamlet is presented to us from a very early stage in the play as the victim of other people's crimes. Another point of view might argue that Hamlet himself is responsible directly or indirectly for most of the deaths that occur in the play, and not all of these can be regarded as deserved. In this reading, Hamlet creates victims rather than being one himself.

To some extent the degree to which our sympathies are engaged by the plight of the victim will determine our reading of the moral issues within the text. In some texts, such as *Atonement* and *When Will There be Good News?*, the consequences of a crime dominate the narrative, and we are given much space to consider the feelings and suffering of the victims. In other texts, such as *The Murder of Roger Ackroyd*, the narrative is largely driven by the search for the criminal. Here, instead of being carefully integrated in the world of the text, the victim is little more than a device to set the plot in motion.

The narrative often represents the victim as an isolated figure, ironically rather like the criminal in this respect. The crime may operate within apparently unthreatening settings of time and place. In *The Murder of Roger Ackroyd*, the setting for the story – the village of King's Abbot – is described at an early stage as being 'very much like any other village'. Gossip and rumour apart, this appears to be an environment free of crime. By the end of the novel, the village remains essentially as it was and no aspect of its social or moral values has been seriously threatened. The murderer, largely acting alone, has been exposed and eradicated. An alternative reading, however, might suggest that something very unsettling has happened. Characters who apparently represent the solid virtues of middle-class England have been shown to have deep moral flaws. If crime can occur within such a seemingly respectable community, then it can happen anywhere.

Brighton Rock opens during a Whitsun bank holiday in Brighton, and the narrative stresses how out-of-place and isolated the victim, Hale, appears: 'With his inky fingers and his bitten nails, his manner cynical and nervous, anybody could tell he didn't belong – belong to the early summer sun, the cool Whitsun wind off the sea, the holiday crowd.' His desperate attempts to escape his pursuers are contrasted with the carefree movements of the holidaymakers along the seafront.

Bodies and corpses

The way in which the corpse of the victim appears in murder stories is often significant. In novels such as those of Agatha Christie, the murder itself may have been violent or bloody, but the description of the body tends to be brief and restrained. In the fifth chapter of *The Murder of Roger Ackroyd*, for example, the corpse of the victim is described simply: 'Ackroyd was sitting as I had left him in the armchair before the fire. His head had fallen sideways, and clearly visible, just below the collar of his coat, was a shining piece of twisted metalwork.' More attention is paid to the murder weapon and the arrangement of furniture than to the victim. Even the funeral is passed over in four sentences.

In *Hamlet*, however, we never escape from the grisly physicality of death. There are constant references to corpses and bodies, and a whole scene takes place around a funeral. In *When Will There Be Good News?*, we are similarly forced to acknowledge the finality of death. After the train crash, Jackson Brodie believes he is going to die, and his 'dying' moments are described in detail from his strangely objective point of view. The plot circles around a series of deaths, recent and long past. The 16-year-old Reggie Chase, who is drawn into the crime investigation, at one point finds herself overwhelmed by thoughts of mortality: 'Reggie thought of Mum, awkward and ill-at-ease at the horrible posh school, Ms MacDonald rattling on about Aeschylus as if Mum had the foggiest. Now they were both dead (not to mention Aeschylus). Everyone *was* dead.' In crime stories such as this, we are required to reflect on the impact and presence of death, and explore the experience of those left behind, the further victims of crime.

Guilt

Some forms of punishment suffered by the criminal in crime stories are largely internal, revolving around the idea of guilt, often within the context of religious belief. Again, we are presented with the idea of solitary suffering, and this may be a factor that influences your interpretation of the text.

Activity

Consider the following examples, from different texts, of the acknowledgement of guilt and responsibility.

- The Shakespearean villains Macbeth and Claudius both murder kings. The murder that Claudius commits occurs before the play begins; Macbeth's murder of Duncan occurs in the first half of the play. In both cases, as the criminals move towards what increasingly seems to be a certain death, they are tortured by guilt over what they have done.
- In *Brighton Rock*, the murderous Pinkie often seems untroubled by any remorse. He is, however, convinced of the reality of a hell that awaits him:

  > 'Of course it's true,' the Boy said. 'What else could there be?' he went scornfully on. 'Why', he said, 'it's the only thing that fits. These atheists, they don't know nothing. Of course there's Hell.'

- The whole of *Atonement* can be seen as an exploration of the complex nature of moral and narrative responsibility. Briony's extended process of atonement for her crime within the narrative is paralleled by her position as narrator. She becomes a metaphor for the moral dilemma of the novelist in terms of the authorial role, mixing and selecting 'truth' and 'fiction' to achieve a particular end.
- You may feel that what is most obvious about guilt in some narratives is its apparent absence. The criminals in Browning's dramatic monologues never express any remorse for their crimes. Peter Grimes is horribly conscious of the ways in which he is being punished for his past deeds, but he seldom hints at any real acknowledgement that he is being justly punished.

The significance of settings

It is important to consider contextual factors when examining the characters' sense of guilt. Narratives operate within particular contexts of time and place, which significantly influence the ways in which we read texts. You should consider those elements in the context of the production of the text that might affect your response as a twenty-first-century reader.

Link

For more on this idea, see Chapter 30 in the NEA section.

The *settings* of the above texts are very different. Shakespeare's plays *Macbeth* and *Hamlet* are set in a historical period before the Norman Conquest, at a time when Scotland and Denmark were often at war. The characters of both plays are influenced by a battlefield morality, where warrior virtues are held in high esteem. Both Macbeth and Hamlet's father are praised for their abilities as military leaders. However, another morality is also at work in these plays. The killing of a king would at that time have been seen as a crime against God, as well as humanity, and religious beliefs lie behind the guilt which the characters display.

Brighton Rock is set in Brighton in the 1930s. The battlefields here are the pubs, streets and racetrack, and the combatants are the criminal gangs who work those areas. Again, a twisted kind of morality operates in this world: you are expected to show loyalty to the members of your gang and keep your mouth shut when questioned by the law. Pinkie's feeling of guilt – if it is guilt – is driven by something else: his Roman Catholic faith. He is caught between a faint hope of repentance and the greater certainty of his own damnation.

'Peter Grimes' is set in rural East Anglia in the early nineteenth century. The central protagonist's crimes are committed against the community in which he lives, but there is a strong sense of Christian retribution at work. The tale emphasizes how as a young boy, he mocked religion, 'when the father in his Bible read / he in contempt and anger left the shed'. A priest is finally brought to hear the dying man's confession, but this confession is largely incoherent, 'a madman's tale'. In his final days he is tortured by spirits, his guilt perhaps metaphorically represented by the supernatural beings whose existence he has previously scorned.

The world of *Atonement* is almost wholly secular. The characters' actions and motivations are often affected by their social status, and their acute consciousness of that status. In the background is the story of another conflict: the Dunkirk evacuation. This episode from World War II provides the counterpoint of a larger and more murderous crime than Briony's – the crime of war.

In crime stories, therefore, guilt can be:

- central to the narrative and **denouement**
- fully, partly, or not at all acknowledged by the criminal
- associated with solitude and isolation
- connected to religious, especially Christian, feeling
- significantly connected to other moral attitudes of the society within which the crime occurs.

Key term

Denouement. The final scene or chapter of a story, when all the loose ends of the plot are tied up.

Activity

Bearing in mind the ideas about guilt discussed above, look at your own texts and:

- consider to what extent your response to the criminals is affected by their expressions of guilt
- decide the degree to which the settings are significant in terms of understanding the nature of the criminals' guilt.

Punishments administered by society and the law

Many crime stories make a distinction between 'law' and 'justice'. 'Justice' can be seen as an abstract moral concept, whereas 'law' refers to a series of rules and punishments set down by specific human societies. Revenge tragedies and American 'hard-boiled' crime stories often operate in societies that are themselves corrupt, and thus can deliver little genuine justice. In Raymond Chandler's *The Long Goodbye*, a lawyer, Sewell Endicott, tells the detective, Philip Marlowe:

> The law isn't justice. It's a very imperfect mechanism. If you press exactly the right buttons and are also lucky, justice may show up in the answer. A mechanism was all the law was ever intended to be.

Extension activity

Raymond Chandler (1888–1959) is recognized as one of the greatest writers of detective fiction. Reading novels such as *The Big Sleep*; *Farewell, My Lovely*; and *The Lady in the Lake* – mostly set in California – will give you an insight into a very distinctive and influential form of crime writing.

The Long Goodbye also explores an aspect of crime and punishment that many stories fight shy of: the nature of prisons. 'Have you any idea what it's like inside?' Robbie asks Briony in *Atonement*. She doesn't know, but neither do we, the readers, in the sense that the novel leaves that long part of Robbie's story untold. In *The Long Goodbye*, however, we are given some insight into prison life, through the experience of Marlowe:

> In jail a man has no personality. He is a minor disposal problem and a few entries on reports. Nobody cares who loves or hates him, what he looks like, what he did with his life. Nobody reacts to him unless he gives trouble. Nobody abuses him. All that is asked of him is that he go quietly to the right cell and remain quiet when he gets there [...] A good jail is one of the quietest places in the world. You could walk through the average cell block at night and look in through the bars and see a huddle of brown blanket, or a head of hair, or a pair of eyes looking at nothing. You might hear a snore. Once in a long while you might hear a nightmare. The life in a jail is in suspension, without purpose or meaning.

In *Oliver Twist*, few institutions emerge with any credit. When Oliver is in the workhouse, he is at the mercy of the overseers, 'the board'; when he is arrested for theft, he is brought before the equally callous Mr Fang (the police magistrate). His period of imprisonment allows the narrator to make this comment on the nature of police cells:

> In our station-houses, men and women are every night confined on the most trivial *charges* – the word is worth noting – in dungeons, compared with which, those in Newgate, occupied by the most atrocious felons, tried, found guilty, and under sentence of death, are palaces. Let anyone who doubts this, compare the two.

However repellent Fagin is, the description of his last hours in the condemned cell, under the shadow of 'the hideous apparatus of death', emphasizes the horrors of capital punishment.

In 'Peter Grimes', through their casual indifference to the suffering of his boys, the townsfolk are shown as being complicit in his crimes: 'None enquired how Peter used the rope / Or what the bruise that made the stripling stoop.' When, belatedly, they seek to exact justice, they are presented as a vengeful mob:

> And there they seized him – a distemper'd man: –
> Him we received, and to a parish-bed,
> Follow'd and cursed, the groaning man was led.

The mob as representatives of a flawed and compromised authority also makes an appearance at various points in *Oliver Twist*. During the flight of Sikes, for example, the pursuing mob of townsfolk are described in terms which suggest that they have much in common with the man they are hunting:

> On pressed the people from the front – on, on, on, in a strong struggling current of angry faces, with here and there a glaring torch to light them up, and show them out in all their wrath and passion. The houses on the opposite side of the ditch had been entered by the mob; sashes were drawn up, or torn bodily out; there were tiers and tiers of faces in every window; cluster upon cluster of people clinging to every housetop.

The uncontrolled emotions of the crowd parallel those of Sikes during his murderous passion. They also show no respect for property. In some ways they are described as eager spectators in a particularly brutal form of street theatre. Dickens is inviting readers to draw another unsettling parallel, between the standpoints of the mob and that of the reader. Both can be seen as gaining pleasure from the idea of pursuit and capture, in which the person pursued is denied any human sympathy, becoming merely the object of a thrilling chase.

The 'justice' handed out by the Ancient Mariner's shipmates, when each 'cursed me with his eye' has to be seen in the context of their earlier reactions to his shooting of the albatross. They initially condemn the Mariner: 'I had done a hellish thing / And it would work them woe', but then almost immediately express approval of his crime: ''Twas right, said they, such birds to slay / That bring the fog and mist'. If the Mariner's morality is presented as flawed, we are not offered any alternative source of human moral judgement that is convincing, until we meet with the character of the Hermit towards the end of the tale.

At an early stage in *Hamlet*, the audience are warned that 'something is rotten in the state of Denmark', and as the play unfolds it is increasingly difficult to have confidence in the operation of human justice. Representatives of the state, such as Polonius, Rosencrantz and Guildenstern, and Osric, emerge as morally compromised through their association with power.

You may have noticed that some crime stories have very little to say about any form of punishment once the criminal has been unmasked. At the end of Browning's 'My Last Duchess', the Duke looks likely to carry on exactly as he has before; Porphyria's lover congratulates himself that 'God has not said a word' against his crime; and in *The Murder of Roger Ackroyd* and *Brighton Rock*, the deaths of the criminals occur before they can be bought to trial. This makes a striking contrast with 'The Rime of the Ancient Mariner', in which an extended description of the Mariner's penance dominates the poem.

Activity

The question of punishment in crime stories is therefore seldom a simple one, and you may feel at times that some unsettling moral questions are raised by the ways in which punishment operates within the text. For example, consider the following.

1. How much confidence do we have in the forces of law and order as represented within the world of the story?
2. Do law and justice at times seem rather separate things?
3. Does the nature of punishment draw some disturbing parallels between the criminal and those who hand out 'justice'?
4. It is in the nature of crime stories that the reader is imaginatively engaged in the pursuit and punishment of the criminal. Are we at times, as readers, placed in a rather uncomfortable position because of this?

Summary

In this chapter you have examined the complex morality that operates in many crime stories, and have seen that:

- it is not always easy to make a confident judgement about questions of guilt and responsibility
- the nature of the punishment handed out to the criminal is at times presented as troubling, and we may even sympathize with the motivations of the criminals
- it is not always easy to decide what we feel about the victim
- the settings of the stories, in terms of both time and place, are always significant in determining our response to the moral issues that have been raised.

20 Crime writing and poetry

In this chapter you will:

- explore the nature and effect of some crime stories that are written in verse.

Key term

Ballad. A long poem that tells a story, and usually has a fast pace, with repetition a common feature.

There is a long history of telling crime stories through verse. From traditional folk songs, to border-country **ballads**, to the city-based broadside ballads that told tales of convicted criminals, poetry has proved to be a popular and successful narrative form for crime fiction.

What are the features of poetry that make it so suitable for crime stories?

- Poetry is a concentrated and condensed form, in terms of both language and structure.
- Poets use patterns of rhythm and rhyme to create relationships between words that rely on sound as well as meaning.
- These two effects have always made poetry a suitable form for oral narrative, and many crime stories in the past were related to a listening audience.
- Poetry is an effective medium for conveying intense feelings and emotions, which are important elements of crime stories.

When you discuss the distinctive features of poetry, check that you do more than simply identify them: analyse those occasions when rhymes, metaphors or images are used to drive home key ideas, and consider exactly which effects are achieved through the placing of key words, in individual stanzas or within the broader structure of the poem.

Ballads

Ballads are verse narratives that tell dramatic and often tragic stories. Many traditional ballads were composed to be sung, and were passed down by word of mouth; their relatively simple language and repetitive structure make them easier to recall. Ballads have the following features:

- They tend to be largely impersonal in terms of narrative voice; only occasionally does the narrator express direct judgement on the characters.
- Action and event dominate the stories. Dialogue also plays an important part.
- Violence in ballads is often both extreme and only partially explained. The guilty may be punished, but this does not always happen. The sufferings of the victims are frequently the focus of the tale.
- Many ballads are based on myth and legend, but are at times essentially true-crime narratives.

Activity

1. To what extent and how significantly do ballad features operate in your poetry text?
2. Explore the **significance** of the features of crime writing in the following ballad.

The Cruel Mother

(A traditional ballad, possibly of seventeenth-century origin)

There was a lady that lived in York
All alone and a loney-O
She proved with child by her father's clerk
Down by a greenwood sidey-O.
As she was walking down her father's lawn,
All alone and a loney-O
She said Mother Mary, pity me,
Down by a greenwood sidey-O.

As she was walking down her father's lawn,
All alone and a loney-O
It was there her three fine sons were born,
Down by a greenwood sidey-O.

She pulled out her little penknife,
All alone and a loney-O
And robbed her sweet sons of their lives,
Down by a greenwood sidey-O.

She's dug a grave by the light of the moon,
All alone and a loney-O
And there she's buried her sweet babes in
Down by a greenwood sidey-O.

As she was out one summer's morn,
All alone and a loney-O
She saw three boys play bat and ball,
Down by a greenwood sidey-O.

O my fine boys, if you were mine,
All alone and a loney-O
I'd dress you up in silk so fine,
Down by a greenwood sidey-O.

O mother dear, when we were thine,
All alone and a loney-O
You did not dress us in silk so fine,
Down by a greenwood sidey-O.

You pulled out your little penknife,
All alone and a loney-O
And took away our own sweet lives,
Down by a greenwood sidey-O.

O cursed mother, hell is deep,
All alone and a loney-O
And there you'll enter step by step,
Down by a greenwood sidey-O.

Commentary

Several characteristic elements of crime writing are evident in this ballad. There is a crime at the heart of the story – infanticide. Most societies consider the murder of a child to be a particularly horrible crime, but in the seventeenth century it was thought of as an urgent social problem because of the number of cases where desperate women took extreme steps to get rid of unwanted children. An Act of 1624 distinguished infanticide from other forms of murder.

The motive for the crime is not explicitly stated, but it would seem to involve the familiar contexts of class and family that operate within crime stories. The woman has been made pregnant by an employee of her father; we may assume that her family would have seen this as a wholly unsuitable relationship. In this version of the ballad, the crime is shown as a brutal one, tersely described. Motivation is clearly passionate, but left under-explored. We are left to guess at the exact nature of the woman's state of mind. As often with ballads, character is presented as slightly stereotypical and one-dimensional.

The victims are characterized as 'fine' and 'sweet': the innocence of the children is emphasized to arouse the audience's sympathy. Setting is carefully used. The precise placing of the story in York suggests that this ballad might have been based on a real event. A further setting in time and place, a grave by moonlight, introduces familiar features of the **gothic genre** into the story. In sharp contrast, it is a summer morning when the woman meets three seemingly ghostly figures. Characteristically, the real and unreal worlds overlap.

The ballad moves on at pace, assisted by the swiftly moving quatrains and refrains; it approaches its conclusion through the use of a passage of carefully shaped dialogue. What are we meant to infer by the woman's words? Partially acknowledged guilt? A bitter sense of what the children's future could have been? Either way, the response to what she says is unflinching. The sons' reply repeats some of the earlier phrases from the ballad, thus emphasizing the brutal nature of her crime. The ballad concludes with a judgement that reflects a religious view of punishment as extending into the afterlife.

Ballads in later literature

Kate Atkinson's *When Will There Be Good News?* makes repeated use of ballad references. The chapter entitled 'Sanctuary' involves a scene involving Reggie's criminal and predatory brother Billy, after which the lines from the nursery rhyme 'Hark! Hark! The dogs do bark, the beggars are coming to town' tellingly end the chapter. The next chapter, ominously, is entitled 'To Brig O' Dread Thou Com'st at Last', a line from 'The Lyke-Wake Dirge', a ballad traditionally sung during a funeral procession. In this chapter, Jackson Brodie catches a wrong train and in doing so takes a journey towards a fatal rail crash. A different line from 'The Lyke-Wake Dirge' comes into Brodie's mind as he thinks about going to the buffet car: 'If ever thou gavest meat or drink, the fire shall never make thee shrink. If meat or drink thou ne'er gav'st nane, the fire will burn thee to the bare bane.' 'That damned dirge', he thinks to himself.

When Will There Be Good News? repeatedly forces us to confront the nature and consequences of death; the way it weaves ballad references into the fabric of the narrative helps to establish the timeless nature of the subject matter.

A famous literary ballad is 'The Ballad of Reading Gaol', written by Oscar Wilde about the execution in 1896 of Charles Wooldridge (sentenced to death for the murder of his wife). The poem describes the reaction of the other prisoners in the gaol to the impending execution and also offers a lengthy and anguished debate about the relationship between the law, justice and mercy.

Activity

Read the opening stanzas below from 'The Ballad of Reading Gaol'. What familiar features of ballads do you notice here?

He did not wear his scarlet coat,
For blood and wine are red,
And blood and wine were on his hands
When they found him with the dead,
The poor dead woman whom he loved,
And murdered in her bed.

He walked amongst the Trial men
In a suit of shabby gray;
A cricket cap was on his head,
And his step seemed light and gay;
But I never saw a man who looked
So wistfully at the day.

I never saw a man who looked
With such a wistful eye
Upon that little tent of blue
Which prisoners call the sky,
And at every drifting cloud that went
With sails of silver by.

I walked, with other souls in pain,
Within another ring
And was wondering if the man had done
A great or little thing,
When a voice behind me whispered low,
'That fellow's got to swing.'

Dear Christ! The very prison walls
Suddenly seemed to reel,
And the sky above my head became
Like a casque of scorching steel;
And, though I was a soul in pain,
My pain I could not feel.

I only knew what hunted thought
Quickened his step, and why
He looked upon the garish day
With such a wistful eye;
The man had killed the thing he loved,
And so he had to die.

Commentary

You will have noticed here some familiar characteristics of ballad literature. The repetition of key words and ideas (such as 'blood', 'the sky', and 'souls') helps to establish a sense of inevitability, a remorseless movement towards the prisoner's death. Contrasting colours carry symbolic significance, and the setting is carefully used to contrast the freedom of the sky and the enclosed prison yard. We are drawn into the man's experience along with the 'other souls in pain' and made to anticipate and imagine the process of hanging. The central idea that 'each man kills the thing he loves' is developed in the famous stanza that follows this extract.

Extension activity

Read the remainder of the poem and explore the contexts of the poem's production, especially Wilde's own experience as a prisoner at Reading Gaol between 1895 and 1897. You may like to compare elements of the ballad with the next poem dealt with in this chapter, 'The Rime of the Ancient Mariner'.

'The Rime of the Ancient Mariner'

In 'The Rime of the Ancient Mariner', Coleridge makes use of the traditional ballad stanza form, quatrains of alternating three- and four-stress lines with an ABAB rhyme scheme. At times, Coleridge modifies this form to give emphasis to particular moments in the narrative. It can be argued that this flexibility of method is paralleled by the shifting and ambiguous morality of the poem. This aspect of the text will be considered later in this section.

The tale also incorporates many of the elements of crime stories with which you should by now be familiar:

- a crime is committed, which shapes the narrative that follows
- the crime can be seen as an offence against religious and moral laws
- the motive of the criminal is not wholly explicable
- much of the narrative is concerned with the consequences of the criminal act
- there is considerable focus on the nature and expression of guilt
- the story opens up questions of justice and injustice in terms of the suffering and punishment that different people endure.

Activity

Read the following extract from 'The Rime of the Ancient Mariner'. In what different ways might this part of the crime story be interpreted?

In this extract, the Ancient Mariner forces a Wedding-Guest to listen to the story of his strange voyage. He tells how his ship arrived at the land of mist and snow. An albatross came through the fog and was at first greeted with joy, but was then shot by the Mariner.

PART THE SECOND

The Sun now rose upon the right:
Out of the sea came he,
Still hid in mist, and on the left
Went down into the sea.

And the good south wind still blew behind,
But no sweet bird did follow,
Nor any day for food or play
Came to the mariners' hollo!

And I had done a hellish thing,
And it would work them woe:
For all averred, I had killed the bird
That made the breeze to blow.
Ah wretch! said they, the bird to slay
That made the breeze to blow!

Nor dim nor red, like God's own head,
The glorious Sun uprist:
Then all averred, I had killed the bird
That brought the fog and mist.
'Twas right, said they, such birds to slay,
That bring the fog and mist.

The fair breeze blew, the white foam flew,
The furrow followed free;
We were the first that ever burst
Into that silent sea!

Down dropt the breeze, the sails dropt down,
'Twas sad as sad could be
And we did speak only to break
The silence of the sea!

All in a hot and copper sky,
The bloody Sun, at noon,
Right up above the mast did stand,
No bigger than the Moon.

Day after day, day after day,
We stuck, nor breath nor motion;
As idle as a painted ship
Upon a painted ocean.

Water, water everywhere,
And all the boards did shrink:
Water, water, everywhere,
Nor any drop to drink.

An illustration by Gustav Doré, in which the dead albatross has been hung around the Mariner's neck

Link

For more about ecocriticism see Chapter 32.

Key terms

Alienated / Alienation. Alienation involves being made to feel distanced, isolated, even hostile. People can experience alienation when they feel that their lives lack full meaning, because they are just part of a process.

Dramatic monologue. A poem where a character speaks her or his thoughts to an imagined, silent listener.

Link

For more on the concept of **alienation**, look at the NEA chapter on Marxism and feminism (Chapter 28).

Commentary

This part of the poem deals with the immediate consequences of the Mariner's crime. In some ways it justifies Wordsworth's comment in his note to the 1800 edition of *Lyrical Ballads* that the principal character in the poem 'does not act, but is continually acted upon'. For much of this section there is little movement, indeed this is an aspect of the punishment visited upon the ship. In the penultimate stanza of the extract, time seems to be suspended, signified by the repetition of the phrase 'day after day'; the ship is 'stuck', and the sun stands still above the mast. This unnatural stagnation is emphasized by the simile that compares the ship to something fictional, unreal, merely 'painted'.

An ecocritical reading of the poem might emphasize this particular consequence of the Mariner's act. The shooting of the albatross was a crime against nature; the initial response of the other mariners acknowledges the interrelationship of bird and environment: 'the bird [...] That made the breeze to blow'. Later, however, they reverse that judgement, using words that ironically echo their original viewpoint: 'Twas right, said they, such birds to slay'. The internal rhyme of 'they' and 'slay' drives home the significance of their abandonment of natural sympathy, replaced by a homocentric view that sees nature as something simply there for human use and benefit.

Another interpretation of the mariners' position might emphasize their **alienation**. The purpose of the mariners' journey is never fully clear, nor is there any evidence of a hierarchy of command on board the ship. The mariners seem to have been taken away from any form of supportive social grouping (perhaps represented by the wedding at the start of the poem). We are told that they 'Were the first that ever burst / Into that silent sea'. This might suggest that the objective of the voyage is discovery, but it might also be imperialist, commercial or even military. Any of these purposes might be considered, in eco-critical terms, crimes against a world that is simply being regarded as something to plunder.

This general uncertainty about the nature of the voyage is paralleled by the nature of the punishment given to the mariners and the associated moral message of the tale. The connection between the crime and the punishment seems a little arbitrary at times. It is the Mariner who kills the bird, but his shipmates who are delivered to Death. There also seems to be a distinction between the positions taken by the Mariner as narrator and the gloss that Coleridge added to the 1817 text. It is the gloss that explicitly states that the Mariner 'inhospitably' kills the 'pious' bird. The gloss is similarly unambiguous about the other mariners' guilt. We are told that by justifying the Mariner's act, they 'make themselves accomplices in the crime'. The main text is never so explicit in delivering moral judgement.

Other forms of poetry

Although ballads are a popular choice of poetic form when telling crime stories, other types of poem are also often used. The next two poems you will look at are 'Peter Grimes', part of a long verse narrative called *The Borough* by George Crabbe, and 'The Laboratory', a **dramatic monologue** by Robert Browning.

'Peter Grimes'

The story of Peter Grimes, like 'The Rime of the Ancient Mariner', deals with the relationship between humanity and nature, and that between the individual and society. Crabbe gives his tale a rural setting in which the fishing community lives in some harmony with the natural environment. Grimes's crimes shatter that local harmony, and their effects are shown in the ways in which the natural world begins to seem hostile and threatening:

> 'The small stream, confined in narrow bound,
> Ran with a dull, unvaried, sadd'ning sound:
> Where all, presented to the eye or ear,
> Oppress'd the soul with misery, grief and fear.
>
> ('Peter Grimes', lines 201–204)

Another way in which 'Peter Grimes' resembles 'The Rime of the Ancient Mariner' is in Crabbe's use of a range of points of view to explore the troubled individual conscience. At different times we see the perspectives of Grimes's father, his employees, the townsfolk, the seamen's wives, and the 'idly curious' summer visitors. Towards the end of the story, Peter Grimes, who has been behaving in an increasingly strange manner, has been seized by his neighbours and begins to tell his story to a priest. The beginning of this story is given below.

'I'll tell you all', says Peter Grimes, just before this passage begins. We now have a temporal shift; the narrative goes back in time, and we are given a participant's view of events that we have previously witnessed only as curious outsiders. The passage deals with the guilty suffering of the murderer, Grimes; his punishment is shown as being both internal and extended.

Activity

Read the following extract from 'Peter Grimes' and compare its treatment of crime and punishment with that of any other crime story you have read.

> 'Twas one hot noon, all silent, still, serene,
> No living being had I lately seen;
> I paddled up and down and dipp'd my net,
> But (such his pleasure) I could nothing get, –
> A father's pleasure, when his toil was done,
> To plague and torture thus an only son!
> And so I sat and look'd upon the stream,
> How it ran on, and felt as in a dream:
> But dream it was not; no! – I fix'd my eyes
> On the mid stream and saw the spirits rise;
> I saw my father on the water stand,
> And hold a thin pale boy in either hand;
> And there they glided ghastly on the top
> Of the salt flood, and never touch'd a drop:
> I would have struck them, but they knew th'intent,
> And smiled upon the oar, and down they went.

'Now, from that day, whenever I began
To dip my net, there stood the hard old man –
He and those boys: I humbled me and pray'd
They would be gone; – they heeded not, but stay'd:
Nor could I turn, nor would the boat go by,
But gazing on the spirits, there was I:
They bade me leap to death, but I was loth to die:
And every day, as sure as day arose
Would these three spirits meet me ere the close;
To hear and mark them daily was my doom,
And "Come," they said, with weak, sad voices, "come",
To row away with all my strength I try'd,
But there were they, hard by me in the tide,
The three unbodied forms – and "Come," still "come" they cried.'

('Peter Grimes', lines 298–327)

Commentary

The following comparisons can be made with 'The Rime of the Ancient Mariner' and *Oliver Twist*.

- As in the 'Ancient Mariner', time and motion seem to freeze, as the guilty man finds himself fixed in one place during 'one hot noon, all silent, still, serene'. Time and events repeat themselves: 'every day, as sure as day arose'. The Mariner is similarly stuck 'Day after day, day after day'.
- Again, as in the case of the Mariner, isolation is described as being an essential condition of the guilty man. Sikes and Fagin, in *Oliver Twist*, are also depicted as being very much alone in their final moments.
- The criminal's guilt manifests itself through the appearance of dreams or visions. Here Grimes sees 'the spirits rise'. They act in unnatural ways, standing on the water and gliding over the surface. The Mariner is subjected to the terrors of Death and Life-in-death, whose boat also moves silently and unnaturally over the water. While on the run from the law, Sikes sees visions of Nancy; Nancy herself earlier talks of a coffin being carried close to her on the street. When told that this is a common occurrence, she replies, '*Real ones* [...] This was not.' In all these cases, the victim of these ghostly manifestations is described as being helpless, unable to resist. Note now the broken rhythm of line 324 (And 'Come,' they said, with weak, sad voices, 'come') and the length of line 327 allow for the insistent repetition of the appeal to 'come'.
- A significant difference between the case of Grimes and that of the Mariner is that the latter is visited by obviously spectral and supernatural beings; the spirits that afflict Grimes seem to represent his family and past employees. The family is a familiar context in crime stories.
- The attempt of criminals to pray is often ineffective. The Mariner 'looked to Heaven, and tried to pray', but cannot do so. Fagin, in the condemned cell, drives away those who try to offer him religious consolation. Grimes prays that the spirits 'would be gone', but 'they heeded not, but stay'd'.

Extension activity

During his life Crabbe enjoyed much popular acclaim, but his work also attracted a mixed critical reception. A review in the *Christian Observer* in 1811 argued that Crabbe was over-fond of 'dealing in low life', and that 'no gleam of hope is allowed to pierce the dungeon which Mr Crabbe exhibits'. Read some more of *The Borough* and consider to what extent you think this view of his poetry is a just one.

'The Laboratory'

Robert Browning's 'The Laboratory' is a dramatic monologue spoken by an anonymous woman who has come to an apothecary's laboratory in order to buy poison with which to kill her love rival. The subtitle '*Ancien Régime*' suggests that the poem is set in France before the French Revolution of 1789. As with many of Browning's poems set in Renaissance Europe, the world in which the action takes place appears to be cultured, but is ruthless and corrupt. Some critics have suggested that the central character is based on Marie D'Aubray, the Marquise de Brinvilliers (1630–76), a notorious poisoner.

Ideas about these contexts need to be carefully woven into your arguments rather than being bolted onto them, and need to clearly assist your interpretation of the text. Stories such as 'The Laboratory' invite careful consideration of contextual material.

Activity

Read the opening and closing few stanzas of 'The Laboratory', below, and consider the significance of some possible contexts in terms of a reading of the poem as a crime story.

I

Now that I, tying thy glass mask tightly,
May gaze thro' these faint smokes curling whitely,
As thou pliest thy trade in this devil's-smithy –
Which is the poison to poison her, prithee?

II

He is with her, and they know that I know
Where they are, what they do: they believe my tears flow
While they laugh, laugh at me, at me fled to the drear
Empty church, to pray God in, for them! -- I am here.

III

Grind away, moisten and mash up thy paste,
Pound at thy powder, – I am not in haste!
Better sit thus, and observe thy strange things,
Than go where men wait me and dance at the King's.

***

X

Not that I bid you spare her the pain;
Let death be felt and the proof remain:
Brand, burn up, bite into its grace –
He is sure to remember her dying face!

XI

Is it done? Take my mask off! Nay, be not morose;
It kills her, and this prevents seeing it close:
The delicate droplet, my whole fortune's fee!
If it hurts her, beside, can it ever hurt me?

XII

Now, take all my jewels, gorge gold to your fill,
You may kiss me, old man, on my mouth if you will!
But brush this dust off me, lest horror it brings
Ere I know it – next moment I dance at the King's!

Commentary

One way of looking at 'The Laboratory' is to consider the features of different genres that seem to be present in the poem. In terms of crime stories, you might have identified the familiar elements of a central crime, a victim, a criminal, a motive and a wider social context, the morals and priorities of which help to shape the action. You might also have seen the poem as a gothic story – set in a laboratory, featuring a sinister scientist, involving extreme emotions, and so on. Both of these approaches will make it easy to identify the woman as villainous, but if – as could be the case – the poem is viewed as a love story or even a form of fairy story, that might encourage rather different interpretations. The story also deals with the evil uses to which scientific knowledge can be put: a frequent subject of science fiction. From this perspective the story has a timeless, or even rather modern quality.

The *ancien régime* setting clearly has a powerful impact on the story. The narrative focus switches obsessively between the different places that force themselves into the narrator's imagination. We start in the laboratory, but move to wherever 'He is with her'. The narrator then imagines 'them' imagining her alone and praying for 'them' in a church. This is a society in which the forms and rituals of religion matter; some readings have argued that the speaker is a nun, thus adding another intriguing element to her jealousy. The references to dancing 'at the King's' acts as a refrain, focusing our attention on a very public, social world, in striking contrast with the secret, claustrophobic environment of the laboratory.

Time and place are important settings here, and the question of time has earlier been shown to be a significant feature of crime stories. The narrative of the complete poem constantly moves back and forward in time. We begin in a dramatic present where the narrator watches the apothecary at work. Her imagination then switches to a parallel present where her lover and rival are together; her use of a frenzied sequence of pronouns – 'He', 'her', 'I', 'they', 'me' – testifies to her obsession. We go back to the present, then to an imagined future where she takes a terrible revenge, then back to 'only last night' (stanza IX), when in a frenzy of jealousy she spied on the two lovers, before a final malevolent anticipation of the moment when she will dance in triumph 'at the King's'.

Summary

In this chapter you have:

- looked at the distinctive contribution which poetry makes to crime literature
- examined some elements of the ballad form
- considered different interpretations of 'The Rime of the Ancient Mariner'
- examined 'Peter Grimes' as a crime story
- looked at some contexts that affect readings of 'The Laboratory'.

Component 2
Texts and genres

Option 2B:
Elements of political and social protest writing

21 An introduction to political and social protest writing

This chapter will:

- consider definitions of political and social protest writing
- introduce some of the key elements of the genre.

Key term

Bildungsroman. A German word referring to a story of growing up, and being educated, in the most general sense of the word.

Notions of genre

As you will have found from your previous studies, genre provides a useful method of categorizing texts. Genre helps to create expectations, and provides a loose framework by which we can begin to judge and understand literature. You will have realized from your study of tragedy or comedy that genres evolve over time, and different writers make use of **conventions** in various ways.

This course regards genre as a broad, inclusive notion; any text in this component could be classified under several headings. *The Kite Runner*, for example, has elements of the adventure story, post-colonial fiction and the **bildungsroman** (see Chapter 26 page 208), among others. In this component, you are primarily exploring your texts as examples of literary political and social protest writing; you are being asked to consider what your texts have to say about issues of power and powerlessness. This chapter will outline some of the features of the genre, but it is important to remember that this is not a checklist to fit all of the texts you are studying all of the time.

What is political and social protest writing?

Although this genre may initially seem new to you, it is likely that you already have a good knowledge of this category. If you have read William Golding's *Lord of the Flies*, you will be familiar with its depiction of social organization and anarchical violence. Likewise, you may have read *Othello* or *Richard II* and enjoyed the study of machination and control. Power struggles abound in popular fiction too: Roald Dahl's *Matilda* focuses on the corrupt control of comic tyrant Miss Trunchbull; *Star Wars* presents rebellion against an evil empire and the ultimate destruction of the Death Star; and *The Hunger Games* is a tale of war, defiance and self-preservation in spite of the Capitol's oppression. These texts and the ones you will study have at their core the issues of power and powerlessness.

Political and social-protest writing offers the reader narratives of dominance, oppression, rebellion and resistance, and has something to say about the way in which societies are organized. It is concerned in part with aspects of gender, class and economic status, in both public and domestic settings. As you read your texts, you should begin by considering how power is represented in them, the effect this has on the characters, and what **significances** arise.

The representation of power

The stories, places and time settings in your texts may range from the historical to the futuristic. You may feel that you recognize the scenarios and issues, but it is essential to remember that they are fictional **representations**, rather than reality. Authors organize their narratives to present power struggles in a way that suits their purposes and the ideas they wish to convey.

Activity

Some of the issues relevant to your study are represented in George Morland's painting called *Execrable Human Traffick* (see below). As its title suggests, it was intended to draw attention to the iniquities of the slave trade in West Africa.

1. What does the painting reveal about conflict, economics and gender?
2. Think about how the artist has organized the image to draw attention to these issues.

◀ **What does George Morland's painting *Execrable Human Traffick* have to say about conflict, economics and gender?**

Commentary

The scene above features a conflict in which race and economics are central. The artist has arranged the material so our attention is drawn to the group of three men in the centre left of the picture, where an obvious power struggle is occurring. Physical coercion is apparent. There is a clear imbalance in power, and although it may seem that this is about white oppression, the black man with the earrings on the right is accompanied by a musket-wielding assistant, perhaps suggesting that a murky trade is being done with the sailors. Other details such as the ships on the left suggest the economic backdrop and invite us to view this as a narrative of financially motivated oppression.

Perhaps the most striking aspect is the human cost of this political struggle. The heart-breaking story at the centre of the painting is the separation of a family, echoing a familiar feature of political texts: the very things that make us human – love and relationships – are threatened by political conflict. There is a sense in which the natural world is being invaded by the corrupt human world and compromised by greed. There is no sense of resistance in this image, only subjugation.

Key term

Agency. The capacity or power to act, rather than be passive.

In terms of gender representation, some of the men in this picture are active characters who occupy familiar roles as aggressor and organizer. They have **agency** and occupy antagonistic roles, being associated with violence. All the white men appear to be touching, gesturing or physically intimidating, in ways which suggest control and dominance. The slaves by contrast are passive, but the need for their subjugation casts them as dangerous. The solitary female is portrayed as a maternal figure whose body language suggests passivity. She lacks agency and is a victim, but interestingly she is placed at the heart of the picture, perhaps asking us to see this as an exploration of the effects of male dominance on the female.

Did you know?

The term 'politics' means 'of the city'. It is Greek in origin, and derives ultimately from *polis* ('city'). Aristotle's eight books entitled *Politics* were concerned with the organization of human communities.

Elements of political and social protest writing

Literature about political and social protest seems a fairly recent classification, and while it is tempting to try to identify the 'first' text of this type, the question of when a genre 'begins' is not really a helpful one. Texts from any age or genre might contain political elements. This course is interested in *elements* of the genre, so you are looking at some *aspects* of political and social protest writing, such as dominance, rebellion, powerlessness, and how these are represented in a variety of stories over time and across genres. You will examine how writers use and represent these elements. In the next activity, you will use a story from the Bible to identify some of the elements of the genre.

Activity

Read the following summary of an episode in Numbers 16 from the Old Testament. What elements of political writing are shown in the text?

- Korah, Abiram, Dathan and 250 other Israelites confront Moses and Aaron, leaders of their community. They want to know why Moses and Aaron are in charge. The protestors seem to want to take over the priesthood.
- Moses tells Korah that God will decide. When God appears the next day, the ground opens and the three main protestors and their families are swallowed up.
- God sets fire to the other 250 men. Moses and Aaron are mistakenly blamed for their deaths by the community. God is annoyed at this, so he creates a plague. Before the plague is over, 14,700 people die.

Commentary

This is a dramatic story illustrating some key ideas about political writing. Here are some ideas you may have noted:

- The central issue is one of power. The narrative is set in motion by a dispute over who rules the community. The dispute is about how society is organized.
- The protest is a form of rebellion, one that involves people grouping together to try to change things. A direct challenge to powerful people is made by the powerless.
- The story is about questioning authority – in this case, the highest power. God's dominance is asserted. A controlling entity is present.

- Punishment and death feature heavily as a way of resolving conflict. The narrative is complicated by confusion; conflict leads to conflict.
- Men are responsible for the dispute – they are the instigators and the victims. Pride and ambition are central. Women and children are merely victims. The individual suffers.
- The ending leaves the reader with some interpretive work to do. There is a victor, but what are we meant to understand by the story? Is this simply a story of good and evil? If so, who is the villain? Is there a hero?

Gender and domestic politics

Not all texts deal with politics on a grand scale. Many writers are interested in the way power structures operate in a domestic setting. Texts from different time periods can give us cause to reflect on the changing values of relationships.

One way of interpreting Shakespeare's *The Taming of the Shrew* is to read it as a narrative in which Katharina, the rebellious 'shrew' of the title, is 'tamed' by Petruchio and turned into an acceptable wife. Despite her outspoken nature, there are times when she falls silent. For some audiences, her bridal humiliation and subsequent taming may feel uncomfortable. After their wedding, Petruchio sees her as a possession, observing:

> I will be master of what is mine own:
> She is my goods, my chattels. She is my house,
> My household-stuff, my field, my barn,
> My horse, my ox, my ass, my anything
>
> *The Taming of the Shrew*, 3.2.218–221

The idea that Kate is owned, controlled and changed by Petruchio is at odds with what many, but not all, modern readers would consider 'normal'. The accepted power structure of marriage and conventional ideas of femininity in the world of the play suggest an unequal division of power, to the female's detriment.

Did you know?

In late medieval times, the Church instituted marriage laws which insisted on monogamy and criminalized non-marital and same-sex intercourse. Sex for any purpose other than procreation was deemed sinful.

Narrative structures

Narratives in political and social protest literature are usually organized around conflict between opposing (often unequal) forces. As we have seen, sometimes there is obvious, open conflict between people or forces accompanied by warfare, violence or threat. In some texts, the conflict manifests itself in frustration and subjugation. The narrative can be seen as a journey from repression towards escape, yet whether the protagonist's struggle ends in victory depends on the point the writer is trying to make. It is not always the case that sympathies are allied with the rebel. Shakespeare's *Henry IV Part I* shows Hotspur's rebellion against the king, but depending on your view, sympathy may be directed towards Prince Hal.

The endings of texts can signal victory, but are often muted rather than celebratory. Nonetheless, endings are a useful place to start when considering the **significances** of the political story.

Activity

Consider how conflict and resolution operate in your texts. You may wish to think about:

- the nature of the conflicts, and where power initially resides
- crisis points in the narrative where conflict reaches a peak
- how much control the protagonist has over proceedings
- what happens at the end of the text: who 'wins' and who is left out in the cold.

The significance of political and social protest writing

Political texts, like those of any other genre, are open to a range of interpretations and readings. How you react to their content will depend partly on your own context and your beliefs about the way societies should be organized. This option will require you to think carefully about debates arising in these texts and what is being signified.

One approach is to apply different reading perspectives, so the critical material outlined in the Critical Anthology and the Coursework (NEA) component of this book provides a good reference point. We will look at the application of these perspectives in subsequent chapters.

Useful initial questions to ask about significance in texts from this genre may include the following:

- What is being shown about the economic situation in the world of the text?
- What is the relative status of the characters? Does this remain constant throughout the story?
- Is there anything to be said about gender and power? Is this a text where men fight and woman are passive or absent?
- Does any aspect of the world of the text change by the end of the narrative? Do you share the protagonist's elation or despair?

In the following chapters you will look more closely at aspects of the genre and apply them to some of the texts you are studying. Even if some of the material is unfamiliar to you, this will be useful practice for Section C (the unseen part of the exam) and help you to refine your knowledge of the genre.

Summary

In this chapter you have learned that political and social protest writing:

- is about power and powerlessness
- is structured around conflict, oppression and resistance
- explores the effects of political structures on the individual
- may be about domestic and gender politics.

The political landscape

22

The texts you are studying are set in a variety of places and time settings. Wherever the action takes place, the storyworld in the genre is one beset by conflict. Yet settings are more than just places where conflicts occur: they are frequently places of **transition** and discord, where the effects of power shifts are etched on the landscape. They are places where economic and power issues are central.

In this chapter you will look at some of the values inscribed in public settings in texts, their significance, and how you might read them. You will apply some theoretical perspectives from the Critical Anthology.

This chapter will:

- explore the public settings of political and social protest texts
- apply theoretical perspectives to our reading of these places.

The significance of names

Place names in fiction are carefully chosen by writers to suggest something about locations. A good example of this is in Charles Dickens's *Hard Times*, where life in Coketown is a largely miserable one. The novel is set in mid-19th-century northern England, in the midst of the industrial revolution. The name 'Coketown' conjures up images of industry, darkness and grime. It seems to suggest that the town is defined by its relationship to industry and little else. The name also draws attention to itself: we are meant to spot its unusual nature and be aware of its **satirical** qualities. As we discover in the novel, Coketown is a place where education is reduced to the acquisition of facts, and the world of work is one of drudgery. It is a place where a powerful minority control the powerless via education and work.

Activity

What meanings do you find in place names in your texts? Remember that the use of 'real' places can often suggest associations from your own cultural knowledge. It is also worth noting that the choice *not* to use a name can be significant in itself.

Opposing worlds

In some of your texts, narratives are organized around competing value systems. Writers often use opposing settings to represent and criticize different **ideologies** or different ways of organizing society. In the following activity, we will look at Coketown.

Activity

Read the following extract from *Hard Times* and think about how the world of Coketown is shown and what is being signified.

> It was a town of red brick, or of brick that would have been red if the smoke and ashes had allowed it; but, as matters stood it was a town of unnatural red and black like the painted face of a savage. It was a town of machinery and tall chimneys, out of which interminable serpents of smoke trailed themselves for ever and ever, and never got uncoiled. It had a black canal in it, and a river that ran purple with ill-smelling dye, and vast piles of building full of windows where there was a rattling and a trembling all day long, and where the piston of the steam-engine worked monotonously up and down, like the head of an elephant in a state of melancholy madness. It contained several large streets all very like one another, and many small streets still more like one another, inhabited by people equally like one another, who all went in and out at the same hours, with the same sound upon the same pavements, to do the same

Did you know?

Urbanization accompanying the industrial revolution resulted in malnutrition and the spread of contagious diseases. In Manchester, the death rate among children under five was 60%.

> work, and to whom every day was the same as yesterday and tomorrow, and every year the counterpart of the last and the next.

Commentary

Among other things, you may have noticed the focus on the dominance of the industrial environment, which seems to represent the ugly heart of Coketown. It's a world that is 'unnatural'. The bricks and canal are discoloured, the smoke 'serpents' suggest threat, and the pistons run ceaselessly. It has the feeling of a world where individuality has been erased. The repetitive nature of life and work has reduced people to automatons. A political point is being made here about the way societies are organized for the benefit of the money men.

This depiction is brought into relief by contrasts with other places in the novel, one of which is Sleary's Circus, a place of freedom and fun. Tellingly, it is erected on a site 'which was neither town nor country'. Its people are transient and live outside the 'rules' of Coketown. In this excerpt, Sissy Jupe is saying farewell to her circus family before she goes to live with the Gradgrinds:

> The basket packed in silence, they brought her bonnet to her, and smoothed her disordered hair, and put it on. Then they pressed about her, and bent over her in very natural attitudes, kissing and embracing her; and brought the children to take leave of her; and were a tender-hearted, simple, foolish set of women altogether.

The circus is a place where people display care towards each other and are at liberty to express feelings. It is a place of love, honesty and spontaneity, and stands in opposition to the values of Coketown, forming a key part of the novel's debate about the world of facts and work versus the world of imagination and fancy. What is being signified is the abnormality of systems which try to control and repress human feeling and instinct, and it is the use of contrasting places which, in part, help to express this. You may have noticed that these two worlds seem to embody conventional masculine and feminine values.

Consider how oppositional worlds are used in your set texts. For example, *The Kite Runner* can be read as an exploration of the **representation** of American freedom versus the repression in Afghanistan by a variety of ethnic, religious, national and social forces; *Henry IV Part I* contrasts the politics of the court with the politics of the tavern.

Activity

Make a list of the settings in your texts. Explore the significance of these places. You might ask the following:

- Which settings are given prominence in the narrative? In which place(s) does the story start and end?
- Are characters allied with specific settings? Do characters feel isolated in their setting?
- Are the settings oppositional? What political values are associated with them?
- Is it possible to see stereotypically masculine and feminine aspects in these places?

Societies in transition: applying Marxist perspectives

One way of reading political and social-protest literature is to see it as a genre about **transition**, where the conflicts that occur revolve around the changeover of social and economic systems. The application of Marxist perspectives can be illuminating in this regard, but as ever, care needs to be taken not to disregard the text at the expense of the theory.

Link

See Chapter 28 for more details.

Marxist approaches suggest, among other things, that narratives can be read in terms of class struggle and economic progression. Therefore, a useful starting question to ask about any political text is whether the conflicts in the story have their roots in economic issues.

What follows is a Marxist reading of Jim Crace's *Harvest* – a story exploring the events of a turbulent week in an unnamed village. Although set in an unspecified past, there are clear echoes of the historical agricultural process known as enclosure, where common land was appropriated by landowners for private benefit. *Harvest* is narrated by Walter Thirsk, who lives in the village and, like the other inhabitants, farms the land. The arrival of Master Jordan (who replaces the benign Master Kent as landowner) signifies a change in the organization of the village's economy.

In the extract below, Master Jordan, the new landowner, is speaking about his plans for the settlement and is breaking the news that rather than grow crops for the benefit of the village, he wants the villagers to farm sheep. He formally introduces Mr Baynham, who has been charged with the task of mapping out the land and planning its redevelopment.

Activity

Read the following extract from *Harvest* and make notes on the way in which the landscape is to be altered and the implications of this for the inhabitants.

> 'This gentleman is Mr Baynham…' Here I heard his steward civilly muttering his greetings. '… and he, you will discover, is adept at preparing land for sheep. This is not the first community to benefit from Mr Baynham's stewardship. Of course, he needs to be acquainted with your land, my land. He will be guided by the charts. Before first snow he will have structured everywhere within these bounds with fences, dykes and walls, as he sees fit. He'll be reclaiming forestry. How can it profit it us that there are trees, an oak let's say, producing shade but not a single fruit to eat, except for beasts? We would be wise to hew it down and trade its timber rather than allow it to defeat the sun, for beauty's sake, at my expense. Likewise, the commons will be cleared and privately enclosed. You're pasture now. These lands are grass. We'll never need another plough.'

Commentary

Harvest can be read as an **anti-pastoral** political novel, which reveals the hardships of rural life. The village is undergoing a change from an economy where goods are produced for the consumption of the villagers, to one where goods are produced for profit. The emphasis is on money and ownership, with

Key term

Anti-pastoral. A **sub-genre** of pastoral, which focuses on the hardships of country life rather than an idealized **representation**.

the land being carved up to suit production. Trees are to be felled for economic purposes, common land is being repossessed and power is concentrated in the hands of the landowner. The losers are, of course, the villagers whose way of life changes for ever.

In Marxist terms, Master Jordan has assumed control of the **means of production** – the land – and will make capital from it. The agent of social change is the exploitation of one class by another, a by-product of which is the **alienation** of the villagers. This means that experience of work will become fragmented as the villagers will simply become links in a longer chain – they won't be able to see who buys their goods. This is a process known as **reification**, which means effectively that people become 'things' whose relevance is judged in terms of economic usefulness rather than their humanity. They have been **commodified**.

Key terms

Alienated / Alienation. Alienation involves being made to feel distanced, isolated, even hostile. People can experience alienation when they feel that their lives lack full meaning, because they are just part of a process.

Commodified. Turned into a commodity that can be traded. Enslavement is an extreme example of commodification of people.

Means of production. The materials and assets needed to make products, e.g. land, factories, wealth.

Reification. Turning something – or someone – into an item of economic use.

Activity

1. Check that you understand the meanings of the key terms used in the commentary above.
2. Write a substantial paragraph in which you give a Marxist reading of the extract from *Hard Times* on pages 173–174. Use the key terms appropriate to this critical approach.
3. Now apply Marxist approaches to one of your set texts. Think about the extent to which the conflicts in the story are motivated by class and status.

The disruption of nature: an ecocritical approach

Ecocriticism, a relatively new approach to reading literary texts, is interested in the natural world and humanity's relationship with it. You may have grown used to writing about nature as a backdrop to events, or how natural events (such as storms) are used by writers to represent the emotions of the characters. Ecocriticism goes beyond this and sees place and nature as a distinct category worthy of study in the same way that class and gender have become. It is motivated in part by a desire to foreground environmental issues. Remind yourself of the ecocritical material in the Coursework (NEA) component of this book (Chapter 32) and the Critical Anthology before you continue.

Ecocritics tend to see humanity as part of the ecosphere, rather than an entity separate from nature, so we might begin by asking how nature is represented in political texts: what are the effects of power struggles on the natural world? In some political texts, the vying for control leaves its visible effect on the landscape. The ending of *Henry IV Part I*, as filmed for the BBC's *The Hollow Crown* series, shows the muddy disarray of the battlefield at Shrewsbury. A disruptive alteration of the natural world is shown in the excerpt from *Harvest* cited above. The coiled 'serpents' of smoke in Coketown and its polluted canal come to symbolize the effects of human actions on nature. It might be said that political events can cause a dislocation between humanity and nature.

Activity

How might you apply an ecocritical approach to the following extracts from *The Kite Runner*? What significances do you find in the relationship between political events and nature?

In these two extracts, Amir (the protagonist of the novel) is returning from America to Afghanistan, his homeland, which has undergone years of conflict. He has spent some years away and has mixed memories of the place. The term *Showari* refers to the Russians, who invaded Afghanistan in 1979, after which Amir and his father left for a variety of reasons. In the first extract, Amir has just arrived in the country. In the second, he arrives in his home town of Kabul. Farid is his driver.

Did you know?

The 1979–1989 Soviet war in Afghanistan resulted in the deaths of over 1 million Afghan civilians; 4% of the population were left disabled by land mines. Child mortality was estimated at 31%.

***The Kite Runner*: Extract 1**

I stepped outside. Stood in the silver tarnish of a half-moon and glanced up to a sky riddled with stars. Crickets chirped in the shuttered darkness and a wind wafted through the trees. The ground was cool under my bare feet and suddenly, for the first time since we had crossed the border, I felt like I was back. After all these years, I was home again, standing on the soil of my ancestors.

***The Kite Runner*: Extract 2**

A haze of dust hovered over the city and, across the river, a single plume of smoke rose to the sky.

'Where are the trees?' I said.

'People cut them down for firewood in the winter,' Farid said. 'The Showari cut a lot of them too.'

'Why?'

'Snipers used to hide in them.'

A sadness came over me. Returning to Kabul was like running into an old forgotten friend and seeing that life hadn't been good to him, that he'd become homeless and destitute.

Commentary

In the first extract, the reader is presented with an image of harmony between humanity and the natural world. There is a balance in nature, with the sky, wind and animals prompting thoughts of belonging. Ecocriticism tends to stress the concept of home as a sense of belonging within the natural world, rather than just a place to dwell, and this seems appropriate to this extract: Amir's physical contact with the ground is bound up with thoughts of time and ancestry. He is 'rooted'. The second extract shows a more disrupted world. The trees have been cut down for the purposes of warfare and survival. Man-made smoke hovers over the scene. You could read in this a reminder of the damage that humanity does to the environment, and a suggestion that political actions seem to go against nature: they scar it. It may be that political texts can be read as stories about male aggression and control of land. If so, it is tempting to see the natural world and the feminine as victims. In some political texts, it seems that the natural world is out of balance. There are many ways in which texts can be approached, and part of the skill of analysis is to decide which are the most revealing for the text at hand, rather than trying to force a reading on a text.

Staging and symbol

As you will know from your previous studies, drama texts are different from poetry and prose in that the performance aspect allows directors and actors to give different interpretations of texts through choices about the delivery of speeches, positioning on stage, and costume, among other things. Sets and physical spaces can represent the political conflicts central to stories; some of the choices made offer a different slant on the issues at stake.

Physical and **ideological** disputes can also be echoed through other non-literal means. Writers often use **symbols** to represent aspects of conflict in political writing, and to add extra layers of meaning and ambiguity. For example, William Blake's use of symbol in his poem *The Tyger* opens up a range of possible political significances in terms of religion and/or revolution. In Dickens's *Hard Times*, the Old Hell Shaft in which Stephen Blackpool is trapped may symbolize the diabolical nature of industrialism.

Symbols rely on readers looking beyond what they are being told directly – but be aware that symbols operate within the context of a text, so although an apple might symbolize temptation in one text, it may symbolize something more positive in another, such as nature's bounty.

Activity

Explore the use of symbol and (where relevant) dramatic method in your texts. What political significances emerge? You might think about the following:

- The points in the text where symbols appear. Are they associated with particular settings or characters? What relevance to issues of power and powerlessness do they have?
- Whether symbolic meanings evolve during the course of the text. Do layers of ambiguity emerge as the story progresses?
- How staging choices affect meanings. How might choosing to set *A Doll's House* or *Henry IV Part I* in different time periods and costumes affect interpretation? You might read reviews of different productions to help you with this.
- How performance can produce different readings. For instance, how should Hal kill Hotspur in *Henry IV Part I*? In gentlemanly combat, or with merciless savagery? How prolonged and emotional should Torvald's reaction be to Nora's slamming door at the end of *A Doll's House*?

Extension activity

Dystopian fiction is a genre which deals with issues of power and powerlessness through presenting grim versions of alternative or future worlds. Research the genre and the types of books and films associated with it. You might start with the film *Blade Runner* and the story it is based on, 'Do Androids Dream of Electric Sheep?'. Other titles of interest might include *Never Let Me Go* and *A Clockwork Orange*. Your study of this genre might inform the choices you make in the Coursework (NEA) component.

Summary

In this chapter you have learned how:

- names of places can hold significance
- writers can use place as a way to represent and explore political views
- issues of economics and power are central
- the natural world and landscape are often adversely affected by political events
- stagecraft and symbol can be used to represent power struggles.

Gender politics

23

Politics can sometimes be regarded as a male pursuit, in the sense that it deals with affairs of state and the politics of public life, which have traditionally been masculine-dominated areas. Yet the texts you are studying aren't just concerned with high politics or masculinity. They explore how the power structures of society affect the individual, and offer insights into how power operates in both public and domestic worlds. Some texts pay particular attention to the power relationships between men and women.

In this chapter, you will learn how the home can be a place of oppression, particularly for female characters. You will explore the ways in which femininity and masculinity are represented, and prepare gender-based readings of your texts.

This chapter will:

- consider power in domestic settings
- explore the representation of **gender**
- apply gender-based critical approaches.

Key term

Gender. The representation of women and men through cultural stereotypes, which can and should be endlessly disputed; the adjectives 'feminine' and 'masculine' and the nouns 'femininity' and 'masculinity' apply here.

Public and domestic worlds

One way of analysing your texts is to ask which characters are associated with the public sphere – the world of work, culture and intellectual life – and which characters are associated with domesticity, home and children. These divisions often operate along gender lines, with male characters performing tasks involving decision-making in the world outside the home, and female characters being concerned with the organization of the home, and social and emotional matters. The association of men with weighty, public situations can mean that the 'female world' is sometimes perceived to be of lesser importance. The authority that men exhibit in public life can also extend to the home, leading to an unequal power balance.

The interplay of public and private worlds can be seen in the following excerpt from *Henry IV Part I*, where Hotspur, the impulsive young rebel, is preparing to take his leave from his wife, Lady Percy. This scene is usually staged in the interior of a castle, giving a glimpse into the private world of husband and wife. Lady Percy is keen to know what her husband has planned and asks why he has not been intimate with her recently. He tells her:

> This is no world
> To play with mammets and to tilt with lips.
> We must have bloody noses and cracked crowns
>
> *Henry IV Part I* 2.3.87–89

In this excerpt, we see the association of the female with 'mammets' (dolls) and intimacy, which contrasts with the male world of violence. Hotspur even refers to kissing as combat (to 'tilt' is to joust), whereas Lady Percy is linked by her husband to emotional and infantile interests. Remember, though, that this is dramatic representation, so while Hotspur clearly believes in high masculinity, this does not mean that Shakespeare, or a director or an audience, have to agree. Lady Percy, along with other women, is less active in the play – appearing in domestic scenes rather than decisive, public ones. At the end of this scene, as Hotspur prepares to depart, the conversation ends as follows:

> HOTSPUR Today will I set forth, tomorrow you.
> Will this content you, Kate?
> LADY PERCY It must, of force.
>
> *Henry IV Part I* 2.3.112–113

Hotspur's words are commanding and demonstrate how his public power infiltrates the domestic world. Much depends on performance, however, and it may be that Hotspur and Kate's words are delivered playfully, sarcastically, or in an embittered fashion. In any case, it seems as if she has little choice but to go along with what's expected of her.

Activity

Consider the places and characters in your set texts.

1. Which characters are associated with public life and which with domestic matters? Are they divisible along gender lines?
2. Do characters behave differently in public and private worlds? Is there a noticeable difference in terms of who controls which sphere?
3. Are enclosed, domestic worlds associated with trivial matters, and public ones with serious issues?

Power and patriarchy: feminist perspectives

A **patriarchal** society is one organized by and for men, and can often result in powerlessness for women. Patriarchy can involve all the structures (such as law, religion and education) which promote and maintain male power. The division of roles into male/public and female/domestic in some cultures means that men's access to institutions of power lends them authority. Access to money, public profile and financial freedom is often denied to females in patriarchal societies.

Feminist criticism examines how patriarchal power is represented, and shows that although people might see patriarchal arrangements as 'natural', they are unjust and designed to serve the interests of those in power. Considering the relative rights of male and female characters can provide a useful starting point in preparing a gendered reading of your texts.

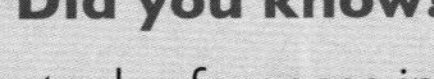

Did you know?

Textual references in the story suggest that *The Handmaid's Tale* is set in a version of Cambridge, Massachusetts. Historically, Cambridge was a Puritan stronghold and was the location of the Salem Witch Trials in the 1690s, an event explored dramatically in Arthur Miller's play *The Crucible*.

As an example, examine the role of the Commander in Margaret Atwood's *The Handmaid's Tale*. Atwood's novel deliberately draws attention to the patriarchal nature of Gilead, a future society where men and women's roles are rigidly prescribed. The Commander is one of the leading thinkers in Gilead. Politically, the leaders have assigned themselves absolute power. The narrator, whose role it is to bear children, lives with the Commander, his wife and female assistants. The Commander's power comes from his position in society and extends into the domestic sphere.

Activity

In the following extract from *The Handmaid's Tale*, the narrator describes a domestic scene where the Commander is preparing to read a story from the Bible to the inhabitants of his house. He is dressed in his black uniform. Serena Joy is his wife. Consider the **representation** of patriarchy in the extract.

> His manner is mild, his hands large, with thick fingers and acquisitive thumbs, his blue eyes uncommunicative, falsely innocuous. He looks us over as if taking inventory. One kneeling woman in red, one seated woman in blue,

> two in green, standing, a solitary man, thin-faced, in the background. He manages to appear puzzled, as if he can't quite remember how we all got in here. As if we are something he inherited, like a Victorian pump organ, and he hasn't figured out what to do with us. What we are worth.
>
> He nods, in the general direction of Serena Joy, who does not make a sound. He crosses to the large leather chair reserved for him, takes the key out of his pocket, fumbles with the ornate brass-bound leather-covered box that stands on the table beside the chair. He inserts the key, opens the box, lifts out the Bible, an ordinary copy, with a black cover and gold-edged pages. The Bible is kept locked up, the way people once kept tea locked up, so the servants wouldn't steal it. It is an incendiary device: who knows what we'd make of it, if we ever got our hands on it? We can be read to from it, by him, but we cannot read. Our heads turn towards him, we are expectant, here comes our bedtime story.

Commentary

The Commander clearly performs the role of patriarch, a role that is part of the wider political structure of Gilead. He is the centre of attention, with the other characters arranged for his benefit. He appears to have the power to judge and decide the roles of the women, and seems both perplexed by their presence and aware of a vague sense of ownership. He has authority, and his wife and the others remain silent. They are anonymized and dressed in colour-coded clothing (as is he) to represent their status. His power is expressed through his control of the environment – he has access to the Bible and is the only one allowed to read. The Bible, as a sacred text, is used to bolster his position. As it turns out, the stories he reads are ones that offer moral judgements about the role of women; they echo the patriarchal values of the society the characters inhabit.

The Commander's ability to speak and act, and to deny the same rights to others, shows where the power lies in the household. The women's role is to listen and accept. They are infantilized by the 'bedtime story' that follows. The control of the language – both in terms of who speaks and who has access to reading matter – might be seen as a form of cultural **hegemony**. His power is related to his status in public life, one shared by other Commanders.

> **Key term**
>
> **Hegemony.** The dominance or control of one person or system by another.

The significance of language

As we have seen elsewhere, names of people and places can be significant. In *The Handmaid's Tale*, for example, you may have noticed that the narrator is named by her relationship to her Commander (she is the possession of Fred, hence Offred), whereas the Commander is defined by his political position. When considering power relationships in literature, the manner in which characters address each other can say something about their status.

In Ibsen's *A Doll's House*, the way in which Torvald Helmer addresses his wife, Nora, reveals much about the balance of power in the play. *A Doll's House*, written in a different social context from Atwood's text, may be read as an exploration of female economic powerlessness. The Helmers live a seemingly comfortable, middle-class existence. Torvald has been promoted to bank manager, and at the start of the play, he gently chastises his wife for her spending habits. Nora has no job, but has a secret in her past: she borrowed money, fraudulently, to finance a trip to help her husband convalesce. (Note that even Nora's secret involves serving her husband.) From this brief summary, you can

Link

See Chapter 28 for a discussion about feminist criticism.

see that money and status are central to their situation, with Nora being the dependent partner. The language used reflects this imbalance. Here are some of the ways Torvald refers to his wife in the opening section of the play:

- 'my skylark'
- 'little spendthrift'
- 'squanderbird'
- 'my squirrel'
- 'my little songbird'
- 'funny little creature'.

Depending on your point of view, you might view these terms as endearing. You might also think that the references to diminutive creatures say something about how Torvald views Nora. The words 'My' and 'little' have connotations of ownership and insignificance. The creatures mentioned are associated with a 'cute' version of nature, which is unthreatening, pleasant to look at and unable to speak. At a later point in the play, Torvald describes her as 'wife' and 'mother', both terms that cast Nora into roles she no longer wishes to have.

In the scene that follows, Nora's secret has been revealed, which leads to an honest exchange of views between wife and husband.

Activity

What is being signified by the word 'doll' in the following extract from Ibsen's *A Doll's House*?

> NORA When I lived with papa, he used to tell me what he thought about everything, so that I never had any opinions but his. And if I did have any of my own, I kept them quiet, because he wouldn't have liked them. He called me his little doll, and he played with me just the way I played with my dolls. Then I came here to live in your house –
>
> HELMER What kind of a way is that to describe our marriage?
>
> NORA (*undisturbed*) I mean, then I passed from papa's hands into yours. You arranged everything the way you wanted it, so that I simply took over your taste in everything – or pretended I did – I don't really know – I think it was a little of both – first one and then the other. Now I look back on it, it's as if I've been living here like a pauper, from hand to mouth. I performed tricks for you, and you gave me food and drink. But that was how you wanted it. You and papa have done me a great wrong. It's your fault that I have done nothing with my life.

Commentary

The word 'doll' opens up a range of meanings. Here are some possibilities:

- A doll can't speak, but can be spoken to.
- Dolls are passive and can be bent into different shapes to suit the will of their owner.
- Dolls can be dressed up to look pretty.
- Dolls are associated with childhood.
- Dolls are toys that can be played with then discarded when they are no longer of interest.
- Dolls have no mind of their own.

All these meanings are reflected in the play as a whole, and in this extract, Nora expresses the feeling that she is a possession of the men in her life. Her father has passed her to Torvald and the experiences are much the same. Nora refers to 'your' house and there is a feeling that her economic dependence has left her powerless. She feels like a 'pauper' and much of her life seems to be an act – she pretends to take on Torvald's views and has 'performed tricks' in exchange for the lifestyle he has offered her. In other words, women are expected to give up power in order to become 'acceptable' in a man's world. They have no control over their destiny and are silenced. Here, however, Nora refuses to be silent any longer. Her departure at the end of the play is her way of reclaiming her identity and economic freedom. This is signified by the way she gains control of language – she speaks, uses and rejects the language used to patronize her. In doing so, she refuses to be a doll and gains **agency**, the power to act.

Did you know?

Until the late 19th century, the legal principle of *coverture* in England meant that on marriage, a woman gave up the right to own property. She became a *femme couverte* ('covered woman') and could only have an education or job with her husband's permission. Any money she earned, or property she inherited, had to be given to her husband.

Activity

Explore the ways in which females are represented in your set texts.

1. Are they passive subjects of male power? Are they silenced?
2. Are they rebellious? Do they have agency?
3. Which terms are applied to them by other characters? Is there any significance in the way they are addressed?
4. Is their situation determined by economic circumstances?
5. Are the contexts of production, i.e. the time when the text was written, relevant to the representation of women?

Performing masculinity

One way to think of gender is to see it as a performance, that is to say that our concepts of masculinity and femininity aren't natural, but are something we learn and perform. Men learn what society thinks is masculine behaviour, such as competiveness, ambition and pursuit of power, and may feel compelled to live up to these expectations. Masculinity, like femininity, is a social construct, and as such is subject to change. The concept of masculinity has altered in Western culture in recent times; the way you think of manhood may influence the way in which you read representations of masculine power in political texts.

For example, *Henry IV Part I* is partly concerned with the growth of Prince Hal, the protagonist, and how he learns to become the type of man who will make a suitable king. In the play, he explores different forms of masculinity – perplexing his father because of his love of friendship and the tavern life, rather than the battlefield. In the end, Hal proves his manhood in battle. The representation of masculinity in promotional material for this play often shows this range of types. Look, for example, at the main publicity image for the BBC's *The Hollow Crown* series, which can be found at:

http://www.amazon.co.uk/The-Hollow-Crown-Mini-Series/dp/B007P3Q95K

or

http://en.wikipedia.org/wiki/The_Hollow_Crown_%28TV_series%29

Here the idea of masculinity is yoked to that of power – in this case regal power. The clothing and props suggest status. The backdrop is one of violence and brooding skies. The way the characters face the audience suggests confidence and perhaps menace. This version of masculinity is one that is easily recognizable and is represented in some of your texts.

Henry IV Part I (and the sequence it is part of) explores the relationships and expectations of fathers and sons. You might consider whether, in your texts, the parent/offspring relationship reveals anything about the nature of power.

Henry IV Part I invites the audience to consider what 'being a man' constitutes, and offers us different versions of masculinity. For Hotspur, the rebellious and engaging young son of Northumberland, masculinity is bound up with violence, power and honour. Bravery and combat are the methods by which a man's worth is measured. His version of honour is contrasted with Falstaff's assertion that 'honour' means pain. Honour for Falstaff is just a word. 'Can honour set to a leg?' he asks, a sentiment which some modern readers who have different views about warfare from Hotspur's might agree with.

Activity

What is the significance of power and masculinity in the following extract?

Before the play begins, Hotspur has captured some prisoners from a battle he was engaged in. Breaking with custom, he has not sent these prisoners to King Henry, something which the king views as an act of defiance. Hotspur has been summoned by Henry to explain his actions, and in this scene he recounts how, at the end of the battle, a foppish lord's manner caused him dismay. A 'pouncet-box' is a snuff container.

> But I remember, when the fight was done,
> When I was dry with rage and extreme toil,
> Breathless and faint, leaning upon my sword,
> Came there a certain lord, neat and trimly dressed,
> Fresh as a bridegroom, and his chin, new reaped,
> Showed like a stubble-land at harvest-home.
> He was perfumed like a milliner,
> And 'twixt his finger and thumb he held
> A pouncet-box, which ever and anon
> He gave his nose [...]
> With many holiday and ladylike terms
> He questioned me, amongst the rest demanded
> My prisoners in your majesty's behalf.
>
> *Henry IV Part I*, 1.3.30–48

Commentary

Hotspur offers two contrasting images of manhood here. One is himself, allied with violence, rage and physical exertion. The other is that of the lord, who is well-dressed, clean-shaven, sweet-smelling and clutching a box of snuff. He speaks in a 'ladylike' way. You may notice that the lord is described by Hotspur in effeminate terms. He is not, implies Hotspur, a 'real man'.

Masculinity is often associated with emotional restraint, competitiveness and victory. Hotspur's values reflect the values of the world of the play, which is in the throes of civil war and power struggles. Depending on your point of view, you might read some political texts as critical of the destructive, masculine scrabble for power. However, it would be a gross oversimplification to read all males as bad and all females as good.

Applying gender perspectives

This chapter has been concerned with the ways in which power and powerlessness in political and social protest writing can be read from the perspective of gender. You might consider some of the following issues as you study your texts:

- To what extent are female characters silenced?
- Do female characters gain agency during the course of the text?
- Is there a division between public life and domestic life in relation to gender?
- How closely linked are issues of power, gender and economics in the text?
- How does the language used by characters reflect power imbalances?
- To what extent could we see political texts as a critique of patriarchy?

Summary

In this chapter you have learned how:

- the abuse of power can take place in domestic settings
- male public power is expressed through social institutions
- language can be a method of repression
- femininity and masculinity are cultural constructs.

24 Radical poetry

This chapter will:

- explore the representation of England, identity and language
- consider how poets depict marginalized figures and powerful entities.

English poetry has a tradition of writers whose work draws attention to political and social matters. Writers such as Milton, Shelley and Spender all wrote verse that was intended to challenge the ways society was organized. Tony Harrison and William Blake can be read as part of this tradition too, in the sense that their work offers radical, often angry comment on matters of class, religion, identity, language and oppression. The poems you will study shed light on the treatment of the dispossessed, allowing those who are normally kept in the shadows to speak or be represented.

Political poetry explores rebellious acts, but can also be rebellious itself. It can encourage dissent and also challenge the forms and **conventions** of literature, attempting to disrupt the cosy world of words. Literature is usually written for – and by – those with privilege, and so in choosing to place marginal figures at the centre and criticize the establishment, poetry becomes a revolutionary force. Whether this translates into action is a different matter, but its intent is to provoke thought. Some of your poems directly mention or echo personal or political events of their time, so it is important to know about the context of production, but it's also important to remember that the text itself is the primary area of focus.

England's green and pleasant land divided

The poetry texts that you will study offer various **representations** of England, its cities, regions and countryside. They appear to work against the romantic representation, prevalent in some holiday brochures, that England is a place of cream teas, cricket and country cottages. This romanticized view of the country is a comforting one, because it suggests ease and civility. In patriotic songs, England is a place of order and fairness, virtue and moral rectitude.

Activity

Consider the political implications of the following lyrics.

> There'll always be an England
> While there's a country lane,
> Wherever there's a cottage small
> Beside a field of grain.
>
> Red, white and blue,
> What does it mean to you?
> Surely you're proud, shout it aloud,
> 'Britons, awake!'
> The empire too, we can depend on you.
> Freedom remains.
> These are the chains
> Nothing can break.

Commentary

In these lyrics, England is a land of order and permanence, where the countryside somehow embodies and protects English values. The Church, the State and the Empire are symbols of power, with the Empire seen as offering freedom rather than restraint. Chains, associated with slavery, are here indicators of unbreakable values and security. There is an assumption in the lyrics that listeners buy into this version of England; if they don't, they are unpatriotic. Above all, the text suggests unity and stability, where the political order is settled and there is no obvious discontent.

The image of a happy, untroubled country is a powerful political tool. It suggests that the political leaders are strong and effective, and implies that anybody who questions the way things are is a troublemaker who wishes to disrupt the peace of the majority. The representation of the country in most literary works is, however, more subtle and questioning; in texts such as Betjeman's poems – which may seem on the surface to celebrate traditional English ways of life – there are subtle ironies that undermine the notion of the uncomplicated pastoral vision. Some of the poems that you will study challenge the myth of a unified society and offer different versions of Britain, where inequality flourishes.

William Blake's 'London' was written and published in 1794, at a time when the British government had introduced curbs on freedom of speech following social unrest in the wake of the French Revolution. The revolution resulted in the overthrow of the French aristocracy and prompted some writers to question the way in which their own society was organized. Blake lived in London, and explored ideas of revolution in several of his writings.

Activity

How are the capital city and its institutions represented in Blake's 'London' below?

You might consider:

- what the word 'charter'd' can mean in the poem
- how the Church and religion are represented
- what is being said about monarchy.

London

I wander thro' each charter'd street,
Near where the charter'd Thames does flow,
And mark in every face I meet
Marks of weakness, marks of woe.

In every cry of every Man
In every Infant's cry of fear,
In every voice; in every ban,
The mind-forg'd manacles I hear:

How the Chimney-sweeper's cry
Every black'ning Church appals,
And the hapless Soldier's sigh
Runs in blood down Palace walls.

But most thro' midnight streets I hear
How the youthful Harlot's curse
Blasts the new-born Infant's tear,
And blights with plagues the Marriage hearse.

Commentary

As you will see in the Coursework (NEA) component (Chapter 28), Marxism suggests that people live their lives imagining that they have choice and freedom, when in reality the options they have are fairly limited. One of the functions of the rebellious poetic voice is to shine a light on injustice and to invite us to recognize oppression. In the 16 lines of 'London', Blake recounts the sights of the city and attacks the institutions of power which blight and control individuals. Much of its criticism is aimed at society's corrupt economic power bases.

A key word is 'charter'd', which has connotations of cartography, control, and legal ownership. London seems to be a place where not only the streets, but also natural things such as the river are owned. Those who oversee these streets are implicitly criticized in the poem: the Church is damned as an institution that permits the suffering of the child sweep (note the grim pun on 'appal'/'pall'), and the Palace (a symbol of the monarchy) is associated with militarism and violence. Depending on how you read the third stanza, it may be suggested that the Palace relies on soldiers who are willing to give up their lives to maintain the current power structures. In short, the soldier's death allows the king to enjoy privilege.

The poem can also generate some interesting readings about sexuality and marriage. One view of the final stanza might be that socio-economic structures result in prostitution: those with limited financial and social opportunities resort to selling their bodies. Prostitution, an economic transaction, corrupts the harlot, the child, marriage and also those men who pay for the prostitute's services. It is also possible to read the phrase 'marriage hearse' as a criticism of social and religious institutions. Marriage is a form of constraint, controlling human sexuality. The Church's support for marriage is a method of maintaining stability and ensuring that people remain monogamous, but it's also an unnatural arrangement amounting to sexual repression. Whether this reading can be convincingly supported by the text is a question you might wish to consider further. You might also explore the idea of sexuality in two more of Blake's poems: 'The Sick Rose' and 'Earth's Answer'.

In 'London', the ordinary people are controlled – 'charter'd' – by institutions, and the 'mind-forg'd manacles' prevent them from seeing the truth of their situation. They have undergone **commodification** and are of use to the ruling elite only as servants and soldiers. Blake's poetry criticizes organized religion, the monarchy, militarism and marriage. It questions everything that society is built upon, and is a wake-up call to the oppressed.

Did you know?

William Blake's *The Marriage of Heaven and Hell* (published in 1790) challenges the accepted thinking of the Church, suggesting that passion is a positive experience and that reason and restraint prevent self-expression. Some Blake scholars view him as an advocate of 'free love', suggesting that State control of human sexual conduct should be removed.

Activity

How are power and powerlessness represented in the poems you are studying?

1. What forms of power are exposed? Who is shown to be dispossessed?
2. What might be said about class, status and gender?
3. Is there anything to be said about institutions?
4. What role do the speakers occupy? Do they observe or are they directly affected by events?
5. Is there any significance in the form and language employed by the speaker?

6. How does the story develop? What is signified by the ending?
7. Is there anything to be said about the context of production? What political events at the time the poem was produced might have influenced its content?

The politics of language

Language has been described as a loaded weapon, in that words bring with them a set of assumptions – they can be 'loaded' with a range of meanings which are there to be decoded. Speech is a political act: not only can words themselves be a method of persuasion, sedition or threat, but the manner in which fictional characters (and real people) speak can ally them with political positions. In Tony Harrison's 'Them and [uz]', oppression and rebellion are linguistic in nature. Several of Harrison's poems explore the tension between the world he grew up in (as the son of a baker in a working-class area of Leeds) and the world of education, with its access to different forms of culture and privilege.

'Them and [uz]' is autobiographical in nature, with Harrison reconstructing his experience of a teacher's judgemental attitude towards accent; in particular, the pronunciation of 'us' as 'uz'. The use of the speaker's native Leeds accent to read Keats's 'Ode to a Nightingale', rather than the Received Pronunciation variant, provokes derision from the teacher, whose values represent the educated elite. All of this is inextricably bound up with class, identity and power – inviting us to consider the complexity of Harrison's position: he is an outsider who feels distant from the grammar-school education he experiences, yet also enjoys a certain amount of privilege via his education.

A range of references in this poem make some demands of the reader. It will help you to know the following:

- ***Richard Hoggart*** was, like Harrison, born in a working-class area of Leeds. He held a range of lecturing posts, becoming Professor of English at Birmingham University. *The Uses of Literacy*, one of his early books published in 1957, explored poverty, class and culture in working-class communities.
- ***Leon Cortez*** was a music-hall comedian and radio performer whose stage act usually began with his catchphrase 'ay, ay'. He wasn't a professor, but Harrison's dedication makes him one. You might like to think why the poet does this.
- ***Demosthenes*** was an ancient Athenian orator whose speeches focused on political matters pertaining to Greece. It is thought that one of the treatments he underwent for a speech impediment was to practise speaking with pebbles in his mouth, often projecting his voice above the roar of the sea.
- ***Daniel Jones*** was a phonetician whose 1918 book *The Outline of English Phonetics* was a description of Received Pronunciation (RP), the accent often associated with privilege and power.

Activity

What is the significance of language, class and power in 'Them and [uz]'? What might be said about names and naming in the poems?

Them and [uz]

(for Professors Richard Hoggart and Leon Cortez)

I

αἰαι, ay, ay! … stutterer Demosthenes
gob full of pebbles outshouting seas –

4 words only of *mi 'art aches* and … 'Mine's broken,
you barbarian, T.W.!' *He* was nicely spoken.
'Can't have our glorious heritage done to death!'

I played the Drunken Porter in *Macbeth*.

'Poetry's the speech of kings. You're one of those
Shakespeare gives the comic bits to: prose!
All poetry (even Cockney Keats?) you see
's been dubbed by [ʌs] into RP,
Received Pronunciation, please believe [ʌs]
your speech is in the hands of the Receivers.'

'We say [ʌs] not [uz], T.W.!' That shut my trap.
I doffed my flat a's (as in 'flat cap')
my mouth all stuffed with glottals, great
lumps to hawk up and spit out… *E-nun-ci-ate!*

II

So right, yer buggers, then! We'll occupy
your lousy leasehold Poetry.

I chewed up Littererchewer and spat the bones
into the lap of dozing Daniel Jones,
dropped the initials I'd been harried as
and used my *name* and own voice: [uz] [uz] [uz],
ended sentences with by, with, from,
and spoke the language that I spoke at home.
RIP RP, RIP T.W.
I'm *Tony* Harrison no longer you!

You can tell the Receivers where to go
(and not aspirate it) once you know
Wordsworth's *matter/water* are full rhymes,
[uz] can be loving as well as funny.

My first mention in *The Times*
automatically made Tony Anthony!

Commentary

Speech and class are used as a way of excluding the narrator from privileged domains: in this case, literature. He is seen as a 'barbarian' who is either silenced or only allowed minor, non-poetic roles such as the Porter in *Macbeth*. This may reflect how in the real world, those in power maintain their status by denying the lower classes access to institutions and opportunities that may alter the power balance.

Note however that Harrison the writer has benefited from his education, a fact that adds to the complexity of feelings in this and other Harrison poems. The speaker's rebellion takes the form of refusal to accept the status quo. By refusing to adapt his language (and therefore his identity), and by accessing (and ironically 'destroying') the privileged world of literature, he becomes powerful. You will also have noticed the irony that he is only able to deflate literature once he has acquired the knowledge his education gives him.

Language in this text is a site of cultural conflict. The use of Harrison's distinctive hybrid voice can be seen as a deliberate attempt both to subvert poetic convention and to fight back against the accepted values of society. The rhetoric is combative in nature, and the message one of rebellion. However, you may also have noticed that the text is written in conventional form, with the use of two 16-line Meredithian sonnets, so there is an ironic interplay between meaning and form. Harrison seems to be writing in both a conventional and non-conventional way: the tools of oppression – language, and the rarefied world of literature – are being used ironically to draw attention to their own prejudices.

Names abound in the text, ranging from highbrow cultural referents (Demosthenes, Keats, Jones, Wordsworth) who are all marshalled to help point out the values associated with speech and power, to the less highbrow but equally interesting Leon Cortez. The linking of the Greek αἰαι to Cortez's catchphrase provides an ironic linguistic link between highbrow and popular culture.

The terms attached to the poet/speaker are relevant. During the course of the narrative he is dubbed 'barbarian' and 'T.W.' (his first two initials) before refusing these epithets and declaring 'I'm *Tony* Harrison'. The closing lines suggest (perhaps with comic exasperation) that there is no escape from the linguistic control of the powers-that-be – even in adult life, he is given a 'wrong' name, being dubbed 'Anthony' rather than 'Tony' by the establishment newspaper *The Times*.

Did you know?

A Meredithian sonnet is a verse form that takes its name from George Meredith, an English poet. The main distinguishing feature is its use of 16 lines, rather than the more common 14 lines found in Shakespearean and Petrarchan sonnet forms.

Titles

The choice of title, the first word(s) that the reader encounters, is often worthy of comment. For instance, Harrison's title 'Them and [uz]' suggests opposition, conflict and language issues. Its orthography seems unusual, leading the reader to expect a text that stands outside of **convention**. It prepares the reader for the two voices in the sonnets, suggesting that the speaker is defining himself against 'them'.

Activity

Look at the titles of some of William Blake's poems in the list below. What significances can you find in them?

Remember that seemingly simple titles can have multiple meanings and associations. You might like to consider links to different genres.

'The Garden of Love'

'A Poison Tree'

'Infant Sorrow'

'The Sick Rose'

'The Divine Image'

'The Little Girl Lost'.

Selling the dream: ideology

In this section, you will consider a Marxist reading of Blake's 'The Chimney Sweeper' and think about the role of **ideology**. Begin by looking at the material on Marxism in Chapter 28 of this book, and also the Critical Anthology, then read the following explanation carefully before proceeding to the poem itself.

Marxist theories

In order for society to function, the majority of people have to abide by a set of values. The thinking and beliefs that underpin these values are often referred to as ideology. According to Marxist theory, the dominant ideology is a way of maintaining the power of the ruling class. Ideology – a set of beliefs and values – is transmitted through law, media and religion, and these mechanisms are controlled by the ruling classes. People generally take these values for granted, seeing them as 'common sense' and 'normal', and don't really question them.

By accepting the dominant ideology, people support the systems that allow the ruling class to stay in power, and keep the powerless in their place. Some versions of Marxism refer to ideology as 'false consciousness', in that the population subscribe to the dominant ideology, thinking they are free, when in reality they are allowing themselves to be controlled. Ideology is like a dream that people buy into, and in doing so they enslave themselves.

Blake's 'The Chimney Sweeper'

This poem, from Blake's *Songs of Innocence*, is narrated by a child. The speaker's mother has died and he has been sold by his father into child labour as a chimney sweep. The practice of using children to climb inside chimneys in order to clean them was a very dangerous one, becoming increasingly common in the industrial era until it was outlawed in 1875. The speaker's childhood has been disrupted and he has become **commodified**. In this poem Blake is denouncing the practice of child labour and also criticizing the Church, which condoned it.

In the second stanza, the speaker tells us about Tom Dacre, a new recruit, whose head is shaven, causing him upset. That night, Tom has a dream. He imagines that thousands of sweepers are locked in 'coffins of black' until they are set free by an angel. Here are the last three stanzas of the poem.

> And by came an Angel who had a bright key,
> And he open'd the coffins and set them all free.
> Then down a green plain leaping laughing they run
> And wash in a river and shine in the Sun.
>
> Then naked & white, all their bags left behind,
> They rise upon clouds, and sport in the wind.
> And the Angel told Tom, if he'd be a good boy,
> He'd have God for his father & never want joy.
>
> And so Tom awoke and we rose in the dark
> And got with our bags & our brushes to work.
> Tho' the morning was cold, Tom was happy & warm.
> So if all do their duty, they need not fear harm.

Texts are open to a variety of readings. Here are some possible ways of interpreting Tom's dream.

1. Dreams are a way of sustaining you. They provide you with a way of dealing with hardship. The pastoral qualities of the dream emphasize the restorative power of nature.
2. Religion will rescue you. It will release you from your bonds, guide you and offer you permanent happiness. It will help you to cope with hardship in this life.
3. Religion, like dreams, offers false promises. It sells you a lie that will fool you into putting up with all manner of horrors in exchange for a place in heaven which, depending on your view, may not exist anyway. Religion is, as Marx pointed out, the opium of the masses.

As you have seen elsewhere in this book, the ambiguous nature of language allows different readings, and so a lot depends on the last line of this text. It seems as if the narrative voice has altered from a childish one to a voice offering a more moralising tone. It may even seem mildly threatening, implying that it's the sweep's duty to get on with things in order to escape punishment. If you follow the implications of the third reading, it appears that Tom and the speaker have accepted the dominant ideology of the Church and imagine that their freedom is assured in heaven, when actually they are being conned into performing their labours as expected by their masters.

It should be noted that Blake had deeply held religious beliefs, but disliked organized religion. How you respond to the third reading proposed above will depend on your own beliefs. One way of seeing this text is as an attack on the hypocrisy of the Church and the inability of disadvantaged people to see how they are being manipulated. As in 'London', their 'mind-forg'd manacles' keep them in their place.

Narratives of dissent

Most stories feature conflict or disharmony as an essential part of the narrative. The narratives of political poetry can position the poet/speaker as some kind of crusader, rather than just a presenter of stories. One way of reading your poems is to see the poet as occupying the role of rebel, as if the speaker is a protagonist in the story of rebellion who holds the mirror up to abuses of power and speaks for the powerless. In the case of Harrison and Blake, it is difficult to separate their poems from their own personal beliefs and context, yet this isn't to say that different voices aren't used, or that language and form aren't consciously crafted to make meaning.

Before you read on, remind yourself about the material on narrative in the Coursework (NEA) component of this book (Chapter 29) We will explore several aspects of narrative method in the following sections and consider some characteristics of poetic method in the poems you are studying.

Shaping story: places and voices

Narrative refers to the ways in which a story has been organized. Narrative is a construction, and part of the skill of studying literature is to see how the process of construction operates. Poems sometimes tell odd kinds of stories, and because of the compressed nature of poetry, significant and meaningful absences occur. Focusing on voices, place and ambiguity in a poem can be a useful place to start thinking about narrative in relation to meaning.

Tony Harrison's 'National Trust' offers a story of physical and cultural conflicts, which references the former mines, Castleton and Towanroath. Castleton is a former lead mine in Derbyshire, the dramatic caverns of which are now a tourist attraction. One of the shafts is known as the 'bottomless pit'. In the poem, we learn of an unsavoury experiment by those in power to see what lies at the bottom of a deep mineshaft. Wheal Coates, Towanroath, is a former tin mine in Cornwall, which is now a visitor attraction owned by the National Trust (an organization set up to preserve and protect places as diverse as stately homes and industrial sites). The poem suggests that those in power don't value the lives, experiences and language of those further down the social scale.

Activity

Read 'National Trust' carefully and consider the following.

1. How are places used in the text? How are double meanings exploited in the references to pits and mining?
2. What is the significance of voices in the narrative? Whose voice is dominant? Who speaks last?

National Trust

Bottomless pits. There's one in Castleton,
and stout upholders of our law and order
one day thought its depth worth wagering on
and borrowed a convict hush-hush from his warder
and winched him down; and back, flayed, grey, mad, dumb.

Not even a good flogging made him holler!

O gentlemen, a better way to plumb
the depths of Britain's dangling a scholar,
say, here at the booming shaft at Towanroath,
now National Trust, a place where they got tin,
those gentlemen who silenced the men's oath
and killed the language that they swore it in.

The dumb go down in history and disappear
and not one gentleman's been brought to book:

Mes den hep tavas a-gollas y dyr

(Cornish) –
'the tongueless man gets his land took'

Commentary

Two settings are used in this text, with the first segment of the poem being centred on Castleton and the recounted story of the convict, and the second location, Towanroath (where it seems the narrator is currently speaking from), being used to make a point about dispossession. Pits are dangerous places and are associated with industry and hard physical labour, usually undertaken by the working classes. They are often seen as places of yesteryear, and in some cases have now become monuments to a bygone age. The places have a significance beyond the literal, though, with wordplay centred on the double meanings of 'plumb the depths' (to explore, but also to experience great sadness), 'bottomless pits' (somewhere you may never return from – Hell, perhaps – but also financial riches) and 'going down in history' (being remembered, descending, but also perhaps being forgotten). There are clear associations between the physical and social position of the lower orders, with the implication being that the men of high status have low morals. You might like to think further about the various meanings that the term 'National Trust' signifies, with its emphasis on the state's care, credibility and protection of its subjects.

The speaker of the text is the dominant voice of the poem. The voice initiates the narrative in a direct, playful way, engaging us with the ambiguous opening line. The tale is then recounted in bitterly ironic terms. We realize that these people aren't 'stout upholders of our law and order' (notice the pun on 'stout'), and there are times when the speaker seems to echo the voices of those involved – the line 'Not even a good flogging made him holler!' sounds like the way in which the men involved would gleefully recount their horrid endeavours. Perhaps the most significant decision is to end the poem with the voice of a Cornish person whose land and language have been appropriated. It's as if literature gives a platform to the dispossessed – but of course the crushing irony is that the line has to be translated for most readers, thereby revealing the central point of the poem: the powerless people have had their language erased. One final piece of linguistic subversion is the dialect use of the word 'took'.

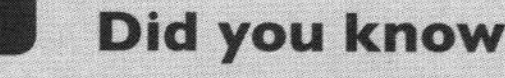

Did you know?

When it was broadcast on Channel 4 in 1987, the filmed version of Tony Harrison's 'V' prompted an outcry about the use of expletives in the poem. Conservative MP Sir Gerald Howarth proposed an early day motion in Parliament entitled 'Television Obscenity'.

Activity

Choose one of your poetry texts and prepare a presentation showing how its language and structural choices assist in the making of political meanings.

You might consider the following:

1. Who is the speaker in this text? What is the nature of power/powerlessness?
2. How are voices used? Are they in subtle or overt conflict with each other?
3. What is the balance between narrative voice and dialogue? Who speaks the last words?
4. Is there a turning point or moment of crisis in the text? Who is affected by it?
5. Are there any ambiguous words in the text? What significances do you find in them?

Connecting texts

In this specification there is no requirement to compare texts, but in section C of the exam you are expected to consider how texts are *connected* via an element of genre. Trying to find specific links and juggling comparisons in a response often leads to forced writing, so instead think of this part of the exam as looking at the (usually) different approaches that writers take to a common element. For example, in this chapter we have looked at divisions in society. You might begin to think how the other texts you are studying represent this.

Another way to connect texts is through critical approaches. For example, in this chapter, and elsewhere in this book, you have applied Marxist perspectives. Considering how different reading positions illuminate the texts you are studying can often prove useful.

The more extensive your reading experiences are, the easier you will find it to make connections between texts. It is therefore essential that your A-level study isn't confined to the texts you are reading for the exam; experiencing a range of political and social protest writing will help to develop your knowledge of the genre, and how it can be used and/or subverted by various authors. Reading is a cumulative process, in which each text you experience extends your knowledge.

Summary

In this chapter you have learned:

- how political poetry centres on disunity
- how titles, voice, point of view and language can shape meaning
- how writers use literary forms to rebel against convention
- how Marxist approaches can reveal ideological assumptions.

Further reading

It could be argued that all modern writing is by necessity political. However, below is a list of some recent novels that are well worth reading for their political ideas:

Americanah by Chimamanda Ngozi Adichie (2013)

Last Man in Tower by Aravind Adiga (2011)

The Catastrophist by Ronan Bennett (1998)

We Need New Names by NoViolet Bulawayo (2013)

The Circle by Dave Eggers (2013)

Billy Lynn's Long Halftime Walk by Ben Fountain (2012)

The Reluctant Fundamentalist by Mohsin Hamid (2007)

The Lowland by Jhumpa Lahiri (2013)

NW by Zadie Smith (2012)

Component 3, on non-exam assessment, has various suggestions for further reading which are relevant to this topic.

Antagonists and institutions

25

In *The Handmaid's Tale*, the narrator observes that the operation of power is about 'who can do what to whom'. This definition neatly draws attention to the fact that political narratives often depict an entity that not only acts as obstacle to the **protagonist**'s desires, but also actively oppresses and exercises power over them. The nature of narrative means that conflict is essential: no **antagonist** means no story in political and social protest writing.

Yet conflict doesn't always have to arrive in the form of a character. Very often, institutions, belief systems or societies act in ways that oppress, and as we have seen already, these issues may be played out on the battlefield or in the home, or both. In this chapter, you will consider the function and representation of antagonising forces, and explore the manner in which dominant entities and systems manifest themselves in the texts you are studying.

This chapter will:

- explore the function of **antagonists** in political and social protest writing
- consider the representation of institutions and society.

The role and significance of antagonists

Throughout your course, you have been considering characters as constructs of the author, rather than as 'real' people. This means focusing on the author's choice of character's names, appearance, speech habits and actions, and what these might signify. You will have seen that one way of opening up readings of character is to place them against literary contexts. For instance, you may have judged Malvolio (in *Twelfth Night*) against the context of comic drama and his role as comic butt. Or you may have evaluated Desdemona (in *Othello*) against the backdrop of tragedy and the conventional roles allotted to women in the genre. Reading character in relation to literary roles such as villain, victim, protagonist and antagonist can be equally useful.

In some texts, the role of an antagonist needs to be uncomplicated for obvious reasons. It would be difficult to imagine a **pantomime** containing a sad scene that revealed some hitherto unsuspected sorrow in the villain's life. Although interesting, this might prove tricky in performance: how would the children know whether to boo or cry? In some literary works, it becomes harder to categorically define the status of characters. Is Frankenstein an antagonist or a protagonist – or both? As we have seen elsewhere, it is this sort of ambiguity that allows different readings to emerge. You might assume that for moral messages in political writing to arise, a clear-cut, unambiguous antagonizing force needs to be established. Yet whether this is always the case in the texts you are studying makes a good starting point for discussion.

Key terms

Antagonist. An antagonist is an opponent, often with some sense of evil, against whom the protagonist must struggle.

Pantomime. In modern culture, a play generally based on a folk-tale or fairy-tale, often performed around Christmas. In theatre, pantomime has a long tradition of a variety of styles.

Activity

Consider the representation of antagonizing characters in your texts. Bear in mind that texts may have more than one antagonist, and where this is the case, there may be distinctions to be drawn between them.

For the purposes of this task, assume that an antagonizing character is one who causes problems for the central character or hero of the story. Make notes on the following areas.

- The antagonists' role in the narrative. When do they appear? What significant events are they involved in? What villainous actions do they perpetrate?

- The character arc of the antagonists. How do they develop or evolve during the story? What happens to them at the end of the text?
- The antagonists' relationship with the central characters. What effect do they have on the protagonists?
- What meanings can you find in their actions? What moral **significances** emerge?

Commentary

Here are some points you may have thought about. Notice that not all of the following observations will fit your texts all of the time, but that is the nature of genre: different texts deal with genre elements in varying ways. And often, when expectations or **conventions** aren't fulfilled, it can be significant and worthy of exploration.

1. The antagonist acts as a catalyst in the narrative

Key term

Plot. The chain of causes and circumstances that connect the various events and place them in some sort of relationship with each other.

One of the functions of an antagonist is to complicate the **plot**. It is his or her actions and involvement in a significant event or events that cause conflict and lead to the climax of the narrative. For example, the arrival of Master Jordan in *Harvest* leads to substantial changes in village life, and ultimately the departure of the villagers. In *The Kite Runner*, Assef's rape of Hassan is the event that determines the shape of Amir's journey – leading ultimately to his return to Kabul. In both of these texts, the antagonist is introduced after the main character's situation has been established.

The antagonist is therefore a destabilizing force, disrupting the equilibrium in the world of the text. Krogstad in *A Doll's House* has a similar effect – you may have noted that he is a character from Nora's past whose reappearance causes problems. Some texts, such as *Hard Times* and *The Handmaid's Tale*, begin from a position where the antagonizing forces are firmly in control. The level of villainy ranges from political indoctrination to murder, but quite clearly the actions of most antagonists are morally questionable. Their transgressions are driven by a desire to gain or maintain power, and so are political in the widest sense.

2. Antagonists can evolve during the narrative

The 'crimes' of antagonists, like transgressors in crime fiction, can increase in magnitude during the narrative. For example, Assef progresses from neighbourhood bully to rapist to murderer. He possesses no redeeming qualities at all. Bounderby in *Hard Times* remains an unfeeling braggart whose only significant development happens when he becomes a victim of his own lies. However, Thomas Gradgrind from the same text develops from a foolish, blinkered man into someone who is able to change.

It may be that finding the ability to change, suffering a reversal, or dying is the fate of most political antagonists. Yet in death, Hotspur in *Henry IV Part I* is highly praised, whereas Worcester's machinations and self-interest make him an unattractive antagonist even as he goes to his end. Also less clear cut is the position of Torvald at the end of *A Doll's House*: do you have sympathy for him? The Commander in *The Handmaid's Tale* also becomes a more ambiguous figure as his relationship with the narrator develops. The position of these characters at the end of the text is worth exploring: you might feel that by the climax of the tale, applying the term 'antagonist' to some of these characters has become problematic. It may be that the death or defeat of antagonists signifies a victory of sorts, whereas their continued dominance usually makes for a less-reassuring ending.

3. Antagonists are inextricably linked to the protagonist

In some texts, the antagonist acts in direct opposition to the hero, often subjecting him or her to physical or emotional oppression. Sometimes, linguistic silencing or even death is meted out. The role of the antagonist therefore has a bearing on the hero, sometimes acting as a contrast to the protagonist. This seems true for Hotspur and Hal in *Henry IV Part I*, where the king draws unfavourable comparisons between Hotspur and his own son, although this changes in the course of the play. In this text and *The Kite Runner*, the hero has to physically confront his opposite number at the climax of the narrative, so it is possible to regard the fates of both character types as linked. A less physical, but equally final confrontation happens between husband and wife in *A Doll's House*.

One of the roles of the antagonist might be to force the hero to go beyond his or her limits or to do things that may be uncomfortable. You will look at the idea of the protagonist's journey in a subsequent chapter, but for now you might consider that some of your texts seem to involve the protagonist having to respond – or perish – in the light of antagonizing actions.

4. Antagonists represent the cruel aspects of humanity

The actions of antagonists reveal uncomfortable truths about humanity and the corrupting power of religious zealotry, dehumanizing systems, and political machination. Political texts therefore have a moral function, warning of the dangers of such behaviours, and the antagonist becomes a vehicle for conveying this message.

One of the methods for undermining the antagonist is to reveal his or her hypocrisy. As noted above, Bounderby's lies about his supposedly humble upbringing confirm our mistrust of him, and Assef's proclamations about the sexual behaviour of the characters he executes in the football stadium in *The Kite Runner* are brought into sharp relief by his own actions. The antagonist comes to represent an **ideology** that is challenged during the course of the novel and revealed to be morally suspect, often to the delight of the reader. In doing so, you might reconfirm that 'your' way of life is morally superior. You might therefore consider the extent to which political texts are ultimately conservative in outlook rather than revolutionary: do they simply tell you what you already know – that power corrupts?

In certain text types, such as the medieval morality play, characters are little more than **personifications** of virtues and vices and never appear more than stock, one-dimensional types. While the texts you are studying might feature rounded, credible antagonists, they also embody the values of institutions or systems that the writer may want you to question. They stand for ideologies that are held up to scrutiny and usually found wanting. For instance, Master Jordan in *Harvest* and Gradgrind and Bounderby in *Hard Times* embody the preference of commodities over human beings.

Did you know?

Agon was an ancient Greek term for a contest, initially the sporting and cultural contests of the ancient Greek games at Olympia. In literary study, the term is used to refer to the contest between protagonist and antagonist in a narrative.

Key term

Colonialism. The process whereby European political forces took over, settled and ruled places such as India, Africa and the Middle East. Countries such as Britain colonized India in the 18th century. The term carries connotations of exploitation: native cultures were repressed, often brutally, and Western imperial forces plundered economic resources.

Applying post-colonial approaches

In the next activity, you will look at a scene from *The Kite Runner* and consider not only the role of antagonist but also how you could apply a post-colonial approach to the text. At this point, it may help to read the relevant material in the Critical Anthology and the Coursework (NEA) section of this book (Chapter 31). Post-colonial criticism essentially explores the effects of **colonialism** on cultures, countries and peoples. Among other things, it can:

- show the ways in which colonized cultures are shown in Western literature – drawing attention to the ways in which writers often misrepresent the colonized as 'other' or homogenous, instead of varied and individual
- focus on texts written by colonized (or formerly colonized) people, thereby giving a different slant on the realities of life in colonized countries.

Post-colonial approaches are therefore political in nature – attempting to criticize colonizers and redress misrepresentation by giving a voice to the oppressed. Some Western literature is accused of patronizing **representations** of 'the East', focusing on common stereotypes about exoticism and the lazy, hedonistic foreigner. You might consider whether similarly reductive images of other cultures still persist in mainstream culture.

The Kite Runner might be read as a text which gives a voice to colonized people, revealing much about the history of foreign invasion and introducing the Western reader to the varied aspects of Afghan culture and its internal divisions. The writer, Khaled Hosseini, is an Afghan American who chose to write his novel in English and publish his text in the West. The novel has also been criticized by some readers as oversimplifying cultural difference for the sake of a sentimental story.

In the following excerpt, the narrator, Amir, and Baba, his father, are leaving Afghanistan. Their country has been invaded by Russia. They are travelling by truck with other people when they are stopped at a checkpoint by a Russian soldier. Karim is the Afghan driver.

Activity

As you read the excerpt below, consider:

- the representation of the antagonist in terms of name, speech, actions and role
- the actions of the other characters in this scene
- how the characters and events might be read from a post-colonial perspective.

The Kite Runner

The Russian soldier thrust his face into the rear of the truck. He was humming the wedding song and drumming his finger on the edge of the tailgate. Even in the dim light of the moon, I saw the glazed look in his eyes as they skipped from passenger to passenger. Despite the cold, sweat streamed from his brow. His eyes settled on the young woman wearing the black shawl. He spoke in Russian to Karim without taking his eyes off her. Karim gave a curt reply in Russian, which the soldier returned with an even curter retort. The Afghan soldier said something too, in a low, reasoning voice. But the Russian soldier shouted something that made the other two flinch. I could feel Baba tightening up next to me. Karim cleared his throat, dropped his head. Said the soldier wanted a half hour with the lady in the back of the truck.

The young woman pulled the shawl down over her face. Burst into tears. The toddler sitting in her husband's lap started crying too. The husband's face had become as pale as the moon hovering above. He told Karim to ask 'Mister Soldier Sahib' to show a little mercy, maybe he had a sister or a mother, maybe he had a wife too. The Russian listened to Karim and barked a series of words.

'It's his price for letting us pass,' Karim said. He couldn't bring himself to look the husband in the eye.

'But we've paid a fair price already. He's getting paid good money,' the husband said.

Karim and the Russian soldier spoke. 'He says ... he says every price has a tax.'

That was when Baba stood up. It was my turn to clamp a hand on his thigh, but Baba pried it loose, snatched his leg away. When he stood, he eclipsed the moonlight. 'I want you to ask this man something,' Baba said. He said it to Karim, but looked directly at the Russian officer. 'Ask him where his shame is.'

[...] The Russian soldier said something to Karim, a smile creasing his lips. 'Agha sahib,' Karim said, 'these *Roussi* are not like us. They understand nothing about respect, honor.'

'What did he say?'

'He says he'll enjoy putting a bullet in you almost as much as...' Karim trailed off, but nodded his head toward the young woman who had caught the guard's eye. The soldier flicked his unfinished cigarette and unholstered his handgun. *So this is where Baba dies*, I thought. *This is how it's going to happen*. In my head, I said a prayer I had learned in school.

'Tell him I'll take a thousand of his bullets before I let this indecency take place,' Baba said.

Commentary

The soldier remains anonymous in terms of name, which distances him from the reader, as does the fact that his words are relayed via Karim, rather than in direct speech. His behaviour is belligerent, conveyed by Hosseini in verbs such as 'thrust', 'shouted' and 'barked', and his demands are designed to show his immorality and exploitation of power. He threatens not only rape but murder, and does so with a smile. Like most antagonists, his actions increase tension and put a physical block on the progress of the protagonists. He certainly seems to embody the cruel aspects of humanity.

Here are five possible ways of reading this excerpt from a post-colonial point of view.

1. The exchange shows the disruption to family life caused by the invasion and can be seen as a **diaspora** narrative. It gives a voice to those who are oppressed: rather than being seen as 'other', the husband and wife become 'real' characters with human feelings and emotions.

Key term

Diaspora. The scattering of a population whose origins lie in a particular geographical area.

Key terms

Binary opposition. The idea that we define words and concepts in relation to their opposite, i.e. 'good' is partly determined by what we understand by 'evil'.

Colonization. The process whereby one country or group of countries seeks to take over another.

Emasculation. Literally castration but, by extension, humiliation and disempowerment.

2. The scene strongly reminds us of the brutality of **colonization**. It tells us that occupying forces aren't benign. They exploit their physical power to subdue the local population.
3. The scene is largely **metaphorical**, with the soldier representing the colonizing force and the woman embodying Afghanistan. The threatened rape symbolizes the invasion of the country. The pleading husband represents the **emasculation** of its people.
4. Instead of portraying the Afghans solely as victims, the courage of Baba reconfigures the straightforward **binary opposition** of oppressor/victim, and offers the reader a way to see Afghans as resistant and morally decent.
5. The 'real' Afghans are little more than anonymous ciphers, only there to act as victims, clearing the way for Baba to act the hero. For some readers, Baba is the embodiment of US values of strength and honour, steadfastly refusing to accept Communist aggression. Baba can be read as a Westerner's acceptable version of the Afghan.

You may like to explore these readings further and decide which reading is most convincing for you before developing a longer written response drawing upon other events in the text.

Institutions I: Religion

In political writing, institutions and the values they represent can be depicted as controlling and immovable forces, which visit misery on the protagonist. Religion can, in the wrong hands, be used for indoctrination and control.

In previous chapters, you have explored some issues surrounding organized religion by looking at William Blake's writing. The next activity is an opportunity to extend your knowledge of the representation of religion to other texts you are studying.

Activity

Remind yourself of the material discussed in Chapter 24 on Blake's depiction of religion (pages 187–188). Using your prose and/or drama texts, explore the representation of religion in political writing. You might consider:

- the exploitation of religion and religious texts to control people
- the extent to which organized religion is complicit in oppression
- the extent to which personal religious beliefs are a sustaining force for embattled characters
- the use of religious references and metaphors.

The following areas may make useful starting points:

- *Hard Times*: the religious significance of the titles given to sections and chapters; the references to the Teetotal Society; the spiritual impoverishment of Coketown's residents
- *The Handmaid's Tale*: the use of biblical texts to support **patriarchy**; the biblical names given to the shops in Gilead and the society itself; the reference to Genesis in the epigraph

- *A Doll's House*: the setting at the time of a religious holiday; Nora's reference to Pastor Hansen; the reference to 'miracles'; the Christian concept of marriage
- *Harvest*: the symbolism of the unfinished church; the punishment of outsiders as a religious **allegory**; references to witchcraft and pagan traditions
- *The Kite Runner*: Amir's personal faith; the divisions caused by faith; the depiction of extreme beliefs; punishment for supposed transgression
- *Henry IV Part I*: references to God, sin and heaven; the delayed religious crusade; the issue of legitimacy and the **divine right** of kings.

Institutions 2: Education

Like organized religion, the education system is often the target of criticism in political writing. Rather than being shown as a way to enlightenment and freedom, it is often seen as a restrictive method of upholding the **ideology** of the establishment. On pages 189–191, you considered the ways in which the anonymous schoolteacher belittles the speaker's accent in Tony Harrison's 'Them and [uz]'. The next activity is an opportunity to further explore the representation of education by looking at an excerpt from *Hard Times*.

Activity

Consider the representation of education, power and powerlessness in the following text. You may wish to think about:

- what is being said, directly or indirectly, about educators and education
- the use and representation of character, point of view, voice and repetition
- the links to other genres and how they are used to represent education.

This is the opening segment from *Hard Times*, in which Thomas Gradgrind (as yet unnamed) offers instruction to a schoolteacher on how to educate children. Gradgrind is a successful industrialist who is in charge of a 'model school'. His values embody what Dickens saw as the dehumanizing effect of industrial labour. The title of this chapter is a reference to a passage from the Gospel of St Luke in the Bible, where the 'one thing needful' is to listen to and obey Christ's word.

Chapter 1: The One Thing Needful

'Now, what I want is, Facts. Teach these boys and girls nothing but Facts. Facts alone are wanted in life. Plant nothing else, and root out everything else. You can only form the minds of reasoning animals upon Facts: nothing else will ever be of any service to them. This is the principle on which I bring up my own children, and this is the principle on which I bring up these children. Stick to Facts, sir!'

The scene was a plain, bare, monotonous vault of a schoolroom, and the speaker's square forefinger emphasized his observations by underscoring every sentence with a line on the schoolmaster's sleeve. The emphasis was

Key terms

Allegory. A sort of extended **metaphor**, where a story or meaning emerges under the surface of some other story. Famous examples are *The Pilgrim's Progress* and *The Faerie Queene*. Some critics have argued that J. R. R. Tolkien's *The Lord of the Rings* is an allegory of the First World War, in which Tolkien fought.

Divine right. The idea that kings are anointed by God; this was reinforced by the religious order in the coronation ceremony.

Did you know?

The Elementary Education Act of 1870 paved the way for universal education in England for those between the ages of 5 and 12. Some sectors of society were not in favour of educating the masses, perhaps fearing that education might cause those at the bottom of the pile to question the status quo.

> helped by the speaker's square wall of a forehead, which had his eyebrows for its base, while his eyes found commodious cellarage in two dark caves, overshadowed by the wall. The emphasis was helped by the speaker's mouth, which was wide, thin, and hard set. The emphasis was helped by the speaker's voice, which was inflexible, dry, and dictatorial. The emphasis was helped by the speaker's hair, which bristled on the skirts of his bald head, a plantation of firs to keep the wind from its shining surface, all covered with knobs, like the crust of a plum pie, as if the head had scarcely warehouse-room for the hard facts stored inside. The speaker's obstinate carriage, square coat, square legs, square shoulders – nay, his very neckcloth, trained to take him by the throat with an unaccommodating grasp, like a stubborn fact, as it was – all helped the emphasis.
>
> 'In this life, we want nothing but Facts, sir; nothing but Facts!'

Commentary

In this text, education and those who deliver it come in for criticism. The reader is shown a character exploiting his position of power to press forward his ideology. Here are some points you may have noted:

- The form of education on offer seems dry, with an emphasis on factual rather than creative matters. There is the sense that children are being encouraged to conform rather than think – here, education's purpose seems to be to 'form the minds' by learning incontrovertible Facts (note the ironic capitalization) rather than learning to question the world. This sort of education will churn out compliant workers fit for the drudgery of industry. The 'plain, bare, monotonous' setting echoes the educational experience.
- The opening speech is used not only to establish the reductive philosophy of Gradgrind, but also to undermine it. The reference to Christ's teaching in the chapter title is obviously an ironic comment on Gradgrind's self-importance and the shortcomings of his rigid views.
- The narrative voice undermines Gradgrind by a sustained focus on his **caricatured** appearance. The repetition of 'square' and references to an 'unaccommodating grasp', his 'obstinate carriage' and 'wall of a forehead' suggest dominance and inflexibility, which have clear links to his humdrum, controlling brand of education.
- Although the character seems to have potentially villainous qualities, the nature of the writing is comic: the light-hearted references to his head 'like the crust of a plum pie' make him seem foolish and narrow-minded. Gradgrind and his limited ideas are being **satirized** – he seems ridiculous, but there is a serious point being made about education and authority. The schoolroom seems little more than a factory.

Key term

Caricature. An exaggerated portrayal of a person or type of person, often for comic effect.

Comparing texts

You could compare any of the excerpts in this chapter with an extract from your own text. Remember that connecting texts does not mean that you need to make direct comparisons; it is often productive to think about the different ways in which writers handle the same political element. Even if the texts in this chapter are unfamiliar to you, regard this as an opportunity to extend your awareness of the genre and practise some of the skills required for section A on unseen texts.

As noted at the end of the previous chapter, in this specification there is no requirement to compare texts, but in section C of the exam, you are expected to consider how texts are connected via genre. To practise this key skill, try the following Activity.

Activity

Connect the extract from *Hard Times* on pages 173–174 to another text that deals with education and/or indoctrination. You could begin by thinking about the connections between this text and Tony Harrison's 'Them and [uz]', which you looked at in Chapter 24 (pages 189–191). Blake's *The Schoolboy* could also be a productive connection, along with some of public scenes in Atwood's *The Handmaid's Tale*. What can be said about educational practices in these texts?

Summary

In this chapter you have learned:

- that antagonists have a range of functions and significance in the genre
- post-colonial approaches can offer different readings of oppression and its effects
- organized religion and formal education are frequently criticized as controlling forces.

26 The political protagonist

This chapter will:

- explore the significance and representation of political protagonists
- explore the significance of journeys and endings in political writing.

Protagonists in political and social protest narratives are central to the text's power struggles. They are often powerless characters who attempt to change or escape their circumstances. They may be agents of rebellion, but not always: some texts call into question the actions of rebels and political machination, and it may be that the central character represents the interest of dominant rather than powerless groups.

In previous chapters, you have considered how your texts represent dissenting or rebellious voices or actions. Some stories feature fairly dramatic upheavals, yet in others the attempts to resist control are more subtle. In this chapter, you will consider the representation of protagonists, their journeys and the significance of closure in political narrative. The success (or failure) of the protagonists' journeys towards empowerment provides key moments: the endings of texts are rich in significance.

The role and significance of protagonists

A protagonist may be defined as the figure the reader identifies with – a 'good' character. However, you will be aware from your previous studies that this is a limited definition, because protagonists can sometimes act in ways that call their 'hero' status into question. In this first activity, you will start by asking questions about protagonists that are similar to the ones you asked about **antagonists** in the previous chapter.

Activity

Consider the representation of protagonists in your texts. Work on the assumption that a protagonist is the leading character in the story, but bear in mind that stories can feature more than one protagonist, and where this is the case there may be distinctions to be drawn between them. Make notes on the following areas:

- The protagonists' role in the narrative. When do they appear? What significant events are they involved in? What heroic and/or rebellious actions are they involved in?
- The character arc of the protagonists. How do they develop or evolve during the story? What happens to them at the end of the text?
- What meanings can you find in their actions? What moral significances emerge?

Commentary

You will find that not all of the following observations about protagonists will fit your texts all of the time. Being able to identify when expectations or **conventions** are fulfilled or denied is a key aspect of genre study, and is one of the ways in which you can begin to find connections between texts. Consider how far the following points apply to the characters in your texts.

1. Protagonists may be victims or outsiders

In most fiction, protagonists are 'doers' – characters who heroically achieve things in the **plot**, with some degree of control over their situation. Prince Hal in *Henry IV Part I* seems to fit this description. However, one role which the political protagonist can occupy is that of victim – a role traditionally associated with lack of power. The establishment of the protagonist as victim or outsider has a narrative significance, because it signals to readers the type of story that they are about to read: a tale about an underdog who must, through his or her actions, endure or escape a situation. This recognizable story type echoes the Cinderella story, where the restricted protagonist must overcome the obstacles to liberation.

The characters' awareness of their victimhood can therefore be a motivating force in a narrative: a refusal to accept the status quo is at the heart of their actions. The narrator in *The Handmaid's Tale* is clearly an oppressed female in a dystopian world. She is the victim of the society in which she finds herself – and she knows it. On the other hand, in *A Doll's House*, Nora's realization that she is oppressed is gradual. Victims are usually subjected to harm, but political protagonists also involve themselves in physically or emotionally violent acts, usually with moral justification.

In the post-2000 texts, narrator-protagonists occupy different sorts of roles. Walter Thirsk in *Harvest* declares himself to be an outsider in the village, despite having lived there for 12 years. We are encouraged to adopt his point of view and generally trust his observations, although we note his acceptance of some violent events. Amir in *The Kite Runner* perpetrates some cowardly acts, yet he may (or may not) retain your sympathy. Protagonists in political texts can be tainted by the power struggles they find themselves in, but this often makes them appear as 'rounded' characters, rather than conventional heroes. You might wish to consider further the idea of flawed or compromised heroes at this point. What prevents them from being deemed 'villains'?

2. Protagonists gain power during the narrative

As you have seen elsewhere, the development of **agency** (the capacity to act) is a feature of political and social protest texts. If political narratives are about the movement from victimhood to empowerment, there must be disruption of equilibrium. Protagonists must escape, survive or become empowered. Protagonists' motives might therefore be seen as broadly similar to those of antagonists: the desire for a form of power.

In Chapter 23 on Gender politics you explored Nora's development in *A Doll's House* (pages 181–183). If you are studying this text, you will be aware that her actions are not always seen as virtuous or morally correct by all audiences. Therefore, whether the acquisition of power in the form of liberty is a positive thing isn't always clear cut: Louisa Gradgrind in *Hard Times* might be read as a tragic figure who achieves some escape from her father's philosophy by the end of the text, but whether this is an entirely happy ending for her is up for debate. In *The Handmaid's Tale*, the narrator's escape is likely to be read as a more obvious form of liberation.

Some protagonists are aligned with powerful groups from the start of the narrative. Their story is about maintaining power, or losing then regaining it. Hal in *Henry IV Part I* is heir to the throne and Amir in *The Kite Runner* enjoys a life of privilege: both these protagonists have to prove themselves in the light of their actions in the early part of the narratives. Protagonists' fates seem to differ too, depending on the nature of the story, but the usual destinations are liberation, success, redemption or reversal.

3. Protagonists represent humanity's desire for freedom and fairness

Reading political and social protest writing as straightforward 'good versus evil' stories might be too simplistic; another way to view these texts is as **representations** of the struggle between competing **ideologies**. Yet you are usually invited to side with the protagonist, and it is worth exploring how the writer achieves this.

Some writers appear to ally the protagonist with the ideas that Western liberal thought sees as 'right', that is: freedom from oppressive institutions; the importance of individual fulfilment; a belief in justice; and the right to live your life in the way you choose. There is a romantic quality to these notions; they somehow embody what we see as fair, humane values. Protagonists in political and social protest writing represent human qualities under threat from unfeeling authority, as you may have noticed during your study of texts such as Blake's poems or *Hard Times*.

There is a **paradox** in this, however: in real life, freedom is only guaranteed by structures of security and power, and it may be that these desires are, in the end, incompatible. Whether they are fully resolved in fiction is an issue you might wish to investigate.

Key term

Paradox. An apparent contradiction that holds some unexpected truth.

Activity

Political protagonists often embody positive human attributes and desires which contrast with the values of political systems. Explore the representation of some of the following in your texts:

- love and sex
- memory
- dreams
- humour

Think about how these aspects are used and represented in the text. Start by considering how they are forms of resistance or insulation against oppressive acts. You might also think about their comic or pastoral qualities – is political fiction a vehicle for exploring the endurance of the human spirit?

Political protagonists and the bildungsroman

A **bildungsroman** is a text concerned with the life journey of a protagonist (often male), usually chronicling a moral education. They are a type of coming-of-age story. You could read *Henry IV Part I* as a form of political bildungsroman in which Hal learns how to handle regal power. Consider the following events in the play:

- Hal's father, Henry IV, bemoans the fact that his son is idling his time away, while Lord Northumberland's son (Hotspur) is the model of honour and manliness.
- Hal spends a lot of time in The Boar's Head with Falstaff, engaging in riotous behaviour.
- By the end of the text, Hal fights Hotspur at Shrewsbury to defend his father's kingship.

Did you know?

'Bildungsroman' is a German word, comprising the terms *Bildung* (education) and *Roman* (novel). Well-known examples include *David Copperfield*, *Great Expectations* and *The Catcher in the Rye*.

Hal's journey is one in which he learns how to be a man of politics. There are some significant points here, however. In becoming a conventional prince, Hal has to choose serious matters such as violence and honour over playfulness and friendship. He reveals that his time spent in The Boar's Head was all part of his plan. If you are studying this text, you might wish to explore further what this play has to say about learning to rule.

The Kite Runner also offers a story of personal development, this time with the focus on redemption. Here is an overview of Amir's journey:

- Amir begins the story in a position of privilege. He witnesses his friend Hassan (the son of his father's servant) being raped, but doesn't intervene, which causes Amir tremendous guilt.
- Unable to handle his guilt, he frames Hassan for theft and loses touch with him. Amir has to leave Afghanistan when the Russians invade. Hassan subsequently dies.
- He is summoned to Pakistan to see an old family friend, Rahim Khan, who recounts the story of Hassan and the misery of his orphaned son. He tells Amir he knows about Amir's guilt and instructs Amir to atone for his sins. Amir does not do this easily.
- Amir returns (as an adult) to Taliban-governed Afghanistan to rescue Hassan's son, which is 'a way to be good again'. In doing so, he has to physically fight the antagonist. He succeeds, but only when aided by Hassan's son.

In both of these texts, there is an assumption that growing up to be a man means becoming noble and making good your previous 'errors' – and demonstrating it through physical actions. There is the sense that taking your place in life means confronting past and current political situations and learning how to deal with them, sometimes violently. You may have noticed that in both these texts, personal matters are bound up with political situations.

Activity

Not all political texts can be classified as bildungsromans, but it can be useful to explore the journeys undertaken by male protagonists and the moral messages that emerge. Choose some male protagonists from the texts you are studying and consider the following.

- The role of previous errors or behaviours in shaping the protagonist's journey. Are they political or personal in nature? Or both?
- What is implied about being or becoming a man. What qualities are associated with manhood? What has the protagonist learned by the end of the journey?
- The role of violence in the text. To what extent do male protagonists have to prove themselves physically?
- Whether personal journeys are always linked to political situations. Does the acquisition of power taint the protagonist?

The rebellious female

In the Critical Anthology and in the Coursework (NEA) section of this book dealing with **gender** (Chapter 28), you will consider some of the ways in which females have been represented in literature. Political and social protest writing offers some complex representations of women, and in this section you will look at the **representation** of rebellious females. It may be that the texts you are reading present less dramatic types of female characters, but remember that developing a wider understanding of the genre and literature generally will help you to make connections between texts and also help you to prepare for the unseen part of the exam.

Activity

Explore the representation of the female in the following extracts.

The events of *Harvest* take place in an unnamed village over the course of a week. Near the start of the novel, three newcomers arrive in the tightly knit community. They (two men and a woman) are suspected of theft. The woman has attracted the attention of the men of the village. Master Kent decides that the men will be put in the pillory, and all three will have their heads shaven. Willowjack is Master Kent's horse.

The following extracts are taken from a longer scene. In the first extract, the narrator gives an account of the woman. In the second, he describes the confrontation between Master Kent and the woman. Consider:

- the manner in which the narrator views the woman – what terms are used to describe her?
- the woman's responses and actions towards Master Kent – what is being revealed about the politics of this society?

Harvest Extract 1

She was a widow, possibly, with all that implies: she would be seasoned and experienced; she would have an unslaked thirst for company. In a village such as ours, where women die before the men, there are plenty of my neighbours who will have seen at once a tempting opportunity. While the women might have cast her as a subject of their kindom or a partner for their sons and might have nieced and cousined her, glad to have their breeding stock enlarged by some black hair, the men there will have chambered her and nested her the moment that she showed herself. Surely that could hardly count as sin. The local women were like land – fenced in, assigned and spoken for, the freehold of their fathers, then their husbands, then their sons. You could not cross their boundaries, or step beyond your portion. But this one, this incomer, was no better than any other wild quarry on common ground. Like any pigeon, any hare, she was fair game.

Harvest Extract 2

One week, disarmed and bald? A modest punishment. And one which by happy chance would keep the woman on our land and separated from her men for long enough for every village hand to try his luck with her. She spat at this point, only at the ground between the horse's hoofs but still a shocking act and one that Master Kent could not ignore without losing face.

> 'Count yourself as fortunate we do not boast a broader pillory,' he said, not looking at her in case she widened her eyes at him again. 'And be thankful that we are too gentle here and careful of our water to duck you in our village pond. But you will lose your hair together with your men. And in the time it takes to lengthen you might consider your disdain for us.'
>
> This time her phlegm reached Willowjack and left a rosary of pearls across her flank.

Commentary

In Extract 1, there is a sense in which the woman is seen as temptation. She is judged as a potential lover, and assumptions are made about her previous sexual experience. The various roles considered for her are sexual partner, family member or producer of children – she is only viewed (by the narrator) in relation to men. The women in the village are 'owned' by their menfolk: terms of physical or legal ownership ('fenced in', 'freehold' and 'boundaries') are used to describe these relationships. The woman is also linked to nature, hunting and consumption ('seasoned', 'quarry', 'pigeon', 'hare' and 'game').

Extract 2 provides an ironic contrast to how the narrator perceives her. In this segment, she refuses to comply willingly and Master Kent seems to avoid her gaze, suggesting a certain power on her part. Her actions seem unfeminine and her spittle coats the Master's horse, not only a symbol of power, but also a part of the natural world. Mistress Beldam, as she comes to be known by the narrator, seems feisty and unwilling to cooperate. The novel has much to say about closed societies and the mistrust of the outsider. If you are studying this text, you may wish to explore further the significance of intrusion, injury and death in the narrative.

Did you know?

Religious texts are often used to justify the supposed subservience of women. In the Bible, I Corinthians 11 decrees that the female is there for the benefit of the male, stating 'For the man is not of the woman; but the woman of the man. Neither was the man created for the woman; but the woman for the man.'

The end of the journey

In this final section, you will consider the **significance** of endings in political fiction. The ending of stories is where actions and morals are affirmed or held up for debate: whether protagonists succeed or fail in their journey is a significant choice made by the author. At its most basic, a story can be seen as a series of events which lead to an endpoint, and it is the final part of a story which usually interests readers most, because it is what they have been prepared for all through the text – it's one of the main reasons why they keep reading.

Readers accrue a store of knowledge about the outlines of stories. It is these story skeletons and other genre knowledge – which you develop all through your reading life – that lead you to expect certain endings.

Some types of story have a clear sense of closure, such as fairy stories where the characters live happily ever after. This type of ending is both satisfying and disappointing: on one level, you might be 'pleased' for the characters, but as a reader, there is no real surprise, no twist or unexpected event – which, ironically, is something that many readers expect to find in a story.

In H. Porter Abbott's *The Cambridge Introduction to Narrative* (2008), a distinction is made between two aspects of closure. These can be summarized as follows:

1. ***Closure at the level of expectations***, which refers to satisfying the expectations generated by genre. In tragedy, you expect deaths at the end, and even though the deaths may be difficult to watch, you are still satisfied because it is conventional to the genre. However, as noted above, anything highly conventional runs the risk of disappointing the reader. Is there a conventional way in which political texts resolve?
2. ***Closure at the level of questions***, which refers to the questions readers generate as they read. At the beginning of a text the questions may be to do with orientating yourself in the storyworld, such as asking about the relationship between the characters, and where the text is set. More existential questions are raised too: in political texts, you might be tempted to ask whether it is ever permissible for a protagonist to kill, or whether there is any form of power which is admirable. Whether all questions are answered in the end is debatable – it would be odd if they were.

In the texts you are studying, it may be useful to apply the above distinctions. *A Doll's House*, for example, could run contrary to expectations – Nora's departure may well come as a shock. We might also be left with some unanswered questions, such as whether it is acceptable for a mother to walk out of the family home. Do we cheer as she leaves? There is, of course, no right response to this sort of question, but your willingness to engage and offer your view is essential to being successful in the exam.

A happy ending would seem ill-suited to tales of struggle. Perhaps a muted or a bleak ending is more effective in making a political point than an uplifting ending. This might justify the view that political fiction is a glum genre, tending towards negative events. In which case, why does the genre remain enduringly popular on stage, in bestseller lists, and on academic courses? Is political fiction morally instructive to the reader? Or does it simply reaffirm what you already think – that your values are 'right' and that power is corrosive? Is it a 'male' genre – or does it offer a critique of manhood? Does it ever foreground powerful women? You may like to pursue some of these questions in your studies.

In this final activity, you will explore the manner in which your texts resolve.

Activity

Consider the endings of the texts you are studying. What narrative, moral and political **significances** emerge? You might think about the following.

- Whether the expectations of genre are satisfied. Remember that your texts may belong to several genres. What are we led to expect? Are these expectations fulfilled?
- The questions left unanswered by the ending. What answers do you as a reader propose? How might different readers respond to the ending? What can the application of different critical perspectives add?
- What is being said ultimately about issues of power and powerlessness? Is rebellion championed? Are powerful people the object of your disgust? Is everything economically determined? How central is gender?

Summary

In this chapter you have learned that:

- protagonists can operate as victims or wielders of power who seek to acquire, maintain or regain power
- the influence of other genres in a text can lead to different expectations
- the endings of political and social protest fiction are seldom straightforward.

Component 3

Non-exam assessment (Coursework): Theory and independence

27 Non-exam assessment introduction

This chapter will:

- introduce the idea of critical theories as tools of reading
- introduce the critical areas covered by your AQA Critical Anthology.

Literature as representation

It should by now be clear, through your reading of other sections of this book, that literature is **representational**. This means that it does not give a definitive view of the world that we can say is 'real' or 'true': instead it offers us versions of the world which we can, up to a point, recognize, depending of course on our own experience of the world in the first place. And because literature gives us versions, these versions must be **ideological** in that they encode various attitudes, values and assumptions.

Literature is representational because it has to be. The very language we use, the words and sentences which make up the toolkit of literature, are themselves arbitrary labels for things and actions, rather than the things and actions themselves. The signs on the page making up the word 'book' have nothing to do with the thing itself, beyond the fact that in the English-speaking world it is quite convenient that we all use the same word. The French, however, use the word *livre*. If language actually *was* what it is labelled, there could only be one world language.

If literature is representational, giving ideological versions of the world, then literary criticism is also ideological, giving versions of texts. These versions arise out of the approaches that critics use to analyse the texts in the first place.

English Literature is a young subject compared to many other academic areas: it is not much more than 100 years old. As work in other subject areas, such as sociology, anthropology, philosophy, and so on began to recognize that a person's view of the world depended in a sense on their own starting point, English Literature as a subject had to acknowledge that depending on the ideology of the critic, and the critical methods used, different readings of a text would emerge.

Some people claim that there is no need to understand critical theories. What they ignore is the fact that all criticism *has* to be rooted in theoretical starting points, and so to claim that you don't need theory to understand a text is itself a (not very sustainable) theoretical viewpoint.

It is worth noting here that Assessment Objectives 3, 4 and 5 for English Literature are all relevant to this issue. The contexts that you as a critic choose to apply, the ways in which you connect texts, the interpretations you make based on your critical reading – all of these work together to form a critical debate. For this reason, although your specific work with theory takes place in the coursework section of your A level, it makes sense to apply theoretical ideas to your answers in all parts of the specification.

Ways of reading

A central idea that runs throughout the Literature B specification, and is especially prominent in the coursework component because of the Critical Anthology, is that literature can be read in different ways. The two examined components take **genre** as a starting point for reading literature. The Critical Anthology looks at other theoretical ways of reading texts.

The Critical Anthology should be used as a guide and a starting point, not as a definitive document. Your work in this book supplements the anthology itself and helps you to work with some of the ideas it contains.

Why study theory?

Understanding critical methods helps when you are faced with literary texts, because it gives you some frameworks to apply. It also highlights an interesting dilemma that we all face when analysing a text: should we, as critics, give a single and very strong reading of a text based on one method we happen to favour? Or should we weigh up various possible readings and understand the central ambiguity of texts and criticism?

Both approaches have a lot to recommend them. Some of the most interesting criticism – whether on books, film, music or other art forms – is committed, controversial and full of attitude. On the other hand, criticism based on an understanding that the work of art can be seen in many equally justifiable ways can be just as interesting, even if it lacks the immediacy of the single approach. There is no reason why, in your coursework, you cannot have a go at both methods, provided that you show you are aware of the frameworks you are applying.

Activity

To begin thinking about some theoretical ways of looking at literature, consider the text below, which is an example of the work of Banksy, who at the time of writing remains an elusive figure in terms of his real identity. His public work, usually in the form of murals, is generally seen as witty and political, but **paradoxically**, given the attitudes that the works seem to convey, they are now often worth a lot of money. A work produced in Cheltenham in 2014, thought to be by him, apparently doubled the value of the property it was painted on.

The work below appeared in Fitzrovia, one of the most exclusive and expensive parts of London, in 2011.

Consider the following critical questions:

1. Is this text pleasing to look at, or is it graffiti that should be removed or painted over?
2. Who in the world of the text has written the slogan? Is this significant?
3. How relevant is the context you have been given above about where this text is situated?
4. How do you respond to the message of the text? What do you think it means?

Key term

Paradox. An apparent contradiction that holds some unexpected truth.

Key terms

Critical establishment. The 'establishment' refers to a dominant or elite group, whose views and behaviour are powerfully influential. The critical establishment therefore refers to a dominant group of literary critics who say what you should read and how you should interpret your reading.

Narrative. How the events and causes in a story are shown and the various methods used by authors to do this showing; exploring narrative involves looking at what the author has chosen to include (or exclude) and reflecting on how these authorial methods shape the way we read.

Reflexivity. The act of referring to yourself. In a literary sense, it involves texts showing and knowing that they are texts.

Commentary

This activity has been designed to introduce some of the critical theories and methods in your coursework anthology. These are referenced in the comments below.

It would be hard to argue that this text is visually beautiful, but then it was probably never intended to be. It is indeed an example of graffiti in one sense, but it is unlikely to be painted over because of its commercial value – not least as a site of tourism. Banksy, who started off as an outsider in the art world, has now been embraced by it and so the **critical establishment** once again makes sure that it is in control of public taste. This critical view draws on aspects of the anthology section called 'Value, Aesthetics and The Canon'.

This work has a **narrative**, because in the world of the picture the slogan has either been written by or is being read by a rat. It is possible to see the **significance** of the rat in several ways: it is a lowly, yet scary creature; it is indestructible as a species, implying that its views cannot be eradicated; as speaker of the central message, it has subtle wisdom. It is also possible to see a playfully **reflexive** element to this work – it is a piece of graffiti talking about graffiti. These critical views draw on aspects of the anthology section called 'Narrative'.

You are told above that the work is situated in Fitzrovia. If you choose to see this context as significant, you will be taking a political approach to your interpretation of the text. From this perspective, the location of the work – among the richest and wealthiest properties in London – is used to make a very political statement about power and the silencing of voices raised in opposition to those in power. These critical views draw on aspects of the anthology section called 'Marxism'.

How you respond to the work and what it means can, if you choose, draw on all three of the above critical comments. In that case, you could argue that the work, and its context, make a clever and powerful statement about the hearing of alternative views. Because of the way the narrative has been constructed, several layers of meaning are possible here. It is the rat that speaks (or reacts), not the artist, and in fact graffiti *is* illegal. However, Banksy is unlikely to be arrested – his works have become valuable and, he implies, they have therefore lost any real power. This work, then, can be seen as a protest about the power of protest.

Link

If you are studying Elements of political and social protest writing (Option 2B), you can make connections here between literature and other forms of art.

Activity

The following extracts are taken from an article about Banksy by Simon Kelner in the *Independent*. Read the extracts and consider the ways in which Kelner (a) writes with a distinctive personal voice and (b) reflects in his views some of the critical issues raised above.

> I don't think there is a better commentator on the mores of the modern world than the incognito graffiti artist from Bristol. As an anti-celebrity celebrity, he's having a joke which shows no sign of running its course. He is a disruptive force in an era of convention, when most public discourse is sanitised for fear of causing offence. And as an artist, his every work makes a statement, designed to subvert the established way of doing things, and bringing art closer to the people. The latest Banksy to have been discovered is, in many ways, the ultimate expression of what we can only assume he is trying to achieve. [...]

> Banksy seeks to enrich our lives culturally and, inadvertently or not, financially. Critics say he is a phenomenon rather than an artist, and it's certainly true that he perfectly embodies our transitory age, a time when public engagement is powered by social media, and big ideas have the lifespan of a mayfly. But, in the end, who cares? Banksy is an original, a product of his time, a subversive force, an inaccessible figure whose work is accessible, and, most of all, an heroic anti-hero.

Requirements of this component

Technically called non-exam assessment (NEA) but more traditionally known as coursework, Component 3 requires you to do the following:

- You must submit two pieces of your own independent work, each between 1,250 and 1,500 words in length.
- One piece must be based on the study of a prose text and one on a poetry text. On the poetry text, a substantial amount of poetry should have been read.
- Each piece of work must link to an area of the Critical Anthology, which must be different for each piece.
- One re-creative response is permitted.

Your AQA Critical Anthology

The Critical Anthology is a distinctive feature of this specification. It is required reading in support of your coursework submission in Component 3, but it can help your work across all the components, including at AS level.

Assessment of your work in this specification is holistic – meaning that the Assessment Objectives are always considered together, and all five of them are best dealt with by responding to literature through a critical approach. Using appropriate concepts and terminology when writing about texts (AO1) is at the centre of everything you do, as is understanding how authors make meanings in their narratives (AO2). Applying critical methods to your reading inevitably leads to working with contexts (AO3). It involves connecting texts, because most critical ideas involve looking across texts (AO4), and by definition it offers a range of interpretations (AO5).

You should, then, be aware of the Critical Anthology from the start of your course, and refer to it frequently. It is not a set text in that it does not have to be covered in its entirety, and it does not say everything there is to say about its chosen areas. It is best seen as a resource to work with, and where fruitful to expand upon, throughout your course.

The coursework section of this book focuses specifically on ideas discussed in the Critical Anthology. It explains some of the central ideas, helping you to develop a deeper understanding of some important ideas. It also at times extends the ideas seen in the Critical Anthology, showing you how you can read beyond it to develop your critical thinking about literature.

Before considering in detail, in the following chapters, the theoretical areas covered in the Critical Anthology, look at the outline below of its central topics. Broadly speaking, the material is concerned with the following three types of critical approach.

Did you know?

The word **'gender'** is often used loosely. Strictly speaking, if you refer to someone as a man or a woman, you are referring to his or her sex. If you want to consider how men and women are represented through aspects of masculinity and femininity, you should use the word 'gender'. Using 'gender' in both instances diminishes the word's specific meaning. See page 220 in the next chapter.

Structural criticism

All literature tells stories, so studying how stories are told can help you reach critical views about what the stories can mean. The study of how stories work, and how they are structured, comes under the category *Narrative*.

Political criticism

The pre-release material looks at four approaches that are concerned with aspects of personal, social and political power. *Marxist* criticism investigates the ways in which texts portray economic and other inequalities, and the extent to which the text challenges these and indicates a need for change. *Feminist* criticism looks at representation of **gender**, and also urges us to consider the implications of inequality. In the past such criticism was especially concerned with femininity, but now it tends to embrace other gender issues such as masculinity.

Political criticism in a general sense investigates aspects of power, and some of the most significant acts of power in the past 500 years have involved the **colonization** of one set of people and their culture by another. *Post-colonial* criticism examines and sometimes re-examines literature, concentrating on the social and political relationships between the colonizer and the colonized, which shaped and produced the literature.

Just as literature and criticism have had to reflect on the potential ramifications of colonialism, they have had to do the same with the potential ramifications of humanity's relationship with the natural world. *Ecocriticism* is an area of criticism which analyses and promotes texts that raise political and moral questions about human interactions with nature.

Key terms

Aesthetic. Relating to the appreciation or consideration of beauty.

Canon. The group of texts that are said to be of particular value and so should be read by all.

Gender. The representation of women and men through cultural stereotypes, which can and should be endlessly disputed; the adjectives 'feminine' and 'masculine' and the nouns 'femininity' and 'masculinity' apply here.

Moral and aesthetic criticism

Here three inter-related topics are considered. In 'Value, Aesthetics and the Canon' you are asked to consider whether it is possible to say that reading literature has any real purpose beyond the recreational, whether in some sense it can be said to be 'good' for you and so have 'value'.

The second topic considers whether it is possible to say that literary texts are beautiful, that is that they have **aesthetic** value, and if so whether it is possible to analyse such beauty. The third part of these connected topics involves the idea of a literary **canon**, a selection of texts deemed to be superior to others which become 'required' reading.

Summary

In this chapter you have been shown why it is worth thinking about critical theories, and you have been introduced in outline to the critical theories you can work with throughout your course, as well as more specifically for your coursework.

Marxism and feminism: politics and power 28

Marxism

Hans Bertens, writing about Marxism, makes the important distinction between Marxist politics, which since 1989 have come to be seen as increasingly irrelevant, and Marxist thinking, which can still be seen as highly relevant. After all, Marx was a philosopher and economist whose ideas were adopted by politicians, rather than a politician himself.

The central ideas of Marxist thinking

Below are some of the central ideas of Marxist thinking, and some of the implications that follow from them for the study of literature.

- Human beings are not free and independent agents, acting as individuals with limitless choices. We are bound to processes of collective thought and action. This is one reason why the **essentialist** approach to literature has to be abandoned in favour of seeing literature as **representational**. Essentialist approaches to literature talk about events and characters as though they are individual and 'real'. Representational approaches to literature understand that there is no such thing as a single 'reality', just endless versions of it, told in endless different ways. The version you are given and the way you read that version are a result of collective **ideology**.
- Part of Marx's review of history involved looking at people's **socio-economic** circumstances, which condition them: we think and behave in certain ways because we have to. The life of the reader and the work of the author are bound together, therefore, by complex contextual connections involving attitudes towards wealth, property, and above all, power.
- Although we like to think we live in a world of choices, this idea of choice is an illusion – our choices are much more limited than we pretend. Literature, at heart, is frequently about conflict and resolution. In Marxist thinking, the history of all societies is the history of class struggles between the oppressors and the oppressed. Marxist criticism looks for evidence of the inevitable in human behaviour and interaction, rather than the significance of individual behaviour.
- Much of the social **discourse** that surrounds us encourages us to believe that we lead our lives as part of a series of choices. The capitalist system appears to offer choices, but Marxism suggests that many of these are illusory. Because there is a gap between what we see as potential in life and what life actually offers us, we are in a sense **alienated** from the world. Marxist approaches to literature look for evidence of such alienation.
- Opponents of Marxist criticism say that it is necessarily political, and so its application forces the reader into looking at literary texts as vehicles for political ideas. A counter-argument is that all critical activity is political, so being open about your political position is surely to be encouraged.

This chapter will:

- introduce you to two of the most influential sets of theories for the study of literature, as seen in Sections 2 and 3 of the Critical Anthology
- introduce you to the key idea of power in literature
- show you how theories can be applied to texts, as you will need to do in your coursework component.

Key terms

Alienated / Alienation. Alienation involves being made to feel distanced, isolated, even hostile. People can experience alienation when they feel that their lives lack full meaning, because they are just part of a process.

Discourse. This is a term used differently in many academic disciplines. Here it is used in the sense of repeated patterns of language use.

Essentialism. Interpreting literature as if it is 'real', peopled by 'real' people.

Socio-economic. The combination of the social and economic conditions we live under. Although the phrase always puts social first, a Marxist view would say that it is economics which determine everything else.

Link

For more on the ways in which stories are told, see the section on **narrative** in Chapter 29.

Activity

In Chapter 1 we looked at the poem 'The Road Not Taken' by Robert Frost, and explored some potential meanings. Look at the poem again (page 13). Write a couple of paragraphs in which you offer a Marxist reading of this poem, based on the theories you have just read about.

Commentary

Given what we have read about the illusory nature of choices, this poem is well suited to a Marxist interpretation. We have already seen in Chapter 1 that the final stanza of the poem presents problems for a simple reading about taking the road 'less traveled by'. If you take the final two lines out of context, as is frequently done in self-help books selling capitalist management solutions, it appears that the poem supports the idea of self-improvement by choosing the less-usual options.

However, if we look at the poem in its entirety, another meaning is possible. For the first three stanzas the narrator makes a great deal out of having a choice to make, but the choice is not really much of one at all. In the final stanza, he says that having made the choice (which was really no choice at all) he will in the future, with an alienated 'sigh', 'be telling' this story as though he did have a viable choice and it made all the difference to his life. In other words, rather than face up to the inevitability of our lives, we make up fictions that we try to believe in – but we can't quite manage to do so.

What has happened as you made this reading, or one similar to it, is that you put yourself into a certain way of critical thinking, and applied ideas from this thinking to a text. You are then faced with a critical decision to make when writing your coursework. Do you keep to this single interpretation, perhaps because you think it's especially significant, or do you at the same time offer another reading which might seem equally viable? Whichever way you go, supply evidence and be clear about the framework you have used.

Feminism and gender

Feminism can be linked to Marxism in that both schools of thought have socio-economic ideas at the heart of their thinking. While Marxism saw working people as historically disadvantaged, it traditionally failed to take much notice of another group who have been especially disadvantaged throughout history: women.

Key term

Sex. The biological differences between men and women.

Marxist ideas on literature have tended to consider how literature *reflects* the social world. Feminism, by contrast, has often taken a stronger line, saying that literature helps to *construct* views of women that are unfair. This is why the difference between **sex** and **gender** is so important, even though the words are often confused in everyday use.

As ideas about feminism developed, it became clear that men too are potentially disadvantaged in that they are expected to perform stereotypical roles that create their own problems. Recently gender studies have tended to look at notions of masculinity, and the way it is represented, as well as femininity.

Central ideas of feminist thinking

Below are some of the central ideas of feminist thinking, and some of the implications that follow from them for the study of literature.

- It has already been stressed that Marxist thinking sees literature as representational. So does feminist thinking, although the latter regards much literature as particularly problematic because literary texts actively create negative stereotypes. Assumptions about the roles and status of women are not essential truths; they grow out of hundreds of years of representational assumptions. In many ways, therefore, Marxist and feminist thinking have much in common.
- Feminists see literature as both reflecting women's lack of power and contributing to it. Lists of set books are dominated by male authors (frequently, dead white male authors) who inevitably reinforce **ideologies** about male superiority and female subordination.
- Feminist critics have focused on language and the way it can promote assumptions about the apparently essential nature of man and woman, with man as the norm and woman as 'the other'.
- Typically, women are stereotyped either positively or negatively (from a male point of view). Women in 'positive' stereotypes are seen as cute but helpless, or angelically unselfish. Women in 'negative' stereotypes are seen as either seductresses or shrews. Typically, therefore, passive women are seen as virtuous, while active women are regarded as dangerous and selfish.
- Our society has adopted many attitudes, values and assumptions based on uncritical notions of gender. It is these assumptions in particular that are dangerous, because they are not even explicitly stated. This is why feminists have been so concerned about aspects of language that seem, by their very structure, to enshrine inequality.
- Early feminists saw personal relationships and the wider world as operating in much the same ways: the personal is the political. This would suggest that women needed to intervene to change their social positions – so in literature, they needed to produce texts that challenged the stereotypes.
- Women authors, especially from earlier times, sometimes struggled to see beyond the stereotypes, because inevitably they were themselves suppressed. Those who wrote critically about the condition of women before the feminist movements of the 20th century are therefore especially prized.
- Many texts seem to assume that the reader is male. Some male authors noted for their daring depictions of the erotic have been seen by feminists as giving a very male-focused view of sex and relationships.
- Focus on gender shows some men in power to be dangerously weak behind their mask of masculinity.

Activity

Christina Rossetti (1830–1894) was a Victorian poet who wrote many poems with women at their centre. One of these is 'A Daughter of Eve'. The website 'Humanities 360' gives the following interpretation of the poem:

> 'A Daughter of Eve' was a sad poem by Christina Rossetti, but one people could relate to. Many individuals have periods in life that they

> regret or wish they could change. This poem brings feelings [of] sadness and regret, which can be difficult to deal with. The poem can also enable readers to find closure with their own mistakes and move on. Despite sorrow, until one is gone, there is still life left to be lived and Rossetti also made this clear in the poem. 'A Daughter of Eve' was a beautifully written poem with an important moral that readers could understand.

In the light of what you have read about feminist thinking above, write your own analysis of the poem below. Think carefully about the ways in which the title and the structure of the poem create metaphors that can lead you to certain meanings.

A Daughter of Eve

A fool I was to sleep at noon,
And wake when night is chilly
Beneath the comfortless cold moon;
A fool to pluck my rose too soon,
A fool to snap my lily.

My garden-plot I have not kept;
Faded and all-forsaken,
I weep as I have never wept:
Oh it was summer when I slept,
It's winter now I waken.

Talk what you please of future spring
And sun-warm'd sweet to-morrow:
Stripp'd bare of hope and everything,
No more to laugh, no more to sing,
I sit alone with sorrow.

Commentary

One way to produce a critical response using material from the Critical Anthology is to do some comparative criticism. This involves looking at the text closely and analysing it by using a critical theory set against another type of critical response. The writer quoted in the Activity clearly regards Rossetti's poem as referring to individuals and their lives in a non-political way. As has been mentioned, it is possible to say that being non-political is itself a political act.

If we look at the title of Rossetti's poem, though, and consider its potential significance, it should immediately be clear that this can be regarded as a poem about women and power. All women are daughters of Eve, and the biblical Eve can be seen as the ultimate rebel against the **patriarchal** world of Adam and God. The narrator of this poem has acted against convention and now suffers for it, as all women must in a male-centred world.

Much of the imagery in the poem can be related to sexual behaviour. The lines 'A fool to pluck my rose too soon, / A fool to snap my lily' imply that the narrator at the time enjoyed sexual experiences which she now regrets. Society expects women to keep their lives and marriages neat, like a 'garden-plot' where flowers are grown to be pretty and well managed. In picking the flowers, in ignoring the garden, the narrator has lived by desire, not convention. The time of the poem is set in the past – these actions were long ago, and the woman has suffered for and is still suffering for what she has done.

The criticism quoted in the Activity says that although there is sorrow in the narrator's life, there is still life to be lived, which is a sweetly optimistic reading of the poem. But the poem uses much darker language than this: our narrator is 'Stripp'd bare of hope' and says 'I weep as I have never wept'.

When applying the Critical Anthology to literary texts, you are not bound by applying only one set of theories at a time. The 'Narrative' section of the anthology points you to thinking about points of view. Consider again the final stanza. How can we interpret the **pronoun** 'you' here? 'You' is a powerfully ambiguous pronoun in English because it can refer to one or many. If we take it here to mean society as a whole, then we can see the narrator accusing the society she lives in of offering silly platitudes about life when the reality for the fallen woman is harshly different.

Possible applications in coursework

This specification is designed to enable you to make individual choices about the texts you write about. The following are some possible starting points, but obviously the more you have read, the wider your range of choice will be.

Choice and its illusory nature

Many literary texts portray people at a crossroads in life, deciding which way to go. No wonder life as a journey is such a popular metaphor in both life and literature. You could explore your chosen text to see whether the choices that people make in the text are 'free' or 'determined'.

Possible poetry texts include collections by Christina Rossetti, Thomas Hardy, Robert Frost, Philip Larkin (including for example 'No Road', 'Deceptions', 'Essential Beauty' and 'The Large Cool Store'), Carol Ann Duffy. Possible prose texts include Hardy's *The Mayor of Casterbridge*, L. P. Hartley's *The Go-Between* and Sebastian Barry's *The Secret Scripture*.

Alienation

We can look in texts for 'outsiders', people who do not fit in, or even for whole texts showing the absurdity of a world without meaning. Possible texts include Mark Twain's *Huckleberry Finn*, J. D. Salinger's *The Catcher in the Rye* and Anne Tyler's *Digging to America*. Many European writers, including some living under Communist regimes, have also written about alienation. You could, for example, look at Milan Kundera's *The Unbearable Lightness of Being*.

Women and power

Many literary texts show women without power. Possible texts include 19th-century novels by men such as Charles Dickens and Thomas Hardy, and more interestingly perhaps by women such as Jane Austen and George Eliot. (Make sure though that you do not opt for any of the set texts listed in Components 1 or 2.) Many novels written after 1960 represent women from a more feminist perspective. You could try novels by Fay Weldon, Jeanette Winterson or Angela Carter.

Remember, too, that feminist critical ideas can be applied to works by men not normally known for being sympathetic to feminist thinking. Novels by Martin Amis and poems by Philip Larkin are among the possibilities.

Women and stereotypes

Possible texts are numerous, right across the spectrum of genre and time. The novels of D. H. Lawrence, reviled by early feminists, could be possible texts, especially *Sons and Lovers*. If you are studying the 'Elements of crime writing' option in Component 2, you could extend your reading in this genre where women are frequently victims of male violence. Poetry by Carol Ann Duffy and Philip Larkin could be contrasted.

Gender

In terms of gender, you can look more widely at the representation of men as well as women. Possible texts include novels by Nick Hornby, men and women in the novels of Ian McEwan, and many more.

Summary

In this chapter you have considered some of the basic principles behind two political forms of criticism: Marxism and feminism. You have also applied these theories to texts, and been encouraged to think about the texts you might choose for your coursework.

Further reading

Books about literary theories can be notoriously complex to read, and often seem to be written for a highly specialist audience. Your Critical Anthology does a good job in providing you with some starting points. If you wish to read further, there are some books aimed at a wider audience. These include:

Barry, P. *Beginning Theory* (2nd Edition, 2002), Manchester University Press

Bertens, H. *Literary Theory: The Basics* (2001), Routledge

Culler, J. *Literary Theory: A Very Short Introduction* (1997), OUP

Green, K. and LeBihan, J. *Critical Theory and Practice: A Coursebook* (1996), Routledge

Introducing narrative: telling stories 29

This chapter will:

- show you why understanding about narrative is important for literary study, and how the study of narrative can help you as much with exam papers as with coursework
- remind you that when stories are told, they are representations of the world, not the world itself
- introduce you to some key ideas about narrative, namely point of view, focus and voices in texts.

The Critical Anthology

The AQA Critical Anthology begins with 'Ideas about Narrative', and of all the sections in the anthology it is this one that can be applied most usefully not just to your NEA, but also to your examined components. For that reason two chapters of this book discuss ideas about **narrative**, some of which go beyond the introductory material in your anthology.

Storytelling

We are surrounded by storytelling, and on a basic level it forms an essential part of how we live. In all cultures, storytelling is a vital part of human connection, and children, of course, are taught from a very young age how to live in their culture by being told stories.

Activity

Note down all the stories you have come into contact with in the past 24 hours. Then share one of them with your class.

Commentary

It is likely that you came up with plenty of examples of stories. The ones most people start with when doing this activity are the set-pieces, coming from quite formal sources such as newspapers and magazines, and informal sources such as conversations about nights out with friends. You may, though, have spread your net wider. It can be argued that many of the visual texts that surround us wherever we go – advertising all sorts of products and services – tell us stories about our lives and our desires. And even the simplest SMS text from a friend might be part of a bigger story.

Story, plot and narrative

In everyday use it does not really matter how we use the term 'story' because, after all, these stories flash past us at a rapid speed. We take from them as much as we want at any given time, and then pass on to the next.

When it comes to studying stories in a more academic way, however, it is useful to sort out some key terms and agree that they will be used in quite specific ways. As is always the case with such terminology, it is not important as such, but using it consistently helps to establish a common way of thinking and explaining – in this case, about how literature works. Understanding the difference between the terms **story**, **plot** and **narrative** can help you to see where to focus your attention when thinking about all the texts you are studying, not just your coursework.

Key term

Story. The various events that are shown.

The English word 'narrative' derives from the word *gnarus*, meaning knowledge – so a helpful starting point for thinking about narrative is to consider the following question when looking at a text: *Who knows what, when do they know it, and how do they know it?*

When studying literary texts, especially if you are looking at aspects of narrative, bear in mind the following simple rule:

It is the author who controls the characters and events in a story. Characters cannot do or say anything other than what the author makes them do.

When exploring texts, it is vital to keep the authors, and their methods of working, at the heart of your considerations.

Points of view

Visual and spatial metaphors

The term 'point of view' is very important when studying aspects of narrative, but hard to define simply, partly because it is a **metaphor** based on a visual and spatial idea. If you are at a football match, and you stand behind the goal, that is your point of view for the game. If you are at the side of the pitch, that is a different point of view, as is the view from the other end of the ground. And it can easily be argued that where you stand affects how you see the game. It depends upon your position, your standpoint. Behind the goal where your team scores gives a different perspective from being at the far end of the pitch. Digital television coverage nowadays allows you to change your angle in the living room.

So where, as readers, we are 'placed' in the telling of the story is vital to the way we interpret it, in just the same way as where we stand in a sports ground can affect our sense of how well we think our team played. Our understanding both of characters and of **narrative gaps** is crucially underpinned by understanding how writers have used point of view.

> **Key term**
>
> **Narrative gaps.** The parts of a story that we are not given, as readers, but which we nonetheless try to supply ourselves.

While the sport analogy above should be clear, you may have noticed that in explaining point of view, other metaphorical terms were used, which also depend on visual and spatial concepts. So we can say everything depends on:

- your point of view
- where you stand – your standpoint
- the perspective you take
- your position
- the angle you take.

These terms can have another level of meaning. They can refer not only to your physical position, but also your position in terms of the beliefs you hold, the ideas you have. To continue with the sport analogy, we might say something like 'whether or not Bobby Smith should be sacked as manager depends on your point of view, but I think he's doing a good job'.

For our purposes, then, looking at point of view is important because it allows us to analyse narratives technically, but also in terms of their ideas and views; how they see the world. Point of view is therefore to do with how a text works and also an indication of the **ideology** in a text. By exploring both these elements we are able to arrive at a more complete reading of the text.

The narrator: first person or third person?

You probably know about first- and third-person narrators from your previous studies. These terms can be the starting points for a more sophisticated way of looking at narratives, and it is useful to consider in a broad sense what the two techniques allow writers to do.

The obvious way to identify whether a text uses first-person or third-person narration is to look at the **pronouns** that are used. Thomas Hardy's poem 'Drummer Hodge', about a dead young soldier in the Boer War, begins with his body being crudely buried on a South African hill ('kopje').

> They throw in Drummer Hodge, to rest
> Uncoffined – just as found:
> His landmark is a kopje-crest
> That breaks the veldt around

We can tell immediately that this is a third-person narrative by the use of 'They' (rather than 'We') and 'His' (rather than 'My'). If we think about point of view as being in part about proximity to the action, then the effect of 'they' instead of 'we' is one of distance, with the third-person narrative being further away from the reader than the first person would be. This tells us that the **focus** of the poem is likely to be Drummer Hodge. Note also that in this case the pronoun 'They' is **unreferenced**. This means that we are not sure who 'They' are – his fellow soldiers, the enemy, a burial party after the battle? This lack of detail makes his burial seem even more casual.

On the other hand, Thomas Hardy's poem 'The Darkling Thrush' begins with the lines:

> I leant upon a coppice gate
> When frost was spectre-gray

This is obviously a first-person narrative, and suggests therefore that the **focalization** could ultimately be on the **speaker** of the poem rather than on the bird named in the title.

Activity

Look at Hardy's poems 'Drummer Hodge' and 'The Darkling Thrush' in full, and consider how the different narrative voices affect what the poems are ultimately about.

There is no commentary with this activity.

Activity

Imagine that you are going to write a story about two people meeting and falling in love.

1. Consider telling it in the first person, from the point of view of one of the two people meeting. What are the advantages and disadvantages of this?
2. Consider telling it in the third person. What are the advantages and disadvantages of this?
3. Can you think of any other ways in which the story could be told?

Key terms

Focus / Focalizer / Focalization. A narrative point of view through which the text is mediated. We see the events of the story from the perspective of the focalizer.

Speaker. It is not possible in a story to say that the narrator of the story is the same as the author. The term 'speaker' makes this distinction clear.

Unreferenced pronoun. A pronoun that is not attached to a specific person or thing. This can lead to creative ambiguity. Just who is being referred to? Advertising frequently uses unreferenced pronouns, especially 'you', which has the added ambiguity of being possibly one person or many.

Study tip

Changing the focus of the narrative, switching the point of view, can be a very useful tool to use as part of a re-creative exercise for your coursework.

Commentary

1. An advantage of the first-person method is that it can be intimate, close to the action, and have a very personal narrative voice. But within this advantage also lies a distinct disadvantage: the narrator can report only on what he or she thinks and feels, and only on action taking place in his or her presence. There are ways around this of course: other characters can relate what they did, and what they think, and devices such as letters, diaries, emails and so on can provide further information. There are times, though, when the narrator can seem almost required to be the novelist, to give the reader necessary information – and at times such as these, the first-person method is at its least effective.

2. The advantage of the third-person narrative is that it offers the author the possibility of taking the narrative anywhere, of observing everything and everyone – but the downside is that this can feel quite remote from the reader and it can lack the personal nature of the first-person method.

3. In reality, authors do not necessarily have to stick rigidly to one method, and there are many ingenious ways to overcome narrative problems. For example, there can be more than one first-person narrator in a novel, with the switch clearly marked in the chapter headings. Or there can be a third-person narrative, but one that changes the point of view, often getting close to different characters one at a time.

Shifting perspectives

Perspectives frequently shift and move within texts – this is certainly the case in novels, but can be seen in poems too. Sometimes, to highlight the different perceptions of characters, and perhaps misunderstandings between them, essentially the same incident is seen twice, first from one character's point of view, then from another's.

The following extracts from *Small Island* come early in the novel. Hortense has arrived in London in 1948 from Jamaica, to be reunited with her husband Gilbert, who has lived in London for some time – and who has failed to meet her at the dock. Hortense has just seen the room they are to live in and is horrified at how small it is. Gilbert, on the other hand, is aware that living in London means you live in small rooms. We, as readers, have an overview of their misunderstanding in a way that the two characters don't.

Activity

How does Andrea Levy show the differing perceptions of the two characters in each of the extracts? Can you see a third point of view here, which involves what the reader could think about this exchange?

Hortense

'Well,' I said, 'show me the rest, then, Gilbert'. The man just stared. 'Show me the rest, nah. I am tired from the long journey.' He scratched his head. 'The other rooms, Gilbert. The ones you busy making so nice for me you forgot to come to the dock.'

Gilbert spoke so softly I could hardly hear. He said, 'But this is it.'

'I am sorry?' I said.

'This is it, Hortense. This is the room I am living.'

Three steps would take me to one side of this room. Four steps could take me to another. There was a sink in the corner, a rusty tap stuck out from the wall above it. There was a table with two chairs – one with its back broken – pushed up against the bed. The armchair held a shopping bag, a pyjama top, and a teapot. In the fireplace the gas hissed with a blue flame.

'Just this?' I had to sit on the bed. My legs gave way. There was no bounce underneath me as I fell. 'Just this? This is where you are living? Just this?'

Gilbert

'Is this the way the English live?' How many times she ask me that question? I lose count. 'This the way the English live?' That question became a mournful lament, sighed on each and every thing she see. 'Is this the way the English live?'

'Yes', I tell her, 'this is the way the English live ... there has been a war ... many English live worse than this.'

She drift to the window, look quizzical upon the scene, rub her gloved hand on the pane of glass, examine it before saying once more, 'This the way the English live?'

Soon the honourable man inside me was shaking my ribs and thumping my breast, wanting to know, 'Gilbert, what in God's name have you done? You no realise, man? Cha, you married to this woman!'

Commentary

Hortense's point of view is given through a number of methods, beyond the obvious one that it is her first-person narrative. Her imperative way of speaking, of giving orders, is contrasted with Gilbert's softly spoken words. The detail of what she sees, especially things that are broken and out of place, suggest someone seeing them for the first time with a critical eye. The repetition of 'Just this' and the giving way of her legs focus on her shock and surprise.

Whereas repeated words from Hortense show her amazement, when Gilbert reports her repetition, he does so with increasing irritation, until we are given, in direct thought, the idea that he is wondering if he should regret his marriage.

As readers we probably do not take sides in this misunderstanding, but we are being offered a third, more indirect point of view to consider – provided, that is, that we pick up the potential meanings on offer. Hortense has supposedly come from a small island, Jamaica, but she is shocked by the squalor she finds in England, when she expected to be impressed. To her, Britain is the small island. One detail in Gilbert's narrative highlights this: when Hortense rubs the window, he does not comment on its significance, and because it is not in her narrative nor does she. But attentive readers will note that she is wearing a glove, a sign of social standing, and after rubbing the dirty window which soils her (white?) glove she repeats her question.

The **semiotics** here suggest that how you view a culture depends on your point of view, and in this novel English readers are being asked to examine the assumptions they make about cultural superiority over others.

Indirect speech and thought

Speech can be directly related in the world of a story, that is the words spoken by the character are given as 'said', and usually they are put in speech marks. Speech can also be related indirectly. Indirect speech is reported by the narrator, giving a version of the words spoken rather than the words themselves.

Indirect speech, sometimes called reported speech, involves some structural changes to the grammar that would be used in direct speech. For example:

- *'Are you in love, Rob?' asked Rachel.* This is attributed direct speech, signalled in part by the use of speech marks.
- *Rachel asked Rob if he was in love.* This is indirect attributed speech.
- *Rob was asked if he was in love.* This version takes Rachel out of the statement altogether. This is **free indirect speech**, and it leaves the situation more ambiguous.

If we transfer this same statement to thought, rather than speech, we will have:

- *'Is Rob in love?' thought Rachel.* This is direct attributed thought.
- *Rachel wondered if Rob was in love.* This is indirect attributed thought.
- *Was Rob in love?* This is **free indirect thought** and again leaves some doubt as to whose voice, in 'thought' form, is being heard here. Is it Rachel thinking about Rob or is it Rob thinking about himself?

Key terms

Free indirect speech. This refers to speech that is embedded in a narrative, so it is unattributed (free) and a report of the speech rather than the actual words (indirect).

Free indirect thought. A narrative technique where a character's thought processes form part of the narrative but are not attributed to him or her.

Note that pronouns and verb tenses change when moving from direct to indirect speech, as does word order. Looking at these indicators is a key way of thinking about how narratives have been organized.

When considering point of view, and which character's thoughts and ideas are being focalized, it is worth considering the use of the free indirect forms of speech and thought, as these forms can be used seamlessly within the narrative.

Activity

The following extract is from a third-person narrative in Kate Atkinson's novel *When Will There Be Good News?*. In this extract, the detective figure, Jackson Brodie, wakes up in hospital after a serious train crash.

1. What direct speech can you find here, and is it attributed?
2. What thought can you find here? Is this thought free or attributed? Is it direct thought or indirect thought?

'Where am I?' Jackson asked a nurse.

'In the Royal Infirmary in Edinburgh,' she said.

'Edinburgh? Edinburgh, Scotland?' Listen to him, he sounded like an American tourist.

'Yes, Edinburgh, Scotland,' she affirmed.

What on earth was he doing in Edinburgh? The scene of some of his greatest defeats in life and love. Why was he in Edinburgh? 'I was on my way to London,' he said.

'You must have gone the wrong way,' she laughed. 'Bad luck.'

He might not know where he had come from but he knew where he was going. He was going home.

Commentary

Most of the direct speech is attributed, with the terms 'affirmed' and 'laughed' being used as attribution in addition to the words 'asked' and 'said'.

One piece of free speech comes when Brodie says 'Edinburgh? Edinburgh, Scotland?'. We know it is him speaking because of the sequence; the nurse has just spoken before.

Of more interest here, though, is the way in which thought is used, and thought is the more dominant mode. The last two sentences, for example, are clearly indirect thought, from Brodie's point of view. The final statement 'He was going home' shows a character who is strong and decisive, not to be confined by the rule of a hospital.

One part of the extract that may have been more difficult to ascribe is the sentence 'Listen to him, he sounded like an American tourist.' There is a deliberate ambiguity about who could be thinking this. Presumably it is Brodie commenting ironically on himself, but it could also be the nurse's thoughts, in which case she is finding her patient rather annoying. Or it could be both.

Using ambiguity

Your Critical Anthology has the underlying theme of ways of reading. One way to use narrative as a starting point is to find creative ambiguity in texts, to find a tension between different interpretations which makes the reading process more subtle.

To recap on what we have found so far, one way in which we receive information or knowledge in a story is through what we are 'told' by characters involved. Areas to consider include:

- Who speaks, to whom and when?
- What are they talking about?
- What information does the talk give (a) other characters and (b) the reader?
- Is the speech direct or indirect?
- Is the speech attributed or free?
- If attributed, is the attitude towards the character contained in the attribution?
- Whose thoughts are accessed?
- Are these thoughts attributed or free?
- Voices in stories can help to establish character traits, and so are part of **characterization**, but also they enable authors to give information.

Key term

Characterization. The way in which an author creates and uses characters, and why.

Extension activity

1. Read Matt Madden's comic book on narrative, called *99 Ways to Tell A Story*. It is a superb way to understand how narrative works – in at least 99 different ways.

2. Start to narrow down the choices of texts you might wish to write about for coursework. As well as potentially allowing the application of other parts of the Critical Anthology, do they also allow you to write about narrative?

3. Consider the novels you are studying in Component 2. Choose a representative section (say, a chapter) and discuss the following issues:

- How is speech used in this chapter of the novel?
- Is attribution used to indicate aspects of character?
- Is thought given in this chapter? Whose thoughts are given?
- Are there points in the chapter where who is speaking/thinking is deliberately ambiguous?

4. Consider the poetry texts you are studying for Component 2 and discuss the following issues:

- To what extent do the poems contain direct speech? What is the effect of this?
- Do the poems have a range of speakers?
- Who is heard and who is not? Is this significant?

Possible applications in Component 3 coursework

All literature contains narrative of some sort, so it would be odd to name specific works as being better for the study of narrative than others. In order to refer to books which you might be studying, this chapter has discussed some of the set texts as examples of key principles. Do be clear, though, that you cannot write about *any* of the AQA-nominated set texts in your coursework.

Remember, too, that you must study one prose text and one poetry text. In the case of the latter you should refer to more than one poem in your answer, unless you have chosen a long narrative poem.

Summary

This chapter has looked at some of the ways in which authors use speaking and thinking voices in texts. One result of this process has been to see that it contributes to creating the point of view of the story. In the next chapter, some further ideas about narrative are explored.

Narrative: places, time and people

30

Representing place

This chapter will:

- explore the potential significance of places in **narratives**, where something significant happens somewhere significant
- explore the significance in narratives of time and sequence, understanding that time in stories can be re-arranged, repeated, speeded up and slowed down
- explore the significance of people in narratives, whether they are central to the story or have a more minor role.

Fictional stories, if they are to represent in some ways the real world, need to be set in significant places. These places can vary in size: they can be rooms, houses, gardens, streets, towns, regions, countries, worlds and even universes. They can be recognizable as places we already know, or based on places we know but also clearly fictional – or completely invented 'new' worlds.

These places all share something in common, however: they are representations of places, not actual places. So, at one end of the spectrum, a highly realistic description of a place that can be found on a map is still a version of the place in words, a depiction by an author of some aspects of the place but not others. At the other end of the spectrum, a completely invented place, one that cannot possibly exist in our real world, will nonetheless possess all sorts of features from our world that we can recognize. And meanwhile, across the rest of the spectrum, authors are taking bits of real places and altering them to suit their purposes.

Stories are condensed versions of reality, shaped to present actions and ideas that tell us something about the lives we lead. Stories need to be set in places if they are to persuade us of their connections with our lives, but at the same time these places can be more than just settings where events happen. Scenes and places frequently carry a significance that goes way beyond being where something merely happens. In their uses of scenes and places, authors take advantage of the possibilities for creating meanings.

Activity

From your own knowledge, and then using research facilities such as the Internet, histories of literature, and so on, make a list of novels that have a place name as a major part of their title. Does the name of this place carry connotations of meaning – significance?

You could extend your search to include films and television programmes, especially soap operas, and again consider the possible significance of the places.

There is no commentary for this activity.

Places in prose fiction

Places have a significant role in **prose** fiction. In a poem, with its concise narrative, specifics of a place can be given, without all the detail of precise location.

In prose fiction, though, there is a greater expectation that places will be filled out in detail. There is more room in novels and stories, and readers have the expectation that places will be described more fully. In novels and stories, people's lives are examined in some detail, and although these lives are fictional, in most cases we expect them to be 'realistic', to represent a world that we recognize. (There are, of course, always exceptions to rules about literature: science fiction and fantasy, for example, tend to describe weird and exotic places, even if in some ways such genres still comment on the world as we know it.)

Not surprisingly, there is a tradition in English Literature of novelists who centre their work on one particular place or area. Charles Dickens frequently writes about London – representing real places with their actual names. Thomas Hardy, though, does something slightly different – although his novels are largely set in and around Dorset, he uses the older name of Wessex for this area, and changes the names of towns, with Dorchester becoming Casterbridge, for example.

Key term

Establishment. The work the author does for the reader at the beginning of the text, or a section of the text, involving the introduction of places, time, people, etc.

Activity

Read the opening paragraph of Jim Crace's novel *Harvest*, below. What aspects of place are **established** here?

> Two twists of smoke at a time of year too warm for cottage fires surprise us at first light, or they at least surprise those of us who've not been up to mischief in the dark. Our land is topped and tailed with flames. Beyond the frontier ditches of our fields and in the shelter of our woods, on common ground, where yesterday there wasn't anyone who could give rise to smoke, some newcomers, by the lustre of an obliging reapers' moon, have put up their hut – four rough and ready walls, a bit of roof – and lit the more outlying of these fires. Their fire is damp. They will have thrown on wet greenery in order to procure the blackest plume, and thereby not be missed by us. It rises in a column that hardly bends or thins until it clears the canopies. It says, new neighbours have arrived; they've built a place; they've laid a hearth; they know the custom and the law. This first smoke has given them the right to stay. We'll see.

Commentary

Although the first-person narrator's voice is not presented in a pseudo-archaic way, we can quickly work out that the so-far-nameless place is in an agricultural setting in the past. The land is 'Our land' and there are customs and laws which give people the right to stay. The smoke the newcomers make, far from being something they want to hide in case they are caught, is deliberately drawing attention to the claim they have staked to residence on common land.

What is established at once is that this is a rural community with customs and laws which, it seems, are known and obeyed by all. This is a stable place where people belong. But then comes the final short sentence: 'We'll see'. This suddenly establishes a sense of doubt, the possibility that all is not going to be stable – and so a sense of potential disharmony is created. This conflict, or disharmony, is of course necessary for the novel to work – if all was harmonious and nothing changed there would be no story to tell.

Symbolism of place

Locations in fiction are necessary arenas for people to occupy and for their actions to take place, but these locations can also carry greater significance. The places not only provide venues where things happen, but throw extra light and significance on events, people and relationships.

In his story *Abyss*, the American writer Richard Ford writes about Howard and Frances, two estate agents who are having an affair while attending a conference.

Instead of going to the conference, they decide instead to visit the Grand Canyon in Arizona.

The Grand Canyon is a vast and colourful gorge cut by the Colorado River over a period of about 6 million years. It is 277 miles (446 km) long, between 4 and 18 miles (6.4 to 24 km) wide, and more than a mile (1.6 km) deep.

The Grand Canyon is described as follows on its national park website, showing that it is not just literary figures who add meanings to places.

> The Grand Canyon is more than a great chasm carved over millennia through the rocks of the Colorado Plateau. It is more than an awe-inspiring view. It is more than a pleasuring ground for those who explore the roads, hike the trails, or float the currents of the turbulent Colorado River.
>
> This canyon is a gift that transcends what we experience. Its beauty and size humble us. Its timelessness provokes a comparison to our short existence. In its vast spaces we may find solace from our hectic lives.

Activity

Read the extract below from Richard Ford's short story 'Abyss'. At this point in the story Frances and Howard reach the Grand Canyon. The story is told in the third person, but here it is very much told from the point of view of Howard.

Answer the following questions:

1. In what ways do Howard and Frances react differently to their first experience of the Grand Canyon?
2. In the light of what you have read already about the significance of place, what use does Ford make of the Grand Canyon in this extract?

> And then, all at once, just very suddenly, he was there; at the Grand Canyon, beside Frances who had her camera up to her face. And there was no way really not to be surprised by it – the whole Grand Canyon just all right there at once, opened out and down and wide in front of you, enormous and bottomless, with a great invisible silence inhabiting it and a column of cool air pushing up out of it like a giant well. It was a shock.
>
> 'I don't want you to say one single thing,' Frances said. She wasn't looking through her camera now, but had begun to stare right into the canyon itself, like she was inhaling it. Sunlight was on her face. She seemed blissed.
>
> He did, however, expect to say *something*. It was just natural to want to put some words of your own to the whole thing. Except he instantly had the feeling, standing beside Frances, that he was already doing something wrong, had somehow approached this wrong, or was standing wrong, even looking at the goddamned canyon wrong. And there was something about how you couldn't see it at all, and then you completely did see it, something that seemed to suggest you could actually miss it. Miss the whole Grand Canyon!
>
> Of course, the right way would be to look at it all at once, taking in the full effect, just the way Frances seemed to be doing. Except it was much too big to get everything into focus. Too big and too complicated. He felt like he wanted to turn around, go back to the car and come up again. Get re-prepared.

> Though it was exactly, he thought, staring mutely out at the flat brown plateau and the sheer drop straight off the other side – how far away, you couldn't tell, since perspective was screwed up – it was exactly what he'd expected from the pictures in high school. It was a tourist attraction. A thing to see. It was plenty big. But twenty jillion people had already seen it, so that it felt sort of useless. A negative. Nothing like the ocean, which *had* a use. Nobody *needed* the Grand Canyon for anything. At its most important, he guessed, it would be a terrific impediment to someone wanting to get to the other side. Which would not be a good comment to make to Frances, who was probably having a religious experience. She'd blow her top on that. The best comment, he thought, should be that it was really quiet. He'd never experienced anything this quiet. And it was nothing like an airport. Though flying in that little plane was probably the best way to see it.

Link

For more on point of view see Chapter 29, page 226.

Commentary

Howard arrives at the canyon after Frances. She is clearly overwhelmed by the experience, or so Howard thinks. She tells him 'I don't want you to say one single thing' and to Howard she 'seemed blissed'. Notice that although they don't say anything, Howard does expect to 'say *something*'. He seems to want to share the experience; she wants to experience it alone.

For Howard, therefore, the experience is unsettling, and in various ways unsatisfactory. Annoyed by being shut out by Frances, he is as bothered by her as he is by the canyon. He considers it possible to miss the whole thing, or on the other hand that it is impossible to get it all into focus. Because so many others have seen it, he finds it 'sort of useless'. All he can think of is that it stops you getting to the other side, whereas Frances seems to be finding it 'a religious experience'.

In other parts of the story, Ford switches his perspective to Frances – we get a sense here that were she to be telling the story it would be very different.

What should be clear, though, is that Ford has used the Grand Canyon as a vehicle to show the two lovers drifting apart, that what lies ahead of them, in terms of their relationship, is an abyss, a chasm. Ford needs to set the story of this failing relationship somewhere, because stories need to be placed. But in choosing this venue, he has given himself the opportunity to make the place stand for more than just a location. The alert reader recognizes the connections between where a story is set and what the story is saying.

Time and sequence

All stories that are told, however fantastic in their genre, need to contain aspects of time. The word 'aspects' is in the plural because even in this broad sense, time can work in at least two ways:

- the time covered by the events within the story
- the broader time that surrounds the story, the time in which the story is set.

For example, if a contemporary novelist writes a love story, the time covered by events might be from the time the couple meet to the time they marry (or divorce?). But if the author wants to write a love story set in Victorian times, other aspects of time are involved: if the story is to appear believable, the author will have to incorporate aspects of Victorian life and attitudes.

In a general sense, then (general, because as always these aspects of narrative overlap), how the author manages time *within* the story is covered by AO2, which looks at aspects of internal authorial method, in this case with a special focus on structure. Meanwhile, how the author manages the time that *surrounds* the story is covered by AO3, which looks at contexts.

Chronology

If we were all to write our stories, whether 'real' or 'imagined', in strict **chronological order**, the first main issue that would arise is that telling a story in strict chronological order can be very dull – one of the first lessons children have to learn when writing stories is not to start at the beginning (and maybe not even end at the end).

You may question whether it is actually possible, with a complex story, to say definitively that it has a beginning and an end, anyway. In a complex world, such hard and fast distinctions are not always possible – and writers, of course, are aware of this.

You might think that the nature of crime fiction would lend itself to a chronological narrative, with the murder at the beginning and the solution at the end. Imagine, though, that you are going to write a piece of crime fiction, which will have a murder as its main crime. Immediately you are faced with all sorts of narrative questions, but for the moment concentrate on aspects of sequence.

Questions you will have to consider include:

1. Does the story start with the body being discovered?
2. Does the story start with the murder itself?
3. Does the story start with the planning of the murder?
4. Does the story start with the detective being called to the case?

If you think this through, it should be clear to you that how you answer these questions potentially points to the type, or **sub-genre**, of crime fiction that you are going to write. If you start with the discovery of the body, you might be writing a forensic novel, where the perpetrator is uncovered through evidence. If you start with the planning of the murder, then the murderer will be known to the reader but not to the detective. If you start with the body and the detective being called to the scene, you could be writing a **police procedural**.

If we take as an example a typical plot line from a detective story, its chronological sequence might be something like this:

1. A murder is planned, for a certain motive.
2. A body is found, which yields evidence.
3. The detective pursues a number of clues and identifies the killer.
4. A violent shoot-out leads to the death of the villain.
5. This leads to another revenge killing.

Key terms

Chronological order. The sequence of events in the order they happen, in a timeline that goes from A, the start of events, to say E, the end.

Police procedural. A crime sub-genre in which the narrative involves the solving of the crime and the identification of the perpetrator.

Sub-genre. A particular type of text within a **genre**; genre can sometimes seem like a Russian *matryoshka* doll, containing ever smaller categories.

It is easy to conceive other ways of presenting the same sequence – for example it could go 4, then 1, 2, 3, 5 or 2, 1, 3, 4, 5. In each case, something different would be foregrounded by the chronology.

Chronology, then, is one way in which the writer of a narrative can influence their reader's response. This can lead to a focus on suspense, where the action and its results are foregrounded, or on character, where feelings are foregrounded, or sometimes both.

Establishing time and sequence

Whereas in a novel we expect some detailed **establishment**, in terms of place, time, people, and so on, in poems we tend to be straight in and out of the story with much less detail. Indeed the effects of the poem are often emphasized by what is not said, by what can be called *meaningful absence*.

As part of your coursework submission you must write about one poetry text and one prose text, but as has already been stressed, what you learn from your work with critical material can, indeed should, be applied in the exam components too. Thinking about how time operates in the narrative of a novel can be exceptionally helpful when it comes to finding meanings and responding to debates.

Modern novels especially use time in different and creative ways. Andrea Levy in *Small Island* takes a non-chronological approach to time – remember there's nothing that says a story has to be told chronologically. The first chapter of *Small*

Activity

Look at the three different comic-strip chains below (A–C), showing how the same murder story can be told in different sequences. Then write an outline for a crime story of your own, and work out different chronological sequences for the key events. If you have the drawing skills, you could story-board your own story as seen here. How would your story's genre change, depending on the sequences you choose? If working in a class setting, you can compare stories with a partner.

There is no commentary for this activity.

B

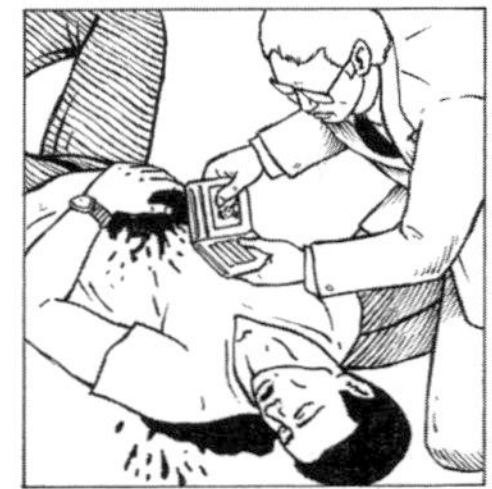

C

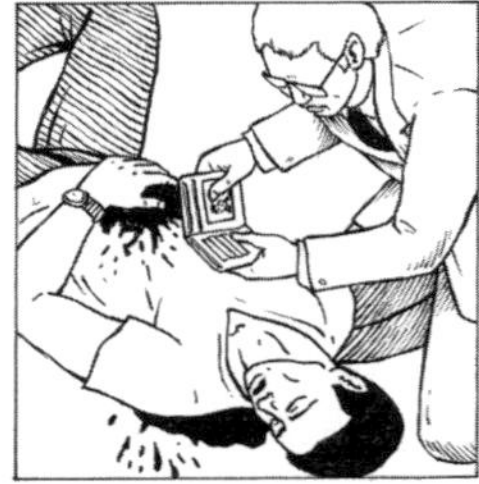

Island is called 'Prologue'. This is followed by a chapter entitled '1948'. Two chapters after this, comes a chapter labelled 'Before'. So within 30 or so pages we have the following headings:

- Prologue
- 1948
- Before.

Each one potentially deals with a different point of time, but with the implication that events are nonetheless connected.

Activity

Look at the opening paragraph of Khaled Hosseini's novel *The Kite Runner.* How are complex elements of time introduced right at the very start of the novel, and how might they be significant?

> *December 2001*
>
> I became what I am today at the age of twelve, on a frigid overcast day in the winter of 1975. I remember the precise moment, crouching behind a crumbling mud wall, peeking into the alley near the frozen creek. That was a long time ago, but it's wrong what they say about the past, I've learned, about how you can bury it. Because the past claws its way out. Looking back now, I realize I have been peeking into that deserted alley for the last twenty-six years.

Commentary

It should be obvious just how many different references there are to time here, starting with the date, which comes before the main text, and including references to 'today', the past in general, the past as a specific moment, and so on.

The significance of all these time references includes the fact that the present cannot escape the past, and that history cannot be escaped from.

Characters and characterization

People in stories

Stories are about people doing things and having things done to them. (There are sometimes stories, especially those written for children, where animals replace people, but they nonetheless have distinctly human qualities.) When looking at aspects of narrative, though, you are not concerned with the characters as such but with aspects of **characterization**. Reminding yourself that a character is not real, does not exist outside the confines of the novel or poem, reminds you that you are looking at how authors achieve effects.

This not to say that as keen readers we do not lose ourselves in a book, and talk and think about characters as though they are real. But that reality is an illusion, a **representation** of people rather than the people themselves. Studying literature is not the same as just reading it – in studying literature you need to analyse rather than describe.

Starting with a name

One of the first things we are given after we are born is a name: the first part is a choice our parents make from a limited collection, the second part is a family name. Most of us have no choice about this, and quite a few of us wish we could change what we have been given. Although our names can say quite a bit about our cultural origins, it feels as though there is something random about the name we end up with.

There is nothing random, though, about the names of characters in literature, because of course they do not really exist. They have been invented, and this offers the author a chance to signal to the reader what sort of person the character is. Names can carry a great deal of significance, in the process saving the author a lot of time and work. There are varying degrees of subtlety in this, depending in part on the genre of the text, but look closely and it is possible to see something significant in even the most ordinary of names – the ordinariness itself sometimes carrying significance. And when there are virtually no names at all – as in Cormac McCarthy's *The Road* – that too is significant.

The process of signification, though, is a cultural one. In other words, the meanings and associations we find in names are not there by nature; they are implied by the author and understood by those readers who have enough knowledge of the culture to make the connections. So when you read a fictional text that comes from a culture other than your own, you may miss the significance of all sorts of things, without necessarily losing the point of the text altogether. Two obvious ways in which cultural references can be lost are through geography and through time. Texts from countries that we are not fully familiar with, and texts from earlier times, require a special effort when reading – and an understanding on our part that we may not be quite getting the whole point.

One author who created a huge cast of characters was Charles Dickens. He often created names which were memorable (important in a complex plot) and which at the same time pinned down the character to a certain physical or emotional characteristic. For example, Silas Wegg (in *Our Mutual Friend*) has a wooden leg and is unpleasantly devious and greedy. While there is no reason in principle why a character called Silas Wegg could not be heroic, it somehow seems unlikely that an author would give a hero such a name.

Activity

Below are some more names created by Dickens. Put them into two lists, one for good characters and one for bad. Then have a guess at what characteristic might be implied by the name of each character.

Thomas Gradgrind	Mr McChoakumchild	Stephen Blackpool
Josiah Bounderby	Charles Cheeryble	Sir Leicester Dedlock
Uriah Heep	Krook	Seth Pecksniff
Wackford Squeers	Miss Flite	Noddy Boffin
Esther Summerson	Ada Clare	Sissy Jupe

Commentary

Good	**Bad**
Esther Summerson (because of summer)	Thomas Gradgrind (hard sounding)
Ada Clare (sweetness)	Mr McChoakumchild (a teacher – as it says!)
Noddy Boffin (eccentricity)	Josiah Bounderby (cad)
Miss Flite (lightness, fragility)	Uriah Heep (creep)
Charles Cheeryble (humour)	Krook (thief)
Sissy Jupe (creative, but maybe a bit naïve – easy to dupe)	Seth Pecksniff (two unpleasant words together)
Stephen Blackpool (more open to question, but solid and dependable)	Sir Leicester Dedlock (intransigent and immovable)
	Wackford Squeers (a different kind of teacher)

Making an appearance

You have seen above that a fictional name can say a great deal about a fictional person. The same goes for the appearance of characters: what they look like, how they dress, their physical gestures, and so forth. Characters in fictional texts are usually described early on, as part of the establishment of the text. Obviously in novels there is plenty of space to do this, whereas in narrative poems a couple of features are often enough to pin down not just what a character looks like, but what they are like in a broader sense.

Just as a name can conjure up ideas about a character's moral qualities, so can a brief description of their appearance.

Activity

Look at the opening stanzas of Samuel Taylor Coleridge's narrative poem, 'The Rime of the Ancient Mariner'. What details about the appearance of The Ancient Mariner are given here? What do they suggest about him as a character?

It is an ancient Mariner,
And he stoppeth one of three.
'By thy long grey beard and glittering eye,
Now wherefore stopp'st thou me?

'The Bridegroom's doors are opened wide,
And I am next of kin;
The guests are met, the feats is set:
May'st hear the merry din.'

He holds him with his skinny hand,
'There was ship,' quoth he.
'Hold off! Unhand me, grey-beard loon!'
Eftsoons his hand dropt he.

> He holds him with his glittering eye –
> The wedding guest stood still,
> And listens like a three years' child:
> The Mariner hath his will.
>
> The Wedding-Guest sat on a stone:
> He cannot choose but hear;
> And thus spake on that ancient man,
> The bright-eyed Mariner.

Commentary

The Ancient Mariner has a 'long grey beard' (signifying age), and a 'skinny hand' (signifying age, but also perhaps a life devoid of pleasures such as food). But it is the eyes that are most highlighted. They are mentioned three times: 'glittering eye' is mentioned twice and 'bright-eyed' once. It would appear that his eyes belie his physical appearance. He may be old and decrepit but inside he burns fiercely in his desire to endlessly tell his story. He is a man possessed by a mission.

Novels can take a more leisurely look at appearance than poems, especially when an important character is being portrayed. The example below is taken from Khaled Hosseini's novel *The Kite Runner*. Near the start of the novel the narrator, Amir, looks back to his childhood and begins to build up a picture of his friend Hassan, who is the kite runner of the title. Hassan is the son of a family servant, but a playmate of Amir. Later in the novel Amir betrays his friend, an action that lives with him for the rest of his life.

Activity

Look at the paragraphs below which introduce the boy Hassan in *The Kite Runner*. Based on these descriptions, what can you work out about the characteristics that the author is establishing?

> I can still see Hassan up on that tree, sunlight flickering through the leaves on his almost perfectly round face, a face like a Chinese doll chiseled from hardwood: his flat, broad nose and slanting, narrow eyes like bamboo leaves, eyes that looked, depending on the light, gold, green, even sapphire. I can still see his tiny low-set ears and that pointed stub of a chin, a meaty appendage that looked like it was added as a mere afterthought. And the cleft lip, just left of mid-line, where the Chinese doll maker's instrument may have slipped, or perhaps he had simply grown tired and careless.
>
> Sometimes, up in those trees, I talked Hassan into firing walnuts with his slingshot at the neighbour's one-eyed German shepherd. Hassan never wanted to, but if I asked, *really* asked, he wouldn't deny me. Hassan never denied me anything.

Commentary

We are meant to form a positive picture of the character. His face is 'almost perfectly round' and there is a sense here that the slight imperfection, the lip, makes him even more attractive. The eyes are again given prominence, but this time they shine, with not one colour but three. The poetic comparisons, the way the boy is in harmony with his surroundings, are also a hint that here is someone special by character.

Hassan's loyalty to his friend is then shown, which takes on much greater significance once we know that his friend will betray him.

The ins and outs of characterization

We have discussed so far two ways of creating characters, both of which are external: names and appearance. Poetry, which often works in briefer and more symbolic ways, makes particular use of these short cuts. But remember that characters are also developed through more internal methods, especially if the reader is given access to a character's thoughts.

Your Critical Anthology has a small section on this area of narrative, headed 'Flat and round characters'. 'Flat' characters would tend to be developed though external descriptions only, whereas 'round' characters would be developed through internal means. It is, of course, perfectly possible, over the length of a full text, for both methods to be used.

Activity

Below is a list of some of the ways in which characters can be presented by authors – in other words, some of the ways in which we get to know about a character. As you consider this list, see whether you agree with the external/internal labels that have been attached. Then consider whether and how the labels apply to characters in your chosen texts.

- How the character is named — external
- What the character looks like — external
- The character's speech habits — external
- What the character does, his or her actions — external
- The character's motives for these actions — internal
- What the character has to say — external/internal
- What the character thinks — internal
- What others say about the character — external/internal
- What others think about the character — internal/external

There is no commentary for this activity.

Extension activity

The two chapters on narrative (Chapters 29 and 30) have looked at various aspects of this very important area in the study of literature. To see how much you have learned, write an account of the narrative methods used by Helen Dunmore in the opening of her novel *The Betrayal*, published in 2010 (shown below). As this is the opening of the novel, there is no context to give – the context emerges as you read.

> It's a fresh June morning, without a trace of humidity, but Russov is sweating. Sunlight from the hospital corridor's high window glints on his forehead. Andrei's attention sharpens. The man is pale, too, and his eyes are pouched with shadow.

It could be a hangover, but Russov rarely drinks more than a single glass of beer. He's not overweight. A touch of flu then, even though it's June? Or maybe he needs a check-up. He's in his mid-forties; the zone of heart disease.

Russov comes close, closer than two people should stand. His breath is in Andrei's face, and suddenly Andrei stops diagnosing, stops being at a comfortable doctorly distance from the symptoms of a colleague. His skin prickles. His body knows more than his mind does. Russov smells of fear, and his conciliating smile cannot hide it. He wants something, but he is afraid.

'Andrei Mikhailovich…'

'What is it?'

'Oh, it's nothing important. Only if you've got a moment…'

His face is glistening all over now. Drops of sweat are beginning to form.

Suddenly Russov whips out his handkerchief and wipes his forehead as if he were polishing a piece of furniture.

'Excuse me, I'm feeling the heat … I don't know when they're going to get around to turning off these radiators. You'd think our patients had all been prescribed steam baths.'

The hospital's radiators are cold.

'I wanted to ask your advice, if you've got a moment. As a diagnostician there's no one whose opinion I respect more.'

Now why is he saying that? Only last week there was an idiotically petty and irritable 'professional disagreement' over a little girl with an enlarged spleen following a serious fall. Russov had gone on about 'scientific accountability' while he tapped his pen scornfully on the table. He hadn't appeared very impressed by Andrei's diagnostic skills then. Andrei spent far too much time with his patients. This was a clear-cut case of splenic trauma following an abdominal injury. The only question was whether it could be treated non-operatively, or whether an immediate operation was advisable.

When it turned out that the child's swollen spleen had indeed nothing to do with the accident, and was due to undiagnosed leukaemia, Russov muttered about 'flukes' and 'all this hands-on mumbo-jumbo.'

But all the same, Russov is a reasonably good physician. Hard-working, responsible and extremely keen to write up as many cases as possible, in the hope of raising his research profile. He's certainly getting noticed. One day no doubt he'll produce that definitive research paper which will unlock the door to a paradise of conferences and the golden promise of a trip abroad. Andrei's gift for diagnosis annoys him. It isn't classifiable and it hasn't been achieved in the correct way, through study and examination. The two men have never become friends.

'So what's the problem, Boris Ivanovich?' asks Andrei.

Russov glances down the corridor. A radiographer is wheeling a trolley-load of X-ray files towards them.

'Let's go outside for a breath of air.'

Commentary

The best way into thinking about narrative is often to consider point of view. Although this is a third-person narrative, and the opening sentence could be seen as a distant third-person narration, clues emerge very quickly that in fact the narrative is from the point of view of the character Andrei. The use of his first name as against Russov's surname, 'The man', and the crucial significance of 'Russov comes close' are clues. If Russov comes close, then he must come close to someone, and that is Andrei.

Names here give us not only the identification of two people, they also give wider clues. They sound Russian, suggesting where the novel is set, and the address of a character by name suggests types of formality if spoken, and relationship if thinking. Note that Russov is only ever 'Russov' when the narrative is via Andrei's thought. Meanwhile, Russov's sweating suggests he is hugely uneasy. Also notice that Russov makes up a reason for the sweating which cannot be true. The short sentence, 'The hospital's radiators are cold', which has a paragraph to itself, carries a lot of significance. It shows us that Russov is not telling the truth, and that Andrei is. It tells us to trust Andrei and not Russov.

The novel's action begins at a specific point in time, a June morning, and a specific place, a hospital. But when we read we look for clues about wider aspects of time and place. We have already worked out the place, Russia, and there is a clue too about the time in which the novel is set. The reference towards the end of this extract to 'the golden promise of a trip abroad' immediately tells us that this is Soviet Russia, even if we had not worked it out from Russov's concern about talking in public.

Why are we not told this directly? If the narrative is from the internalized point of view of Andrei, the novelist cannot make him think 'And here I am in Soviet Russia' – at least, a good novelist can't! Instead the novelist has to keep an eye on a consistent internal life for the character whose perspective has been chosen, while at the same time giving the reader enough clues to work out how the story is developing.

Characterization goes a long way towards helping the story here. If we assume that Andrei can be trusted (not all narrators can be – but that is not the case here), then we are presented with two paediatricians of contrasting methods who have little in common professionally, yet it is the one who is in official favour who seems to be wanting advice. Andrei cares about his patients and spends time with them. It doesn't get him officially recognized, but it would seem that the ambitious Russov, at a point of crisis, has to turn secretly and out of hearing to Andrei for help.

What is that crisis? It is well worth reading this novel to find out.

Possible applications in Component 3 coursework

Most literature is about people in some way or another, but it is possible to find texts that rely heavily on place and/or time for their particular effects. Your research for the activity on page 233, for example, will give you some ideas about novel titles that include the name of a place. Look also for titles that refer to time, such as Kazuo Ishiguro's *Remains of the Day,* David Nicholls's *One Day,* J. L. Carr's *A Month In The Country*, and many more.

In order to refer to books you might be studying, this chapter has used some of the set texts as examples of key principles. Do be clear, though, that you cannot write about *any* of the AQA-nominated set texts in your coursework. Remember, too, that you must study one prose text and one poetry text. In the case of the latter, you should refer to more than one poem in your answer (unless you have chosen a long narrative poem).

Extension activity

1. In starting to narrow down the choices of texts you might wish to write about for coursework, you could consider texts that are especially striking in the way in which time and place are used. Remember that studying narrative shows you how stories are told, but there are still plenty of other things that you might want to say about the text. It is perfectly possible that in writing about a post-colonial text, for example, you will refer to its narrative.
2. Consider the novels that you are studying in Component 2. Choose a representative section (say, a chapter) and discuss the following issues:
   - How is time used in this chapter of the novel?
   - How is place used in this novel?
   - How does the author develop aspects of characterization?
3. Consider the poetry texts that you are studying for Component 2 and discuss the following issues:
   - To what extent do the poems contain characters? What is the effect of this?
   - Do the poems have specific and significant references to time?
   - Do the poems have specific and significant references to places?

Summary

This chapter has looked at some of the ways in which authors use people, places and time as part of their narrative strategy in texts. One result of this process has been to see how these aspects contribute to the significance that can be found in the story.

Post-colonial criticism

31

What is post-colonial criticism?

As you might expect from a relatively new area of theory, interested in how language is used to express power, the very term 'post-colonial criticism' is itself disputed. The word 'post' seems to imply, for example, that all colonialism is in the past, and that post-colonial critics will be looking at an historical rather than a dynamic process. There is also an implied sense that all colonialism, at least in retrospect, can be seen to be a damaging and harmful process.

If the term itself is disputed, why was it thought necessary to name such a school of criticism in the first place? As with Marxism and feminism, this is a political form of criticism with a specific focus, in that it looks at a particular political phenomenon, in this case the forcible takeover by one country of another. Such a takeover has severe political consequences, often leading to re-drawn and inappropriate national boundaries, severe economic consequences as wealth is diverted to the colonizers, and severe cultural consequences as languages and traditions are forcibly changed. Historically, such takeovers were military and cruel; more recently some have been cultural and less obvious.

Post-colonial criticism looks at writing that is the product of such processes. As with Marxism and feminism, with which it often has much in common, it seeks to explore the consequences of **colonization** from the starting point that the process is essentially negative, certainly for the colonized and frequently for the colonizers too. So, as with Marxism and feminism, it looks to privilege views and voices that are frequently not heard in the mainstream.

This chapter will:

- introduce you to an influential theory for the study of literature, as seen in Section 4 of your Critical Anthology
- show you how some of the theory can be applied to texts, as you will be able to do in your coursework component.

Approaches to post-colonial criticism and suggested reading

Many different types of text, covering many different types of situation, can be looked at through the lens of post-colonial criticism. It is likely that if you are interested in this area, you will be working with a **prose** text, but some poetry is appropriate too. Here are some areas of post-colonial criticism:

Absence

As you will see in the Critical Anthology's section on Edward Said ('Post-colonial criticism; an example'), post-colonial criticism can engage with the study of **canonical texts** where there is a key **absence**, this absence stemming from the fact that those living alongside a colonial system don't recognize it as such. Post-colonial criticism therefore looks afresh at such texts.

Possible texts include: Daniel Defoe, *Robinson Crusoe*; Jane Austen, *Mansfield Park*; Emily Brontë, *Wuthering Heights*.

Key terms

Absence. Something (a person, a voice, a point of view) that is not in a text, but whose absence from the text can be seen as significant.

Canonical texts. Texts that have a special status and are often seen as 'great' and enduring works of literature.

Living with colonialism

Post-colonial criticism can comment on texts written by authors living within, or having experience of, countries that have been colonies. The definition of a colony can be broad. Much Irish writing is studied from this perspective, for example.

Possible texts include: E. M. Forster, *A Passage to India*; Joyce Carey, *Mister Johnson*; Paul Scott, *Staying On*; Chinua Achebe, *Things Fall Apart*; William Trevor, *Fools of Fortune*; W. B. Yeats's poetry.

Migrant writing

Post-colonial criticism can refer to the study of modern texts about countries that are now independent but still hugely influenced by the colonial experience. This can include the study of migrant writing, produced by authors who have left their homeland for various reasons, and what is sometimes called 'dispersed or diaspora writing' produced by authors living usually in Britain or the US but with strong connections to Africa, Asia or other areas.

Possible texts include: Mohsin Hamid, *The Reluctant Fundamentalist*; Aravind Adiga, *Last Man in Tower*; Monica Ali, *Brick Lane*; Salman Rushdie, *Midnight's Children*; Jhumpa Lahiri, *Interpreter of Maladies* (short stories) and *The Lowland*; Taiye Selasi, *Ghana Must Go*; NoViolet Bulawayo, *We Need New Names*; Chimanda Ngozi Adichie: *Americanah*; Derek Walcott's poetry.

Ethnicity and race

Post-colonial criticism can refer more broadly to the study of literatures grouped by their authors' ethnicity and race.

Possible texts in Black writing including: Toni Morrison, *Beloved*; Ralph Ellison, *Invisible Man*; Maya Angelou's poetry; Grace Nichols's poetry.

Your task in approaching this area

In your A-level work you are applying theories to texts, not studying the theories in their own right. In one sense you do not need to know all the variant forms of post-colonial criticism, because you are applying some ideas to just one text. The fact that the term is so disputed, and so problematic, can work to your advantage because it opens up plenty of possibilities to write with a fresh and personal voice about specific aspects of texts. One example would be to focus on the way names are used, and the significance of names. For examples of this see below.

The first of two short examples of how post-colonial criticism works is based on a key moment in Daniel Defoe's novel *Robinson Crusoe*, first published in 1719. This is a text that is an established 'classic' but which can be seen in a new light if read through the lens of post-colonial criticism. One way to apply such criticism is to explore the **attitudes**, **values** and **assumptions** contained within the text.

Key terms

Assumptions. A set of beliefs which are not questioned, but taken to be right and/or true.

Attitudes and values. Attitudes are views you hold and values are views which you believe to be morally right.

Activity

The following extract is taken from the beginning of the chapter where Robinson Crusoe, who has been marooned on an island for many years, describes for the first time another inhabitant, whose life he has just saved. What assumptions about power and control are contained in the way Robinson Crusoe describes one of his first meetings with Friday? How do you respond to these assumptions?

I Call Him Friday

He was a comely handsome fellow, perfectly well made; with straight strong limbs, not too large; tall and well shaped, and, as I reckon, about twenty six years of age. He had a very good countenance, not a fierce and surly aspect; but seemed to have something very manly in his face, and yet he had all the sweetness and softness of an European in his countenance too, especially when he smiled. His hair was long and black, not curled like wool; his forehead very high and large, and a great vivacity and sparkling sharpness in his eyes. The colour of his skin was not quite black, but very tawny; and yet not of an ugly yellow nauseous tawny, as the Brasilians, and Virginians, and other natives of America are; but of a bright kind of a dun olive colour, that had in it something very agreeable, tho' not very easy to describe. His face was round and plump; his nose small, not flat like the negroes, a very good mouth, thin lips, and his fine teeth well set, and white as ivory. After he had slumbered, rather than slept, about half an hour, he waked again, and comes out of the cave to me; for I had been milking my goats, which I had in the enclosure just by; when he espy'd me, he came running to me, laying himself down again upon the ground, with all the possible signs of an humble thankful disposition, making a many antick gestures to show it. At last he lays his head flat upon the ground, close to my foot, and sets my other foot upon his head, as he had done before; and after this, made all the signs to me of subjection, servitude, and submission imaginable, to let me know how he would serve me as long as he lived. I understood him in many things, and let him know I was very well pleased with him; in a little time I began to speak to him, and teach him to speak to me; and first, I made him know his name should be Friday, which was the day I saved his life; I called him so for the memory of the time; I likewise taught him to say Master, and then let him know, that was to be my name; I likewise taught him to say yes and no, and to know the meaning of them; I gave him some milk in an earthen pot, and let him see me drink it before him, and sop my bread in it; and I gave him a cake of bread to do the like, which he quickly comply'd with, and made signs that it was very good for him.

Did you know?

Although *Robinson Crusoe* is not widely read these days, it has a place in our culture because many people know of the idea of a 'man Friday' or a 'girl Friday'. There is also a popular workplace notice that reads 'the only person to get everything done by Friday was Robinson Crusoe'.

Commentary

This is a first-person narrative, so we cannot automatically assume that what Crusoe says is what the author Defoe believes too. But where an author wishes to undermine the attitudes shown by a character, readers are usually given hints that we should not agree with the values held by the character. This is not the case here.

Here are some of the attitudes held by Crusoe:

- His long description of Friday makes Friday a mixture of human and animal. He is 'well made' and almost compared to a working animal; the description of his mouth sounds like something that might be written of a horse, for example.
- Crusoe places a huge significance on physical appearance, and his judgements of what makes an attractive appearance are based on European standards.
- He accepts without question that Friday sees him as superior, and that he is indeed superior to him.
- He seems to have no interest in where Friday might have come from, where his family is, and so on. He assumes he has saved Friday's life.

- In naming him Friday he does several symbolic things. He assumes the man has no name already and that it is in his power to give him one, an English word. But to show that he is not really an English person, he names him after a day of the week.
- He assumes the language of communication will be English, and the first words he teaches him are about servitude and obedience. English therefore becomes the language of power.

Crusoe does not seem in any way embarrassed by the attitudes he has. They come naturally to him. This absence of self-criticism, this assumption about the natural order of things, would be noted by post-colonial critics. Crusoe is just one man in one story, but if we extrapolate from this we can see from this single literary representation how colonists thought. Europe – and in this case England – is regarded as the centre of the world, and its standards are those by which all things are judged. England is acknowledged to have history and its culture is regarded as superior, while the colonized have no culture worthy of consideration. The way Crusoe tells his story, always assuming that his point of view is right and that as the kind master he is helping the willing Friday too, reveals how colonists saw only the positive in what they were doing.

Did you know?

A likely source for Defoe's story was the real-life marooning on an island of the sailor Alexander Selkirk. His account of his life and rescue was much publicized at the time Defoe was writing.

In the activity above you saw how post-colonial criticism can be applied to a classic text. In the next activity you will work with a modern text, *We Need New Names* by NoViolet Bulawayo, a Zimbabwean by birth who moved to America when she was 18.

Activity

Read the following extract, bearing in mind that it forms the opening of the novel. It is narrated by a young girl named Darling, aged ten. In what ways are you as a reader surprised by what you read here?

Hitting Budapest

We are on our way to Budapest: Bastard and Chipo and Godknows and Sbho and Stina and me. We are going even though we are not allowed to cross Mzilikazi Road, even though Bastard is supposed to be watching his little sister Fraction, even though Mother would kill me dead if she found out; we are just going. There are guavas to steal in Budapest, and right now I'd rather die for guavas. We didn't eat this morning and my stomach feels like somebody just took a shovel and dug everything out.

Getting out of Paradise is not so hard since the mothers are busy with hair and talk, which is the only thing they ever do. They just glance at us when we file past the shacks and then look away. We don't have to worry about the men under the jacaranda either since their eyes never lift from the draughts. It's only the little kids who see us and try to follow, but Bastard just wallops the naked one at the front with a fist on his big head and they all turn back.

When we hit the bush we are already flying, scream-singing like the wheels in our voices will make us go faster. Sbho leads: *Who discovered the way to India?* and the rest of us rejoin, *Vasco da Gama! Vasco da Gama! Vasco da Gama!* Bastard is at the front because he won country-game

> today and he thinks that makes him our president or something, and then myself and Godknows, Stina, Sbho, and finally Chipo, who used to outrun everybody in all of Paradise but not anymore because somebody made her pregnant.

Commentary

Much of the surprise will come from what will be, for most readers, an unfamiliar culture that is not mediated for you in any way by an adult or authorial voice. The use of the child narrator works especially well here. You are pitched immediately into a set of names of people and places, some of which you recognize and others you don't. But even when you do recognize them, they are unsettling. 'We are on our way to Budapest' clearly does not refer to the capital of Hungary.

Paradise, you can probably work out from the reference to shacks, is the ironic name given to the shanty-town in which the children live. The children are hungry, but this is not the casual hunger of a missed meal. In Robert Mugabe's Zimbabwe, they are virtually starving.

The children's names, with their mixture of English words (reminding us of Defoe's Friday perhaps) and African names are also unexpected. Are these their real names? Are they nicknames?

Most of all, though, it is the lack of any obvious sentimentality that surprises and shocks. The little child is casually 'walloped', and Chipo cannot run so fast now because 'somebody made her pregnant'.

What we can see from this brief opening extract is that this novel is looking at life in an African country, Zimbabwe, from within. The children are having fun, the adults are socializing. The novel does indeed go on to show a country deeply damaged by its past, but with a culture that remains strongly resilient.

Re-creative possibilities

Texts studied through the lens of post-colonial criticism can be especially receptive to re-creative responses, because by definition they often contain absent or marginalized voices, or deliberately one-dimensional perspectives. In the two examples above, for example, it would be possible to create a voice for Friday that would give a very different view, as would an adult perspective of the story told by ten-year-old Darling.

Summary

This brief account of post-colonial criticism has detailed some of the ways in which you can apply this critical method, shown you how it operates in two very different kinds if texts, and has suggested some reading options that you could choose.

32 Ecocriticism

This chapter will:

- introduce you to an increasingly important set of theories for the study of literature, as seen in Section 5 of your Critical Anthology
- show you how the theories can be applied to texts, as you will need to do in your coursework component.

What is ecocriticism?

Although literary critics have always been interested in the significance of places and settings in narratives (see Chapter 30), the critical approach known as ecocriticism is a relatively new way of looking at literature. As with so many of the theories that we have looked at here, its ideas extend well beyond literature; students of geography, history, sociology, and so on will also be engaging with ecotheories.

Many of the other critical theories that we have looked at involve reading texts through a sense of social organization and political power. For example, Marxism looks at aspects of social class and hierarchy, feminism looks at the way gender impacts on life and literature, post-colonial theories look at the impacts of imperialism. What distinguishes ecocriticism from these other theories is that it takes as its central concern the very earth itself. It encourages readers to see literature as not in some way apart from the material world, but as a vital part of the complex system that makes up the earth.

Literature can be a vehicle for raising awareness of what the earth means to us, and what we are collectively doing to it. The world we live in, our physical environment, is the basis for everything else, and of course we ignore its destruction at our peril. It should come as no surprise, then, that ecocriticism is closely allied to the wider political concerns of the ecology movement.

If ecocriticism is essentially political, in that it sees the destruction of the natural environment as a potential disaster, it is not surprising that its basic tenets can be linked to other ideas in your anthology. If you think carefully about the complex dynamic involved, whereby some essentially post-industrial countries in the West lecture newly emerging industrial countries in the East about their environmental records, you will understand that both Marxist and post-colonial ideas can be considered alongside ecocritical ones. And given that the earth is often seen as a mother figure, it is possible to put gender studies alongside ecocriticism to examine whether women write about the physical world in different ways from men.

Study tip

When working on your coursework responses it is important to understand that you are allowed to work within more than one theoretical approach at any given time.

Ecocritical approaches can be used to explore texts in all of the main three literary genres. Poetry offers a very rich set of possibilities in that it is often specifically about nature. In stories and novels, you can explore the way in which physical setting is significant to wider potential meanings. In drama, you can consider how the stage is used to represent the world.

Approaches to ecocriticism and suggested reading

Study tip

Remember that the theories described in the Critical Anthology are not simply reserved for this section of your course. Where relevant to the question, they can be applied equally to the study of your examined set texts.

All criticism in this area shares the basic starting point that human culture is connected to the physical world, and so it both affects the physical world and is affected by it. Contemporary theory would add here that our effects on the physical word are negative, and that if we are not careful the effects on future generations will be negative too. This broad definition means that there is potentially a huge amount of literature for you to choose from. It is important, though, that your choices – both in terms of texts and tasks – have a specific focus and are not just in some general sense about nature.

Here are some ways of using ecocritical ideas, and some possible texts to get you started.

A new view of classic texts

Ecocritical approaches can be used to look afresh at many **canonical texts**. Many classic English novels, from their titles onwards, use places – and the interaction of the human and the natural – as a vital part of what they have to say. Some examples are Jane Austen's *Mansfield Park*, George Eliot's *Middlemarch*, and Elizabeth Gaskell's *North and South*. Meanwhile, a classic tale of humanity in the wilderness is *Robinson Crusoe*, already referred to in Chapter 31 on post-colonialism.

American literature can be an especially fertile area to explore, because of the size of the country, its natural wildernesses, its sense of the frontier, of escaping to a natural world that is purer and more moral than the social world, and so on. Mark Twain's *Huckleberry Finn* and James Fenimore Cooper's *The Last of the Mohicans* are two examples. A seminal work of American literature is Henry Thoreau's *Walden*, which describes an experiment in living alone by a lake. It connects the natural world with the spiritual, and was inspired by transcendentalist ideas.

Nature writing

There are many examples of literature that can be loosely termed nature writing – that is, writing that puts nature at the forefront of its concerns. Such writing is obviously a rich source of possible study, but you do need to be careful that you devise a challenging task, and one that does not merely echo the natural description.

The work of many poets can be explored, and it is worth remembering that you could collate your own selection of poems on which to base your response. William Wordsworth is the most obvious of the Romantic poets to consider, but other nature poets of the 18th and 19th centuries include Samuel Taylor Coleridge, John Clare, James Thomson, Thomas Gray and William Cowper. An example from Wordsworth is considered below.

Many poets of the early 20th century place nature at the forefront of their work. Thomas Hardy, A. E. Housman, Rupert Brooke, Edward Thomas, Robert Frost and D. H. Lawrence are just a few of these. At a time of great social, political and military upheaval, their poems often use nature to look for deeper and unchanging certainties, finding nature a positive force if only we can stop and look at it.

In terms of prose texts, a number of novelists have placed creatures at the symbolic centre of their works. Henry Williamson's *Tarka the Otter*, Gavin Maxwell's *Ring of Bright Water* and Jack London's *White Fang* and *The Call of the Wild* all do this, and for a really challenging read you could try Herman Melville's *Moby Dick*.

Environmental change

A third grouping of texts to consider is those that openly address issues of environmental change, sometimes through comparisons between the naturally idyllic and the humanly mismanaged, sometimes more generally through contrasts of the rural and urban, and sometimes as open statements of a point of view.

In some cases, such as poetry by William Blake, *She Stoops to Conquer* by Oliver Goldsmith, and *Tess of the d'Urbervilles* by Thomas Hardy, you cannot use these texts as part of your coursework, because they appear on the examined set-texts lists, although you can of course apply relevant ecocritical ideas to your exam work on these texts. But you can use other works by these authors; all of Hardy's novels openly address issues of rural life, usually with a subtle interplay between celebration and struggle.

Richard Adams's novel *Watership Down* has a clear ecological agenda, while Graham Swift's novel *Waterland*, while not solely about ecological issues, has many relevant ideas about the possible end of the world.

Poetry is also a rich field, with the possibility of your making your own selection. Poets of the past 50 years for you to consider include R. S. Thomas, Owen Sheers, Norman Nicholson, Philip Larkin (see below) and Mario Petrucci. A useful anthology is *Earth Shattering: Ecopoems*, edited by Neil Astley (Bloodaxe Books, 2007).

To begin thinking in ecocritical terms, first consider the following activity – focused on a poem by Wordsworth. The questions are framed to be ecocritical in their focus.

Activity

The poem below by Wordsworth is a sonnet, so expectations are created by its genre that it will raise a problem in the first eight lines, and then resolve the problem in some way in the final six.

Note that Proteus was an ancient Greek sea-god, sometimes known as the Old Man of the Sea. Triton was another sea-god, who by blowing his conch shell could calm or raise the waves.

1. What central problem does Wordsworth identify here, and how does he elaborate on it?
2. To what extent does Wordsworth offer a solution to the problem?
3. This poem is often cited to show how literature can be explored with an ecocritical focus. What would you say, from your work on this poem, are some of the key things to look for when working with ecocritical ideas?

> The world is too much with us; late and soon,
> Getting and spending, we lay waste our powers:
> Little we see in Nature that is ours;
> We have given our hearts away, a sordid boon!
> The Sea that bares her bosom to the moon;
> The winds that will be howling at all hours,
> And are up-gathered now like sleeping flowers;
> For this, for everything, we are out of tune;
> It moves us not. – Great God! I'd rather be
> A Pagan suckled in a creed outworn;
> So might I, standing on this pleasant lea,
> Have glimpses that would make me less forlorn;
> Have sight of Proteus rising from the sea;
> Or hear old Triton blow his wreathèd horn.

Commentary

The problem identified by Wordsworth is that we humans are too concerned with 'getting and spending' – with material things. Wordsworth was writing during the major upheaval of the Industrial Revolution, but he makes it clear that we have always been like this through the phrase 'late and soon'. 'We have given our hearts away', 'we are out of tune' with nature, which should move us spiritually but 'moves us not'. Note that the sea is personified as female. The winds can howl 'at all hours' but the implication is that we cannot hear them because we are too obsessed with our possessions in the material world.

You will note, though, that not quite all humans are in this state; in the crucial ninth line we see a pronoun shift from 'us' to 'I', which suggests that the narrator of the poem stands apart from the general mass of humanity. It is suggested that he can appreciate nature more fully.

In the traditional sonnet framework, a problem is established and in some way resolved, but it is hard to see that there is much of a resolution here. After the religious reference to 'Great God!', which is partly an exclamation and partly a call for help, Wordsworth looks back to a pre-Christian time when pagans and their gods were more in tune with nature. He seems to be calling for a change in attitude, but doesn't expect it to happen.

What this poem helps to show us as potential ecocritics is that we can look at texts and decide whether humans relate to the natural world in any constructive way. Are literary characters too intent on manufactured material possessions, and therefore oblivious to nature? And worst of all, are humans destroying nature so that they can achieve their material goals? You might also ask whether ecotexts, and the criticism of them, are essentially pessimistic, railing against what is happening but not really expecting to change anything.

Some further thoughts

You might have had some other thoughts as you read this poem, especially if you remember some of the other theoretical issues you have dealt with. One might be the thought that Wordsworth is very Anglocentric; that is, he seems to see the world from a very English perspective. You do not have to look to the past to find societies that are in tune with nature: you just need to look further afield than Europe. Another issue might be that this is all very nostalgic, harking back to a perfect time which even he admits might only be mythical. And finally, there is a strong sense in this poem of the narrator's feeling of superiority; he is a lone voice surrounded by flawed humanity. A cynic might say that it's quite easy for a poet living on a private income to spend time and energy appreciating nature, but not quite so easy for a worker in a mill town, for example. All these thoughts can of course be countered, and that could be part of the way in which you could frame your independent tasks.

The next activity looks at a poem by Philip Larkin, which belongs in the third category suggested above – it openly and directly addresses issues of environmental change. Written in 1972, it addresses many of the environmental concerns that we would recognize today. It needs, though, to be studied as a piece of literature that has attitudes and values contained within it, rather than as an argument about a rightful cause.

Activity

Working either on your own or in a discussion group, make notes on the following questions about the poem below.

1. What is the significance of the title of the poem? Can you find any other references in the poem that are **intertextual** (refer to other works or sayings)?
2. In what ways is the narration of this poem conversational and informal? What effect does this have?
3. How is the word 'just' used in this poem?
4. Who and what are blamed by the narrator for the environmental ruin that is written about here?
5. In what ways is it possible to critique this poem using some of the other theories that you have learned about?
6. How would you compare Larkin's poem to Wordsworth's sonnet discussed previously?

Going, going

I thought it would last my time –
The sense that, beyond the town,
There would always be fields and farms,
Where the village louts could climb
Such trees as were not cut down;
I knew there'd be false alarms

In the papers about old streets
And split level shopping, but some
Have always been left so far;
And when the old part retreats
As the bleak high-risers come
We can always escape in the car.

Things are tougher than we are, just
As earth will always respond
However we mess it about;
Chuck filth in the sea, if you must:
The tides will be clean beyond.
– But what do I feel now? Doubt?

Or age, simply? The crowd
Is young in the M1 cafe;
Their kids are screaming for more –
More houses, more parking allowed,
More caravan sites, more pay.
On the Business Page, a score

Of spectacled grins approve
Some takeover bid that entails
Five per cent profit (and ten
Per cent more in the estuaries): move
Your works to the unspoilt dales
(Grey area grants)! And when

You try to get near the sea
In summer...
        It seems, just now,
To be happening so very fast;
Despite all the land left free
For the first time I feel somehow
That it isn't going to last,

That before I snuff it, the whole
Boiling will be bricked in
Except for the tourist parts –
First slum of Europe: a role
It won't be hard to win,
With a cast of crooks and tarts.

And that will be England gone,
The shadows, the meadows, the lanes,
The guildhalls, the carved choirs.
There'll be books; it will linger on
In galleries; but all that remains
For us will be concrete and tyres.

Most things are never meant.
This won't be, most likely; but greeds
And garbage are too thick-strewn
To be swept up now, or invent
Excuses that make them all needs.
I just think it will happen, soon.

Commentary

1. The title 'Going, Going' refers to the phrase traditionally used by auctioneers as they are about to close a deal ('Going, going, gone'). It suggests a selling of something for profit. 'There would always be' echoes the patriotic song 'There'll always be an England', which the narrator is doubting, at least in the traditional sense of England – 'shadows', 'meadows', 'lanes', and so on – that he favours.

2. This is a serious poem in that it expresses concern over environmental decay. Yet the language of the poem is often very informal and almost off-hand. 'Mess it about', 'Chuck filth in the sea', and 'snuff it' are just three examples. The effect of this is in part up to you, the reader. It might be said to create a subtle tension between the serious and the not serious, and perhaps suggest a sense of inevitability and despair. For others it might seem just a bit too easy and trite, or **paradoxically** rather superior in the way it looks down on other people.

3. The word 'just' has many uses in contemporary English, some of them as part of an everyday register, rather like the voice adopted by the narrator. The first use 'Things are tougher than we are, just' places the word at the end of one line and so makes it have a possible double meaning, depending on which phrase it is attached to. The second use 'just now' suggests something recent; and in the last line the word has a number of possibilities, depending in part on how you emphasize it. It can imply that the narrator's thoughts are a relatively minor matter (which is what most people in the poem are represented as thinking) or it can sound important (as the narrator seems to believe).

4. and **5.** The blame for what is happening is attached to a number of groups: ordinary people with their 'greeds', who want more in terms of houses, cars, roads, and so on, businessmen looking for profit, the 'crooks and tarts' who are presumably the politicians who let this happen. But as we have seen with the Wordsworth poem, criticizing the ways of the modern world, and looking back to a nostalgic and patriotic better time, can leave you open to criticism, not least that the world you want to preserve is elitist and provides comforts for only a few.

6. There are many similarities between the two poems, but there are some differences. Larkin is much more specific in the way he describes decline, and in saying what he approves and disapproves of. He does not describe Nature with a capital N as a sort of mystical force, and he identifies social reasons for what is happening.

Summary

This brief account of ecocritical theory has detailed some of the ways in which you can apply this critical method, shown you how it operates in two poems, and has suggested some reading options that you could choose.

Literary value and the canon

33

Section 6, entitled 'Literary value and the canon', comes at the end of your Critical Anthology for good reason. It is not a theory in its own right, more of a challenge to some of the assumptions that sometimes underpin the study of English Literature. Does English Literature, knowingly or not, privilege certain types of reading, and perhaps also certain types of readers? In asking this question there is a clear underlying sense that 'English Literature' privileges a certain social class and its interests, against those who might be equally interested in literature (with a lower-case 'l'). Here then, once again, we are at an interface between the study of literature and the politics of social class.

This chapter will help you consider:

- why some books are seen as more important than others
- whether this process should be challenged.

The central ideas

Various sources are used in the Critical Anthology's material. The ideas are synthesized for you below, and are meant to be thought about and challenged. They make for useful discussion topics in class, which in turn could lead to some ways of writing about texts in your coursework component. These ways of writing could be 're-creative' in the sense that they will not necessarily be academic essays; indeed, they could be in the form of articles or journalism.

- The word 'aesthetic', which was originally to do with ideas of beauty, became connected to 'good taste', so in fact represented no more than one elite group's idea of what they liked.
- Artists, including writers, were said to make beautiful things and artisans to make useful things. This placed beauty above usefulness.
- The legacy of the two points above is that in the study of literature there is a canon of 'great' texts, which is placed above popular writing and mass media. One result is that the idea that writers such as Shakespeare and Dickens were highly popular is now played down. The idea of a canon belongs to elitist notions and needs to be challenged.
- In addition to claims about their beauty, texts in the canon have been said to be 'valuable'.
- Three types of value have been identified. Texts are said by some to be of value because:
  a. they are complex and so offer challenges to the reader
  b. they use elegant and carefully chosen language – a special sort of 'literary' language
  c. their subject matter is serious, moral and philosophical, giving readers insights into fundamental ideas.
- The canon tends to be dominated by dead, white, upper-class males.
- Who gives authority to the canon in the first place? Is the very idea of a canon part of self-perpetuating elitism?
- 'Alternative' canons have been suggested, based on writers who challenge the orthodox.
- Some more modern types of criticism have focused on readers' responses, especially the pleasure to be found in reading.

- Michel Foucault claimed that the very idea of Literature is meaningless, but sustained by writers and critics in mutual self-interest. The critics fill in the gaps that the authors couldn't in the first place.

Activity

1. Review the fiction, poetry and drama you have read so far as part of your reading curriculum in school. To what extent have you enjoyed the texts? Why do you think they were chosen? Would you recommend them? You can go as far back as you like, including infant years, but try also to consider your reading for AS or A level.
2. To what extent have you been free to choose your own reading, and to what extent has it been given to you as a requirement? Has this made any difference to how you view the text?
3. Choose a text that you really like that is not on A-level specifications, and ask yourself the questions:
   - Could it under the present rules be studied as an A-level text?
   - Are there reasons why it would make a good choice as an A-level text?
   - Would making it an A-level text spoil it for you, or enhance its qualities?

Creating suitable tasks

As has already been made clear in this coursework section, you need to be working independently on your choice of texts and tasks. If you wish to use Section 6 of the Critical Anthology, you come up against an interesting conundrum. The official requirements for A level decree that any texts you study must be 'literature of sufficient substance and quality to merit serious attention', so it could be said that if you wish to argue a case in favour of a text that is not part of the canon, you and your text are in danger of falling outside this category. This is not to suggest that you cannot tackle a task that argues in favour of a text, but it does mean that you need to be careful about the text you choose. Here are some broad ideas – but make sure that you come up with your own specific tasks.

1. Argue in favour of a text that could be studied at A level. The safest way to approach this might be to argue in favour of something very contemporary.
2. Write an article in which you explore whether a text that shows the harsh realities of life can be said to be 'beautiful'.
3. Choose a text and then, in an article, discuss some questions and answers that best show the text's qualities. In doing this you could also refer to some of the other critical theories.

Summary

Even if you do not specifically use this section of the Critical Anthology as part of your coursework, it is well worth considering some of the ideas that often lie beneath the surface of your study, and are at the root of the way in which our exam system works.

Preparing for the examinations

This section provides some useful hints to help you with your final preparations for your AS or A level English Literature examinations. Some of these hints apply equally well to all of your exams, whatever the subject. They are based on the assumption that you have worked hard up to this point and that you have read the texts and know them well.

The examination requirements

One obvious way of preparing for your English Literature exams is to use this book. Take each of the chapters in turn and apply its focus to the actual set texts that you have studied. At this stage, make sure that you know what the precise requirements for your various exams are. What follows is a checklist of requirements.

> **EXAMINER'S TIP**
>
> Always make sure that your preparation and revision involve a specific task – with a specific amount of time allocated to it and a clear end result. Revision involves looking over something that you have done already, which is important, but it is equally important to do something new – to prepare some thoughts and ideas about topics that have not been covered so far.

AS level

(The requirements for the 'Aspects of tragedy' and 'Aspects of comedy' options are the same.)

Paper 1 (closed book)	Paper 2 (open book)
Section A: You respond to a passage from a Shakespeare play and how it relates to the play as a whole.	**Section A:** You answer an essay question on a poetry text. As part of the question, you will be given some poetry to comment on specifically.
Section B: You answer an essay question on a set-text play.	**Section B:** You answer an essay question on a prose text.

A level

(The requirements for the 'Aspects of tragedy' and 'Aspects of comedy' options are the same in Paper 1; and the requirements for the 'Elements of crime writing' and 'Elements of political and social protest writing' options are the same in Paper 2.)

Paper 1 (closed book)	Paper 2 (open book)
Section A: You respond to a passage from a Shakespeare play and how it relates to the play as a whole.	**Section A:** You respond to an unseen prose text, stemming from your chosen genre.
Section B: You answer an essay question on a Shakespeare play.	**Section B:** You answer an essay question on a single text.
Section C: You answer an essay question connecting two set texts.	**Section C:** You answer an essay question connecting two texts.

The examinations themselves

The variety of questions

It should be obvious from the outlines of the examination requirements above, that this specification has different types of questions, including:

- questions with text
- essays on single texts
- essays connecting texts
- unseen material.

Each of these types of question requires subtly different approaches, as well as having common ground. The common ground is provided by the outline mark scheme, which requires you to debate meanings based on an application of all of the Assessment Objectives. The difference in question types is in part a matter of focus. It is vital that your revision includes practising for each of the different question types.

Open-book exams

One of the core requirements of these exams – in all but the unseen critical question – is that you can demonstrate your detailed knowledge of the texts you have studied. It would be wrong to assume that an open-book exam replaces the need for a good knowledge of the text.

Open-book exams allow you to respond to questions by checking broad issues, such as the organization of scenes or chapters, or stanzas. Also, with a poetry text, you can fairly easily find and examine the detail of a specific poem that you may need for an answer. However, for novels and plays, the situation is very different – within the available time, you cannot afford to spend ages looking for a specific passage in a long novel or play. Therefore, it is vital that you come into the exam room mentally equipped with a good stock of quotations and references for all of your exams, so that you can quote and make references relevantly and quickly in your answers.

! EXAMINER'S TIP

As a general rule, short concentrated bursts of work – followed by periods of relaxation – are much better than spending long stretches of time revising, which deliver little in terms of an end product.

Providing evidence

Quotation

One form of textual evidence is direct quotation, and you are far more likely to use this with the poetry than the prose fiction.

Quotation can involve quoting chunks of text, but it can also involve integrating words or phrases into your own syntax. So, while you could quote from 'The Rime of the Ancient Mariner' by writing:

> *Coleridge begins the poem with a narrator describing a wedding scene:*
>
> *'It is an ancient Mariner,*
>
> *And he stoppeth one of three.'*

You could also write:

> *In his opening lines, Coleridge immediately identifies the strange behaviour of 'an ancient Mariner' by the fact that 'he stoppeth one of three.'*

The second method is often better, because it lets you get on with your argument while at the same time demonstrating that you know the text well. Practise this method of quoting and you will soon find that you become adept at it.

Reference

Equally effective, though, can be reference – especially when you are writing about a novel. Reference is when you show awareness of an event, a character, a place, etc., by referring to it with knowledge rather than using the exact words written by the author.

If we continue to use the lines above from 'The Rime of the Ancient Mariner' as an example, if you were to refer to them you would write something like:

> *Coleridge's use of a wedding scene at the start of the poem, and the immediate reference to an ancient mariner who inappropriately stops every third guest, sets up the strange narrative that is to come.*

Reference has particular value when you are dealing with novels, where direct quotation can be difficult in either a closed- or open-book exam.

To summarize, here is a list of points to bear in mind when you are using quotation and reference:

- You should support your arguments with frequent and relevant textual evidence.
- Quotations should be brief.
- Quotations should be accurate.
- The best quotations are embedded in your own sentences.
- Reference to the text can also help to give evidence, and close references can often work better than quotations.
- Quotations and references should never stand alone – they should be used to support particular points that you are want to make.

EXAMINER'S TIP

Always make sure that your focused stint of work leaves you ***better informed*** about the key topic than you were before you started. And also make sure that you have a ***written record*** of what you have prepared, so that you can glance over it in the final few days before the exam.

And finally...

It is common among students to talk about dreading exams, but this can sometimes be overplayed. Exams are a fact of the system we are all in, so we might as well make the most of them.

If you are well prepared, the exams should be seen – in part anyway – as a chance to show what you know. And the nature of English Literature as a subject also means that you should find some space in your head to think in the exam itself.

It is never really appropriate to say 'good luck' to someone before an exam, because exams are not about luck. They are about being well prepared in advance, and thoughtful on the day itself.

EXAMINER'S TIP

At some points in your preparation programme, actually write some sample exam answers and show them to your teacher for feedback and guidance.

Glossary

Absence. Something (a person, a voice, a point of view) that is not in a text, but whose absence from the text can be seen as significant.

Adage. A frequently used saying that sets out a general truth.

Aesthetic. Relating to the appreciation or consideration of beauty.

Agency. The capacity or power to act, rather than be passive.

Alienated / Alienation. Alienation involves being made to feel distanced, isolated, even hostile. People can experience alienation when they feel that their lives lack full meaning, because they are just part of a process.

Allegory. A sort of extended **metaphor**, where a story or meaning emerges under the surface of some other story. Famous examples are *The Pilgrim's Progress* and *The Faerie Queene*. Some critics have argued that J. R. R. Tolkien's *The Lord of the Rings* is an allegory of the First World War, in which Tolkien fought.

Alter-ego. A second self, similar to but in crucial respects different from the first person.

American Dream. The idea that everyone has opportunities, in the comparatively new country of America, to achieve material success and financial rewards.

Antagonist. An antagonist is an opponent, often with some sense of evil, against whom the protagonist must struggle.

Anthropomorphic. With imagined human qualities.

Anti-hero. A character with heroic or attractive qualities who does not fit the usual criteria for heroism.

Anti-pastoral. A **sub-genre** of pastoral, which focuses on the hardships of country life rather than an idealized **representation**.

Archaic. Having the features current in a much older period.

Aside. A brief **soliloquy**, where – within a longer sequence of dialogue – a character speaks a short line aside, as if privately, to the audience – revealing their true thoughts about events on stage.

Assumptions. A set of beliefs which are not questioned, but taken to be right and/or true.

Attitudes and values. Attitudes are views you hold and values are views which you believe to be morally right.

Ballad. A long poem that tells a story, and usually has a fast pace, with repetition a common feature.

Banishment. A form of punishment where an individual is forced to stay away from a particular area, or even to stay out of the country, on pain of death.

Bathos. An abrupt transition in style from high to low, intended for ludicrous effect.

Beast fable. A story involving beasts or animals, usually with a moral applicable to human beings.

Bildungsroman. A German word referring to a story of growing up, and being educated, in the most general sense of the word.

Binary opposition. The idea that we define words and concepts in relation to their opposite, i.e. 'good' is partly determined by what we understand by 'evil'.

Blank verse. Unrhymed verse.

Body politic. The nation, symbolized by the monarch as head of state.

Bourgeoisie. The wealthy, middle-class individuals in a society.

Canon. The group of texts that are said to be of particular value and so should be read by all.

Canonical texts. Texts that have a special status and are often seen as 'great' and enduring works of literature.

Caricature. An exaggerated portrayal of a person or type of person, often for comic effect.

Carnivalesque. Related to a literary form that subverts dominant forms by using humour and chaos; it has its origins in festival culture, which itself subverts the normal order of things.

Characterization. The way in which an author creates and uses characters, and why.

Charade. An absurd pretence.

Chorus. In Greek drama, a group of performers who comment with a collective voice on the play's action; in later dramas, the chorus could be a solitary performer, who assists the audience by providing narration.

Chronological order. The sequence of events in the order they happen, in a timeline that goes from A, the start of events, to say E, the end.

Classical tragedy. Plays written in ancient Greece or Rome, or in a similar style.

Clown. A person who behaves comically, a buffoon.

Colonialism. The process whereby European political forces took over, settled and ruled places such as India, Africa and the Middle East. Countries such as Britain colonized India in the 18th century. The term carries connotations of exploitation: native cultures were repressed, often brutally, and Western imperial forces plundered economic resources.

Colonization. The process whereby one country or group of countries seeks to take over another.

Comedy of manners. A text which satirises the behaviour of a certain social group or groups.

Commodified. Turned into a commodity that can be traded. Enslavement is an extreme example of commodification of people.

Conceit. An extended and ingenious simile.

Conscience. Judgement that assists us in deciding right from wrong.

Contemporary tragedy. Plays written in the late twentieth or twenty-first centuries.

Conventions. The accepted rules, structures and customs that we expect to see in a specific **genre** of writing.

Critical establishment. The 'establishment' refers to a dominant or elite group, whose views and behaviour are powerfully influential. The critical establishment therefore refers to a dominant group of literary critics who say what you should read and how you should interpret your reading.

Cross-dress. To take on any form of disguise that presents one gender as another.

Decadence. A process of decay in moral standards, revealed in undignified and wasteful behaviour.

Denouement. The final scene or chapter of a story, when all the loose ends of the plot are tied up.

Destiny. The path one takes in life, and its eventual destination, which often seem mysteriously assigned to us.

Detachment. A lack of connection with the processes occurring around oneself.

Diaspora. The scattering of a population whose origins lie in a particular geographical area.

Diction. In the sense in which Aristotle uses it, this means the composition of the verse.

Discourse. This is a term used differently in many academic disciplines. Here it is used in the sense of repeated patterns of language use.

Disorder. The inversion or destruction of the normal order in a society.

Divine right. The idea that kings are anointed by God; this was reinforced by the religious order in the coronation ceremony.

Domestic tragedy. A drama set in a household, apparently without grand or ambitious themes.

Dramatic monologue. A poem where a character speaks her or his thoughts to an imagined, silent listener.

Emasculation. Literally castration but, by extension, humiliation and disempowerment.

Enlightenment. A state of wisdom or knowledge, usually based on fact and experience rather than belief or superstition.

Epic tragedy. Plays with a grand or ambitious theme.

Essentialism. Interpreting literature as if it is 'real', peopled by 'real' people.

Establishment. The work the author does for the reader at the beginning of the text, or a section of the text, involving the introduction of places, time, people, etc.

Extradiegetic. Extradiegetic narration is when the narrator occupies a position above and apparently superior to the story they narrate. *Oliver Twist* is an example of such a narrative, where the narrator seems to have a sort of omniscience – access to characters' thoughts and an ability to know what is happening in different places at exactly the same time. In the case of this text, the narrator can also be called **heterodiegetic**.

Farcical. Relating to farce, a type of entertainment that depicts improbable situations and ludicrous pretence.

Fate. A pattern of predetermined and unstoppable events that affect one's life.

Focus / Focalizer / Focalization. A narrative point of view through which the text is mediated. We see the events of the story from the perspective of the focalizer.

Folly. Foolishness.

Framing device. A structure that helps introduce and/or conclude a play, offering a context for its performance.

Free indirect speech. This refers to speech that is embedded in a narrative, so it is unattributed (free) and a report of the speech rather than the actual words (indirect).

Free indirect thought. A narrative technique where a character's thought processes form part of the narrative but are not attributed to him or her.

Gender. The representation of women and men through cultural stereotypes, which can and should be endlessly disputed; the adjectives 'feminine' and 'masculine' and the nouns 'femininity' and 'masculinity' apply here.

Genre. A way of categorizing texts. Genres can be arranged around ways of writing (such as poetry/drama/prose), around content (such as crime, politics) around purpose (such as satire) and so on. In a most general sense, genre involves grouping texts by type – and so connecting texts. There are many ways of grouping literary texts. They can be grouped in many ways through their connections with other texts, with which they have things in common. In most cases, generic groupings are not fixed, so thinking about genre involves connecting with other texts.

Gothic. A **sub-genre** of literature devoted to horror and the supernatural.

Hegemony. The dominance or control of one person or system by another.

Heroic couplets. A verse form found in epic poetry, where the lines are in rhyming pairs.

Heterodiegetic. A heterodiegetic narrator does not take part in the narrated action.

Homodiegetic. A homodiegetic narrator takes part in the narrated action.

Hybridization. The fusion of two or more concepts.

Iambic pentameter. Refers to the stress and length of a line of poetry. The 'iamb' part refers to pairs of syllables that are unstressed/stressed, and the 'pent' part refers to the fact that there are five pairs of syllables in each line. A classic line of iambic pentameter is the first line from Gray's *Elegy*: 'The curfew tolls the knell of parting day'.

Idealism. A philosophical idea that the ideal state of humanity is possible.

Ideology. A view of the world held by a particular group of people at a particular time.

Imitation. In Aristotle's theory, this means acting like or being like the real world.

Intertextuality. The relationship that a text may have with other texts. In structural and post-structural theory, texts are often regarded as referring to other texts or to themselves, rather than to any external reality.

Intradiegetic. An intradiegetic narrator operates on the same level as characters in the story, so is different from the **extradiegetic** narrator who occupies a position above the story.

Laughing comedy. This is often compared to **sentimental comedy**, which was seen as socially mild and inoffensive. Laughing comedy claims to show life as it is, with human follies shown up for what they are.

Liberal idealism. A set of philosophical and political ideas concerned with creating a progressive society based on humanity moving from the dark into the light.

Lyric poetry. The medium in which classical drama is written.

Magical realist. A **genre** of writing in which magical and strange elements are part of what is otherwise realist writing.

Magnitude. The presence of the ambition in tragedy to deal with an event that is sufficiently serious.

Malapropism. A comical confusion of words, such as saying 'expedition' instead of 'exhibition'.

Means of production. The materials and assets needed to make products, e.g. land, factories, wealth.

Metaphor / metaphorical. A literary technique that involves the transfer of meaning, with one thing described as being another (e.g. education is a journey, as in the metaphor 'I'm stuck' or ' I am making good progress'). There are many types of metaphor, but in a broad sense metaphor involves the linking of something with something else that is otherwise not related to it.

Metre. This is the basic rhythmic pattern in a particular piece of poetry.

Midwest. A geographical area of the USA, centred broadly between the Great Lakes in the east and the state lines of North Dakota, South Dakota, Nebraska and Kansas in the west.

Misogynistic. Showing a hatred or distrust of women.

Mock-heroic. Parodying heroic verse.

Modern tragedy. Plays written in the late nineteenth or twentieth century.

Moralism. The promotion of conventional (and usually outmoded) morals or values upheld by a society.

Moralistic novel. A novel with a moral message for the reader, usually about how to lead a better life.

Motifs. Repeated elements that usually have a symbolic function.

Narrative. How the events and causes in a story are shown and the various methods used by authors to do this showing; exploring narrative involves looking at what the author has chosen to include (or exclude) and reflecting on how these authorial methods shape the way we read.

Narrative gaps. The parts of a story that we are not given, as readers, but which we nonetheless try to supply ourselves.

Narrative realism. Narrative style that aims to faithfully represent real life.

Oedipal. An adjective deriving from the Greek legend of Oedipus, who unknowingly murdered his father and married his mother. It refers to the repressed desire of a son for his mother and thus rivalry with his father.

Omniscient. An omniscient narrator operates from 'above' the story and seems to have a higher narratorial authority in relation to it. There is a sense that such a narrator knows 'everything' about the story (the word 'omniscient' comes from the Latin for 'all-knowing'). The narrator of Dickens's *Oliver Twist* falls into this category.

Pantomime. In modern culture, a play generally based on a folk-tale or fairy-tale, often performed around Christmas. In theatre, pantomime has a long tradition of a variety of styles.

Paradox. An apparent contradiction that holds some unexpected truth.

Parody. This is the copying of a specific text (or **genre**) for a comic and sometimes satirical effect.

Pathos. The depiction of suffering, an appeal to the reader's emotions.

Patriarchy A social system run by men for the benefit of men.

Personification. The attribution of human feelings or ideas to a non-human concept.

Platonic. Connected with the thinking of the Greek philosopher Plato. A 'Platonic conception' is an unreal, impossibly ideal version of something.

Plot. The chain of causes and circumstances that connect the various events and place them in some sort of relationship with each other.

Police procedural. A crime **sub-genre** in which the narrative involves the solving of the crime and the identification of the perpetrator.

Post-modernism. A movement in art and literature away from modernism, and characterized by a new understanding of historical events.

Pretentious. Claiming exaggerated merit or importance.

Primogeniture. The right of the first-born son of the monarch to succeed to the throne.

Pronoun. A word that stands for and replaces a noun.

Prose. Passages of text that are not in verse.

Protagonist. In dramatic terms, the first major character who offers a particular view. The protagonist is often seen in opposition to the **antagonist**.

Reasoning. The case being staged and the opinions being put forward by the characters.

Reflexivity. The act of referring to yourself. In a literary sense, it involves texts showing and knowing that they are texts.

Reification. Turning something – or someone – into an item of economic use.

Representation / representational. The process of showing versions of the world, rather than the real world itself. Literature can only ever be representational.

Repressive. Authoritarian, preventing people from finding fufilment.

Revel / revelling. Lively enjoyment or merrymaking.

Reynard Cycle. A series of medieval stories centred on a fox, Reynard.

Ritual. A repeated, traditional series of actions used for ceremonial or festive purposes.

Satire / Satirical. A **genre** that criticizes people or systems, usually in a comic or witty way.

Scots. The dialect spoken in lowland Scotland.

Semiotics. The study of signs and how they work. Signs can be visual (a red light on a traffic light worldwide means stop) and can also be verbal (a Rolls Royce car, at least in British culture, could signify social class and wealth for example). Semiotics, then, looks at the significance of connotations.

Sentimental comedy. This is often compared to **laughing comedy** and is usually seen as socially mild and inoffensive. Laughing comedy claims to show life as it is, with human follies shown up for what they are.

Sex. The biological differences between men and women.

Significance. Your course of study, and this book designed to aid you in your course of study, are aimed at helping you to become an independent and active reader who can find relevant significances in your literary reading. Significance involves weighing up all the potential contributions to how a text can be analysed (such as the way in which the text is constructed and written, contexts which can be applied, aspects of **genre**, possible theoretical approaches) and then finding potential meanings and interpretations.

Slapstick. Physical comedy (a term invented in the 20th century but applied to the past); it involves falling over, blows and collisions.

Socio-economic. The combination of the social and economic conditions we live under. Although the phrase always puts social first, a Marxist view would say that it is economics which determine everything else.

Soliloquy. A speech where a character tells or confesses thoughts to the audience, unheard by other characters. Soliloquies are often used in tragedies because they tell us why particular characters are doing something. In films, this is often presented as a voice-over to imitate the thoughts inside a character's mind.

Speaker. It is not possible in a story to say that the narrator of the story is the same as the author. The term 'speaker' makes this distinction clear.

Story. The various events that are shown.

Sub-genre. A particular type of text within a **genre**; genre can sometimes seem like a Russian *matryoshka* doll, containing ever smaller categories.

Sub-plot. An additional or second plot that often parallels events of the main plot of the tragedy.

Symbol / symbolized / symbolism. This involves suggestion or connection between things, rather than direct comparison. A symbol is often repeated, or part of a bigger scheme of suggestion. The meanings of symbols are not fixed.

Transition. A process of change or development.

Trickster. A practical joker, sometimes clever at disguise, who may be a thief or liar.

Unreferenced pronoun. A **pronoun** that is not attached to a specific person or thing. This can lead to creative ambiguity. Just who is being referred to? Advertising frequently uses unreferenced pronouns, especially 'you', which has the added ambiguity of being possibly one person or many.

Vignette. A short, impressionistic scene, providing insight.

Index

080414